CATHOLICISM IN THE ENGLISH PROTESTANT IMAGINATION

Nationalism, Religion, and Literature, 1660–1745

This study examines the role of anti-Catholic rhetoric in late seventeenth- and early eighteenth-century England. This role was long neglected, being at once obvious and distasteful, a reproach to the heirs of the Enlightenment who prided themselves on their tolerance and did not want to confront its origins in intolerance. Raymond Tumbleson discusses how the fear of Popery, a potentially destabilizing force under the Stuarts, ultimately became a principal guarantor of the Hanoverian oligarchy. The range of authors discussed runs from Middleton, Milton, and Marvell to Swift, Defoe, and Fielding, as well as numerous pamphleteers. Crossing traditional generic, disciplinary, and chronological boundaries, this book examines hitherto neglected relationships between poetry and prose, literature and polemic, the Reformation and the Augustan age.

Raymond D. Tumbleson is Assistant Professor of English at Kutztown University, Pennsylvania. He has published articles in journals including *Literature/Film Quarterly*, *Journal of the History of Ideas*, *Genre*, *Studies in the Novel*, *Persuasions*, and *Prose Studies*.

"A Scheme of Popish Cruelties." Broadside, 1681

CATHOLICISM IN THE ENGLISH PROTESTANT IMAGINATION

Nationalism, Religion, and Literature, 1660–1745

RAYMOND D. TUMBLESON

CAMBRIDGE
UNIVERSITY PRESS

PUBLISHED BY THE PRESS SYNDICATE OF THE UNIVERSITY OF CAMBRIDGE
The Pitt Building, Trumpington Street, Cambridge CB2 1RP, United Kingdom

CAMBRIDGE UNIVERSITY PRESS
The Edinburgh Building, Cambridge CB2 2RU, United Kingdom
40 West 20th Street, New York, NY 10011–4211, USA
10 Stamford Road, Oakleigh, Melbourne 3166, Australia

First published 1998

Printed in the United Kingdom at the University Press, Cambridge

Typeset in Baskerville 11/12.5 pt [CP]

A catalogue record for this book is available from the British Library

ISBN 0 521 62265 4 hardback

To my parents

Contents

Illustrations

Acknowledgments

I would like to thank Marshall Brown, Thomas Lockwood, and especially Robert Markley (who directed the dissertation whence this book began) for their assistance in the revision of this work, and also the staffs of the British Library, Harvard libraries, William Andrews Clark Memorial Library, Huntington Library, Burke Library of Union Theological Seminary, and University of Washington Library. Versions of portions of this volume have appeared as: "The Triumph of London: Lord Mayor's Day Pageants and the Rise of the City," in *The Witness of Times*, ed. Katherine Z. Keller and Gerald J. Schiffhorst (Duquesne University Press, 1993); "'Dark and Dirty Party-Writers': Jeremy Collier, Elkanah Settle, and the Ideological Appropriation of Morality," *Transactions of the North-West Society for Eighteenth-Century Studies* 18 (1989–90): 39–50; "Of True Religion and False Politics: Milton and the Uses of Anti-Catholicism," *Prose Studies* 15 (1992): 253–70; "The Novel's Progress: Faction, Fiction, and Fielding," *Studies in the Novel* 27 (1995): 12–25; "Reason and Religion: The Science of Anglicanism," *The Journal of the History of Ideas* 57 (1996): 131–56; and "'Family Religion': Popery in Defoe's Domestic Regime," *Genre* 28 (1995): 255–78. The dust-jacket illustration, "Six Godly Martyrs," appears by courtesy of the Burke Library of Union Theological Seminary in New York; the frontispiece, "A Scheme of Popish Cruelties," is from the Huntington Library collection; and "The Poisoning of King John" and "The Proud Primacy of Popes" derive from the University of Washington. All of the illustrations are from the 1684 edition of John Foxe, *Acts and Monuments*, except for "A Scheme of Popish Cruelties," a 1681 broadside pasted into an edition of [Gilbert] *Burnet's History of His own Times* at the Huntington. Finally, I thank the William Andrews Clark Memorial Library, Houghton Library of Harvard University, Pennsylvania State System of Higher Education, and National Endowment for the Humanities for grants which facilitated my work.

Canonicity and catholicity
the universal church of literature

And Gregory and John and men divine

Who rose like shadows between Man and god
Till that eclipse, still hanging under Heaven,
Was worshipped by the world o'er which they strode

For the true Sun it quenched.[1]

Samuel Johnson's "Life of Dryden" celebrates its subject in part as "the father of English criticism," but still more for his securing as a poet the triumph of "the new versification" over "savageness," a triumph emblematized in his "fix[ing] the limits of poetical liberty" in translation.[2] Before beginning the discussion of Dryden's literary significance, Johnson, noting the poet's frequent pecuniary embarrassments, speculates that his stipend as Laureate may have sometimes not been regularly paid, because "In those days the oeconomy of the government was yet unsettled."[3] This study takes as its subject that inauguratory juxtaposition, the simultaneous "settling" of poetry, of criticism, and of "the oeconomy of the government" in the transition from the seventeenth to the eighteenth century. The interrelationships of ideology, theology, and literature form an essential but neglected dimension of this transition. Protestant prejudice against Catholicism in the England of the late seventeenth and early eighteenth centuries has suffered from the purloined letter syndrome: everyone can see that it is there, and assumes that what is so obvious can contain no mystery to explore or significance to expound. As England's pre-Reformation history receded into myth and Protestantism became identified with the English nation, Catholicism became doubly stigmatized as both alien, what the vain French and wicked Italians practiced, and frighteningly familiar as the accompaniment of absolutism. Catholics in Europe were foreign, different and hence necessarily (by the logic of nationalism) inferior, but instead of being distant and alluringly available for exploitation, like the indigenous peoples of the Americas, they were close and threatening – Bloody Mary, Philip II, Louis XIV, James II. As Islam was to Europe at large, Catholicism was to England an unconquerable threat of externality, an unassimilable other: the cultural paranoia that manifested itself overseas in colonialism was deployed domestically in religious politics of persecution and plots.

This volume traces the history of anti-Catholic rhetoric in England in its last period of major political influence, from the Restoration of Charles II in 1660 to the final failure of Jacobitism after the battle of Culloden in 1746. Catholicism began this period largely overlooked in the clash between a newly triumphant Anglicanism and a Puritanism that was just beginning to define itself as institutionally separate from the Church of England, following the purges of the ministry of the Interregnum and Restoration. In John Bunyan's *Pilgrim's Progress*, Giant Pope hides in his cave unseen, a vanquished evil like Giant Pagan, in contrast to the Anglican establishment's busy and murderous Vanity Fair. Under the pressure, however, of Charles's pro-French foreign policy, French expansionism under Louis XIV, and the conversion of James Stuart, heir presumptive to the crown, to Catholicism, in the 1670s fear of Catholic designs upon English Protestant liberty rose ultimately to the credulous fever of the Popish Plot, when London burned the Pope in effigy. In 1530 England was Catholic; in 1688 James II lost a throne undermined by popular loathing of Popery and tyranny, two words relentlessly linked by anti-government writers. The prejudice created by an intersection of religious fervor and political interest long endured. In 1745, Henry Fielding revived the familiar bugbear on behalf of his political patrons, dwelling on spoilation, slaughter, and foreign domination as the concomitants of Catholic rule to rally public opinion behind the Hanoverian regime when Charles Stuart, Bonnie Prince Charlie, approached London. A few years later, he set *Tom Jones* during "the '45." In her 1769 play, *The Sister*, when Charlotte Lennox wished to find a respectable reason for a young lady to escape from the care of an older female relative, an action requiring extraordinary justification to avoid being scandalous, she found a reason in the aunt's attempting to convert her charge to Catholicism. Gothic novels such as Ann Radcliffe's *The Italian* and Matthew Lewis's *The Monk*, along with such nonliterary events as the Gordon Riots in 1780 and the continuance of Catholic disability laws into the nineteenth century, reflect the persistence of a deep fear and hatred of Catholicism in England. The political significance of anti-Catholicism dwindled as the struggle for supremacy between crown and Parliament ebbed, but it remained available as a nationalistic topos.

I

This study encompasses works both canonical and obscure because anti-Catholicism must function as both text and context in a study of so broad a phenomenon. The movement to historicize literary studies in recent years has been driven by a recognition that the gatekeepers of fame have acted not as benignly neutral arbiters of taste but as human beings who possess agendas beyond the placing of a period. Exclusions can reveal as much as inclusions; to rest content with reading a few selected works is to accept, without examination, the process by which those works came to eclipse their contemporaries. Further, one cannot discuss the relative positions of individual Restoration and Augustan works within a temporally localized canon without proceeding to the next level of generalization, to considering the position of that periodized canon within the larger canon of English literature as a whole. That position is still a secondary one. Although its editor, J. Paul Hunter, is an eminent eighteenth-century scholar, the current edition of *The Norton Introduction to Poetry* appears to have been composed in accordance with the old conviction that what falls between Milton and Blake is not poetry: Dryden, Swift, and Pope alone get a page each in a 500-page volume.[4] The Restoration and Augustan periods are what lie between the glory that is the Renaissance of Shakespeare and Milton and the grandeur that is the novel. They are the omitted, the disappeared. The question is why; why is this period incommensurable with "real" poetry, almost with literature? A strong hint lies in Jerome McGann's observation, following Terry Eagleton, that literature is "an ideological form *per se.*"[5]

One might begin with the names: Restoration and Augustan. The Restoration was, of course, a political event, the end of England's only attempt at a republic, and the end also of a period of intense sociopolitical experimentation that resulted in something much like the institutional formations that still rule Britain.[6] (How an *English* republic led to *British* governing institutions has been much discussed among historians in recent years; this study specifically addresses England, noting the other three nations' internal politics only in the context of their effect on England, how the English saw them, not how they saw themselves, a limitation not intended to deprecate the value of the latter.[7]) What was restored, however, was the throne of the Stuarts, that is, of a monarchy possessing both an institutional and a popular basis independent of Parliament, of the political nation, of the "natural rulers," of the propertied. This independence of the crown, as distinct from the crown-in-Parliament, constituted the principal institutional question at issue in Europe's intragovernmental conflicts of the seventeenth century, both in England, where Parliament won, and on the Continent, where the decision usually went the other way. Johnson's whispered remark to Boswell at a time of unrest that the present monarchy, the Hanoverians, had no friends, that the Stuarts had those who stood by them as late as 1745, may seem the eccentricity of the grand Cham of Macaulay's caricature; but Boswell gave final shape to and published his *Life of Johnson* after the French Revolution had made Jacobitism seem a whimsical relic of a past age, and even in his childhood "the '45" – or the last Anglo-Scottish war, as it might be called – was just a memory. Study of the Restoration was long deprecated because of the "immorality" of the period: J. Douglas Canfield and Robert Markley have observed that that immorality consisted largely of ongoing anarchic energies unspent and displaced in the Interregnum.

The term "Augustanism," with its Classical allusion to the man who found Rome brick and left it marble (and found it an aristocratic republic and left it a military dictatorship) encapsulates an aestheticizing of the political. "Neoclassicism" carries the aestheticizing process a step further by removing even the distant political allusion (in Latin, like one of Gibbon's dirty footnotes, lest the vulgar be corrupted/informed) of Augustus's name. A period of decisive change, of the formation of both the modern British polity and novel, is rendered into a marmoreal bust. The Restoration and Augustanism are what follow what Jonathan Dollimore calls the "demystification of political and power relations and the decentring of 'man'"[8] of Jacobean tragedy and the zero hour of civil war. The "long eighteenth century" functions in traditional literary studies to fit the systemic shock of the Civil War into a teleology of national and cultural redemption. In this view, Interregnum fanaticism and Restoration cynicism cancel each other out, eliding the triumphal progress of English literature, of Western Civilization, more or less directly from Shakespeare through a deified, and thus isolated and depoliticized, Milton to the rise of the novel. Restoration, Augustan, and Neoclassicism are terms less descriptive than deceptive; they operate as a rhetorical maneuver to substitute Whig history, a destiny of foreordained greatness, for history without an adjective to delimit possibilities of interpretive conflict.

The principle for the selection of subject texts in this study is to combine extended scrutiny of a few works with briefer incorporation of numerous others less central to the project of relating religious controversy to social and ideological evolution. The number of directly relevant theological tracts alone in the late seventeenth century is well up into the hundreds, while an extraordinary range of other works, perhaps most abundantly November 5 sermons, are also potentially apposite. Thus this volume necessarily arrives at both breadth and selectivity, a selectivity that some-times consults considerations of canonicity, but that more often dispenses with such customs to focus on less-known texts that are more significant for the purpose at hand. Even when familiar authors are examined, the center of gravity of the examination is commonly not their more accustomed works, not by chance but precisely because sectarian polemicism has not comported comfortably with the emphasis on good breeding that has underwritten the aestheticist approach to literature: Arnoldian "touch-stones" were indefinable yet unmistakable to the initiated in exactly the same fashion as whether one were a gentleman.[9] Milton's is a name known to all, but his *Of True Religion* is all but unknown because unlike *Areopagitica* it is difficult to enlist in a justification of the institutions of modernity according to standards developed over subsequent centuries; Defoe's *Religious Courtship* has similarly seemed flotsam from an unusable past. Middleton's pageants tend to be regarded, if at all, as minor appendages to his plays, which leads to oversight of their function within the larger currents of thought and action in his time, a function which their presence in this study highlights. Elkanah Settle, on the other hand, is simply almost entirely forgotten, a joke for his odd name, commonly noted, if at all, only for being attacked both in *Absalom and Achitophel* and in *The Dunciad* – and yet his corpus remarkably unites strands of religious, dramatic, and political history. In the first wave of 1980s new historicism, efforts at historicization often tended to combine historicist methodology with a continuing *a priori* assumption of the superior importance of the famous: Charles D. Tarlton, for instance, notes the inconsistency between Richard Ashcraft's presentation of Locke's *Two Treatises of Government* as "just another Whig pamphlet" and his "unspoken acceptance of *Two Treatises's* greater significance."[10] Eschewing such inconsistency, then, this volume deliberately addresses the obscure, not out of whimsicality, but because their far from purposeless obscuration has acted to conceal the ideological structure within which they operated, the anti-Catholicism that is an embarrassing cousin for secularizing modernity to have at its table.

The first chapter scrutinizes two phenomena of early modern national-ism as embodied in one formerly central text and one set of thoroughly obscure ones. These seemingly wildly opposite works function comple-mentarily. The once-canonical text, John Foxe's *Acts and Monuments*, has been marginalized by secular successors embarrassed by such a prototype of modernization. This critique of religious authoritarianism relies upon secular authoritarianism as its agent of reform; it implies that the Romish independence of clerical from secular authority acts as the direct cause of the grisly persecutions obsessively portrayed through most of its two thousand folio pages, and in consequence exalts the role of the monarch as the only force capable of defying papal tyranny. The smaller and less familiar works are the brief librettos, as they might be called, for the pageants performed for the inauguration of a new Lord Mayor of London in the sixteenth and seventeenth centuries. While the era of celebrity of any one pageant was far briefer than that of *Acts and Monuments*, they were performed and paraded yearly for all the capital to see for over a century and a half. The pageants of Thomas Middleton in the 1610s and 1620s reflect a covert struggle by the city to subjugate both the monarchy and the world to its nascent regime of metropolitan capitalism – in both senses of "metropolitan," city versus country and metropolis versus colony. The plotting Continental Papist functions as the obverse to the guileless, hapless (alien but exploitable) non-Europeans of City of London Mayoral pageants; both are opposed to the enterprising but honest Englishman, whose freedom is always threatened by the one and whose destiny is to conquer/civilize the other for their own good. The Tudor absolutism lauded for its decisive action in erasing the premodern Church becomes in turn itself an obstacle to the increasing ambitions of the Jacobean commercial classes. Religious disputes and commercial rivalries prove intimately related; the destruction of one enemy only generates more enemies.

The second chapter analyzes the functioning of anti-Catholicism as a political weapon after the Restoration by the use of two examples drawn from familiar authors and addresses the relationship between the fame of the poets, Milton and Marvell, and the obscurity of these polemics. In his last pamphlet, *Of True Religion*, Milton attempts to align his personal hostility towards hierarchy and orthodoxy of all sorts – monarchy, Catholicism, and Anglicanism alike – with popular hostility to Catholicism. Milton represents a transitional figure: in this tract he attempts to demonstrate the continued validity and vitality of Interregnum religious politics under the secularizing conditions of the Restoration. In contrast to the older writer, the younger takes the position of an ameliorationist reformer in a straightforwardly political opposition to the crown. Where Milton's object is religious and transformative, in *An Account of the Growth of Popery and Arbitrary Government* Marvell plays a realpolitiking gradualist who only fills his first few pages with religious animosity to draw the reader on to follow his account of intragovernmental maneuvers sympathetically.

Until the recent increase of attention given to their prose, as the traditional segregation of the literary from the political has come into question, Milton and (especially) Marvell were long better known as poets than as polemicists, nor is this distinction yet extinct; particularly in university literature departments, they often remain primarily literary figures, fundamentally different in kind from the myriad of other pamphleteers contemporary with them. Milton's notoriety in his own day was, however, that of a radical agitator and Cromwellian apologist, while until the nineteenth century Marvell was remembered chiefly as the principled M.P. from Hull. The de-emphasizing of their political activity at the moment of their emergence into canonicity, for Milton three centuries ago, for Marvell one, reflects the need of the progressive Enlightenment conception of modernity they helped establish to erase its historical origin in the Protestant sectarian critique of Catholicism. To operate in the canonical economy, a poet must be departicularized.

In the third and fourth chapters, pamphlet wars of the Restoration receive an extended scrutiny as an essential bridge between what might be called the late premodern situation of the first chapter and the oppositionalist position of anti-Anglican anti-Papism in the second, on the one hand, and on the other the predominance which anti-sacerdotalism commands by the early eighteenth century. These two chapters operate complementarily because the battle between Dissenters and Anglicans of the third chapter, as to which is more distant from Catholicism under Charles II, produces the redefinition of Anglicanism articulated in the pamphlet warfare between Anglicans and Catholics under James II. The third chapter examines competing logics of religio-political conspiracy, particularly the intensifying cycles of anxiety culminating in the Exclusion Crisis. In a cultural movement coding the evolution of kingship from Dryden's baroque vision in *Absalom and Achitophel* to Addison's depersonalization of sovereignty, a multiplicity of uncanonical and frequently antiliterary texts enact one of two narratives of deception and betrayal: to Dissenting pamphleteers the Church of England is a crypto-Papist design for clerical dictatorship, while Anglicans make counteraccusations that Nonconformists, like Catholics, endanger order by placing religious above civil authority, and suggest Jesuit infiltration of sects. Reflecting a social embedding of paranoid narrative, both maneuver to smear their opponents as less perfectly opposed to Papism than themselves. The fourth chapter carries this examination forward to the more elaborate pamphlet warfare between Anglican and Catholic clergy under James II. Under a Catholic king, Anglican clerics were unable to concentrate on the ongoing struggle against Nonconformism; caught in a two-front war, they found that as they held off the Papists the Dissenters outflanked them to obtain toleration. Instead of being able to rest confident that the gagged Papist menace was more distant than the Dissenter challenge, Anglicans had to rearticulate a coherent theological justification of Protestantism against its primordial enemy. One method by which they did so was by bringing the reason of experimental science to the aid of theology, turning a full circle only a generation after the founders of the Royal Society had relied upon plenary theology to validate the premises of their scientific reason. This chapter examines what "reason" represented and its role in simultaneously justifying the Church of England and undermining its monopoly of worship, as well as validating and subverting monarchy.

The ferocious audacity of Restoration drama was intimately related to the violence of the period's intertwined religious and political divisions; consequently, it was following the political resolution of the Glorious Revolution that a moral reform campaign began to gag the stage, to tame its potential for social disruption. As de Tocqueville observed, the invisible coercion of public opinion, where "the body is left free, and the soul is enslaved," proved at least as strong as the open censorship of absolutism before it.[11] In the fifth chapter, this interrelationship of polemic and drama is exemplified in the career of Elkanah Settle, a varied writer of theatrical and controversial works who took a central role in both the pamphlet and stage wars of the Exclusion Crisis and the moral-reform struggle that began in the 1690s, but who has become thoroughly decanonized precisely for his intermingling of the political and the aesthetic. While divisions by genre were recognized at the time by no less an authority than the censor, Roger L'Estrange, who in the Term Catalogues separated works by type, critics should perhaps be wary of a classification system with such a precedent. Although clerical writers dominated argumentative controversial literature, poets and playwrights chose sides as well, Thomas Shadwell and Elkanah Settle writing for the Whigs, Dryden, Behn, and Nathaniel Lee for the Tories. (The terms Whig and Tory originated at this time.) To distinguish between a literary realm of atemporal formal concerns and a nonliterary of ephemera is to belie the reality in which the two commingled. The decade from 1678-1689 generated a tremendous outpouring of argument and produced the constitution under which the British government still functions. All issues were religious issues; the modern world of "economists and sophisters" that Edmund Burke denounces in his *Reflections on the Revolution in France* was in the late seventeenth century as yet nascent. Questions of faith and works incorporated also those of control of taxation and the military. Paul Kleber Monod has claimed that "The [1688] Revolution was the victory, not of timeless conceptions of 'liberty,' but of virulent anti-Catholicism."[12] A nationalistic Protestantism generated popular support for dynastic change that the gentry co-opted to impose the supremacy of a landed oligarchy which endured in full force as the "English ancien regime" until 1832, and to a considerable degree into this century. What has made this ancien regime difficult for liberal scholars to identify as such is that, defining itself against Catholicism and French absolutism, it founded its legitimacy upon the same bases of modernity and reason as liberalism itself.

The final chapter discusses the last stages in the process whereby anti-Catholic sentiment evolves from an instrument of destabilization under the Stuarts to a bulwark of the Hanoverian status quo. It begins with Swift's failed effort to return the High Church position to its strength under Charles II by, ironically, secularizing public discourse, a paradoxical strategy rendered necessary by the loss of sacramental kingship to the Protestant Succession. Whig writers are less constrained. In *Religious Courtship*, Popery defines the boundary of Defoe's regime of domesticity. In a 180-degree turn from the agitprop of Milton and Marvell, Fielding employs anti-Catholicism, from the wartime scaremongering of *The True Patriot* to the subtler measures of *Tom Jones*, to align the government with virtue. The subversive has become the conservative; as with Communism in this century, a rhetoric of radicalism becomes a mystification of rule. Picturesque and sentimental writers occasionally invoke the Catholic bugbear in their task of consolidating the new order, with its supplanting of the court by the country manor as the center of culture and of public man and public spaces with the cult of domesticity. By identifying and tracing the progress of this ideological inversion, this work is locating in a specific historical process and period the transition from the Renaissance to the modern world which Stephen Greenblatt identified as a general, unlocalized matter in his *Shakespearean Negotiations*. A key point of rupture in the ideological coherence of the new Whig order is its dependence on intolerance in the name of tolerance, its suppression of Catholicism on the not entirely baseless grounds that unrepressed Catholics would repress Protestants. As England becomes more confident of its strength as a world power, and as the machtpolitik of domestic policy and international relations ceases to be defined in sectarian terms, the hatred of Catholicism loses its day-to-day political centrality; nonetheless, at moments of crisis, most notably 1715 and 1745, Papism remains available as the ultimate evil against which the Georges guard.

The scope of this study, then, is considerable, but, in Pope's revised words, "not without a plan": at its center lies the role of Restoration contestations between Anglican and Dissenting rhetorics of Christianity in the development of the distinction between modern and premodern across all of intellectual life, from politics to science, from theology, once the queen of sciences, to the birth of literature as something antithetical to theology and theory alike.[13] One item necessary to define before proceeding further is what is meant by Protestantism. Besides confining itself to the British Isles, this study additionally must distinguish not only between the Church of England and the Nonconformists but also between the often doctrinally conservative pre-Civil War Anglicanism of Henry VIII, Elizabeth I, or Archbishop Laud and the post-Interregnum Church that shifted its ideological basis significantly if quietly (as discussed in the fourth chapter) so as to avert the accusations of proto-Papism that had so damaged its cause under Charles I. By the later seventeenth century, the evil of Popery was so entrenched in the popular mind – compare one of Shakespeare's friars to even courtier-laureate (and later Catholic-convert) Dryden's Spanish Fryar – that the Church of England could not afford to be identified with that other apostolical church: that way lay the fate of Laud. In Restoration England, Catholicism and Protestantism did not function in a dyadic system, but rather in a triangular one where the tension between those two poles was frequently of less immediate political importance than the antagonism between the Church and the sects. Both Anglicans and Dissenters sought to delegitimize each other by asserting their rivals' similarity to Catholicism, with the result that "true religion," true Protestantism, tended to equal the faith of the person doing the defining: like today, Protestantism was already a house with many mansions, but unlike today few of its tenants acknowledged each other's right to live there. In the language of Michel Serres, if Catholicism acted as the "other" to the Church of England, Dissent acted as its "other self." The self produces the other as a projection or externalization of scapegoated aspects of the self; the "other self" generates a confirmation of this model, although this figure – the "parasite" – can also serve as the "other," in which case Catholics and Protestants might, as in the royalist army, "otherize" the Protestant Dissenters.[14] The widespread popular fear of "popery and tyranny" was not unfounded; the Catholic Church of the seventeenth century was not gentle towards Protestants within its power, and across the Continent monarchs were aspiring towards absolutism; but behind the calls for a united front (to borrow a phrase) against the Popish menace operated a political and ideological dynamic less benign than its inheritors have portrayed it.

Defoe and Fielding are the heirs to Whig polemicists, such as Marvell and Settle, who uncoupled the equivalence between crown rights and property rights which Dryden stressed in *Absalom and Achitophel* (lines 769–84), so that Fielding could portray the Pretender as a threat to property and sexual virtue in both *Tom Jones* and his pro-government propaganda during the Jacobite uprising of 1745. The ideological mechanism that enabled that uncoupling, making the cause of oligarchy a moral and popular crusade, was the demonization of Catholicism. Bishops but no Pope, lords but no king: thus the aristocracy preserved the arch of hierarchy while knocking out its keystone, subduing both populace and crown – and, together with that sometime-sacred crown, the Church of England as well. To legitimize their half-revolution, the Whigs back-dated it to the dissolution of ties to Rome and of the monasteries, the destruction of the one public institution powerful enough to staff and finance royal absolutism, to silence the memory of the more recent and radical revolution that abolished bishops and lords as well. Milton became the poet of the Whig sublime, Protestantism a justification of aristocratic domination. Rhetorical continuity disguised political inversion.

II

Protestant hostility toward Catholicism functioned as a constitutive element in the emergence of nationalist and imperialist ideology in seven-teenth- and eighteenth-century England. This animus – energized by first allegations and then legends of Irish rebellions and massacres – served to sacralize and mobilize the opposition to the Stuarts in the Civil War, the Glorious Revolution of 1688, and the Jacobite rebellions of 1715 and 1745, and acted as the primary medium of rhetorical continuity between Commonwealthsmen and the defenders of septennial parliaments and rotten boroughs. Both seventeenth-century rebels and eighteenth-century establishmentarians fought for liberty, a liberty defined positively as the absolute value of property rights against a crown that until the Civil War still retained feudal privileges of land tenure, besides prerogative at large, and negatively as the absence or antithesis of Popery. The latter definition validated the former, glossing elite self-interest with a religious idealism able to appeal to all Protestants. This "ideal polemical tool,"[15] as Peter Lake has called anti-Papism, demands to have its history told because it is the founding hatred of a doctrine that professes to feel no hatred and not to be a doctrine – the complex of market economics, imperialism, and liberal progress that constitutes modernity. What Georg Lukacs termed "the inner process of differentiation which is to transform revolutionary democracy into compromising liberalism"[16] predates the barricades of Paris in June, 1848, appearing first in the metamorphosis of Whiggism from insurrectionary movement to justification for oligarchy. When, as Hayden White observes, Gibbon began his *Decline and Fall* in amusement at "ignorant monks celebrating their superstitious ceremonies in a church that stood on the ground where a pagan temple had once stood,"[17] he was positioning himself consciously as a champion of Enlightenment in "an essentially unhistorical struggle between humanist reason and feudal-absolutist unreason."[18] The dichotomy between rational English observer and "ignorant [Continental Catholic] monks celebrating their superstitious ceremonies," however, conflates religious and national superiority in a secularized coding that arose first in sectarian terms. The critique of unreason by reason offered by Gibbon, and many subsequent chroniclers of the Enlightenment, recapitulates the critique of Papism by Protestantism; as we shall see in the fourth chapter, almost every Anglican polemic under James II takes as its two heads arguments from scripture (and perhaps church history) and from "reason." It serves the purposes of each of these successive permutations of bourgeois ideology "to posit its own thinking, its own good sense as a Nature which any doctrine, any intellectual system would offend."[19]

This sectarian dichotomy is the obscured original of the one Edward Said sees as central to the colonialist and orientalist mentality, a "*positional* superiority" privileging the European subject over the foreign other that conceals itself in "the general liberal consensus that 'true' knowledge is fundamentally nonpolitical."[20] Oppositions of first and third worlds reiterate a cultural logic first developed to justify English Protestant exceptionalism; the duty of Europe's foremost Protestant power to champion the faith against the Catholic menace elided into a duty to spread Christian civilization among heathen savages. (Catholicism was of course also usable as a complement to the colonization efforts undertaken by Catholic nations such as France and Spain, but this volume leaves analysis of those relationships to other scholars; one country is subject enough for one book.) When Said quotes Gibbon's remark that Islam's zenith was "coeval with the darkest and most slothful period of European annals," he does not note that Gibbon's view of that period descended directly from the Reformation critique of the medieval Church.[21] Said observes that "Islam became an image . . . whose function was not so much to represent Islam in itself as to represent it for the medieval Christian . . . to *stage* the Orient and Europe together in some coherent way, the idea being for

Christians to make it clear to Muslims that Islam was just a misguided version of Christianity."[22] Similarly, English Protestants constructed a view of Catholicism that suited their need for a demonic external threat capable also of the subtlest internal betrayals; the easy medieval progression of ideas whereby Mohammed as a heresiarch must necessarily possess limitless depravity reproduced itself in the Protestant opinion of the Pope.[23] Michelet's fear that "the Orient advances, invincible, fatal to the gods of light by the charm of its dreams, by the magic of its *chiaroscuro*,"[24] resembles the Protestant dread of the irrationalist potency of an unsuppressed Catholicism, a dread that kept penal laws against Catholics in effect for centuries.

What is anti-Catholicism? It is the ghost in the machine, the endless, neurotic repetition by self-consciously rational modernity of the primal scene in which it slew the premodern as embodied in the archetypal institution, arational and universal, of medieval Europe. Second only to anti-Semitism in power and longevity, it is a myth of iniquity whose pitiless prelatic villain has remained consistent for half a millennium, from John Foxe's martyrology to Dostoyevsky's Grand Inquisitor. In the seventeenth century hostility toward Catholicism represented the common ground between Anglican and Dissenter that, more than any other factor, ended the rule of the Stuart dynasty. Edward Terrar triumphantly cites local studies to demonstrate that most Catholics suffered less from sectarian oppression than from the economic marginalization they shared with poor Protestants.[25] Although it is a legitimate achievement of such studies to prove that Catholicism was not confined to genteel circles, the fact that anti-Papist propaganda had little immediate impact on Catholic commoners reflects not the insignificance of this propaganda but the incommensurability of its goals with a focus on the Papist next door. This propaganda took the clergy – or foreigners – as its target, not those poor lay fools deluded by Romish subtlety.[26] The object was to identify Papism with alien Irish barbarism, French despotism, and corrupt Roman luxury. Directing attention to the indistinguishability of the English Catholic poor from their Protestant neighbors would have been counterproductive for the half-conscious program of identifying Protestantism with a coherent English nation. The immediate personal tolerance of "Some of my best friends are Catholic" must be kept distinct from the impersonal, indeed dehumanizing, image of the Church as a vast conspiracy.[27] The very names "Papist" and "Romish" locate that Church as foreign; the universalist assertion implicit in the name "Catholic" is one Protestant writers never allowed to be legitimate.

Anti-Catholicism does not retain today the central importance it once possessed, but the shape and rhythm of its anxieties find later echoes. What has been said before influences what can be said now, and literature, shaped by its exclusions, is necessarily what can be said. As Terry Eagleton has argued, what constitutes literature is not a neutral, technical question, but on the contrary one necessarily implicated in society's self-definition, its rationalizations and discourses of power.[28] Jochen and Linda Schulte-Sasse note the utility of a national enemy against which to unite a people in the service of "the reproductive needs of powerful centralized states as they developed since the Golden Age in Spain, the late seventeenth century in Great Britain, the eighteenth century in France and Germany, and the late nineteenth century in the United States."[29] The Papacy served as such an emblem of evil against which a modern, centralized nation-state could be organized in England, justified by an ideology of capitalism, nationalism, and Protestantism. As Eagleton remarks of the Enlightenment inventors of the term "ideology," "the appeal to a disinterested nature, science and reason, as opposed to religion, tradition and political authority, simply masked the power interests which these noble notions secretly served."[30] Tenison's *Sermon of Alms* gives an idea of what those interests might be when he cautions against "unprofitable (not to say, very injurious) profuseness" that might contribute to "the *great grievance* of a numerous unmanag'd Poor."[31] He demands, "That Charity may be prudent, let us avoid all *pride* of heart which dealeth out the measures of it to the unqualified and unworthy," and, prefacing two pages devoted to the horror of shamming beggars, conjures "Let us conquer *foolish pity* and irrational compassion" (50, 51). This sermon, although it grudgingly allows that charity is permitted, devotes all its energy to warning against the dreadful sin of generosity. Max Weber claimed that the attitude of Stuart Anglicanism lay nearer to the forgiving medieval attitude toward begging than to the harsh Puritan one, but he was thinking "especially in the conceptions of Laud."[32] If the executed, pre-Civil War Archbishop Laud represented the "forgiving" Stuart Church, perhaps the post-Glorious Revolution Archbishop Tenison equally represented its less forgiving successor.

Condemnation of charity accompanied condemnation of Popery. Tenison's hostility toward "a numerous unmanag'd poor" resembles Buckingham's toward Irish Catholics.[33] Suggestively, Tenison's sermon was published bound with John Williams's 1688 anonymous *An Apology for the Pulpits*, an indignant reply to John Gother's *Good Advice to the Pulpits*, a Catholic apologetic which quoted numerous intemperate Anglican diatribes against Rome from the period before James II's accession as proof of the questionable quality of clerical loyalty.[34] Williams, who himself had published *The History of the Gunpowder Treason* in 1678, cannot deny Gother's facts, and so counterattacks, accusing him of attempting "to incense the Government of the Nation" (2) against the Church of England and of quoting sermons written "20 years since, and the rest in the years 78, 79, 80" (3). Williams's pamphlet reiterates the customary Anglican assaults on Catholicism, beginning with the great argument of Catholic "Doctrines of the Peoples Power over Princes, of the Lawfulness of Resisting, or of a foreign Jurisdiction over their Soveraign [sic]" in contrast to Anglican doctrines of "the Rights of Princes, and the Subjection and Obedience of the People in all lawful Cases" (3). This double monument to loyalty and miserliness appeared in January, 1688; within a year William III, who would make Williams a bishop and Tenison an archbishop, was in London.

Anti-Catholicism acted as the mechanism of cultural reproduction necessary to mobilize autonomous subjects in the service of the centralized state; it supplied the other, the enemy. Terence N. Bowers celebrates John Foxe's *Acts and Monuments* as "radical Protestant literature," saying that it encourages "independence" and "honors their ["poor, humble people"] transgression into the realm of texts – a realm that had long been the preserve of a secular and ecclesiastical elite."[35] To call a work placed in every church by order of the sovereign "radical" seems a strained interpretation; the strain becomes even more evident when secular and ecclesiastical elites are casually joined together as though they were one. There is no need to question Foxe's sincerity to see that the secular elite used Protestant enthusiasm to appropriate to their own uses the assets of the ecclesiastical establishment, which is to say that the government and the wealthy exploited a popular movement to enrich themselves at the expense of the only institutions (however inadequate) of education and social care in their society. Nor did gentry appropriation of ecclesiastical property end with the outright confiscations of the Reformation. The practice by which laymen controlled clerical benefices, "livings," enabled an ongoing siphoning away of vast sums. Richard Brown observes that numerous churches were ruinous by 1700, and a majority of incumbents remained nonresident still in 1812, at which latter date one £800 living was tended by a clergyman allotted only £55, leaving the other £745 for the living's owner.[36] If a church is only so much property, it is to be exploited as profitably as possible, like any other property. In the seventeenth century, the combination of popular religious enthusiasm and elite self-interest became volatile, to the point where there seemed a danger at midcentury that the enthusiasm would escape the control of the self-interest. It did not, however, and instead anti-Popery became the principal propaganda weapon of what J. C. D. Clark has called "the English ancien regime, 1660–1832."[37] That this period corresponds to what English departments call the long eighteenth century (plus the Romantic period) is no more coincidental than that anti-Popery has been almost entirely, one might say scrupulously, avoided as a subject for literary study. It is the antithesis of the literary – a bitterly partisan, vastly voluminous, minutely contemporary mass of ephemerae.

John Bender has asserted that "until recent revisions of critical methods by feminism, new historicism, and cultural materialism, Anglo-American investigation of eighteenth-century literature proceeded largely within deep-rooted postulates – within a frame of reference – that fundamentally reproduced Enlightenment assumptions themselves."[38] In Parliament-ruled Britain, and in America with our bewigged-savant Fathers, the Enlightenment *is* the ancien regime. To examine hatred of Catholicism is to question the existing structures of a society that assumes its perfect rationality and justice. While exploring old mystifications, however, examinations of the past need to be careful to refrain from undue eagerness to construct new ones, a new Whig history, the manufacture of yet another "usable past" impressed to validate the present, or rather an imagination of the present. As J. G. A. Pocock observes, "Given the world-wide failures of revolutionary dialectic, it should seem that the destruction of history as a process justifying the present is a programme for emphasizing irony and contingency, for inviting the inhabitants of the present to conduct their affairs in the knowledge of how very easily things might have been otherwise, and of how complex and contradictory were the processes that have made them what they are."[39] Modernity critiqued the pre-modern as postmodernity critiques the modern; the contemporary *fin de siècle* succeeds the smashup of the racing car which Futurism supposed more beautiful than the Winged Victory of Samothrace. In the words of Brook Thomas, it is the task of a historicism that can claim to be new, to be not merely repeating the motions of its predecessors, "to acknowledge the contingency of its own ideas and beliefs."[40] In the aftermath of the wars of secular religion of the twentieth century, we should remember that we know only our own ignorance, that

> History to the defeated
> May say Alas but cannot help or pardon.[41]

CHAPTER ONE

Constructing the nation, constructing the other martyrology and mercantilism

With the Reformation Christendom was lost.[1]

> ... that vast metropolis,
> The fountain of my country's destiny
> And of the destiny of earth itself,
> That great emporium ... [2]

This first chapter establishes the political and economic contexts that conditioned the development of anti-Catholicism in sixteeenth- and seventeenth-century England. Catholicism acted as the demonized antagonist in opposition to which English nationalism first crystalized.[3] To understand the process by which religious hostility participated in the mutation of traditional into capitalistic society is crucial to understanding the world we have inherited. The two central myths of modernity are progress and nationalism. Both operate as binaries; the new and improved requires the old and inferior, the native the foreign, to provide a boundary. If England was the first country to evolve a recognizably modern political culture, as Liah Greenfeld suggests, one significant reason is that local circumstances facilitated the fusion of these two "others" – the outmoded and the alien – into a single horrific villain, the Catholic Church, "the very masterpiece of *human* wisdom" in Macaulay's words (emphasis added).[4] To be called a masterpiece of wisdom may not seem the worst insult, but to qualify this wisdom as human is to annihilate, in particular, the principle of apostolic episcopal succession common to both the Catholic and Anglican churches, and, more generally, the divine character of its institutional-ization essential to any church. Macaulay continues with high praise that is more obviously low damnation, saying of Catholicism that "among the contrivances which have been devised for deceiving and oppressing mankind, it occupies the highest place."[5] The process of rationalistic modernization begun in England continues, metastasizing in conjunction with capitalism throughout the world. Discussing the evolution of

Hinduism from traditional doctrinalism to a political movement charged with nationalistic passions, Daniel Gold notes how Western and Hindu fundamentalisms share "a feeling that one's world is being colonized, taken over by an alien power that is secular and perhaps demonic."[6] This transformation of religious *ressentiment* into aggressive nationalism occurred first, at least as an agent of spectacular social transformation, in post-Reformation England.

This chapter will examine the construction of a modern England in one famous, if now little read, work and two sets of less well-known treatises. The yoking together of these apparently heterogeneous texts is deliberate, enforcing a mutual implication of religious and secular discourses, which are also political and mercantile ones, traditionally regarded as unrelated. John Foxe's *Acts and Monuments*, the most important text of the English Reformation besides translations of the Bible, exalts kingship as the necessary mechanism for destroying the inherited Church of his time. In his volumes, monarchy is the one hope for the eradication of old abuses. The later and less known works next discussed, which consist of a few pages each as opposed to Foxe's thousands, are published scripts for pageants performed to celebrate the inauguration of London's Lord Mayors. Thomas Middleton wrote seven of them early in the seventeenth century, and Elkanah Settle rather more at the century's end. Middleton's pageants enact and celebrate the importance of commercial London, particularly its lengthening colonial grasp; Settle's pageants, the last ever performed, ratify redundantly a civic power already incontestably established after the Glorious Revolution. Foxe's modernizing monarchy abolishes the medieval institution of the Church, and in the process undermines itself as the other principal institution of governance. Into the gap the city's fiscal power grows. The Lord Mayors' London represents the nucleus of the modern world.[7] In an England transforming its self-image from a marginal European island, which in the mid-sixteenth century had at last lost the final remnant of its Plantagenet French possessions, to a world power, the other against which it defines itself begins to expand from the Continental Catholic menace to include innocent and harmless non-Europeans waiting eagerly to be exploited. A defensive posture in European affairs finds a complement in overseas aggression. The "revolutionary" impact of radical Protestantism melds into a nationalism that releases itself in oppression in Ireland and transoceanic capitalism. As Christopher Hill observes, "The regiments in Ireland remained the most radical in the English army ... Yet in retrospect the Cromwellian conquest of Ireland looks less like a religious crusade than the first of those colonial wars which

were to occupy England for the next two and a half centuries."[8] Religious
radicalism authorizes imperialism.

I

There can be no better starting point for examining the enduring logic and
effect of Reformation anti-Papism than Foxe's *Acts and Monuments,* a
frequently reprinted work that remained in circulation for centuries. If the
primary target of this work is the satanic evil of Rome, its secondary theme
is the sacred value of monarchy.[9] *Acts and Monuments* mentions superstition
and idolatry in Romish practices, but it focuses overwhelmingly upon
"such killing and slaying, such cruelty and tyranny shewed, such burning
and spilling of Christian blood, such malice and mischief wrought, as in
reading these Histories may to all the World appear."[10] The three massive
folio volumes of the 1684 ninth edition, a reprinting of a pre-Civil War
edition of 1632, begin with enough prefatory material to make a book of
substantial bulk. The first introductory section after the title page is "The
Kalendar," a listing of the days of the year, one month per column, two
columns per page, with a martyr or martyrs assigned to each day; the
names are not Roman or Greek, but modern and English. A lengthy
Chronology comes last in this prefatory matter, before pagination begins
with the preface upon "the difference between the Church of Rome that
now is, and the Ancient Church of Rome that then was" (1.1). The third
date in the Chronology is *Anno Christi* 33, the anniversary of when "*Tiberius
Caesar* hearing of Christs Miracles, Resurrection and Ascension, moves
the Senate to receive and adore Christ for a God" (n.p.). The sinister
princeps of Tacitus and Ben Jonson's *Sejanus* becomes for Foxe an early
witness (the root sense of "martyr") to the glory of God, but the Senate
rejects the proposal "because contrary to the Laws of the *Romans* (so they
said) he was received for God, before the *Romans* decreed the same," and as
punishment Rome receives 300 years of tyrants, few of whom avoided
dying "an ill end" (n.p.). The prince is visionary, but the legislature
foolish, so the nation suffers. Foxe is paying court to the one power, the
monarchy, able to break the control of the transnational institution of
the church, and at the same time identifying Protestantism with national
independence.

Particularly while discussing the period before the Reformation, the work
returns repeatedly to the crucial importance of the monarch and to the
horror of the Pope's usurpation of power over secular heads of state. The
first book quickly disposes of "The Ten first Persecutions in the Primitive

Church," then the second and third conflate national and sacred history in the centuries between Constantine and 1066. Having started with "A Table of the Saxon Kings, which ruled alone from King Egbert unto William Conqueror" (1.150), the third book ends by stressing three circumstances to observe: "The religious zeal and devotion of Kings, both in giving to the Church, and also in correcting the manners of Churchmen. Secondly, the dissolute behaviour and wantonness of the Clergy, then abusing the great Donations and Patrimonies of Princes bestowed upon them. Thirdly, the blind Ignorance and Superstition of that time ..." (1.191). The contrast between good, if priest-deluded, kings and villainous clergy forms the subject for the illustrations to "The Fourth Book, containing Other [sic] three hundred years from *William Conqueror*, to the time of *John Wickiffe*, wherein is described the proud and mis-ordered Reign of *Antichrist*, beginning to stir in the Church of Christ" (1.192). These woodcuts portray the Emperor Henry standing for three days and nights outside Canusium (1.202), "Pope Alexander treading on the necke of Frederick the Emperour" (1.231) – below which begins a twenty-five-page discussion of Thomas Becket, a proud prelate obstinate to his king – and, occupying a full page, a series showing a monk's poisoning of King John (facing 1.291). Henry keeps his crown, but stands barefoot outside a shut gate while two mitred figures smirk atop the town wall, behind them two tonsured monks, and in a window a third man in a mitre dallies with a woman, in contrast to the family of the abased monarch, whose wife and child accompany him. As England's premier medieval saint, and a martyr on behalf of the Church against the crown, Becket requires thorough demolition, not the visual representation of hagiography; Pope Alexander's image takes his place. So does King John's, an innocent king supposedly murdered by a cleric in place of Becket, a sainted cleric murdered by a king. If illustrations are expensive and rare in *Acts and Monuments*, full-page ones are much more so, with not half a dozen in over 2,000 pages. That the relations of crowns and mitres occupy so large a proportion of this severely limited pictorial budget suggests the importance of the issue. Let us examine how two of them depict the relation of monarchs and the Church as a usurpation of secular authority by clerical ambition.

The poisoning of John crowds six panels onto one page (see illustration 1). The style is spare; the celebratory gorgeousness of an illuminated manuscript would be not only technically unfeasible but counter to the austerely daunting purpose. The first picture depicts "The Monke absolved to poyson King John": in a bare room, one tonsured and robed figure kneels on the floor before another, who frowns on a thronelike chair,

"The Poisoning of King John" from *Acts and Monuments*, 1684

his hands upon the bald spot of the kneeler. After this image of alien hieraticism comes the mixing of the poison, then its presentation to the king, pictures of the king and monk who each "lieth here dead of [yᵉ.] poison," and the celebration of the Mass. Each panel captures an important moment. The first and last frame the treachery in its institutional approval, both before and after the murder. In the last, communion becomes a memorializing of a murder in the sense opposite to that customarily incarnated: the monks celebrate the killer instead of the killed; the Mass thus becomes a black mass, a satanic rite marking the absolute apostasy of Rome from Christianity. The second and fifth panels respectively introduce and conclude the action proper, showing a monk fanatical enough to kill and to die for the institution symbolized in the first and sixth. In the third panel, the largest and most elaborate, the monk offers the poison in a wassail bowl; four figures are distinctly delineated, the most in any of the six pictures, drapery appears behind the king, and the windows are decorated. The only picture which lay and clerical figures share, this is the central image of the sequence: when Catholicism encounters an unsubmissive king, treachery and murder result. Next, crown and scepter at his side, the king is mourned by the only other layman on the page (beards mark their difference), not by clerics; they attend to their own. As the Mass metamorphoses to an offering to Antichrist, so the slain monarch becomes aligned with Christ, a witness, a martyr like the many who will follow in Foxe's account. It is in the context of such a tradition of iconography that the story that a Jesuit plot lay behind the execution of Charles I becomes plausible. The depiction in the last panel of "A perpetuall Masse sung daily in Swinsted [Abby] for yᵉ. Monk that Poysoned King John" identifies the crime as not individual but corporate. The encroachment of ecclesiastical upon secular power, encoded in the poisoning of King John, signals the onset of "the proud and mis-ordered Reign of *Antichrist*, beginning to stir in the Church of Christ." After that, in Shakespeare's words, "Nothing but bonfires."[11] Nearly every picture that follows depicts burnings alive, with some floggings for variety.

For Foxe, the humiliation of kings leads inexorably to the burning of heretics. Beginning with "The Fifth Book, containing The last Three Hundred Years from the loosing out of Satan" (1.452), *Acts and Monuments* reaches its great and obsessive subject, the hideous cruelty of Rome, repeated with variations for hundreds of pages in one account after another. Two of the few exceptions to the sanguinary rule for the illustrations occur at the start of book nine and near the end of the first volume. The ninth book, concerning the reign of Edward VI, opens with a scene proclaiming "The Temple purged," where a banner reading "Images" burns instead of a human figure: the fire of demonic persecution has become that of purification (2.1).[12] The illustrations return from the spectacle of auto da fes to the earlier subject of the opposition of crown and Church; near the end of the first volume, a two-page spread displays popes' "rising up from faithfull Bishops and martyrs to become Lords and Governors over Kings and Kingdoms" (between 884 and 885) (see illustration 2). The images represent Papal usurpations upon and insults to crowns, including King John's offering of England to the Papal legate and a reprise of Emperor Henry at the gate. The two-page spread depicts the evolution, or rather degeneration, of popes from "faithfull Bishops and martyrs to become Lords and Governors over Kings and Kingdoms." The "tortures" imposed on Christians by a heathen magistrate yield to "Constantine the Emperor embracing Christian Bishops" between the first and second panels; in the third the bishop of Rome sits beside the emperor, and the other nine are devoted to grotesque and sordid degradations inflicted upon monarchs by proud popes or legates. Hats and beards signify cleric and lay positions, and hand-held emblems power; in every scene at least one person wears a crown, miter, or papal tiara. In the first drawing, a persecuting pagan ruler carries a sword and is escorted by soldiers in helmets and bearing pikes, but has a crown very similar to a miter: this one evil secular ruler in the sequence wears quasi-Romish headgear to encourage viewers to identify him with the ecclesiastical abuses that follow, instead of with the Christian kings whose crowns, all similar, resemble those of contemporary monarchs. In the second, only the emperor's head is covered: as in the English court, subjects go bareheaded in the royal presence, and the king's hand holds a staff of authority that has replaced the sanguinary pagan's sword. In the third, the first miter appears, on the bishop advanced to the emperor's side, and some functionary (secular by his beard, which only clerics in this sequence eschew) standing beside the ruler also wears a fantastical hat; the ruler still holds his staff of power, but the bishop's book, surely a Bible, balances it. The spiritual power is beginning to encroach. Suddenly, in the fourth panel, the king has laid down his crown and staff to kiss the papal toe; this abjection accompanies the first appearance of the word "Pope," his triple tiara, two keys in his hand that symbolize his power, and other clerics in supporting roles. The medieval church has emerged full-blown. The rest of the pictures reiterate variations of the fourth, crowns abased and tiaras exalted. The cumulative effect suggests an arrogant upstart, this nobody of a bishop seizing and then abusing the scepter of rule from a temporal power that remains

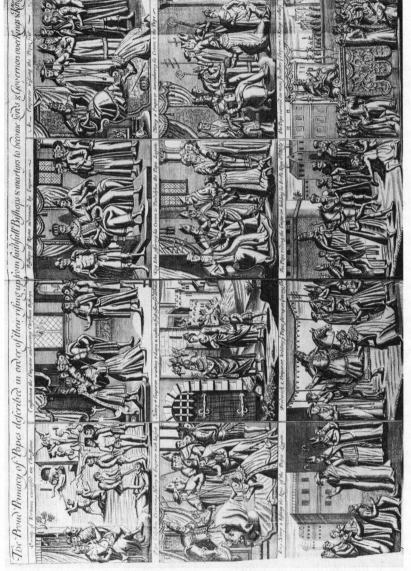

"The Proud Primacy of Popes" from *Acts and Monuments*, 1684

unchanging in its benignity after the first frame. To correct abuses, the secular power must convert Peter's keys back into a scepter. The Pope is the original Tartuffe, a canting parasite who uses piety to cloak his designs to overthrow the rightful master of the house. Papal outrages against monarchs embody the clerical imposition upon the body politic.

Yet a double edge resides in the allusion to John: his grant to Rome, while in theory a humiliation, in practice enabled the Pope to declare the Magna Carta void on John's behalf as "audacious wickedness whereby the Apostolic See is brought into contempt, the royal prerogative diminished, the English nation outraged."[13] Civil war ensued. No such war follows in this updated version of Foxe's work, however, although it includes, as the title says, "Additions of like Persecutions which have happened in these Later Times." Featuring the Bartholomew Day's Massacre, the Armada, "Foreign Martyrs," and "Gunpowder Treason," the "Later Times" stop at 1620. Because the 1684 edition is a reprint of one from before the Civil War, England appears as still standing confidently united against the Popish threat; it need not take into account that a monarch supreme in Church and state is alone with his people, unable to appeal to a supranational authority to validate his own. *Acts and Monuments* projects the historical moment of the Reformation – when a prince could use his secular power to seize control of the spiritual power that had come up for grabs amid the questioning of inherited religious institutions – into a transhistorical truth. The three huge illustrated folio volumes of the 1684 edition, published under the direct patronage of the Stationers Company, represent a substantial investment; that the last two complete editions of the *Acts and Monuments* in the seventeenth century appeared in 1641 and 1684 suggests that, from being a manifesto of Tudor monarchism, it had become a reproach to the Stuarts for neglecting their duties as Protestant champions. A king who does not defy the fires must be kissing the papal toe. In 1641 the Civil War was beginning, with London the great redoubt of Parliamentary strength; in 1684, following the Exclusion Crisis, open resistance by the city against the crown had been effectively prohibited. Both editions act as banners to rally the faithful against the king, like Parliament in the Civil War, in the king's own name.

II

Foxe's synthesis of a heroically Protestant kingship proved ultimately unable to continue to cohere as the dynamics of imperial expansion came into conflict with a monarchy no longer able to control them after the suspected Stuarts succeeded the apotheosized Queen Bess. Only the crown could have unleashed the accelerated circulation of capital caused by the confiscations of Church property, but once Henry VIII had seized (and largely squandered) the booty, events progressively escaped the royal orbit. As Mark Goldie observes, "The Whigs steadily secularized an eschatological drama, inherited from the canonical works of early English Protestantism, and especially from John Foxe. It was a vision in which the temporal sphere, whether embodied in a Godly prince or a Godly people, gradually asserted its rights against the pretensions of a usurping clergy."[14] Foxe's work exemplified the "godly king" of the Reformation literature of Edward's reign, but this type became within a century the "royal Antichrist" of Puritans: from usurping clergy to usurping crown proved, by the time of the Civil War, an irresistable gradation of ideas.[15] Secular hierarchical authority could destabilize its ecclesiastical counterpart, but in the process ultimately destabilized itself. Motions toward emancipation and toward enserfment, however, cannot cleanly be divided; to resist or subvert one system is necessarily to prepare for another. A new authority was incubating in the city, that "image of the future" where one is "a stranger and an agent," a commercial authority whose emergence tracks the fading of feudal ideological structures, Caroline crown and Laudian Church alike.[16] An annual ritual symbolized this new authority, the pageant that celebrated the inauguration of a new Lord Mayor. If Foxe the religious polemicist promulgated a self-consciously modern and English difference from the foreign and archaic as represented by Papism, then Middleton the civic publicist re-coded that difference into a new universalism in the service of mercantile interests. Between the Reformation and the apotheosis of commercial London, "The older providentialist languages of imperialism had been transformed into a pretence to enlightened rationalism."[17] In his pageants, a modernity that in Foxe had consisted of the abolishment of Papist abuses acquired the active dimension of visiting commercial abuses upon other peoples; condemnation of the corruption of the spiritual for material ends opened the way to the pursuit of materialism without any spiritual pretext at all.

London's first recorded Lord Mayor's Day pageant occurred in 1535, its last in 1701.[18] That the rise of these pageants coincided with the 1530s disestablishment of Catholicism in England suggests the displacement of an impulse toward popular processional and festival from its newly disallowed religious varieties into secular form. A populace deprived of saints' days was offered an alternative. The decay and then the cessation of the pageants reflects the delegitimization of folk culture as it was overcome by what Max Weber in his classic study called "the *summum bonum* of this [Protestant] ethic, the earning of more and more money, combined with the strict avoidance of all spontaneous enjoyment of life."[19] With its origins in the medieval Midsummer Show, the festival had already become the principal civic event of the city by the earlier date; by the later it had become a vestigial localizing anachronism in a national and international metropolis. London, with a population of only 50,000 under Henry VIII, grew to 160–180,000 by 1600, and continued to increase in the seventeenth century at a rate much beyond that of the country overall, while such English regional centers as York, Bristol, and Norwich remained relatively static in population, none over 20–30,000.[20] It was in the heyday of the elaborate Lord Mayor's Day pageant, then, that London advanced beyond its medieval status of first among equals, the principal city of the realm, to another order of magnitude, to being the city, no adjective needed. An example of conspicuous consumption on a municipal scale, the pageant asserted the importance of the city in the awkward adolescence of its economic explosion from local to global center. By 1701 there was no need anymore to enact symbolic Triumphs of London, because London had triumphed.

The class of great merchants from among whom the Lord Mayor was chosen, recognized as the masters of the city, put on spectacles to symbolize their dominance; these extravaganzas functioned not only to impress the generosity and legitimacy of their rule upon their social inferiors, however, as Theodore B. Leinwand proposes, but also to advance a claim to what amounted almost to an alternative sovereignty.[21] Thomas Middleton asserts at the opening of *The Triumphs of Truth*, his first Lord Mayor's Day pageant in 1613, "that there is no subject upon earth received into the place of his government with the like state and magnificence as is the Lord Mayor of the city of London."[22] He repeats the vaunt, with some variation in the wording, in the first sentences of his last two pageants, *The Triumphs of Integrity*, 1623, and *The Triumphs of Health and Prosperity*, 1626. David Bergeron has argued that *The Triumphs of Truth* may be likened to a stage comedy in its moral design; but civic pageantry is closer to the masque in its political purpose as an enactment of dominance, and Middleton's subsequent pageants display an awareness that his new genre differs from those popular on the stage.[23] Further, whereas the structure of *The Triumphs of Truth* is an anomaly even among Middleton's own other Lord Mayor's Day pageants, the purpose of these foremost city spectacles remains as true to itself as Polonius could ask.

They emerged when London was beginning to become the national metropolis, and they ceased once, in Raymond Williams's formulation, city had conquered country, once mercantile imperialism and the cash nexus had absorbed the traditional economy and polity. The pageants of Middleton and Elkanah Settle reflect respectively the ideological posture of the city at the peak of the pre-Civil War political struggle and after its final victory in 1688.[24]

Power and its means of legitimation have become a contentious subject in studies of English Renaissance theater. Stephen Greenblatt has suggested that power perpetuated itself in the Renaissance by conjuring a demonized opposition, as accusations of atheism became a necessary means to uphold orthodoxy, and more generally by provoking and then releasing anxiety. When James followed a set of grisly public executions with pardons announced upon the scaffold, he won vast applause.[25] In contrast to such ceremonies of affirmation as those ritually theatricalized pardons, Franco Moretti and Jonathan Dollimore see tragedy as subversive of the social order. If, as Moretti claims, "the historical 'task' effectively accomplished by [tragedy] was precisely the destruction of the fundamental paradigm of the dominant culture," and if, as Dollimore argues, such a work as *The Revenger's Tragedy* subverts authority by inverting the relation of masque and antimasque in courtly entertainments, the question remains just what the paradigm and authority are.[26] As Albert Tricomi observes, Middleton's *A Game of Chess*, with its adversarial metaphor for politics, exposed the falseness of the crown's pretense of ruling impartially from atop a stable order instead of being one of multiple factions competing for power.[27] The court and the country have long been conventional terms for the principal opposites, the "two warring cultures,"[28] but the foremost stronghold of resistance to the court throughout the seventeenth century, politically, financially, militarily, and literarily, was London.[29] Nor did king and Parliament alone possess authority and a cultural paradigm. Every year the ruling elite of the city celebrated their power and wealth with a pageant on the day of the inauguration of the Lord Mayor. Like the royal masques, these pageants provided a performative affirmation of authority, but the authority affirmed was in covert competition with that of the crown.[30]

Middleton, whom Ben Jonson called "a base fellow," held the office of City Chronologer for the last years of his life, and throughout his career was identified with the city.[31] Jonson wrote occasionally for the city, but principally for the court; his masques fill 400 pages. Middleton's one masque, on the other hand, was *The Inner Temple Masque*; the 1603

Magnificent Entertainment: Given to King James to which he contributed was a welcome by and in the city to the new monarch; and the lone "entertainement" he wrote for performance in Whitehall to honor the installation of Charles as Prince of Wales in 1616 was *Civitatis Amor. The Cities Love* (*Works*, 269). When he wrote a piece for a royal audience, then, he wrote not directly for the court but as a way for the city to address the court. Middleton's fame for *A Game of Chess*, the "learned exercise 'gainst Gundomore" and the biggest hit of the Jacobean stage, resembles that of Settle for *The Female Prelate*, an anti-Catholic tragedy of the Exclusion Crisis, and for his political pamphleteering on behalf of Shaftesbury. Middleton, however, enjoyed no such lapse in the censorship as Settle did during the Exclusion Crisis, and Charles I had greater powers than Charles II to restrict and punish authors and their patrons, so we cannot be certain whether the performance of *A Game of Chess* was the result of catching the Master of the Revels napping or, as Thomas Cogswell claims, deep and devious royal machiavellianism.[32] Censorship necessarily creates uncertainty of meaning.[33] Nonetheless, if a writer had to be circumspect in his criticisms, he remained free to praise, and whom he praised and for what can supply a perspective not found elsewhere.

After the indefatigable Anthony Munday, who had at least partial responsibility for fifteen, Middleton was the next most prolific writer of Jacobean Lord Mayor's Day pageants, producing seven: *The Triumphs of Truth*, 1613; *The Triumphs of Honor and Industry*, 1617; *The Triumphs of Love and Antiquity*, 1619; *The Sun in Aries*, 1621; *The Triumphs of Honor and Virtue*, 1622; *The Triumphs of Integrity*, 1623; and *The Triumphs of Health and Prosperity*, 1626. All but the first are the same length, occupying eighteen pages in the spacious nineteenth-century Bullen edition, except the last takes only fifteen. Of the eighteen or fifteen pages, the first six, being largely or entirely blank, could be compressed into one. Thus the forty pages of *The Triumphs of Truth* are not only twice but almost three times as long as any of the rest. This first of Middleton's pageants also possesses a structure anomalous among his other works in the same genre, but not among masques and plays. The later pageants simply recount a progress through a series of set pieces, describing an emblematic scene, then giving the speech recited there in honor of the new Lord Mayor by Expectation (*Love and Antiquity*, 316), the Queen of Merchandise (*Honor and Virtue*, 358), or whatever the presiding figure is in that display, and then moving on to the next scene. There is no interaction and no opposition.

It is unsurprising that a playwright's first pageant should have much reminiscent of the playhouse about it. *The Triumphs of Truth*, unlike

Middleton's later pageants, provides an Error with one long and two short speeches, a sidekick Envy who has two lines, and the ongoing activity of their both being "chased before" the mayor in his processional (*Truth*, 250). After Envy says his two lines, "Learn now to scorn thy inferiors, those most love thee, / And wish to eat their hearts that sit above thee," Zeal directly addresses Error and Envy, crying, "Bold furies, back! or with this scourge of fire, / Whence sparkles out religious chaste desire, / I'll whip you down to darkness" (*Truth*, 244–45). It is tempting to read such lines satirically, particularly when one recalls that Middleton wrote the not particularly naive *A Chaste Maid in Cheapside* at almost the same time; and yet such a reading would at once place the speech at odds with the very purpose of the pageant and require the supposition that Middleton was covertly laughing in their faces at a body of influential men for and to whom he was to continue to write paeans until the year before his death. If intentional satire becomes an untenable hypothesis, an inadvertent bleeding over from his satiric comedy is more plausible. Satire to panegyric can be an awkward transition. Every ringing affirmation suggests that a denial is being outshouted, and an oligarchy of merchant princes could hardly avoid generating resentment among those they ruled. Envy is quickly hushed up, but its mere appearance, and the necessity that it be silenced, as Duke Vincentio silences Lucio in *Measure for Measure*, reminds those present of something that suits awkwardly with full-throttle praise. A dialogic structure cannot help but introduce uncertainties and ambiguities.

Playing the part of Satan in the wilderness, Error tempts the new Lord Mayor to abuse his trust:

> Great power this day
> Is given unto thy hand; make use on't, lord,
> And let thy will and appetite sway the sword; . . .
> The worth of every office to a hair,
> And who bids most, and how the markets are,
> Let them ["Gluttony and Sloth"] alone to smell; and, for a need,
> They'll bring thee in bribes for measure and light bread;
> Keep thy eye winking and thy hand wide ope,
> Then thou shalt know what wealth is, and the scope
> Of rich authority; ho, 'tis sweet and dear!
> Make use of time then, thou'st but one poor year,
> And that will quickly slide, then be not nice:
> Both power and profit cleaves to my advice;
> And what's he locks his ear from those sweet charms,
> Or runs not to meet gain with wide-stretch'd arms?
>
> (*Truth*, 242–43)

For Error to appear to tempt the new Mayor implicitly admits that, unless merchants equal Christ in virtue, they may at times succumb. Despite all his subsequent chastisement, Error has revealed, in a way that cannot be entirely expunged, the fallibility and potential for corruption of the officeholder and his class, since he and they necessarily achieve their positions through "power and profit." Thus David Bergeron's argument that *The Triumphs of Truth* has the same moral design as a comedy may be recast: *The Triumphs of Truth*, borrowing much of its structure from comedy, the form in which Middleton had been used to write, in the process inadvertently borrows in part the self-doubting, self-destabilizing dynamic of the stage. That the introduction of this dynamic resulted from inadvertancy, or a failed experiment, appears from his never again introducing dialogue or humor into his pageants; he had learned that the inaugural ceremony of the Lord Mayor was not a stage, and was not a fitting place to give even devalued speech to the excluded. Comedy would compromise the dignity of the event. Captives do not get lines in triumphs. A pair of zanies "chased before" the Lord Mayor would depreciate his authority, and release the subversive energies of popular carnival into an occasion intended to reinscribe a particular, mercantile form of authority.[34]

Middleton's subsequent pageants display his mastery of this lesson, and the frequency of his selection to write them shows the appreciation of his patrons. After *The Triumphs of Truth* in 1613, he did not compose another pageant until *The Triumphs of Honor and Industry* in 1617; but thereafter, having demonstrated that he had mastered the requirements of the genre, he got most of the commissions until his death. His period of favor from 1617 to 1623, during which he wrote the pageant in 1617, 1619, 1621, 1622, and 1623, was perhaps broken by *A Game of Chess*: even if that play did have court backing, such support would have had to be surreptitious or the satire would have lost the aura of sensational daring that made the show the hit of its generation. In contrast to the incorporation of a mobile Zany into *The Triumphs of Truth*, in *The Triumphs of Honor and Industry* the several symbolic tableaux are presented without destabilizing connectives, and all speeches are serious and directed to the Lord Mayor and audience. The contents of those speeches exemplify what Oliver Goldsmith at the zenith of England's first colonial empire a century and a half later called "The wealth of climes, where savage nations roam, / Pillag'd from slaves, to purchase slaves at home."[35] "The first invention" shows

A company of Indians, attired according to the true nature of their country, seeming for the most part naked, are set at work in an Island of growing spices; some planting nutmeg-trees, some other spice-trees of all kinds; some gathering the fruits, some making up bags of pepper; every one severally employed. These Indians are all active youths, who, ceasing in their labours, dance about the trees, both to give content to themselves and the spectators.

After this show of dancing Indians in the Island, follows triumphantly a rich personage presenting India, the seat of merchandise. This India sits on the top of an illustrious chariot; on the one side of her sits Traffic or Merchandise, on the other side Industry . . . (*Honor and Industry*, 297–98)

While no image so openly coercive as an overseer appears, the Indians do not merely work but are "set to work." Further, although India sits at the top and center of the chariot, the figure that gives the speech for this tableau is Industry, a speech whose theme is praise of Industry itself: "Behold this ball of gold, upon which stands / A golden Cupid, wrought with curious hands; / The mighty power of Industry it shows" (*Honor and Industry*, 299). The Indians labor, dance to display their contentedness, and remain mute, while voice is reserved for those who have set them to work. The difference between non-Europeans, who are only sources of "Traffic or Merchandise," and Europeans, who have individuality and the empowerment of speech, is underlined by the next display, the "Pageant of Several Nations," in which a Frenchman and a Spaniard salute the new Lord Mayor and the Society of Grocers in their respective tongues, with translations supplied as well (*Honor and Industry*, 300–1). France and Spain were of course the foremost Continental powers, as well as major trading partners with England. Power is a precondition of speech; no Error or Envy here requires silencing. Moreover, the pepper, nutmeg, and "spice-trees of all kinds" betray that the setting of the scene lies specifically in the *East* Indies, the province of not the government but the East India Company – a convenient symbol of the power and influence of the merchants and the city.

One pageant differs suggestively from the others. The 1619 *Triumphs of Love and Antiquity* celebrates "the noble Fraternity of Skinners" (*Love and Antiquity*, 313), a less internationally oriented company than the Grocers, and Sir William Cockayne, of the Cockayne project, whom Heinemann calls the only "creature of the Crown" among the ten city merchants to whom Middleton dedicated works.[36] This pageant features no colonial trade; it is instead remarkable for what follows the customary recitation, a brief one in this case, of past Lord Mayors of the same fraternity as the incoming. "[I]n the Parliament of Honour," on the "mount of royalty," Antiquity celebrates at length the fact that "Seven kings, five queens, only one prince alone, / Eight dukes, two earls, Plantagenets twenty-one" have been "of this fraternity made free, / Brothers and sisters of this Company," more than of any other company (*Love and Antiquity*, 323, 324). Afterward, three and a half pages go to listing every one of the royal "Brothers and sisters." A polemical nuance may be inferred from the fact that Middleton's next pageant, the 1621 *Sun in Aries*, his only one whose title does not begin with "The Triumphs of," starts, unlike any of his others, by rejoicing that "Pisces being the last of the signs, and the wane of the Sun's glory, how fitly and desiredly the Sun enters into Aries, for the comfort and refreshing of the creatures, and may be properly called the spring-time of right and justice" (*Sun in Aries*, 341). Middleton's other pageants all open with an exclamation at the wonder and the glory of the ceremony itself, this with rejoicing at a new season, which could be read as criticism of the old, of the antiquarianism of his own previous pageant. A more solid evidence than the calendrical that *The Triumphs of Love and Antiquity* differs in its object of praise from the rest of his pageants lies in what it does and what it does not contain. It contains the long list of "Plantagenets twenty-one"; it does not contain a reference to overseas adventures. Nor, unlike *The Triumphs of Integrity*, does it declare that "'tis the noblest spendour upon earth / For man to add a glory to his birth," better "Than to be nobly born and there stand fix'd" (*Integrity*, 387). When employed by a royalist, Middleton could pass for a royalist.

Two years later, in 1621, he returned to his customary imperialist orientation. Middleton wrote *The Sun in Aries* for the Company of Drapers, whose traditional patron or representative was Jason for his capture of the Golden Fleece. Jason fetched the Fleece from Colchis, a barbarian ("barbaros," non-Greek) kingdom across the Black Sea, and was politically able to repudiate his wife (according to Seneca's *Medea*, which being in Latin was more available to the Renaissance than Euripides) because she was a foreigner. The epithalamium for his new wife which the Chorus sings – in Seneca's *Medea*, unlike Euripides', the wedding does take place – expresses pleasure that at last he is getting a proper Greek wife, not an outlander. In *The Sun in Aries* Jason makes the first speech: "I am he, / To all adventurous voyages a free / And bountiful well-wisher, by my name / Hight Jason, first adventurer for fame" (*Sun in Aries*, 340). The governing metaphor of his address is that the mayoralty is "a year's voyage," a "great expedition" that "goes for honour, life's most precious trading" across the sea of state (*Sun in Aries*, 340–41). Honor does not reside in idle state with kings, queens, and dukes, but is a prize sought abroad by trade. The 1626 *Triumphs of Health and Prosperity*, again for the Drapers, recycles the use of Jason but only as the type for "Sir Francis Drake, England's true Jason . . . / Never returning to his country's eye / Without the golden fleece of victory"

(*Health and Prosperity*, 406). Both *Sun in Aries* and *Health and Prosperity* celebrate the imperial wealth of London and construct it as the theological seat of British power, the true inheritor of the classical imperialism of Greece and Rome; its merchants rule the seas and foreign lands, where the power of the court is confined to England.

The 1622 *Triumphs of Honor and Virtue*, like that of *Honor and Industry* written for the Grocers, returns to "the Continent of India" for its first scene (*Honor and Virtue*, 357). In this scene,

> a black personage representing India, called, for her odours and riches, the Queen of Merchandise, challenging the most eminent seat, advanceth herself upon a bed of spices, attended by Indians in antique habits: commerce, adventure and traffic, three habited like merchants, presenting to her view a bright figure, bearing the inscription of Knowledge, a sun appearing above the trees in brightest splendour and glory. (*Honor and Virtue*, 358)

The presentation of the "Queen of Merchandise" utilizes the symbology of the commodification of women to express the commodification of colonial peoples. In the posture of the exotic Queen of the East whose archetype is the Cleopatra of legend (not that of history), she submissively presents herself as sexual object and colonial subject, and hence doubly other. Unlike "India, the seat of merchandise" in *The Triumphs of Honor and Industry*, she is permitted to speak, but only to delegitimize her own claims in favor of those of European adventurers.

> I that command (being prosperously possest)
> The riches and the sweetness of the east,
> To that fam'd mountain Taurus spreading forth
> My balmy arm, whose height does kiss the north,
> And in the Sea Eoum [sic] lave this hand,
> Account my blessings not in those to stand,
> Though they be large and fruitful, but confess
> All wealth consists in Christian holiness.
> To such celestial knowledge I was led,
> By English merchants first enlightened . . .
>
> (*Honor and Virtue*, 359)

The fantasy is the same as that which Greenblatt finds in Thomas Harriot's 1588 *A Brief and True Account of the New Found Land of Virginia*, that heathen natives will be so swept away by Christianity that they will enrich Europeans for no other reward than that of being converted.[37] Not only soldiers "desire . . . to live by the sweat of other mens brows": a small trader can grow to a great merchant only by capitalizing on the labor of others.[38] In practice, colonial peoples quickly tired of, and rebelled against, so one-sided an arrangement, but Middleton's pageants, after *The Triumphs of Truth*, permit only a single point of view, that of London's merchant elite, whoever the putative speaker. His deliberate univocality, so in contrast to his theatrical writings, affirms the right of that elite to rule; his text silences or co-opts alternative voices.

III

This propagandistic fixedness of purpose persists in the last Lord Mayor's Day pageants at the end of the seventeenth century, but altered circumstances altered content. The Civil War crippled royal independence, and the Glorious Revolution all but ended it. In the place of a Stuart crown attempting to emulate Continental absolutism, in King William the city at last had a monarch who like the Lord Protector would fight for English trading interests, and who, also like Cromwell, had no indefeasible hereditary right to reign. The monarchy had been tamed. With the end of the necessity for a strong symbolic assertion of the power and dignity of the city, the end of the pageants was approaching. In the few years before inertia permitted changes in forms to catch up with changes in power relations, however, they continued, but in a lighter vein, eased of their previous politico-metaphysical urgency.[39]

The official City Poet of London (as Middleton had been City Chronologer), Shaftesbury's chief propagandist during the Exclusion Crisis, and the former master of ceremonies of London's Pope-burnings in 1679 and 1680, Elkanah Settle wrote all the pageants in their last decade of publication, from 1691 to 1701. The 1698 pageant, *Glory's Resurrection: Being the Triumphs of London Revived*, was the first pageant after the custom had been allowed to lapse for the two preceding years, and the only Lord Mayor's Day pageant Settle wrote that was not entitled *The Triumphs of London*. *Glory's Resurrection* has four pages of dedications, six of text, and five of pictures. As his *Empress of Morocco* was the first English tragedy to be published with illustrations (the "sculptures" which provoked John Dryden's indignation), so in this endeavor Settle embellishes all he can to conceal that he is commemorating a dying mode of communal performance. The dedications laud the Goldsmiths for having, "after a three-Years Cessation, reviv'd the Customary *Splendor* of the *City* on this Solemn Occasion," and the Lord Mayor because "*Charity* and *Hospitality*, those two Illustrious Ornaments of Magistracy, Your Lordship has resolved to recal from their late *Banishment*."[40] There is no further mention, however, of any charity or hospitality other than that of holding the pageant – we may recall

Tenison's view of almsgiving – and no invocation of illustrious and generous previous Lord Mayors. Settle's expression, "recal from their late *Banishment*," and his governing metaphor of resurrection echo the rhetoric of providentialist panegyric following the Restoration.[41] In the place of neglected or forgotten civic traditions, he redefines the city as supplanting the country by rewriting the royalist myth of national redemption into a teleology of municipal victory.

In *Glory's Resurrection*, the actual text to be spoken is vanishingly slight, fifty-four lines in heroic couplets, broken into four speeches of eleven to twenty lines each, plus a twenty-four line "Song" at the end which has no apparent place in the pageant and which may well have been added afterward to pad out an exceedingly thin volume. Two of the speeches and the song place primary emphasis on "*Britain*'s Dread *Caesar*" (*Glory's*, 6) and little more than append the Lord Mayor: "So Rules Great WILLIAM: So, my Lord, shall You" (*Glory's*, 2). The Third Pageant, however, "A Triumphant CHARIOT of Gold," efficiently compacts its politico-historical logic into a small space:

> Justice of old by long Oppression driven,
> Left the Tyrannick World and flew to Heav'n.
> But when Great NASSAW, *Albion*'s Scepter bore,
> Our Laws and Rights sent kindly to restore,
> She visited the *Albion* World once more.
> Thus whilst our *Caesar* yields a Trust so large,
> As proud *Augusta* to Your Guardian Charge.
> As He from Heav'n His Sovereign Justice drew;
> He's Heav'ns Vicegerent [sic], his Vicegerent, You.
> *Astraea* then must here her Pow'r resign,
> Her brightest Glories in Your Hand shall shine.
> You'll best, my Lord, my Righteous Ballance hold,
> No Poise so even as in the Scales of *Gold*.
>
> (*Glory's*, 4)

Under the Stuarts, that is, municipal liberties and oligarchic privileges were invaded, but after the Glorious Revolution and the coming of William III the "natural rulers," those of London among the rest, were able to seize uncontested local supremacy in their respective districts. Lord Mayors did not presume to call themselves viceregents under James I. The only dialogue in the volume occurs in the Second Pageant, "The GOLDSMITHS Laboratory":

> ST. DUNSTAN. The Trumphs of this Day, deserv'd so well,
>   When Fame shall in Recorded Story tell,
>   Those Oracles of Truth –

DEVIL.   Can You speak Truth?
ST. DUNSTAN. Peace, snarling Devil! Thus I'll stop your Mouth.
                        [Catches him by the Nose]
                                    (*Glory's*, 3)

Glory's Resurrection can incorporate farce because, even more than *The Triumphs of Truth*, it makes no metaphysical claims. Nothing is threatened by the subversions of dialogue – a dialogue in which the Devil only gets four words – because a festival in the streets is no longer imbued with any kind of meaning. Also, a saint could hardly be invoked with serious reverence only a decade after the expulsion of James II, so the Devil's role is to disrupt the disruptive, to pre-empt audience suspicion of any spokesman with a miter and crosier, as the illustration portrays St. Dunstan. Whereas Middleton used a satiric humor in *The Triumphs of Truth* that proved too disruptive, too dangerous to the solemnities of hierarchy, to be continued in his later pageants, Settle's nose-tweaking slapstick threatens nobody. Settle praises the Lord Mayor, the Goldsmiths, the city, King William, everyone he should, but no sense of London as a community and distinct entity remains. Lord Mayors of past centuries are not recalled; the Lord Mayor is not reminded to look after the poor as part of his duty; London is no longer a place apart but an integral part of the kingdom it has done so much to remake in its own image. All that is left to do as the communal world recedes into the private is to get rich and cheer on the crown-in-Parliament, because city, crown, and Parliament have become united against the threat of France. By the time Settle comes to write them, the ideological work of the pageants has already been accomplished, by the upheavals of the seventeenth century and the advent of an emphatically Protestant king with an aggressive foreign and mercantile policy.

Thomas Middleton wrote Lord Mayor's Day pageants when they were at their peak of magnificence and significance, when they asserted the right of the merchant elite to rule the city to both crown and crowd. He gave rhetorical embodiment to the legitimation they required. Next to Middleton the author of cynical comedies and subversive tragedies stands Middleton the apologist for an emergent bourgeois imperialist ideology. Whatever his undercuttings of the royal mystifications of masques and aristocratic power in his theater work, the evidence of his pageants indicates that he was not implacably hostile to all authority. Once those he had hymned dominated the nation, the sort of poetry he had written as a symbolic reinforcement of their position became archaic, rooted as it was in the very precapitalist system they had overthrown. Once mercantile

interests felt secure of their power, the pageants became obsolete because
their historical moment at the transition between the medieval and the
modern was over, because the city had consummated its hostile takeover of
the crown. It is fitting that it is in the last Lord Mayor's Day pageant ever
published that Mercury says:

> Let Schoolmen in their Academies sit,
> And fancy their Learn'd Heads claim all the Wit.
> All vain Mistake. Search where true Learning lies:
> The MERCHANT is the *Witty* and the *Wise.*
> *Philosophers,* who Nature's Depths explore,
> Seek but for Airy Treasure; they, no more
> But view the Mines. The MERCHANT digs the Oar.
> Let Book-learn'd Heads survey the Golden Strand,
> Like cold *Platonick Suitors* distant stand.
> To warmer Joys does the brisk MERCHANT press;
> They but read Worlds, He pushes to possess.[42]

Subversive ambiguities collapse with what they have been undermining;
in the new world where money justifies itself, the merchant need no longer
disguise his acquisitiveness with a doctrine subtler than "dig[ging] the
Oar" and "push[ing] to possess" the "Golden Strand." Wit and wisdom lie
in wealth, so wealth does not need poetic confirmation. The two
Middletons do not stand independent of each other; to subvert one order
is to construct another. The apparently contradictory sensibilities of the
cynic and the panegyrist illuminate both one another and the apparitions
of victor-written history. Middleton's Lord Mayor's Day pageants form
the logical prelude to both Settle's articulation of disarticulation and the
subsequent suppression of the pageants altogether: by muting every voice
but that of power, the word ultimately conspires to silence itself.

IV

Foxe and Middleton are both engaged in constructing a modern identity
whose center of gravity evolves – or perhaps it might be more accurate
to say a changed identity, new in contrast to what precedes it, even if it
presents itself as a return to authentic origins, "more orthodox than
orthodoxy," in Terry Eagleton's phrase[43] – in contrast to the illegitimate
innovations which Protestants made a standard reproach of Papism. A
crown that enters the Reformation cast by proponents of reform as a
champion of religious emancipation has become, after a management
shake-up, the enforcer for "the brisk MERCHANT," who has been liberated

from any moral constraint whatever beyond pursuit of profit. Discussing the relation of Protestantism to the "rational capitalistic organization of labor," Weber returns repeatedly to its sacralization of labor itself, as when he contrasts Richard Baxter's sense of work as a calling, an end in itself, with Thomas Aquinas's higher valuation of contemplation.[44] Pageantry that at first carries forward a medieval communal tradition, in the process providing an outlet for popular festivity now banished from religion, expires with the sense of locality of a city expanding into Wordsworth's metropolis, a "great emporium" where everything is for sale, including "slaves, and souls of men."[45] It is in the erosion of traditional communities, in the acidulousness of an expanding market economy, that nationalism evolves as a communion of the decommunalized, a colossal projected union compensating for individual alienation and anonymity.

In a role reprised in legitimist guise in 1715 and 1745, anti-Papism served in 1688 to enable an oligarchic *coup d'état* and disguise it as a popular revolution; once the takeover was consummated, however, so powerful a continuing popular sentiment became suspect as still possessing the potential for destabilization.[46] Noting that the Gordon Riots of 1780 were the largest "civil tumult" in England since Monmouth's Rebellion in 1685, which was also animated by anti-Papism, Ian Gilmour condemns the riots as "purely coercive," aimed at "undo[ing] the alleviation of injustice," and "a total failure. So far from bringing revolution they revived the ministry."[47] As he notes, however, the rioters specifically attacked prosperous Catholics, bypassing poor ones, and chose targets more suited to pursuers of revolution and peace with America than nihilistic destroyers.[48] The popular unrest strengthened the government because it provoked anxiety among the gentry at the spectacle of a populace unleashed. What seems to disappoint Gilmour about the riots is that they ensured their own futility by continuing to express popular grievances and class resentment in archaic terms of religious enmity that, never perfectly accurate, had become ludicrously irrelevant to the ministries of George III, who throughout his life opposed toleration of Catholics and who exclaimed while reading Johnson's *Journey to the Western Islands* that "I protest, Johnson seems to be a Papist and a Jacobite!"[49] George III was no Papist or Jacobite, but he was a monarch pursuing widely resented policies, and the remembered synonym for tyranny remained Popery. The protesters were attacking the Hanoverian regime with the very logic upon which it had been founded because they possessed no alternative rhetoric of opposition with such universal appeal.

"The law of political power always works best when it is invisible," as

Eagleton observes, however, and with the disappearance of the Stuart threat hostility toward Catholicism was becoming conspicuous as an anachronism embarrassing to a gentry for whom confessional differences had lost value as a method of indoctrination.[50] The problem with his argument that a colonial situation undermines Gramscian hegemony, because a "visibly alien" law will not readily be internalized, is that he optimistically skips over how difficult it is to "pass through" nationalism, and if a people does not "pass through" in a teleology of emancipation they will repeat the violence to which they were subjected, like a battered child who matures into a batterer.[51] The declaration of the Henrician Act in Restraint of Appeals to Rome that "this realm of England is an empire" retained an aptness that perversely persisted after the sense of "empire" changed: at the time of the Reformation, the Henrician claim to "empire" was an assertion of the nation's sovereignty over itself, of its freedom from external authority, but the power of the Protestant rationale for independence was such as to extend itself into a justification for the subjugation of other peoples. Liberation leads into another prison. The origin of the British empire is itself "An emancipatory politics."[52]

Although Linda Colley focuses more on the perennial warfare with France in the eighteenth century than on religious issues, she also notes the importance of "The Other in the shape of militant Catholicism" as well as "a hostile Continental European power, or an exotic overseas empire" in the creation of a sense of common nationality among the previously separate countries occupying the British Isles.[53] Competition with other European powers, principally but not only France, provided a patriotic justification of expansion abroad as defensively necessary in the context of intra-European competition. The old saying that the British empire was acquired as an afterthought possesses a partial validity, however, to the degree that the acquisitiveness of Middleton's merchant princes found justification in the defensive posture of Foxe's Protestants under siege by horrific Papists. A thousand individual and national acts of opportunistic aggression found an originating rationale in the crusade against Catholicism. The blood of the martyrs was the seed of colonialism. If Middleton's Company of Grocers does not profit by the "Queen of Merchandise," the Spaniard and Frenchman who stand ready might. In the eighteenth century, Robert Clive began England's first campaign in the conquest of India to frustrate French designs that threatened English trading interests. Rome, too, acquired its empire by a series of "defensive" wars.

CHAPTER TWO

Of true religion and false politics
Milton, Marvell, and Popery

We mean to souse old Satan and the pope;
They've no relations here, nor friends we hope.[1]

This chapter scrutinizes how Milton and Marvell employ anti-Catholic rhetoric so as to begin the detailed investigation of the role of anti-Papism in the seventeenth century with two familiar figures in an unfamiliar aspect. My discussions of each are constructed around suggestive juxtapositions within their corpuses that are usually ignored in critical discourse. Milton's *Of True Religion*, one of his most neglected pamphlets, nevertheless is the only controversial work he published after the Restoration, the period of *Paradise Lost* and *Samson Agonistes*, and addresses the same issue, toleration, as the much more familiar *Areopagitica*. Marvell's "Upon Appleton House" and *An Account of the Growth of Popery, and Arbitrary Government in England*, respectively one of his most famous poems and a prose tract that has not been reprinted in over a century, are apparently altogether dissimilar works of the sort that have kept constructions of the poet and prose writer Marvell distinct. Nonetheless, they share a common deployment of anti-Catholic rhetoric that communicates an underlying unity readable in the seventeenth century but deliberately repressed since. No poet and polemicist has been so closely associated with Milton over the centuries as his friend, assistant under Cromwell, and fellow "poet-patriot," Marvell, yet the connection is more often confined to biographical discussions than permitted to inform examinations of their works. If the distance seems too wide between Marvell's characteristic tetrameter couplets and Miltonic blank verse, however, perhaps we should consider what we may learn from an earlier critical tradition that celebrated Marvell as a politician mediating between the divine Milton and his people. As Nahum Tate, William III's poet laureate after Dryden's dispossession for religious and political unreliability, wrote, "Great *Milton's* Shade with pleasure oft look'd down, / A Genius to applaud so like his Own."[2]

Examining Milton as a post-Restoration anti-Papist pamphleteer presents him in a different context than he usually assumes. His last tract, *Of True Religion*, excited no interest at the time of its publication in 1673, and has attracted surprisingly little since, compared to the attention given his earlier prose.[3] When it has been treated, as recently by Reuben Marquez Sanchez, Jr., the context in which it is set has tended to be limited to Milton's other works. But *Of True Religion* is a work deeply and deceptively involved with the larger contemporary political context; under a pretense of simply supporting a general Protestant tolerance, it covertly continues the war against royalty, episcopacy, and orthodoxy which Milton had waged so long before.[4] Written in the spring of 1673 as a reaction to the February 4–March 29 session of Parliament that passed the Test Act in response to the "no Popery" furor that followed Charles II's promulgation of the Declaration of Indulgence on March 15, 1672, *Of True Religion* renews with tactical modifications the argument Milton had earlier made in *A Treatise of Civil Power* for religious tolerance.[5] Its radical implicit agenda, however, extends beyond a merely defensive plea for toleration. *Of True Religion* has been mistaken for a more moderate work than Milton's screeds of the Civil War period, without sufficient allowances being made for the greatly different circumstances of its composition, for the necessity of indirection and encoding after the Restoration. In its cautious strategizing it thus parallels the late epic and dramatic poems, whose ambiguity permitted them to be drafted after 1688 to serve as both pillars of Whig order and "republican" testaments. In contrast to the retired Milton's caution, necessary in a politically suspect apologist for regicide, the M.P. Marvell enjoyed considerably more opportunity to participate in active politics, and in consequence has been divided by a formalist criticism unable or unwilling to reconcile aspects assigned separately to the "Renaissance" or "Restoration." Like the neglect of *Of True Religion*, the bisection of Marvell reproduces in miniature the subject of this study: the obscuration of anti-Catholic anti-literature as a whole by a post-Enlightenment literary and political culture intent on effacing its sectarian origins.

This discussion follows the lead of those in *Politics, Poetics, and Hermeneutics in Milton's Prose* that "stress precisely those elements and issues that allow us to break down this partitioning" between the Miltons of prose and verse.[6] The partitioning, however, is not only that between the poet and the controversialist but also that between the poet-controversialist and the England of the Restoration. The institutionalized classification of Milton with the Renaissance by English departments tends to obscure the chronological fact that *Paradise Lost* appeared contemporaneously with *Annus Mirabilis*. Perhaps partly in consequence, extant scholarship on *Of True Religion* remains as close to nonexistent as is possible with an original work by Milton. Nathaniel Henry oversimplified the status of religion in England before 1688, but nonetheless his sweeping point that Milton wrote not "as a philosopher presenting an individual, personal, theoretical view" but "political propaganda devoted to the program of a party" may serve as a corrective to idealizing views of the poet.[7] Far from expressing a liberal belief in the equal rights of all viewpoints, it should be remembered, Milton states that "we have no warrant to regard Conscience which is not grounded on Scripture" (*Of True Religion*, 432). Sanchez's essay, the first extended analysis of the pamphlet since Henry's over forty years ago, sees it as important "as the last (public) example of the manner in which Milton attempted to perform his role as God's chosen teacher to the English people."[8] The Milton of Marquez perpetuates the atemporal prophet who "attempts to communicate with an audience of the not-so-distant future – with a Parliament, and an England, whose position on religious toleration might not be so parochial as that of his immediate audience" and who warns of "the danger of politicized religion"(36). This Milton is the decontextualized Whig saint canonized in the eighteenth century, not the intensely political, and therefore inevitably "parochial," author of the seventeenth. In the 1670s as in the 1640s, Milton's religion remains politicized; nonetheless, unlike Marvell's, it is not subordinate but superior to secular considerations.

Fredric Jameson cites Max Weber as viewing "the charismatic and militant moment of heroic protestantism as something like a vanishing mediator between the older traditional societies in the process of ruthless disintegration, and the newer secular or desacralized world of capitalism and the market system," and proceeds to read this intermediate status as embodied in *Paradise Lost*.[9] Milton left more direct evidence, however, than that in iambic pentameter of his position amid the transformations of seventeenth-century England. The threat of Catholicism, as embodied in the future James II, was the central political issue of the 1670s and 1680s. A comparison of Milton's 1673 *Of True Religion* to Andrew Marvell's 1677 *An Account of the Growth of Popery, and Arbitrary Government in England* indicates the radical divergence between his writings and those of active politicians. The controversies of the time insistently link religious and political issues in a way that exemplifies the status of religion as a "master code," in whose terms all other disputes were expressed, in seventeenth-century England. Marvell's title, with its verbal equation of "Popery" and "Arbitrary

Government," seems a locus classicus of this coding. The crucial ideological difference, however, between Milton and Marvell is precisely that for the older writer politics is an aspect of religion, whereas for the younger religion is an aspect of politics. For him, there are no theological principles more important than Parliamentary maneuverings, no causes beyond the immediate and pragmatic, and religious language serves only as drapery for secular concerns; more concerned with purity than victory, Milton holds to the good old cause.

In his fidelity to his vision in defiance of changed circumstances, Milton drifted away from a gathering secularization of public life as the era of religious wars waned, a secularization exemplified by Marvell's pamphleteering. At the conclusion of *The Experience of Defeat*, Christopher Hill admits that he had anticipated returning to Milton as a central figure in both politics and culture.

> When I started writing this book I had not thought that Harrington and the Harringtonians would become so central: I had expected to end with Milton. We have seen that there was a wide variety of reactions to the experience of defeat. But two variants emerge. Once we get beyond the immediate agony of the Restoration, Harringtonianism appears to take over. Defeat further fragmented and depoliticized the saints: their answer could only be rewards in the after life, or Milton's blank assertion that good must win in the end.[10]

For Hill, after the Restoration Milton becomes a peripheral figure politically, regardless of his canonical centrality, with only a "blank assertion" of revolutionary chiliasm to set against the schemings of the Machiavellians. N. H. Keeble, however, protests against

> the impression [that] remains that Puritanism peters out after the Restoration, its religious and cultural life henceforth a backwater . . . The contrary seems rather to be the case: political defeat was the condition of cultural achievement.
>
> It is that proposition which this study advances: the literature of Puritanism, far from being left over from an earlier age, was generated by the Restoration experience of persecution and nonconformity. Milton and Bunyan appear as exceptions only so long as we accept the court's confident assertion of the universal hegemony of its taste and measure by the Caroline rule.[11]

Keeble and Hill are not so irreconcilable as they might seem. Keeble is discussing cultural events and literary phenomena, Hill the overtly political, writing that directly confronts issues engaging society at large.[12] Where the political historian is disappointed, the literary historian finds a beginning: their approaches and emphases differ, but both rest upon a similar substratum of factual agreement underlying the interpretation. The emergence of a separate literary and cultural tradition, as Keeble suggests, is not contradictory to but, on the contrary, complementary to a withdrawal from the political mainstream. To become the other, to be denied expression, paradoxically empowers.

By remaining preoccupied with the division between orthodoxy and independency within the Protestant bloc, Milton kept his integrity at the cost of immediate political relevance. More successful pamphleteers, such as Marvell, focused on the Catholic threat as a rallying cry to unite all Englishmen (besides the tiny non-Protestant minority). That the Stuart court stridently proclaimed its unchallengeable hegemony after 1660 does not, of course, prove that such a hegemony existed; rather the reverse. Insecure in a power so recently re-established, the court balanced its campaign between a positive propaganda and a negative system of censorship and spies, between John Dryden and Roger L'Estrange, but neither could stem the flow of public feeling as the memory of the major generals became more distant and the threat of Louis XIV and James Stuart more ominous.[13] In 1673, amid the first great flux of the anti-Catholic hysteria that would culminate in the Exclusion Crisis, Milton published *Of True Religion*. The full title of this work is *Of True Religion, HAERESIE, SCHISM, TOLERATION, And what best means may be us'd against the growth of POPERY*. Mary Ann Radzinowicz claims that, "The occasion of the work was Milton's discovery that popular support existed for his own profoundest convictions." She perceives correctly that rising anti-Catholic sentiment presented him with an opportunity to re-enter public debate, after long exclusion as the champion of regicide, with a position that, if pursued "carefully" might lead toward a "common ground between himself and Parliament."[14] But he and they were headed different ways.

I

In the history of Marvell criticism, the prosewriter and poet have seemed to preclude each other. Marvell's reputation constitutes perhaps the most striking instance of critical inversion of any canonical figure in English literature; he has not merely been sometimes eclipsed and sometimes celebrated, but has possessed two entirely different reputations at different times and based on different works. While reprints and studies of his lyric verse multiply, his prose has until recently gone unread, and the latest complete compilation remains Alexander B. Grosart's in 1875, although a modern edition of *The Rehearsal Transpros'd* does exist.[15] Few Marvell collections since Grosart's *The Complete Works in Verse and Prose of Andrew*

Marvell M.P. include the "M.P." in the title. The critical tradition has been so amnesiac that in 1980 Harold Tolliver in a review essay was surprised to find "that earlier critics presented very partial versions of him. They ignored the lyric poet almost entirely and even the verse satirist and saw primarily the prose satirist and patriot whom Swift admired and emulated."[16] Apparently, that later critics have reversed the polarity and seen only the poet does not seem "partial" to him. The reaction had already begun in Grosart's time; a review of his edition regrets that "he who was Milton's friend and a sweet poet of nature and of sentiment has been the accredited author of many satires full of loathsome obscenity and virulent malice."[17] The political activity that had been Marvell's glory in the older tradition becomes an embarrassment once he becomes consecrated as a "serious," canonical poet. The literary and the political are antithetical: "And the singer of an April mood, who might have bloomed year after year in young and ardent hearts, is buried in the dust of politics, in the valley of dead bones."[18] While twentieth-century critics may repudiate the sentimental rhetoric with which their Victorian predecessors whitewashed Marvell as a "singer of an April mood," they have continued the disjunction between poet and pamphleteer inaugurated by those predecessors, until Tolliver is puzzled to discover that the pamphleteer was ever considered significant.[19] A disjunction once deliberate has become habitual.

In recent years, historicizations of Marvell have been attempted, but unless his partisan political agenda is integrated with his theological context, which in the seventeenth century defines the ideological, such efforts must be partial.[20] Michael McKeon begins his study of Marvell by arguing for the poetry's "consistency" – he mentions that *An Account of the Growth of Popery, and Arbitrary Government in England* displeased the government, but otherwise does not discuss the prose – and concludes that "Marvell's most central concerns have not altered" from "the circumspect observer of the 1650s to the Protestant patriot of 1678 and posterity." McKeon's analysis, however, lacks a mechanism motivating Marvell's "progress" from seeing "not Dutch liberalism but French absolutism ... as the model of what was to be feared most at home." It is not by chance that McKeon uses the passive voice: the question of who is to do the fearing is thereby sidestepped. Marvell's position remains consistent because in both periods he is championing not "English freedoms" but the upper-class dominance that is coded as such freedoms.[21] At Appleton House, Marvell is an aristocrat's retainer; in Parliament, he represents those with the means to exercise the franchise. The significance of his use of

Catholicism in "Upon Appleton House" and *An Account* is what it has to tell us about his ideological positioning; concerning Papism, he is no more "circumspect" in the 1650s than the 1670s. As Jean-Luc Nancy observes, "ideology is the blind spot where a system of thought no longer brushes against its own deconstruction, where it does not let go of the obvious, of a meaning already present to itself."[22] Popery is pre-eminently the blind spot of seventeenth-century Protestantism. The connection between *An Account* and "Upon Appleton House" is their employment of Catholicism as a bogey, an ultimate incarnation of evil against which Marvell can rally all Protestants, no thought necessary, no dissent allowed. To doubt the "obvious" urgency of the Popish menace would be to cast doubt upon one's own attachment to the Protestant cause, which is synonymous with the nation; by invoking that menace, Marvell supplies an unchallengeable justification for his political agenda. Although very different, so much so that they have hardly been regarded as the work of one hand, both works have related objectives and strategies. The tract operates to undercut the legitimacy of Charles II, the poem to uphold the legitimacy of the gentlemanly counter-dominion, embodied in Appleton House, that over-threw Charles I, and both works identify the cause of gentry rule with Protestantism. A true king is a defender of true religion who enjoys the support of his people; as on the Continent, monarchy requires religious sanction. The political function of arousing popular fear of Popery is to deprive the crown of that sanction, and it is as an actively political intelli-gence that Marvell, the pamphleteer *and* poet, deploys religious hatred as a tool of the trade. Marvell's ongoing goal is to promote the power of the propertied, such as the Fairfaxes or Parliamentary electors, and his con-sistent device to disguise that class aggression, whether against the lower orders or the crown, as the national interest is attacking Catholicism.

An Account of the Growth of Popery, and Arbitrary Government in England, by the member for Hull, Andrew Marvell, indicates the tactics of the Parliamentary opposition during the 1670s. Marvell had long been a formidable critic of the government, and this pamphlet like others of his sold well and excited attention. The *London Gazette* offered a reward of £50 for discovery of the printer of this anonymous work, and £100 for that of the author, much above the usual blood money of shillings or a few pounds.[23] On the title page, "Popery" is in letters twice the height of any other word; "Growth" and "England" are next in magnitude; and "Arbitrary Government," the remaining words of significance, are in letters again barely over half the size of those of "Growth" and "England." The second period of the title, however, in fine print occupying no more

space than "Popery" alone, tells the real subject: "More Particularly from
the Long *Prorogation*, of *November*, 1675, Ending the 15*th* of *February* 1676, till
the Last Meeting of *Parliament* the 16*th* of *July* 1677." Whereas Milton
focuses seriously on religious issues for their own sake, and is willing to
affront the Anglican majority to make his case, Marvell reduces Popery to
a device for arousing popular attention and alarm. Nor was Marvell
unique in employing such a rhetorical sleight of hand. A more extreme
example may be found in the anonymous *The Papacy of Paul the Fourth. Or,
the Restitution of Abby Lands and Impropriations, An indispensible condition of
Reconciliation to the Infallible See*: the lengthy subtitle, sure to grab an English
eye (and not confined to small print), has no relation to the text of the
pamphlet, which is a history of the Continent in the sixteenth century that
devotes only a paragraph or two to England.[24] Marvell is typical of
Restoration political pamphleteers in his willingness to enlist religious
prejudice in the service of a secular dispute, a practice that climaxes in the
sensational allegations of the Popish Plot. The religious aspect of his title
operates not in any spiritual sense but as a code for political concerns.

The text repeats this strategy of secularizing the religious. A short introductory paragraph claims that, "There has now for divers years a design
been carried on to change the lawful Government of England into an
absolute Tyranny, and to convert the established Protestant Religion into
downright Popery."[25] The next two pages praise the English constitution,
under which, unlike in the tyrannies "of our neighbor nations[,] ... the
subjects retain their proportion in the Legislature" and the king's "very
Prerogative is no more than what the Law has determined" (248–9). What
ensues gives a demagogic caricature of Catholicism as "such a thing that
cannot, but for want of a word to express it, be called a Religion" but
rather "the bold imposture of priests under the name of Christianity," a
fraud "deliberately contrived, knowingly carried on" (250–1). After a half-
dozen pages of such general-purpose libel, the subject modulates to the
threat posed by Catholicism to governments because of its independence
of the temporal power, its counter-sovereignty, a state within the state
(257). In particular, rehashes of Queen Mary and the "Gunpowder
Treason" culminate in the observation that, were Catholicism restored
with its pre-Reformation landholdings, "no considerable estate in
England but must have a piece torn out of it upon the title of piety, and the
rest subject to be wholly forfeited upon the account of Heresy" (258–60).
Following this alarmist appeal to private interest, the remaining 150 pages
give a minute account of recent English Parliamentary transactions
and governmental infighting. Michael G. Finlayson points out that

seventeenth-century English Protestantism found its common ground not in doctrine but in anti-Catholicism.[26] Because an attempt to define or defend any theological position is unnecessary to Marvell's partisan purpose, and would only limit the appeal of his case by offending those with different beliefs, he plays to his audience by confining his remarks on religion to that with which almost every English Protestant will agree. Unlike *Of True Religion, An Account of the Growth of Popery* is not interested in Popery at all except as a device for generating popular excitement and mobilizing the landholding classes against the crown. Marvell exploits a generally perceived equivalence between "French slavery" and "Roman idolatry" (261), but for him Catholicism is only a crowd-pleasing teaser, a Bloody-Mary shirt to be waved to catch the reader's attention and then be put away. In contrast to Milton's concern with scripture and spirituality, doctrinal niceties of faith and idolatry are not on the agenda for Marvell. He redirects Anglican hostility from Dissent to Popery with more success than Milton precisely because he prefers demagogy to theology. As Conal Condren notes, "Breaking the nexus of confidence between Church and King[,] as Marvell correctly saw, was the essential thing."[27] To undercut the crown successfully, religious issues must become synonymous with political ones, as in the Civil War. Marvell's "doubly indirect" strategy, as Annabel Patterson calls it, of attacking Popery instead of defending the Church of England is designed to enable him to unite all Protestants against, in William Lamont's phrase, "Kings who betrayed their imperial role."[28]

To recognize "the centrality of religious issues" in the seventeenth century, it is not necessary to dismiss anti-Popery as mindless emotionalism, "a knee-jerk response to a non-existent popish threat."[29] On the contrary, the importance of the animus toward Catholicism consisted precisely in its power as an organizing principle of binary opposition: the polarity of true Protestants and antichristian Catholics recapitulated, intertwined, and in the process amplified binaries of reason and unreason, English and foreign. If Renaissance literature performed theatricalizations of authority upon a social model focused around the court, this centralization occurred not only onstage but also in Francis Bacon's formal garden and Ben Jonson's great house. An aesthetics of spectacle and spectatorship, such as many critics have suggested is central to Renaissance literature, implies a polarization of authority and subjection. A spectacle, however, requires spectators, which before mass communications in turn necessitated the physical assembly of a crowd; but a crowd, as Elias Canetti observed, is apt to become a mob if not controlled.[30] A country house and garden occur frequently as an idyllic setting for conversation in the Rennaissance, whether the storytelling of Boccaccio's *Decameron* or the philosophical dialogue of Erasmus's "The Godly Feast." A conversation operates on a smaller and hence less unstable scale than the mob action of spectacle, as a manor is more manageable than a metropolis. As Don Wayne notes, Jonson's "To Penshurst" domesticates the aristocratic command center of agricultural production that is the premodern great house into something that begins to be recognizable as the modern "home."[31] Authority is localized and sentimentalized, but remains authority. Where Bacon's enormous and elaborately formal garden represents princely power, Jonson's Penshurst celebrates the regional aristocratic fiefdoms within the monarchical economy of power, and Marvell's Appleton House completes the process of divergence by recasting familial gentry authority as actively opposed to the institutional organization of the nunnery. As in *An Account* Marvell attempts to discredit Charles II by identifying his "Tyranny" with "Popery," so in "Upon Appleton House" he revises the Renaissance tradition of the garden or great house as an image of authority, and authorizes the revision by identifying the old order with Catholicism in the Thwaites episode. John N. King observes that "during the century following Edward's reign, the godly king had become the royal Antichrist in the eyes of Protestant radicals."[32] Appleton House's more secure foundation upon the ruins of a nunnery defeats Bacon's purely secular garden.[33]

One of Bacon's longer essays, added to the post-impeachment third edition of 1625, "Of Gardens" begins with the declarations that "God Almighty first planted a garden" and that "I do hold it, in the royal ordering of gardens, there ought to be gardens for all the months in the year, in which, severally, things of beauty may be then in season."[34] He then launches into several pages listing times of greenness, blooming, and fruit-bearing for year-round use, "*ver perpetuum*" (192), as he quotes Virgil. The concatenation of plant names common enough in themselves creates an opulence of enumeration in cumulative effect:

For December and January and the latter part of November, you must take such things as are green all winter: holly, ivy, bays, juniper, cypress-trees, yew, pineapple trees; fir trees, rosemary, lavender; periwinkle, the white, the purple, and the blue; germander, flags, orange trees, lemon trees, and myrtles, if they be stoved; and sweet marjoram, warm set. (190)

One after another such mustering of species and varieties adds to the riot of luxury; yet the effect of sprawling profusion is held in order by an organization into months, with a separate section for flowers. The bounty of a courtier's vision of a kingdom is replicated in these multiple rich gardens that are yet organized by and for the royal pleasure. The task of organization, however, has only begun, for the other two-thirds of the essay addresses exactly how these potentially unruly subject-plants should be arranged in a garden whose "contents ought not well to be under thirty acres of ground" (193). A heath of six acres, green and side gardens of four, and central main garden of twelve provide the primary divisions, with alleys, hedges, arches, and fountains subdividing. Space is there to be controlled, and on a "princelike" (193) scale, with a control both visible and strenuous.

Lesser ornaments that play no part in the layout, in the architectural design of space, seem to him unworthy of notice. He dismisses "knots or figures, with divers colored earths" as "toys; you may see as good sights many times in tarts" (193, 194): a small detail of decor may be equalled by a smaller establishment; a royal garden must focus on the disciplined mass of an army. In his conclusion he owns that

. . . I have spared for no cost. But it is nothing for great princes, that for the most part are taking advice with workmen, with no less cost set their things together, and sometimes add statues and such things for state and magnificence, but nothing to the true pleasure of a garden. (198)

The pleasure he describes has a contradictory nature. Concerned with individual satisfaction, he condemns stagnant pools as "unwholesome" (195) and rates the "state and magnificence" of statues as insignificant, and yet the whole is professedly suited only for "great princes." The essence of his design lies in its overwhelming display of wealth and control on a scale that no one less than a prince can match; the garden he projects is on the order of Versailles; and yet he avows that such a vast display of royal splendor has no political purpose but is created only for personal comfort. His aesthetic anticipates that of Edmund Burke's *Philosophical Enquiry* in its implicit awareness that "A clear idea is therefore another name for a little idea"; that "terror is in all cases whatsoever, either more openly or latently the ruling principle of the sublime"; and that pain is stronger than pleasure and "always inflicted by a power in some way superior."[35] Bacon's garden exercises a sublime infliction of terror by a superior power, the absolutist monarch – but that monarch is "absolutist" rather than "absolute," performing an omnipotence he does not possess and forbidden by the restraint of the same Parliament that impeached Bacon from even openly admitting that his garden symbolizes an overawing power.

In leaving the Jacobean triumphalism of Bacon's ornate formal garden for "Upon Appleton House," we enter a world transformed. Marvell reprises the subject of Ben Jonson's "To Penshurst," the relation of a country house with the land and society about it, but that relationship has been redefined. Penshurst is a semi-mythical domain, "Where Pan, and Bacchus their high feasts have made" (line 11), whose nearest approach to the possession of a past is the salute to "his [Sidney's] great birth, where all the muses met" (line 14).[36] Penshurst embodies a paradisal present exemplifying aristocratic ideals. Vassals deferentially gather in a miniature of the court; at a feast "Thy tables hoard not up for the next day" (line 71); and "thy good lady" gains "The just reward of her high huswifery" (lines 84–85) when the King and Prince arrive without advance notice to find "not a room, but dressed, / As if it had expected such a guest!" (lines 87–88). The contrast drawn at the poem's end between this perfect house and "proud, ambitious heaps" is that "their lords have built, but thy lord dwells" (lines 101, 102): those inferior grandees have committed an act defined in and so limited by time, the building of a house. What has been built may be torn down; what has a past must have a future. Because the lord of Penshurst "dwells," he is impervious to time. Serving in the household of a retired Parliamentarian commander after years of civil war, and in a house that had been a priory, Marvell could not easily ignore the ongoing "building" of history. Patsy Griffin has recently attempted to recuperate the episode of Isabel Thwaites, Thomas Fairfax, and the nuns (stanzas 11 through 35) as an integral part of "Upon Appleton House."[37] Daniel P. Jaeckle expresses more doubt as to whether the episode's violent resolution and bias can be assimilated to a formal perfection.[38] Both articles begin with an acknowledgement that the episode has proven the most problematic part of the poem to recent critics.[39] Marvell's accusations that the nuns are devious, greedy, and unchaste form neither part of a formal necessity, however, as Griffin would seem to suggest, nor the jarring discordancy that disturbs Jaeckle. They do possess a coherence and necessity, but of a theological and political rather than formal nature. Marvell's Appleton House, unlike Penshurst, needs a history; the fantasy of an eternally bountiful present has been violated by the Civil War, and Marvell constructs a past to justify the suddenly vulnerable present. The past he constructs is specifically Protestant, because the Parliamentary cause of Fairfax derives its least controversial sanction as the championing of "true religion."

So large a portion of a work is difficult entirely to ignore, but nonetheless the nunnery passage of "Upon Appleton House" has, like Marvell's prose, been relatively neglected. A. D. Cousins little more than mentions the nuns as "a hedonistic and narcissistic little community organized and maintained by human artifice, not by divine grace, and so dystopian rather than at once Christian and ideal," in contrast to the "type of Protestant heroic virtue," Fairfax.[40] Cousins does not discuss how this contrast embodies, in quite typical fashion, the Reformation dichotomy between true Protestant religion and false Catholic superstition, nor does he explore Marvell's agenda in this substantial section of the poem. Omitting the nuns entirely, Douglas D. C. Chambers sees a different location for Fairfax, who had retired from public affairs to a politically suspect antiquarianism, in the binary economy of the poem.[41] The nun episode may be reconciled to Chambers's account by supposing that a Fairfax aligned with antiquarianism may, like a backsliding Stuart, be exhorted to live up to his anti-antiquarian, anti-Papistical duty. What it cannot be reconciled to is John Rogers's idealizing "historical" account in which "Fairfax, in his retirement, devoted solely to the virtues of the household, has without the least trace of aggression or violence purged England of its corrupt monarchy" – an account which, unsurprisingly, does not so much as mention the Thwaites episode, with its aggression and violence displaced from the Civil War to an ur-Reformation.[42] Regardless of whether the poem praises or warns Fairfax, the function of the nuns is inescapably to anchor Appleton House in recent history, in the demarcation of the recent from what precedes it, to enforce the ineluctability of the modernity of post-Reformation, post-Stuart England. The coding that enforces this disjunction is sexual; in the nun episode, history is sexuality.

In Marvell's narrative, which rests upon the common basis of Protestant polemic that characterized Catholicism as corrupt and unnatural, England is the virgin rescued from Papist sterility by Protestant virility. "Upon Appleton House" equates Protestantism with heterosexuality and Catholicism with a monstrous regiment of lesbians. The story of "the blooming virgin Thwaites" (line 90) and the contest for her allegiance and wealth between the brides of Christ and her future husband, while not expressly pornographic, parallels sexual and religious alignment in a suggestive manner, nor is it unique in exploiting the possibilities of titillating fantasy available in nunneries.[43] In its first four lines, the eleventh stanza effects a transition from the descriptive present of the poem to its narrational past, from "While with slow eyes we these survey" (line 81) to "The progress of this house's fate" (line 84). The "progress" begins:

> A nunnery first gave it birth
> (For virgin buildings oft brought forth);
> And all that neighbor-ruin shows
> The quarries whence this dwelling rose.
>
> (lines 85–88)

"A nunnery" is the starting point from which progress must depart; the following, parhenthetical line announces both the libidinousness concealed behind putatively chaste walls and, in its use of past tense, that such goings-on are at an end, a point that "neighbor-ruin" underlines and links to concrete geography. A story is beginning of a radically different, and worse, time, a past of Catholic corruption that blends into the royal regime ended in part by a later Fairfax. This story consists of twenty-five stanzas of the poem's total of ninety-seven, and, of those twenty-five, twelve and a half, exactly half, convey the "thoughts long conceived" of one of the "subtle nuns" (lines 96, 94), her verbal seduction of Thwaites. The nun flatters Thwaites's appearance in a manner that suggests courtship:

> "Some of your features, as we sewed,
> Through every shrine should be bestowed.
> And in one beauty we would take
> Enough a thousand saints to make."
> (lines 133–36)

Idealization of the female body is removed from its usual place in procreative male desire to an all-female society which propagates only images of saints, and to whose inverted holiness "'Twere sacrilege a man t'admit'" (line 139). The seductive blandishments continue: "'Each one your sister, each your maid'" (line 154), "'such fair hands as yours'" (line 160), "'Your voice, the sweetest of the choir'" (line 161). So do such hints of sinful indulgence as "'The rule itself to you shall bend'" (line 156) and "'Here pleasure piety doth meet'" (line 171), culminating in the promise that

> "What need is here of man? unless
> These as sweet sins we should confess.
>
> "Each night among us to your side
> Appoint a fresh and virgin bride"
> (lines 183–86)

The editors gloss the "'sweet sins'" of line 184 as referring to the "'arts / Still handling Nature's finest parts'" (lines 177–78) of the preceding six lines: flowers, clothes, amber, pastries. Although individually these feminine domestic adornments might seem innocent, though antithetical to the asceticism of the monastic ideal, in the aggregate they amount to the "luxuriousness" always regarded as morally dangerous in the seventeenth century.[44] The "'as sweet sins,'" moreover, could refer forward as well as back, however, to what might be done with "'a fresh and virgin bride'": sins involving her "'handling Nature's finest parts,'" "'All night embracing arm in arm'" (line 191), might be as sweet as with a man.

The suggestions of lesbianism have the backing of a longstanding tradition, in both anti-clerical Catholic and Protestant erotica, of locating sexual improprieties in convents. A sensualism progressing from the self-indulgent to the criminal has one final concomitant: "'Our abbess too, now far in age, / Doth your succession near presage'" (lines 157–58). Thwaites may not only join but lead a household without men. To avert such a threat to patriarchal order as a female head of household, for Fairfax to "valiantly complain" (line 202) – a farcically unmanly coupling of adverb and verb – would accomplish nothing, as indeed his twenty-two lines do, a speech a fifth as long as that of the nun. While he talks he lies upon a level with the nuns, whose "loudest cannon were their lungs; / And sharpest weapons were their tongues" (lines 255–56); or, rather, he comes short of them with such woman's weapons. As he has a precontract, a court grants him "the lawful form . . . / To hinder the unjust divorce" (lines 234, 236), inverting the precedent of "lawful form" by which Henry VIII was given a divorce. (That the object of Fairfax, like that of Henry, is to propagate a "great race" [line 248] the next stanza is devoted to proclaiming.) More successful at action than at talk, as befits a man, Fairfax, "waving these aside like flies . . . away her bears" (lines 257, 265). Whether Thwaites wants to go with him when he finds her "weeping at the altar" (line 264), whether her tears are of sorrow at imprisonment or of fear of his carrying her away, is left ambiguous, because with her recuperation into the patri-archal economy of property transmission her desires become irrelevant. She is safely reduced to a conduit for the transmission of property, for what Eve Kosovsky Sedgwick has called "male homosocial desire."[45] The stanza that begins with his abduction of her ends with the dispossession of "The wasting cloister with the rest" (line 271). The dissolution of the monasteries arrives as a cleansing of a social anomaly in which women might live independently of men, and the proper reincorporation of their property into an estate transmitted to heirs male. As a feminine social–political order, a nunnery is inherently unnatural, and this violation of natural order is conflated with antichristian Catholicism – "such a thing that cannot, but for want of a word to express it, be called a Religion" – as a threat to a patriarchy that is synonymous with Protestantism. Like a king an emblem of authority, Fairfax rescues history itself, performing the restoration of order in England as symbolized by Appleton House, a centrifugal force for maintaining a controlling virtue.

"'Twas no religious house till now" (line 280), as the Thwaites episode concludes, because it had been dedicated to a corrupt religion. Marvell's poem exerts the same organizational violence as Bacon's scheme for an imperial garden, but, instead of being unitary, authority is dichotomized into two warring camps, the false Catholic and the true Protestant. Metaphysical poetry, which Johnson described "as a kind of *discordia concors*; a combination of dissimilar images, or discovery of occult resemblances in things apparently unlike," seemed to him "not successful in representing or moving the emotions" because it lacked "uniformity of sentiment."[46] The bifurcation of authority in "Upon Appleton House" represents not "uniformity" but the collapse of Bacon's absolutist model into opposed polarities; it couches that representation in terms that align the nuns with the Stuarts and Fairfax with the Tudor kingship, a true kingship because a Protestant one. Because the Stuarts betrayed the Protestant cause, which is the English cause, Parliament is the true heir to Elizabeth. As the premodern monarchy collapsed in the Civil War, Marvell is collapsing its poetics by carrying verbal violence to the logical endpoint of portraying the old order's demise. He acts as undertaker to the prerevolutionary discursive and historical regimes, denying the legitimacy of Stuart monarchy yet simultaneously subverting the very logic of subversion itself by resolving the deconstructive process of decomposition into a new beginning. Yet this replacement logic also bifurcates; subversion itself forms half of a dialectic with other forms of idealization. Because his literary engine of demolition is not geared toward defining what form his new beginning will take, Marvell adopts the Reformation intact as a model of completed historical action. Configuration of the present as the timeless past of John Foxe's *Acts and Monuments* solves the problem of what happens after the moment of rupture by positing the present as itself the consequence. In the mid-seventeenth century such a depiction of Protestant revolution, literally re-formation, as the status quo possesses considerable justification, but as a model it remains adhered to long after it has become remote from the historical situation. In "Upon Appleton House," hostility to Catholicism provides a focus for resistance, an ideology in opposition to that of royal and ecclesiastical authority but equally dichotomous, equally ready to impose a division.

II

To move from such a frame of reference to Milton's *Of True Religion* is to experience discontinuity greater than can be accounted for solely by the few years separating this pamphlet from Marvell's. For Milton, religion remains more than a patriotic slogan. His faith has political consequences, but remains the master, not the servant, of those consequences. *Of True Religion* begins:

It is unknown to no man, who knows ought of concernment among us, that the increase of Popery is at this day no small trouble and offence to greatest part of the Nation; and the rejoycing of all good men that it is so; the more their rejoycing, that God hathe giv'n a heart to the people to remember still their great and happy deliverance from Popish Thraldom, and to esteem so highly the precious benefit of his Gospel, so freely and so peaceably injoy'd among them. (417)

This opening falls recognizably within the same realm of public discourse as Marvell's *Account*. Milton starts by asserting the universal interest and importance of his subject, a gesture of inclusion, though modified by the ambiguous "good men." They here seem to be anyone who is against Catholicism, but, as he progressively defines his position, they dwindle to an ever smaller faction. Initially, however, he is inviting his presumably Protestant readers to welcome with him the Gospel and "happy deliverance from Popish Thraldom," neither of which they are likely to oppose. He proceeds,

Since therefore some have already in Publick with many considerable Arguments exhorted the people to beware the growth of this Romish Weed; I thought it no less then a common duty to lend my hand, how unable soever, to so good a purpose. (417–18)

That a topic has been treated of repeatedly may seem an odd recommendation for its being handled again, but with this denial of originality, with the homely image of himself as a gardener, and with the self-deprecation of "how unable soever," Milton is stressing how ordinary he and his tract are, just plain English sense. He uses a similar strategy in the rest of the paragraph, where he avows that, "I will not now enter into the Labyrinth of Councels and Fathers, and intangl'd wood which the Papist loves to fight in, not with hope of Victory, but to obscure the shame of an open overthrow . . . And such manner of dispute with them, to Learned Men, is useful and very commendable: But I shall insist now on what is plainer to Common apprehension" (418–19). Milton does not claim his stance is the right one as a general matter of esthetic principle; it is only the right thing to do when writing for a general audience. Thomas N. Corns observes that from 1649 Milton's prose style becomes less ornate, and conjectures that this is the effect of maturity, a recognition that "a brilliant style" is not after all "what is needed in polemic" as he "checks his exuberance and restricts himself to a more functional prose."[47] What is functional, of course, depends on the audience and its expectations. Pamphleteering differs from epic verse.

Although very possibly the work of the printer, not the blind author, the title page of *Of True Religion*, it may be noted, disingenuously de-emphasizes "toleration" by placing it in smaller type than "haeresie" and "schism" above and "Popery" below. The thrust of the pamphlet is in fact to appeal for universal Protestant tolerance; heresy, schism, and Popery form subordinate parts. The text proper follows a similar strategy, with the first paragraph couched in a manner apt to lead the reader to expect some straightforward Catholic-bashing. As I suggested above, while doctrinal questions divided English Protestants, their common hatred of Catholicism united them. Milton is employing a populist stance to encourage the reader to respond sympathetically to the more idiosyncratic matter ahead.

After making his initial claim to represent a Protestant Everyman, Milton begins his argument: "True Religion is the true Worship and Service of God, learnt and believed from the Word of God only" (419). This sentence marks an abrupt shift from the general prolegomenon of the first paragraph; it is a statement few Protestants could fault, but marks clearly that the terms of debate, unlike in Marvell's pamphlet, will be religious. Milton's development of the idea, moreover, is radical. "No Man or Angel can know how God would be worshipt and serv'd unless God reveal it: He hath Reveal'd and taught it us in the holy Scriptures by inspir'd Ministers, and in the Gospel by his own Son and his Apostles, with strictest command to reject all other traditions or additions whatsoever" (419). So much is, he observes, maintained by all Reformed churches, specifically the Church of England in its Thirty-Nine Articles. So far no bishop could quarrel. But Milton's strategy is to force these agreed-upon premises to what he envisions to be their utmost conclusions. If "the Rule of true Religion is the Word of God only" and "Faith ought not to be an implicit faith, that is, to believe, though as the Church believes, against or without express authority of Scripture," then "no true Protestant can persecute, or not tolerate his fellow Protestant, though dissenting from him in som opinions, but he must flatly deny and Renounce these two his own main Principles, whereon true Religion is founded; while he compels his Brother from that which he believes as the manifest word of God, to an implicit faith (which he himself condemns) to the endangering of his Brothers soul, whether by rash belief, or outward Conformity: for *whatsoever is not of Faith, is Sin*" (420–21). Milton makes the logical leap from condemnation of explicit faith to the necessity of absolute toleration – of Protestants – through an intermediary step which he suppresses. The major premise in his syllogism is that implicit faith is sin, the conclusion that all Protestants must tolerate one another. The suppressed minor premise, suppressed because it would provoke violent objection from any supporter of the established Church, that connects the other two is that everyone must have absolute freedom to determine for himself in all points of doctrine. The single proviso is that "he who thinks himself in the truth professes to have learnt it, not by implicit faith, but by attentive study of the Scriptures and full perswasion of heart" (436). As this statement, from near the end of the pamphlet, indicates, Milton does eventually proceed to expressing what he at first suppresses, after preparing the reader, and the way he takes to that preparation is through his distinction between heresy and schism.

In Milton's definition, "Heresie therefore is a Religion taken up and believ'd from the traditions of men and additions to the word of God. Whence also it follows clearly, that of all known Sects or pretended Religions at this day in Christendom, Popery is the only or the greatest Heresie ... Heresie is in the Will and choice profestly against Scripture; error is against the Will, in misunderstanding the Scripture after all sincere indeavours to understand it rightly" (421, 423). Heresy, then, is such a "choice profestly against Scripture" as to compel another to implicit faith or "outward Conformity," while schism is venial "and may also happen to a true church," being only mistakes, like those of the friends of Job, "in some Points of Doctrin" – such mistakes as those of "Lutherans, Calvinists, Anabaptists, Socinians, Arminians" (423–24).[48] By this logic the heretic is the high-church prelate, while the ejected minister, whatever his beliefs, so long as in his own opinion they are based on scripture, is only a schismatic and in comparison innocent. If Milton finds any interpretation of the Bible dangerous, he omits to say so; to admit that any personal interpretation could be wrong would be to endorse persecutors of the beliefs of others. He does not make explicit the parallel between "the obstinate Papist," "he who is so forward to brand all others for Hereticks" (421), and the similarly obstinate Anglican. He does not need to make it explicit, nor under the censorship would doing so be safe.[49] More to the point, Dissenters had hopes of substantial religious toleration from the bill "for ease" passed by the Commons but not finally enacted before the session of Parliament ended, so Milton had a strong motive not to insult Anglicanism too openly.[50] The parallel is present for the reader to perceive, but also disguised for the reader to ignore.

To the principal argument that Catholicism, and any other established church that imposes "a command or a Prohibition, and so consequently an addition to the word of God, which he professes to disallow" (428), is heretical, Milton briefly appends the customary Protestant denunciation of Catholic "Idolatry," with a topical twist. The Pope "hath not ceas'd by his Spyes and Agents, Bulls and Emissaries, once to destroy both King and Parliament; perpetually to seduce, corrupt, and pervert as many as they can of the People," language that might pass for an ordinarily zealous account of the "Babylonish Yoke," were it not for the Biblical quotation used to support it:

Ezekiel 8. 7, 8. And he brought me to the door of the Court, and when I looked, behold a hole in the wall. Then said he unto me, Son of Man, digg now in the wall; and when I had digged, behold a Door, and he said unto me, go in, and behold the wicked Abominations that they do here. (430–31)

In light of the popular anxiety about Catholic influence at the Stuart court, an anxiety antedating the Civil War but given new urgency by the conversion of James to Rome and the Declaration of Indulgence, the mention here of a "Court" as a site of "wicked Abominations" can hardly be accidental. Given the court's reputation for immorality, Milton's argument for moral reformation as a means to avoid Popery also has political meaning. "The last means to avoid Popery, is to amend our lives: it is a general complaint that this Nation of late years, is grown more numerously and excessively vitious then heretofore; Pride, Luxury, Drunkenness, Whoredom, Cursing, Swearing, bold and open Atheism every where abounding: Where these grow, no wonder if Popery also grow a pace" (438-39). And where should "these" grow, but in the court of wicked abominations, which had of late years been restored?

Milton is reintroducing covertly into public discourse the radical critique he had once been able openly to propound. Later in the same paragraph as the "wicked abominations" appears the sentence, "Whether therefore it be fit or reasonable, to tolerate men thus principl'd in Religion towards the State, I submit it to the consideration of all Magistrates, who are best able to provide for their own and the publick safety" (430). The phrasing of this statement echoes the full first period of the title of *The Tenure of* KINGS *and* MAGISTRATES: *Proving, That it is Lawfull, and hath been held so through all Ages, for any, who have the Power, to call to account a Tyrant, or wicked* KING, *and after due conviction, to depose, and put him to death; if the ordinary* MAGISTRATES *have neglected, or deny'd to do it.* As the title couples kings and magistrates, so to Milton a king is not only the supreme magistrate but, like Popery, something for all magistrates not to neglect but to "consider," and by implication act against. The utmost Interregnum radicalism is still possible; the agenda is open. It is open, however, only for those who can catch a faint allusion, for the earlier work is not one to which allusion other than hostile would be appreciated by the authorities. It would also have frightened a propertied elite with even less fond, and closer, memories of the New Model Army than of Laud. That Milton felt no fondness toward a Stuart is not surprising, but his antiprelatic and republican principles no longer fell within acceptable political discourse. He had to speak in code.

Because idolatry, if public, is "grievous and unsufferable scandal giv'n to all consciencious Beholders" and, if private, "great offense to God," the task remaining for its opponents is "how to remove it and hinder the growth thereof" (430–31). Four means are proposed. "[F]irst we must remove their Idolatry, and all the furniture thereof, whether Idols, or the Mass ... If they say that by removing their Idols we violate their Consciences, we have no warrant to regard Conscience which is not grounded on Scripture" (432). The second means is "to read duly and diligently the Holy Scriptures ... [although] most men ... through unwillingness to take the pains of understanding their Religion by their own diligent study, would fain be sav'd by a Deputy. Hence comes implicit faith" (433–34). The third is to "tolerate," "patiently hear," and "seriously read" "all opinions at least founded on Scripture" (that is, excluding those of Catholics), because "If he who thinks himself in the truth professes to have learnt it, not by implicit faith, but by attentive study of the Scriptures and full perswasion of heart, with what equity can he refuse to hear or read him, who demonstrates to have gained his knowledge in the same way? ... This is the direct way to bring in that Papistical implicit faith which we all disclaim" (436–37). The fourth and last is "to amend our lives ... For God, when men sin outragiously, and will not be admonisht, gives over chastizing them, perhaps by Pestilence, Fire, Sword, or Famin, which may all turn to their good, and takes up his severest punishments, hardness, besottedness of heart, and Idolatry, to their final perdition" (438–39). That London had suffered since the return of the king by pestilence, fire, and sword (the plague, the great fire, the burning of the fleet in the Medway and other disasters of the Second Dutch War) was notorious, and commonly seen by Dissenters as God's judgment on the wicked. What could be the end of impenitence but, in the tract's last words, "the worst of superstitions, and the heaviest of all Gods Judgements, Popery" (440)? Less toleration of Popery, more toleration of Protestant sects, minds full of the Bible, and cleanly lives: such is Milton's program. Toleration, dwarfed on the title page by words of broader appeal, has engulfed and absorbed heresy, schism, and Popery.

Although *Of True Religion* seems at its beginning to be addressing a subject of general topical political interest, Milton refuses, except obliquely, to be drawn beyond questions of toleration and a doctrine that soon reveals itself to be radical. He progressively confines his audience to those with an interest in doctrine and stake in toleration, a much smaller portion of the political nation, "the people" in the seventeenth-century sense, than would endorse a politically charged attack on Catholicism. After a beginning that could be Anglican, his case has narrowed to the specifically Nonconformist. Unlike Marvell's pamphlet, Milton's "had no perceptible effect."[51] The propertied classes valued Protestantism as synonymous with English freedom, freedom from foreign domination and freedom from centralized government.[52] Or as Richard Baxter put it, "The rich will rule in the world, and few rich men will be saints."[53] Milton began his career as a polemicist amid the radicalization of the Civil War; with the arrival of the Commonwealth, he became central to public discourse, holding office and writing official publications. In *Of True Religion*, he ends his pamphleteering once more on the fringe, along with the nonconformism whose toleration he argues.

If Milton's political concerns have become parochial by the time of his last pamphlet, another way of saying the same thing is to observe that what speech is politically normative depends on who controls politics. In the Laudian England of the 1630s Milton was so disaffected from national institutions that he made no attempt to enter public life; as the range of the politically possible became increasingly open to penetration from below and outside in the 1640s, his prominence increased.[54] His Bible-based method of argument in *Of True Religion* was, after all, still closer to what a nation of churchgoers and auditors of sermons was used to than the classical schemata of political theory such as that of James Harrington. In 1689 *The Tenure of Kings and Magistrates* was anonymously republished as a defense of the deposition of James II under a new title, *Pro Populo Adversus Tyrannos: Or the Sovereign Right and Power of the People over Tyrants*, with all allusions to Presbyterians deleted but otherwise largely unchanged, its biblical basis untouched.[55] Some apologist for the new government must have thought its arguments still usable. Nonetheless, as Roger Pooley points out, political language after the Restoration was tending to become secularized, because the principle of individual property rights was becoming strong enough to stand without religious support.[56] What ultimately marginalized Milton in 1673 was his remaining preoccupied with the Civil War's issues of religious liberty, his continuing at Weber's charismatic and militant moment of heroic Protestantism between the traditional and the modern at a time when the political nation was moving onward. This preoccupation persists in *Of True Religion*, which treats Catholicism as a religious issue calling for scriptural quotation rather than a political issue calling for talk of the rights of Englishmen, Bloody Mary, and a standing army. Ironically, his very contemporary irrelevance and inability to propose his views openly facilitated the rise of his posthumous reputation, his post-1688 canonization as a Whig poet and later his accessibility even to an Episcopalian interpretation such as C. S. Lewis's.

III

When *Paradise Lost* appeared, the republican revolts of Charles II's first years had been suppressed, and the widespread public discontent that followed the Third Dutch War and the transpiring of the conversion of James to Rome had yet to begin; the Stuart government seemed at its strongest. Political alienation was the sine qua non of Milton the poet, and *Of True Religion*, as his only prose tract published after the Restoration, provides a unique look at Milton's public political evolution in the period of the final works. The passing of Christianity as a totalizing system capable of explaining all aspects of life was a necessary part of the evolution from patriarchal to contractual society, from aristocratic to bourgeois hegemony, part of the desacralizing of the world embodied in the execution of Charles I. As a republican and regicide, Milton may be presumed to have disapproved of the divine right of kings to rule; yet he remained insistent upon the right of the divine word to be the last word in public affairs, upon the primacy of faith over this-worldly concerns. Younger and more cynical, Whig polemicists such as Marvell transformed Milton's revolutionary logic of the right to divorce a wife, purged of his tortured theological justifications, into a right of the political nation, that is, effectively, the propertied, to divorce the king; and the end of the progression was politics' divorce from God, the original of patriarchal authority. The weapons loosed at Satan in the end felled God.

The noncanonical Milton has implications for the canonical. Consider the relation of *Of True Religion* to *Paradise Lost* and Milton's juvenile Latin exercises – one of his last and some of his first works, and also his most celebrated and among his least. Of the Latin pieces in his 1645 *Poems*, four are epigrams on the Gunpowder Plot, one honors the inventor of gunpowder, and another is the longest Latin work in the collection. At 226 lines, "In Quintum Novembris" is the 1645 volume's longest poem in any language except "On the Morning of Christ's Nativity" – whose 244 lines are so much shorter than Latin elegiac verse that the number of syllables is significantly fewer – and of course *Comus*. The parallel between a conclave of devils to subvert paradise and a demonic council to betray "pius extrema ... Iacobus" is obvious; less obvious is the retention in the later poem of the polemical edge, but an edge turned, of the earlier.[57] Satan's cohorts are not the only plotters against Heaven, but Charles II's court of "wicked Abominations" contrasts with the schoolboy's "pius extrema ... Iacobus." The final stage of the future history which Michael reveals to Adam in the last two books of *Paradise Lost* comes when, after the Apostles die,

> in thir room, as they forewarn,
> Wolves shall succeed for teachers, grievous Wolves,
> Who all the sacred mysteries of Heav'n
> To thir own vile advantages shall turn
> Of lucre and ambition, and the truth
> With superstitions and traditions taint,
> Left only in those written Records pure,
> Though not but by the Spirit understood ...
> What will they then
> But force the Spirit of Grace itself, and bind
> His consort Liberty; what, but unbuild
> His living Temples, built by Faith to stand,
> Their own Faith not another's: for on Earth
> Who against Faith and conscience can be heard
> Infallible? yet many will presume:
> Whence heavy persecution shall arise
> On all who in the worship persevere
> Of Spirit and Truth ...[58]

The condemnation of "grievous Wolves" employs the language of the traditional Protestant indictment of Rome, but here there is no "antistes Babylonius" (Babylonian high priest; that is, the Pope) and "pugiles Romae per saecula longa fideles" (fighters loyal to Rome through long centuries) as in "In Quintum Novembris," nor does the celebrated "two-handed engine at the door" of "Lycidas" appear.[59] No Popish foe is named to be triumphed over at the Reformation; indeed, that rupture central to the Protestant myth of English destiny as embodied in such texts as the *Book of Martyrs* – and "Upon Appleton House" – goes entirely un-mentioned, and certainly the Stuart on the throne receives no praise for exemplary piety, because "heavy persecution" continues, and is still directed against "Faith and conscience" as before. The parallel between Rome and the Church of England here hinted is the same one developed at more length and with greater explicitness a few years later in *Of True Religion*. Neither is any day of reckoning foretold "till the day / Appear of respiration to the just, / And vengeance to the wicked, at return / Of him so lately promis'd to thy aid": Anglican oppression follows Papist tyranny seamlessly; Milton's pre-revolutionary genuflections of loyalty and revolutionary hope have both ended.[60] *Paradise Lost* remains within the system of Protestant typology in which history moves within a line from Israel to contemporary affairs, but the poem denies the church militant the reassuring leap to the church triumphant in either its royalist or anti-royalist forms. The one would have been personally repugnant, the other politically unsafe.

In a return to polemical combativeness, *Of True Religion* plays to popular anti-Papal prejudices to score points in an internecine quarrel among Protestants. If this tract is one of the least canonical works by a most canonical author, another pamphlet by Milton, though like *Of True Religion* obscure till long after his death, has since enjoyed much greater celebrity: *Areopagitica*, the most widely circulated of his prose works. Two essays by one author argue for tolerance; one is celebrated, one ignored. To answer why, begin with titles: *Of True Religion* suggests a theological tract; the full title, *Of True Religion, HAERESIE, SCHISM, TOLERATION, And what best means may be us'd against the growth of POPERY*, sounds even grimmer to the modern, secular ear – not only seventeenth-century theology but seventeenth-century bigotry. It is not the stuff of which Arnoldian transhistorical touchstones are made. *Areopagitica*, on the other hand, although exotic, is a classical reference, a much more humanistic, gentlemanly, and putatively apolitical way of speaking than rants about Haeresie, Schism, and Popery. The full title improves upon the partial in appeal as much as the full title of *Of True Religion* worsens post-Enlightenment trepidations: *AREOPAGITICA; A SPEECH OF Mr. JOHN MILTON For the Liberty of UNLICENSED PRINTING, To the PARLAMENT* [sic] *of ENGLAND*. A speech to Parliament has a dignified sound; the prominent appearance of Milton's full name lends the cachet of his poetry to the work more boldly than the discreet "The Author J. M." at the bottom of the post-Restoration title-page; but the core of the subtitle's attractiveness resides in its substantive phrase, "for the Liberty of Unlicens'd Printing." Great poet-revolutionary calls for liberty of printing: the expression trips off the tongue with the delighted ease of a headline.

As John Illo irascibly but accurately observes, however, Milton is not a "liberal or a social democrat,"[61] but a radical Puritan. *Areopagitica* mocks

Imprimaturs "under the hands of 2 or 3 glutton Friers" – for Milton, as for
Foxe and every other Protestant polemicist who mentions monasticism, a
monk must be a hypocritical sensualist – and in his pocket history of
censorship tells of "the Popes of *Rome* engrossing what they pleas'd of
Politicall rule into their owne hands, extended their dominion over mens
eyes, as they had before over their judgements, burning and prohibiting to
be read, what they fansied not."[62] In *Areopagitica*, Milton condemns censorship as what Catholics do, and so necessarily wrong and improper for
Protestants, as in *Of True Religion* he attacks religious intolerance on the
same grounds. Yet he is perfectly ready to censor and "extirpat" Catholics:
"I mean not tolerated Popery, and open superstition, which as it extirpats
all religions and civill supremacies, so it self should be extirpat, provided
first that all charitable and compassionat means be us'd to win and regain
the weak and the misled" (349). The latter part of the sentence, which
seems at first to soften the rigor of the former, on closer scrutiny only confirms its harshness: "extirpat" means just what it says. If only prohibition
of public worship and printing were intended, there would be no need for
"charitable and compassionat means [to] be us'd to win and regain the
weak and the misled" before imposing such measures. Such charity and
compassion suggest something approaching the choice Spain offered to its
Jews. Even if so drastic an interpretation is refused, Popery and "that also
which is impious or evil" (349), or in other words everything but
"Protestant theism,"[63] in Illo's phrase, is to be prohibited.

Nonetheless, though the intolerance that Illo locates in *Areopagitica* is
present, on casual reading – and, for much the greater part of the work,
even on close reading – the tract does communicate a sense of liberation,
unlike *Of True Religion*. Whereas the later pamphlet lashes a wicked
generation with scriptural quotations and dire warnings to mend their
erring ways "to avoid, the worst of superstitions, and the heaviest of all
Gods Judgements, Popery" (440), the earlier celebrates London as "a City
of refuge, the mansion house of liberty" (340) and rhapsodizes that
"Methinks I see in my mind a noble and puissant Nation rousing herself
like a strong man after sleep, and shaking her invincible locks" (344).
Rudimentary biographical criticism might suggest that in 1673 Milton was
"On evil days though fall'n, and evil tongues,"[64] whereas in 1644 "But
to be young was very Heaven."[65] The change inheres not in Milton alone,
though; thirty years of disillusion intervene between the moment of
revolutionary euphoria and the Cabal. The apocalyptic allure of revolution has long since become a central myth of progressive modernity, and
Areopagitica's lyrical panegyrics to liberty are brilliant with ecstatic hope. In

the glow, a little intolerance of counterrevolutionaries can be overlooked as unimportant – an unwillingness to overlook it can even seem hostile to the myth of revolution itself, which, whether Glorious, American, French, or Russian, is fundamental to all post-Enlightenment regimes. To a degree, such an overlooking is understandable, and even inevitable. Perhaps the decisive difference, besides the generational, between the old and new historicisms is the articulation of an awareness that objectivity is impossible, that the present creates the past in pursuit of a contemporary agenda, that scholarly pronouncements can have no absolute truth value. The canonical is what constitutes a usable past. Thus, as women enter a previously male-dominated profession in such numbers as to alter its gender dynamics, the importance of female writers of the past increases and their role alters. Our Aphra Behn is not Pope's smut-peddler: his past was what suited his purposes; ours is what suits ours. Unlike *Of True Religion, Areopagitica* has provided a past whose glamor has helped under-write Whiggism and liberal democracy: to adapt Johnson's words on Shakespeare, it supports an opinion with arguments, and supplies a faction with invectives.[66] As critics we must remain, however, conscious of our purposes, lest we become what we oppose.

IV

Another poem of Marvell's, besides "Upon Appleton House," that directly touches upon Catholicism is "Flecknoe, an English Priest at Rome." Flecknoe, a "poet, priest, and musician," lives in "a chamber, as 'twas said, / But seemed a coffin set on the stairs' head," and is "so thin / He stands, as if he only fed had been / With consecrated wafers: and the host / Hath sure more flesh and blood than he can boast."[67] As in "Upon Appleton House" and *An Account of the Growth of Popery, and Arbitrary Government,* in his satirical portrait of a Catholic priest Marvell is not conducting a theologi-cal argument but attacking a social deviancy with which he associates Catholicism: Popery is the inseparable companion of tyranny, nuns are scheming disruptors of sexual bipolarism, and Catholics are poor – "wooden shoes" were a frequent reproach – which proves the superiority of Protestantism. As remains the case among some American evangelicals today, material prosperity is a visible badge of God's blessing. The Protestant mockery of Catholic poverty that underlies Marvell's "Flecknoe" becomes generalized in the Catholic Pope's *Dunciad* into a nondenominational attack on bad, and thus impoverished, writers. Material success proves aesthetic success for the gardener of Twickenham as it proved spiritual success for Weberian Protestantism. In place of the historical specificity of "an [exiled] English Priest at Rome," Pope substitutes a vast swarm, abundantly named but in such number as to disintegrate, but for a few, into an anonymous mob of Dunces swarming about the Kingdom of Dulness. The figure of the starving poet living in a garret and vain of his "ill made" verses becomes secularized from Marvell's "propitiary priest," but is still recognizable.[68] The metaphor of poverty remains; the slight single story becomes archetypal, though, as one poor (in both senses) poet becomes a race, and that race itself approaches metaphor in the fourth book. Pope displaces historical issues into aesthetic and apocalyptic frameworks, so that particular struggles transmute to "And Universal Darkness buries All."[69] Another poem of his, "The Universal Prayer," supplies a suggestion as to his motive to universalize the particular: only a universal prayer could be shared by a Catholic in a Protestant country.

That universal implies its own particular, however. The longtime Grub Streeter Johnson observed of Pope that "it would be hard to find a man, so well entitled to notice by his wit, that ever delighted so much in talking of his money ... The great topick of his ridicule is poverty: the crimes with which he reproaches his antagonists are their debts, their habitation in the Mint, and their want of a dinner. He seems to be of an opinion, not very uncommon in the world, that to want money is to want every thing."[70] Pope's reiterated appeal to the disdain in which the prosperous hold the destitute may be seen at least in part as a strategy that anticipates the logic of shared upper-class interest that later resulted in the passage of Toleration Acts alleviating and then repealing the penal laws against Catholics.[71] Brecht's dictum that in capitalist societies the only crime is poverty becomes in Pope a covert manifesto of liberation from sectarian intolerance. Anti-Catholic prejudice, which did so much to bring about the execution of one king and the exile of another, was an instrument of domination dangerously susceptible to becoming an instrument of destabilization. The archaism that critics pass over with embarrassed haste in Milton and Marvell, their sectarianism, is precisely what makes them politically radical, even revolutionary. The religious passion that mobilized both rich and poor against the Stuarts remained powerful enough to threaten the Hanoverians should they ever get on its wrong side. Better to count your gold, enjoy your grotto, and let sleeping hatreds lie, as Pope urges – until they're needed, to mobilize a disaffected populace, when Bonnie Prince Charlie lands, the year after Pope's death.

CHAPTER THREE

The "king's spiritual militia"
the Church of England and the plot of the Plot

As Popery and Treachery go hand in hand, while Popery is kept under; so Popery and Tyranny are inseparable Companions, when Popery gets the upper hand.[1]

Jonathan Scott has likened Restoration England to a "traumatized patient."[2] It was a nation not singly but doubly traumatized, however, haunted by contradictory nightmares, on the one hand Marvell's "popery and arbitrary government" and on the other the chaos of the Interregnum. The following discussion extends into noncanonical writers the preceding chapter's examination of the Dissenting and anti-royalist deployments of anti-Papist rhetoric by Marvell and Milton; additionally, though, it introduces the counterpoint of Anglican replies that seek to parallel Dissent and Catholicism. My purpose is to trace the evolution, through the reign of Charles II, of the Protestant tradition of excoriating Rome and to assess the significance of that tradition for the Church of England. Restoration Anglican anti-Catholic rhetoric reached its crisis in the Popish Plot agitation at the end of the 1670s, only to be transformed in the 1680s. Since Charles's unpopular pro-French position in the Third Dutch War and the revelation of the conversion of the Duke of York, the future James II, to Catholicism, both early in the 1670s, the government faced increasing opposition. Public jubilation over the Restoration, already paling, virtually ceased.[3] A refusal to recognize that opposition could have any legitimacy had been the principal reason why Charles I lost his realm and then his life, and a system in which the king still had nearly absolute executive discretion, although Charles II was quite as dependent as his father on Parliament for adequate funds to run his administration, would have to end in a resolution one way or the other; almost inevitably, one side would have to become predominant. The same dilemma was played out in other European states; what was anomalous about England was that Parliament won, a victory in large measure attributable to popular suspicions of Popery and Tyranny, suspicions which played crucial roles in not just the Exclusion Crisis but also, with more success, the outbreak of the Civil War and the final collapse of the Stuart regime in 1688.[4] The Church of England prided itself on both the Protestant purity of its doctrine and its "loyalty"; it combined the theoretical freedom of the Protestant individual conscience with a hierarchal structure designed to ensure that no radical applications of that conscience would disturb the political status quo.[5] What constituted that status quo would itself come into question, however, under James.

Two confessional divisions existed in England, one between the Church of England and Dissenters and one between all Protestants, that is to say, almost the entire population, and Catholics. Only the Catholic bogey could unite both factions of Protestants to sink their differences and act jointly, whether against James II or Louis XIV. The fervent royalism of the Church of England after 1660 had a remote origin in the crown's central role in the English Reformation, as celebrated by John Foxe, but a more immediate one in the common dangers faced by throne and Church in the Interregnum. As Thomas Fuller wrote in 1655, "*An Ingenious Gentelman some* Moneths *since in* Iest-earnest *advised me to make hast with my* History of the Church of England, *for fear (said he) lest the* Church of England *be ended before the* History *thereof.*"[6] After 1661, a ministry purged of all who refused to swear submission to king and bishops supported with few exceptions and almost without limit a crown that seemed its essential bulwark against Popery on one side and "enthusiasm" on the other. No sooner had the professions of loyalty reached their utmost pitch in the Tory counteroffensive after the Exclusion Crisis, however, than the brief and reckless career of James ended the possibility of an Anglican autocracy on the model of the Lutheran states of Germany – such as Hanover. A confessional state presumed its capstone to be of the state faith; for the head of the Church not to belong to the Church violated the homology of Church and crown that was central to the Restoration ideology of the 1660s. For the head of Church and state to belong to the most hated of heresies could only exacerbate the tension, undermining his legitimacy. It became difficult to maintain that "the Power of the King" was "The best fence against Popery" when the king not only was Catholic but openly favored his own faith.[7] For an adherent of the national enemy to function simultaneously as the emblem of the nation, if possible at all, would have required extreme tact, not James's highly visible floutings of both political and religious custom. James thus posed an intricate and ultimately insoluble problem in theological politics. As the properly Protestant restorer of monarchy and the true church in 1660, Charles II was much more easily supported by what a 1648 tract (republished in 1681) by a royalist clergyman called "the King's spiritual militia, and the most powerful, as commanding the consciences of subjects."[8]

I

This chapter examines a nonliterature of polemic that performs a vital role in the history of English institutions and discourses as a connection between the legitimistic triumphalism that greeted the return from exile of Charles II and the more nationalistic triumphalism that followed the Glorious Revolution. Under the Stuarts the monarch functioned as the ultimate manifester of what Jürgen Habermas has called the "publicity of representation"; H. G. Gadamer has similarly asserted that a lord "displayed himself, presented himself as an embodiment of some sort of 'higher' power."[9] Like Catholicism founded upon apostolic succession rather than individual inspiration, yet like other Protestant sects with doctrine based on the word, on the transparency of scripture, the Anglican Church sought to defend its own "sacramental character" in that of the king. Habermas notes that "Under the Stuarts, up to Charles II, literature and art served the representation of the king";[10] one reason for this celebration of sovereignty is that the monarchy, unlike the Church of England, before the Glorious Revolution still retained its representational character.

If the many panegyrics to William III have received far less attention than those to Charles II, one reason, besides (or perhaps causing) their generally dismal quality, may be that they attempt to represent the negation of representation; under William, panegyric, as in the later scorned laureate efforts of Cibber or Southey, applies the epic language of personal praise to the inaugural reign of the impersonal era, of permanent institutions rather than mortal monarchs. As Johnson commented, Addison's then-celebrated figure of the angel in *The Campaign*, who, "pleased the Almighty's orders to perform, / Rides in the whirlwind, and directs the storm," adds nothing to the poem; it merely reproduces the figure of the commanding general expanded to celestial, inhuman, size.[11] Addison's angel seems to take independent action yet has nothing to do, because if it did that would smack of superstition and credulousness of miracles; nature is mechanism on the Protestant battlefield, as the king (except the "King in Parliament") seems to act without acting in the constitutional state. Perhaps the early pindarics of Swift suggested he would never be a poet to his cousin Dryden, as the legend has it, because he was attempting

to write panegyric under a regime incapable of praise. To be a constitutional monarch is to be constitutionally incapable of doing more than
appearing to preside over action that proceeds regardless; the king as hero
is twin to the king as divine.

In Dryden's *Absalom and Achitophel*, the plotters receive copious description, the "Godlike David" none besides his divinity and philoprogenitive
promiscuity.[12] For David's allegorical analogue, Charles II, the first was
axiomatic in royalist ideology and the second not only notorious but
fundamental to the question of the succession that triggered the Exclusion
Crisis – or as some historians have called it, the re-eruption of the
Restoration Crisis, 1660 proving only a temporary resolution.[13] David
takes only two actions in the poem: near the beginning, "With secret Joy,
indulgent David viewed / His Youthfull Image in his Son renew'd"
(31–32), and, at the end, "from his Royal Throne by Heav'n inspir'd, / The
God-like David spoke" (936–37). His initial "indulgent" silence permits,
authorizes, the plotters' intrigues; his speech abruptly and entirely halts
them. Neither action involves activity; the first is an abstention from
action, the latter a speech that itself constitutes action, an inaugurating
divine word that creates its own reality. The poem concludes with a bare
six lines after he ceases speaking:

> He said. Th'Almighty, nodding, gave consent;
> And Peals of Thunder shook the Firmament.
> Henceforth a Series of new time began,
> The mighty Years in long Procession ran:
> Once more the Godlike *David* was Restor'd,
> And willing Nations knew their Lawfull Lord.
>
> (lines 1026–31)

Like the Almighty, David, permissive or strict, need only consent, and in
response sedition erupts or "willing Nations knew their Lawfull Lord." In
the scheme of the poem, legitimacy presumes inactivity; for a king to have
to take visible action would undercut his own authority by admitting that
majesty in itself lacks efficacy as an agent, that majesty might need an
agent rather than possessing sufficient power in its gesture. He must make
that endangering gesture, however, to secure his power, and by doing so
foreclose all further action. For subjects to counter the king's express word
would revive the turmoil of the 1640s, but for him to have to commit himself to stating that word gambles his sovereignty on its ability to silence
opposition. Ideally, the king is mute, but in an unideal world his plenary
voice is necessary to restore, at the poem's end, the perfect silence that pre-
ceded its beginning. The poem encompasses the moment of a threatened

lapse of sovereignty, the irruption and silencing of a discourse of treasonous conspiracy where any discourse must be treason against silence. Action is what happens in the absence of the king; the purpose of kingship is to prevent action. The legitimacy of Charles II is the legitimacy of possession; it relies not on a transcendent indefeasible hereditary right but on the fact of the danger of change, the fragility of the society whose capstone he is.[14] It consists in an incapacity of the people, not a capacity of the king; the alternative to paralysis is chaos.

Dryden's schematic of English kingship possesses a significant similarity to Walter Benjamin's situating of the role of the prince in the German *Trauerspiel* of the seventeenth century. As "the representative of history," who holds "the course of history in his hand like a sceptre," the baroque monarch has as his supreme duty the avoidance of "the state of emergency."[15] The "state of emergency" is that exceptional condition in which the sovereign will have to act. The Exclusion Crisis was a "state of emergency." *Absalom and Achitophel* at once affirms and denies the possibility of such a condition, of the necessity of sovereign action that compromises sovereignty. The emergence into emergency of tragedy must be avoided because it would retell the history of Charles II as the history of his father, and yet the possibility of that emergence must be suggested to remind the nation of the danger of social dissolution involved in challenging the sovereign silence. As in the plays Benjamin examines, the image of the monarch appears divided between the martyr and the prince regnant, but, unlike in the *Trauerspiel*, Dryden's monarch is not a usurper but possessed of rightful title and kingly justice. The sovereign act is absolute in Dryden, and for that very reason invisible. Where Addison's vast and impotent angel spectacularly "Rides in the whirlwind" without actually contributing to the action of the poem, Dryden's David inaugurates and concludes the action yet cannot participate in it because his presence, holding "the course of history in his hand like a sceptre," is so overwhelming as to preclude all action. Powerlessness and omnipotence possess equivalent dramatic value. Intrigue cannot touch the true king, but neither can the true king intrigue.

The need of *Absalom and Achitophel* for plot and resolution was a need that extended beyond questions of form to the political situation which the poem attempted to explain and manipulate. The succession had to be decided, and so did the larger question of whether king or Parliament would prevail, and the decision would be shaped by which of two opposing propagandas proved the more persuasive. Competing conspiracy theories controlled the political discourse of the Exclusion Crisis: either Charles II and Protestantism were indeed threatened by a hellish Popish Plot or Commonwealthsmen were once more maneuvering to plunge the nation into civil war. As Samuel Weber notes, "The baroque drama thus depends upon a plot that is based not upon a sovereign subject but upon a masterful organizer or promoter (*Veranstalter*) ... The plot is replaced by plotting."[16] The sovereign is not a subject because to remain sovereign he must, like Addison's angel, not act, and action is the province of the subject; in both *Absalom and Achitophel* and the *Narrative* of Titus Oates, as in the *Trauerspiel*, instead action consists of the intrigues of the disloyal plotters. The watershed of the reign of Charles II, the Popish Plot gained its effectiveness as a fictional organization of political reality from its replacement of plot with plotting. The relation of representation and sovereignty underwrites the dynamics of Restoration piety and polity. The absolutist king was the sole and conspicuous guarantor of peace; the pretensions of Charles II to divine right had as basis the very visibility of the fragility of his regime, the recent memory of civil tumult in the absence of a royal center.

II

The Popish Plot agitation demanded belief in incredibilities to avoid scrutiny of fundamentals: a labyrinthine narrative of conspiracy evolved to concretize the dread of Popery that alone could sufficiently overcome memories of the Civil War to challenge the desperate, the *necessary*, loyalty to the crown of *Absalom and Achitophel*. Between fears of major generals and of auto da fes, loyalty became at once essential and impossible. England was a kingdom whose only experience of not being a kingdom was the chaos followed by military dictatorship of the Interregnum, "'a dissolution of government' ... so disturbing that the articulate classes dreaded nothing so much as its recurrence except what they meant by 'popery.'"[17] By claiming to be protecting Charles II against Jesuitical assassins, attacks against the character and prospects of Charles's brother could be justified as inspired by solicitude for the royal safety. As the anonymous *A Letter to Mr. S a Romish Priest* observed, "You cannot but know withal that to believe Him [Charles] inclinable to you [Papists], is to Commit Treason in your Hearts, since that to say so, is declared Treason by an Act of Parliament."[18] To doubt "the firm Resolution of the King to Defend the Church of England" (2) was to cast into question the stability of the Restoration settlement that checked the insecurities of midcentury, because that settlement was founded on a mutual reliance of the hastily reassembled royal and ecclesiastical structures as guarantors of stability. In such circumstances, incredulity suffices as evidence of treachery:

> malicious and violent Enemies of the Protestants in *England*, who here have endeavoured to make us believe there has been no such Plot contrived by the *Jesuits* and *Papists* in *England*, or else that the Plot is only of the making and contriving of those you call Sectaries and Fanaticks in *England* . . . . And these sort of men are very sedulous in raising divers Objections, and endeavour to lessen the Evidences, and asperse the *Judges*, calumniate both Magistrates and People, and by all manner of unjust ways and contrivances seek to instill into the Minds of people that there is no such grand Conspiracy, and that it is only a subtle and politick way of some *great ones in England*, to make new Combustions and Insurrections there, by which means either to set up the *Presbyterian Party*, or to bring in again a *Second Commonwealth*.[19]

In the ever-widening, self-justifying logic of paranoia, to question the conspiracy is to reveal oneself as part of it: "by their obstinacy they may persuade them ["the people"] into a belief that there is no Plot, till the Sword is at their Throats."[20] Anyone might be the enemy. Stories of Jesuits going about stirring up trouble disguised as members of various sects were staples, nor was William Lloyd alone in seeing priests "disguising themselves like Hectors, or mingling with Gentlemen, to poyson the Clubs and Coffee-Houses with Phanatick Discourses, or even with Atheism it self, to destroy all Religion that they may have their will upon ours."[21] One faced an enemy unprincipled on principle: "The Jesuits Creed" in one pamphlet concludes with an admonition that "*He commits the Sin against the Holy Ghost, who doth not, when he can, betray and deceive the Hereticks.*"[22] The situation is so desperate that to pause to reason might be fatal: *A Full and Final Proof of the Plot*, after noting in its Preface that "'tis well known, after your Conspiracies are discovered, your first Artifice is to insinuate an Opinion of your Innocence," owns frankly that "seeing we cannot distinguish between Truth and Falsehood, it behooves us passionately to embrace both together for our own safety and preservation . . . in Cases of this moment and weight relating to the Body-Politick, 'tis better that now and then an Innocent suffer, than that all the Malefactors escape."[23] They could not "distinguish between Truth and Falsehood" because of contradictory anxieties over anarchy and despotism, a "*Second Commonwealth*" and "*Papists.*"

For the king to be a Papist destroyed the symmetry of clerical and monarchical power that underlay Anglican enthusiasm for Charles II. Royalism and Anglicanism were both ideologies of hierarchy that legitimated centralization, but their mutual reinforcement relied upon the convergence of secular and religious hierarchies in the person of the king, a convergence which numerous pamphlets asserted. Without that convergence, without the axiomatic equation of Church and king, the Restoration settlement lost its demonstrative authority and degenerated into uncertainty; if king were set against Church, the principles of religious and secular authority would work to undermine instead of support each other. The explosion of popular fear that found expression in the Popish Plot reflected a desire for a resolution that would satisfy the contradictory impulses to be both loyal and firmly Protestant. Titus Oates entitled his fable *A true Narrative*, and that was the need he, like Dryden in contrary fashion, was supplying: a narrative that would reconcile the impulses to preserve a Protestant monarchy. A murderous and treasonous Popish Plot, by combining threats to the king, nation, and religion, justified and directed popular anxiety; the plot of the Plot succeeded as a technique of mobilization because it offered loyalist, patriotic, and religious anxieties a single enemy. In the terms of T. S. Eliot's condemnation of *Hamlet* as "an artistic failure," the Popish Plot succeeded in "finding an 'objective correlative'; in other words, a set of objects, a situation, a chain of events which shall be the formula of that *particular* emotion."[24] Its formula triumphed so brilliantly as to produce numerous successors in the decades to come, from the Rye House Plot to Atterbury's in the 1720s. The plot of the Plot, however, required an identity of Church and king to remain isomorphic.

The Popish Plot of 1678, with its fiction of a Catholic conspiracy for (in the words of Titus Oates) "the Reduction of Great Britain and Ireland, and all His Majesties Dominions by the Sword (all other wayes and means being judged by them ineffectual) to the Romish Religion and Obedience," was not, it should be remembered, the first such discovery of treachery.[25] By the outbreak of the Civil War, or war of the three kingdoms, political and religious tensions were inextricable from one another, and "a particularly virulent form of popish plot theory had come into existence, which combined secular and religious grievances in an all-embracing explanation."[26] At the end of 1641, as events moved toward the crisis of January 4, 1642, when Charles I attempted to arrest Pym, Hampden, and three other Members of Parliament, Parliamentary propaganda assumed a threefold thrust, against Papists, prelates, and courtiers. The House of Commons' *Remonstrance* of December 15, 1641, declared its three enemies to be:

1. The Jesuited Papists who hate the Laws, as the Obstacles of that change and Subversion of Religion, which they so much long for.

2. *The Bishops, and the corrupt part of the Clergie, who cherish formality and super-stition, as the natural effects, and more probable supports of their own Ecclesiasticall Tyranny, and Usurpation.*

3. *Such Councellors and Courtiers, as for private ends have engaged themselves to further the interests of some forrain Princes or States, to the prejudice of his Majesty, and the State at home.*[27]

The third charge most openly prepares for the escalation of hostilities from words to blows, but the two preceding are properly placed first because they are essential preconditions to the final one. *His Majesties Answer To the Petition which accompanied the Declaration of the House of Commons* assures readers "that for the preserving the peace and Safety of the Kingdom from the designs of the Popish partie, We have, and will still concur with all the just desires of Our people, in a Parliamentarie way," but distinguishes resistance to Popery from "the depriving of the Bishops of their Votes in Parliament."[28] Puritan pamphleteers, in contrast, sought to cast the bishops as cryto-Papists: "In that Reforming Parliament [of 1530], the Prelates pretended to be fearfull of the destruction of the Church, and the ceasing of that glory in which this kingdome then was, and therefore pretended to take great care for both. And thus our Prelates imitate them."[29] Like the royal *Answer* to the Commons' *Petition* and *Declaration*, the *Petition and Remonstrance* of the twelve bishops accused of treason avows "that they do abhominate all Actions and Opinions, tend-ing to Popery, and the maintenance thereof," but protests that "whereas they have been at severall times violently Menaced, Affronted, and Assaulted, by multitudes of people, in their coming to perform their Services in that Honourable House [of Lords]; and lately chased away, and put in danger of their lives, and can find no redress or protection, upon sundry complaints made to both houses in these particulars." Because of this mob action, they request "your Majesty and the Peers" to declare null the actions taken in their compelled absence since December 27, 1641.[30] With populace and Parliament aligned against bishops and king, polarization was approaching levels that would precipitate civil war. What whipped people into the frenzy required to start violence, however, was a Papist menace concretized in Irish horror stories and a rumored "Popish plot" in London itself.

What had happened on December 27 was a "great uprore ... First occasioned by some words between the late Bishop of Lincolne (now Archbishop of Yorke [John Williams]) and some London-Apprentices" and the transpiring of an account that a Frenchman stopped by the watch late on Christmas Eve, who claimed that he had been out "to celebrate the

Eve of Christmas, which he said, was a work of the night. Then they demanded of him, if he had not been about some Popish plot against us."[31] The immediate context that lent plausibility to fables of Popish massacres was – beyond longstanding stories of the Gunpowder Plot and Romish treachery – the stream of sensational accounts emerging of the Irish rebellion:

they soone entred the house, and murdered all that were in it to the number of 15 servants and children: when they had done this bloudy deed they took the old gentlewoman, and hanged her upon the walls before the gate, ripping up her belly, and so cruelly in an inhumane manner tooke out her bowels, and wrapped them about her necke, and then would have fired the house, but could not, it being all stone-worke.

Then they batred down the house, and so marched off away toward Kilmouth, who presently took the town, and batring down the houses about their eares, murdering all the protestants that they could meet with, besetting the town round about, to the intent that none should escape there hands: thus they murdered them all in a cruel manner, some having their quarters torne in pieces, deflouring the women, and hanging their quarters upon the walls, and hanging some up by the heeles, whipping them to death, and others tare the flesh from their bones with pinceeres, and hanging little children upon hookes by the throate, thus when they had searched the Towne in every house, and tooke armes for 300 men, in like manner dealt they with Iormoy, and Cormock; for there they ripped children out of their Mothers wombes, and hanged them np [sic], & trampled them under their feet.[32]

Stories of Irish atrocities supply urgency to the Parliamentary cause, an urgency that spills over into angry mobbing of prelates identified with Popery and suspicion of a royal government permeated with traitors. A *Petition* from the municipal government of London to Charles I connects "the prevailing progresse of the bloody Rebels in Ireland," Papist "Designes, tending to the uttter [sic] ruine of the Protestant Religion, and of the Lives and Liberties of Your Majesties loyall Subjects," and "the mis-understanding betwixt your Majestie and Parliament."[33] More bluntly, an account not couched as an address to the king – after describing the great rallying of armed men to guard Parliament after Charles's attempted intervention there – describes the royal proceedings as "but a design of the Popish party, to put an interruption in the proceedings of Parliament, that no relief may be sent to *Ireland*, but that more Protestant blood may be shed there."[34] After "his Majesty having placed himself in the Speakers Chair, did demand the Persons of divers Members of the House," the Commons established one committee to review "how our Priviledges may be vindicated, and our Persons secured," but also another "to consider of the Affairs and relief of Ireland."[35] What motivated the populace to mobilize to defend Parliament was less its spuriously backdated "Priviledges" than alarms of Papist "prodigious conspiracies."[36] The revolutionary mobs at the start of 1642 poured into the streets of London agitated by anxieties resembling those of the mobs that Ian Gilmour deplores as reactionary, or at best futile, in the Gordon Riots of 1780: to defy the Popish menace.[37] Similarly, once military action commenced in England, "Taking their cue from the House of Commons, which reiterated at every crisis that it was acting 'to maintain and defend ... the true reformed Protestant religion ... against all Popery and popish innovations,' almost every despatch reporting the progress of the armies described Charles's forces as 'papistical' or 'jesuited' or 'Romish.' "[38] In the Exclusion Crisis, anti-governmental agitators attempted similarly to use alarms of Popish crimes to undermine royal authority. As Mark Goldie notes, "the parallels with 1641 were on every lip," but "this time the church party won," for the most part precisely because of the example of what had happened before.[39]

III

While the Civil War had convincingly demonstrated the practical limitations upon monarchical absolutism in England, the very success of that demonstration, when coupled with its alarming consequences, left resistance to authority without a generally accepted theoretical rationale. The repeated, and futile, republican conspiracies and rebellions of the early 1660s testify rather to the impotence of what Richard L. Greaves has called "the radical underground" than to its effectiveness. Their achievements of "preserv[ing] the revolutionary ideology of the preceding decades" and foretelling "government under law, freedom, and toleration" are the achievements of martyrs and prophets, keepers of the flame, not of political actors in their own time.[40] In the absence of an undiscredited logic of resistance, though, there was still the traditional enemy to focus opposition. In an inversion of the Parliamentary propaganda, including his own, of the early 1640s, which claimed "that all Cavaliers were Papists or crypto-Papists," William Prynne by that decade's end was popularizing the theory that Papists had taken over the Army.[41] Following Prynne's lead, Peter Du Moulin's account of how Jesuits contrived the Civil War and the execution of Charles I conflates the two bugbears of regicide – repeatedly identified as a Romish tenet – and Popery. *The Great Loyalty of the Papists* begins:

When the businesses of the late bad times are once ripe for an history, and Time the bringer forth of truth, hath discovered the mysteries of Iniquity, and the depths of Satan which have wrought so much crime and mischief, it will be found, that the late Rebellion was raised and fostered by the Arts of the Court of *Rome*. That Jesuites professed themselves Independent, as not depending on the Church of England; and Fifth-Monarchy Men, that they might pull down the *English* Monarchy, and that in the Committees, for the destruction of the King and the Church, they had their Spies and their Agents. The *Roman* Priest and Confessour is known, who when he saw the stroke given to our holy King and Martyr, flourished with his sword, and said; Now the greatest enemy that we have in the world is gone.[42]

What made "our holy King and Martyr" so great an enemy to Rome was, by Du Moulin's account, only that he had promised upon his marriage to deliver England into Popery and then reneged upon that promise. The mere absence of betrayal might seem a feeble "achievement" to set against the acts of Elizabeth or Cromwell, but Elizabeth had become a golden-age heroine whose name was used as a reproach to the Stuarts, while Cromwell's was not a name for loyal Churchmen and royalists, or any opposition that wanted to avoid accusations of regicide and republicanism, to mention kindly. The portentous style and promise of future revelations conceal the lack of substance to the assertion that the "King and Martyr" is a martyr to the Protestant cause. While preposterous on its face to a modern reader, such a pairing of the two terrors of the Church of England, the enthusiast and the Jesuit, made a deeply reassuring – which is to say, anxiety-provoking – emotional sense. For Independents to be disguised Jesuits closes the gaps of historical causality into a unified conspiracy theory: England did not blunder into tearing itself apart but was subverted by Jesuitical treacheries. Similarly, Titus Oates alleged that "And *Milton* was a known frequenter of a Popish Club. Who more forward to set up *Cromwell*, and to put the Crown of our Kings upon his head, than they? Give me leave to tell Your Majesty, that his new fangled Government was contrived by a Popish Priest, and *Lambert*, a Papist for above these thirty years."[43]

To link Commonwealthsmen and Papists also had the advantage of contradicting the equivalence frequently drawn by Dissenters among episcopacy, royalism, and Popery. A 1659 pamphlet argues against "calling in the late Kings Son" on the grounds that "his affection, if not his interest, is so linked with the *Episcopal* and *Romish* party" and that "Yea, all the *Papists* of *England* appeared for the King in his warres against the Parliament . . . they have been the mortal enemies of Parliaments."[44] To a Commonwealthsman, "the *Episcopal* and *Romish* party" was one group, not two. Also in 1659, Isaac Penington wrote that

The persecuting Spirit changeth its cover often, but still retains its nature, hunting after the life and pure power of the Spirit, in the Children which are begotten of God . . . This, this is the Lords charge against thee, *Thou art for the Protestant name* (it is now become thy interest, and a goodly covering in thy eyes) *but against the Protestant Spirit*, which the Lord calleth to follow him further and further from all the things of Popery, and from all the things like Popery . . . Shall we not testifie against the Popish Spirit, and Popish Practises, and all new inventions of the same spirit (though they get never so fine a covering) in the Church of *England*, as well as against them in the Church of *Rome*? . . . *the Church of England was a Church built up of force, setled by force, upheld by force, her Ministers maintained by force, her Order, Unity, Uniformity, and Government forcible, and the free pure spirit of life can have no scope in her.*[45]

The Church of England, retaining a "persecuting Spirit," has a "Protestant Name" without a "Protestant Spirit." That is to say, as an established church the Church of England is necessarily intolerant; the "Popish Spirit" is the spirit of hierarchy that contradicts the urgings of "*the free pure spirit of life.*" The short tract that concludes with this denunciation of a government-controlled church as "of man's inventing wisdom, then against Christ, then of Antichrists spirit" begins with a reaffirmation of the mutually reinforcing millenarian and revolutionary hopes of mid-century: "And this is the thing which the Lord hath determined to do, both particularly in persons, and generally throughout the earth; namely to pull down the Mighty from their Seats, and to exalt the humble and meek."[46] Such chiliastic egalitarianism, the application of religious passion to the subversion of this-worldly power, is precisely what the Restoration's re-imposition of ecclesiastical and civil hierarchies was intended to restrain. A religious settlement was designed as the guarantor of civil order.[47] In the next year, in *The Root of Popery Struck at*, Penington attacks Protestant national churches as "Daughters of Babylon" (that is, Rome) for "Their taking upon them Authority over mens Consciences" and "abridging mens liberty in things wherin God hath left them free" by "setting up a Church-building, Government, and Discipline by the Magistrates Power."[48] His radical rejection of authority, of all constraint upon spiritual liberty as intolerable, is the same that Milton expresses years later in *Of True Religion*. In a tactic similar to that of Milton's pamphlet, Penington's full title suggests a more interdenominationally and specifically anti-Catholic project than the text bears out: *The Root of Popery Struck at, And the True Ancient Apostolick Foundation discovered, in some Propositions to the Papists, Concerning Fallibility and Infallibility.* Where the title promises an assault on Catholicism alone, whose pretensions to infallibility all Protestants opposed, the text delivers a condemnation of the Church of

England. In the absence of a credible Catholic threat, the Protestant factions continued their century-long, and recently intensified, civil war.

As might be expected, such an equation of their Church with the "triple tyrant" excited indignant Anglican replies. The threat inherent in such accusations was potentially devastating; if the Church of England could be successfully identified with Papism by its enemies, then its credibility as a Protestant and therefore national church would be destroyed. The episcopacy had been abolished in the 1640s, after all, on the grounds of its being a Popish institution. The anonymous 1663 *Philanax Protestant* repeats the charge that a "dangerous Papist" holds that "*any man may rid us of a tyrant*" and exclaims that

> They teach that the Magistrate hath nothing to do in matter of Religion, hath no power to restrain or punish any man in any matter that hath but the colour and pretence of Religion . . . In vain do you Govern if these men and these positions be endured: one mans Religion is to revile authority, the others Religion is to rebel: anothers Religion is to raise scandal upon all publick establishments, anothers religion is to refuse all manner of oaths whether of Allegiance or Supremacy &c. anothers Religion is to deny all ordinances, ministry, Church duties . . . [49]

As Nonconformist attacks seized on points of genuine structural similarity between the Church of England and Rome, so this pamphlet exploits the great superiority of Anglicanism to both Nonconformity and Papism, its loyalty, which is to say its subordination to civil authority, a subordination that ensures it will not license insurrection. Tendencies toward regicide, rebellion, and resistance to authority could be imputed in 1663 to other faiths than the Catholic, after all, and indeed here again the full title provides directions: *Philanax Protestant or Papists Discovered to the King As guilty of those Traiterous Positions and Practises which they first Insinuated into the worst Protestants and now Charge upon all. To which is added Philolaus Or Popery discovered to all Christian People in a serious diswasive from it.* Unlike the titles of Penington and Milton, however, which seek to attract Anglican readers by seeming to focus on Rome instead of the Church of England, *Philanax Protestant* openly admits "the worst Protestants," as well as Papists, to be among its targets. It expects no audience to cross over from the the other side of the sectarian divide; it feels no need of such crossover, confident in the superior numbers and position of orthodoxy. After the violent antipathies and mutual proscriptions of the Interregnum, Dissenter and Anglican are irreconciliably estranged. The pamphlet does, however, intend to return fire on the crucial question of who is more distant from Rome; it accepts with its opponents the premise that the truest Protestant faith is that which is most distant from Rome. Writing under the Commonwealth, Hobbes had carefully refrained from any more overt attack on Protestants than a hint that "it is not the Romane clergy onely, that pretends the Kingdome of God to be of this World, and thereby to have a Power therein, distinct from that of the Civill State."[50] It was precisely on its not being "distinct" from "the Civill State" that the Restoration Church of England based its unacknowledgedly Hobbesian claim to a unique "loyalty."

Still, to cast Charles II as the champion of the Protestant cause became more difficult as he matured from barely known romantic exile to French ally (and, unknown to the public, stipendiary). A serious and recurring charge against all the Stuart monarchs remained that they were "soft on Papism"; a 1660 pamphlet, *Englands Faiths Defender Vindicated,* attacks "a most foul, damnable and scandalous Aspersion," that in exile Charles II had "renounced the Protestant Religion" and "embraced Popery."[51] A Catholic Charles II could never have been restored. Instead, this pamphlet constructs a heroically resistant Charles, after the model of Peter du Moulin's version of the Royal Martyr his father: "large Promises have been made to him by most Popish Potentates (the Pope himself) for establishment of him in his Throne and Dignity, provided he would renounce his Religion" (3). Blandishments failing, "seeing their subtilty could have no prevalency over his spirit, or their temptations draw him from the Truth, to embrace their blinde and most damnable Errors, they at last contrive to force him" (6). To suggest that Charles could turn Papist would be treason legally because for him to do so would be treason culturally. As the foremost Protestant power, England had a providential role to rescue true religion from the Popery and tyranny of Continental absolutism.[52] In the seventeenth century as more recently in our own, Europe was divided into two camps, the "Protestant interest" and Catholicism, and ideology gave the dispute a universal dichotomizing power.

Even (or especially) in cold wars, however, countries may be subject to internal disputes, and, besides Dissenter distrust of monarchs and monarchy, Protestants at the time of the Restoration were bitterly divided over doctrine and discipline. All, though, inherited Catholics as traditional villains. The panic of the Exclusion Crisis intensified until it collapsed under the double weight of the absurdity of the specifics alleged and the ominous parallel with the 1640s. Once popular hysteria had had time to flag, the task of the Stuart propaganda counteroffensive was made easy by particulars so extravagant that the general issue of whether the regime could be trusted was easily avoided. After sardonically remarking that

"Priests of all Religions are the same," Dryden could strike a posture of magesterial dispassionateness in *Absalom and Achitophel* by declaring:

> From hence began that Plot, the Nation's Curse,
> Bad in itself, but represented worse;
> Rais'd in extremes, and in extremes decry'd;
> With Oaths affirm'd, with dying Vows deny'd.
> Not weigh'd or winnow'd by the Multitude;
> But swallow'd in the Mass, unchewed and Crude.
> Some Truth there was, but dash'd and brew'd with Lies,
> To please the Fools, and puzzle all the Wise.
> Succeeding times did equal folly call
> Believing nothing, or believing all.
>
> (lines 99, 108–17)

If "Priests of all Religions are the same," no faith would seem worth valuing over another, and what the "multitude . . . swallowed . . . crude" could be too crude for a gentleman to respect. A pose of genteel superiority to a political–religious enthusiasm gained in credibility after the opposition had rested its case upon wild accusations and perjuries.[53] Dryden is offering support of the crown as a broad ideological consensus that transcends the factionalism of politicized religious passions; it was on such a basis that Charles II was restored in the first place, and if the opposition could be made to appear outside that consensus Charles's position remained unbeatable. The Whigs could be accused of threatening to reintroduce rebellion as well. A 1681 pamphlet, *The Two Associations*, parallels a paper seized at Shaftesbury's arrest with a 1643 Parliamentary pronouncement that begins, "Whereas there hath been, and now is in this Kingdom a Popish and Trayterous Plot for the subversion of the true Protestant Reformed Religion and Liberty of the Subject."[54] Popery was so explosive a charge, summoning up the apocalyptic "struggle between Christ and Antichrist" of the Civil War, as to threaten social order.[55] By discrediting the proponents of what would come to be called the Protestant Succession, the extravagancies of the Popish Plot ultimately facilitated the accession of James II at the death of his brother. Nonetheless, the accusation of the Exclusion Bill, that "if the said duke should succeed to the imperial crown of this realm, nothing is more manifest than that a total change of religion within these kingdoms would ensue," remained countered only by royal promises, which could be and in fact soon were broken, and by popular opposition to Popery and tyranny.[56] After the Plot, opponents to James II could no longer simply hurl fantastic and unsubstantiated accusations; like Nonconformists after the Restoration, when memories of the New Model Army were still fresh, they needed an untainted rhetoric of resistance.

IV

Doctrine could not do the job. J. F. McGregor observes that "Traditional doctrinal definitions were obviously inadequate in dealing with the chaotic mass of religious speculation during the 1640s and 1650s";[57] strictly formulated doctrines such as the Thirty-Nine Articles of the Church of England presuppose a hierarchy to formulate a coherent theory and an obedient institution to follow the line laid down from above. Doctrine is an ordering principle; if not coercive it is apt to wander individualistically. Like Milton's *Of Christian Doctrine*, Henry Stubbe's *Account of the Rise and Progress of Mahometanism*, not published until 1911, indicates how far from orthodoxy independent minds could wander while arguing from the agreed Protestant basis of the appeal to scripture and "primitive" Christianity.[58] In the course of surveying the history of Christianity before Mohammed, his introductory chapter casually tosses off the grossest heresies by asserting that early Christians "were Millenaries, and did beleive and expect the temporal Reign of the Messiah," knew of no Holy Ghost or Trinity, and retained Jewish and pagan rituals and modes of church governance – such as communion and baptism.[59] His St. Paul, "the Apostle of the Uncircumcision, who became all things to all them that he might gain them to the Church, did comply with their weaknesses and prejudices" in a manner reminiscent of the elastic Jesuit of Protestant lore.[60] Stubbe's private speculations undermine much of the conventional Protestant appeal to the "primitive Church" by identifying corruptions ordinarily claimed to be late Papal insinuations as of Apostolic date. Nonetheless, when attacking Thomas Sprat's *History of the Royal Society*, he begins with language we have encountered before:

Never was there any sort of People that by so many Artifices endeavoured to insinuate themselves and their *Religion* into all places and countryes, as that of the *Papists*: there is no *Treaty* or *promise* can secure an *enemy* from their secret *underminings* ... I speak not this to reflect upon the *Society*, who have found so great *encouragement* from that *party*, by the concurrence of their *persons* and *purses*: and so freely keep a *correspondence* with them from beyond seas: I only say, that as such an *entercourse* is not unknown to the *Congregatio de propeganda fide*, so (whatever Mr. *Sprat* suggests) they do not apprehend the *constitution* to be any way to the *prejudice* and *dis-service* of their *Faith* and *Church*. I believe it is not displeasing to *them*, to see how *friendly* the *Protestants* and Papists converse together in this *Assembly*: and it must needs raise their *hopes* of bringing things to a *closer union*, when they perceive that *strangeness*, that ought to be, and *hath been* betwixt them, taken off, and to read addresses commencing with **Holy Father** . . . [61]

Stubbe accuses the Society of being a crypto-Catholic front, a collection of fellow travellers, dupes manipulated by the agents of a foreign conspiracy into compromising the religious independence of England. The Royal Society is fraternizing with the enemy. An education directed toward technical subjects is just what Rome wants Protestants to receive, Stubbe goes on to assert, so that they may not be able to contend in theological disputes with Catholics. He has left the private realm of unpublished manuscripts, where one may assert or question anything, for public controversy, where disagreement is betrayal and an appearance of conformity, at least on the essential point of opposition to Rome, is essential to keep up morale and even to gain a hearing.[62]

Stubbe, as it happens, has received considerably more recent notice than most other controversialists of the period. James R. Jacob has made a determined effort to rescue Stubbe from the charge of being a turncoat, of betraying the Good Old Cause by turning from "late Interregnum republican theorist" to "detractor of all things modern and progressive, especially the Royal Society."[63] Jacob is correct to distinguish between experimental science and what we today consider progressivism, and particularly between political radicalism and the careful grounding of the Royal Society in a "traditional religion" that "was tantamount to popery."[64] Stubbe is not making an original charge, however; what he is doing is fitting the Royal Society as an ally of the Church of England into a pre-existent discourse of condemnation of that Church by religious independents. When Jacob notes that, for Stubbe, "the past to which he appealed constituted a source of primitive purity against which to set, measure, and reform the corruptions of the present," he does so without acknowledging the extent to which Stubbe is echoing the standard Dissenting tactic of applying to Anglicanism, as an established church, an attack originally devised against Rome.[65] Declaring that "Stubbe's description of the Roman Catholic Church established by Justinian is worthy of Hobbes and doubtless owes not a little to *Leviathan*,"[66] Jacob refuses to confront the degree to which the accusation is altogether derivative that the Christianity of Mohammed's day was

ignorant, . . . debauched, and perfidious, and addicted to legends more than the sound doctrine of the Gospel . . . Christianity was then degenerated into such a kind of paganism as wanted nothing but the ancient sacrifices and professed polytheism, and even as to the latter there wanted not some who made three gods of the Trinity, others made a goddess of the Virgin Mary, the reverence to the saints differed little from that of the pagans to their heroes and lesser gods.[67]

The passage does possess one extraordinary feature which suffices to denote it as belonging to the realm of private speculations rather than public discourse: its avowed unitarianism. With that one admittedly large exception, the passage is orthodox doctrine fit for any cathedral of the Church of England; all Protestants agreed that Rome had become corrupt, "The Proud Primacy of Popes," in Foxe's phrase, by the seventh century; that corruption represented the primary justification for the Reformation. Whether an English Protestant is "radical" or "conservative," to follow Jabob's somewhat archaizing but not entirely invalid imposition of modern secular categories on the Dissenter/Anglican divide, or even an advocate of "secular religion" before Toland, opposition to Rome remained a constant.[68] Even if Stubbe is indeed, like Milton, "a radical critic of the Restoration settlement" who has "resorted to subterfuge" to continue to gain a hearing after 1660, however, Jacob's simplistic equation of secularism with an axiomatically virtuous progress acts to validate the liberal tradition upon which science, along with other disciplines, *after* the Restoration period has grounded itself.[69] Jacob begins no fewer than four of his eight chapters with quotations from Henry Neville's *Plato Redivivus*, all of them typically dire Nonconformist warnings against the Papistical tendencies of the Church of England, but indicates no awareness of the degree to which such discourse signifies not an unqualifiable emancipation but the transferral of regime from visible to invisible articulations of hegemony. His radicalism is our mainstream.

The tradition in which Stubbe is participating is not, after all, itself an entirely innocent one of an unproblematic and undifferentiated "radicalism." Even when arguing for freedom of the press in *Areopagitica*, Milton excepts, "I mean not tolerated Popery, and open superstition, which as it extirpats all religions and civill supremacies, so it self should be extirpat, provided first that all charitable and compassionat means be us'd to win and regain the weak and the misled."[70] In his view of Popery as too dangerous to tolerate Milton is entirely orthodox; as for Stubbe, J. A. I. Champion notes that he endorses "Moslem violence . . . in the extirpation of idolatry."[71] Violence to suppress idolatry, however, was not a matter only of distant history. The Irish horror stories that proved so useful to the Parliamentary cause at the beginning of the Civil War continued to be valuable to opponents of the Stuart regime, particularly as formulated in Sir John Temple's *The Irish Rebellion*, a volume which successfully translated broadside urgency into the seeming garb of history and so perpetuated it into future decades and even centuries. He denounces

the malignant impressions of irreligion and barbarism, transmitted down, whether by infusion from their ancestors, or natural generation, [that] had irrefragably stiffned their necks, and hardened their hearts against all the most powerful endeavours of Reformation: They continued one and the same in all their wicked customes and inclinations, without change in their affections or manners, having their eyes enflamed, their hearts enraged with malice and hatred against all the English Nation, breathing forth nothing but ruine, destruction, and utter extirpation.[72]

To reject Reformation is to refuse to become English, to be "enraged with malice and hatred against all the English Nation"; religious and national enmity become identical. The consequence is "indeed fit for a Martyrology" (109), a series of atrocities as lurid as anything in the earlier pamphlets, such as,

that many young Children were cut into quarters and gobbets by the Rebels, and that eighteen *Scottish* Infants were hanged on a Clothier's tenterhook, and that they murdered a young fat *Scottish* man, and made candles of his grease; they took another *Scottish* man and ripped up his belly, that they might come to his small guts, the one end whereof they tyed to a treee, and made him go round until he had drawn them all out of his body, they then saying, that they would try whether a dogs or a Scotch mans guts were the longer. (123)

Such dehumanizing of Irish Catholics into monsters did not end with the 1640s. George Fox follows Temple in 1667 by devoting the longest chapter of *The Arraignment of Popery* to "An Abstract of the Bloody Massacre in Ireland."[73] Such narratives of Irish bestiality update *Acts and Monuments'* obsession with Catholic cruelties. The nature of Catholic violence has shifted, however, from the hieratic flames and faggots of Foxe's woodcuts to a pornographic grand guignol that revels in random brutality, with women, especially if pregnant, and children the favored targets:

In *Queens* County, an *English* man, his Wife, five Children and a Maid, were all hanged together.

At *Clowns*, seventeen men were buried alive; some were wounded, and hanged upon Tenter-hooks.

In *Castle-G[C?]umber*, two Boys wounded, and hung upon Butchers Tenters. Some hanged up, and taken down to confess money, and then murdered. Some had their Bellies ript up, and so left with their guts about their heels.

In *Kilkenny*, an *English* Woman beaten into a Ditch, where she dyed; her Child about six years old, they ript up her belly, and let out her Guts. One they forced to Mass, then they wounded him, ript his belly, took out his guts, and so left him alive.

A *Scottish* man they stript, and hewed to pieces; ript up his Wifes belly, so that her

Child dropt out. Many other Women with Child, they hung up, ript their bellies, and let their Infants fall out; some of the Children they gave to Dogs.

In the County of *Armagh*, they robbed, stripped, and murthered abundance of *Protestants*, whereof some they burned, some they slew with the sword, some they hanged, some they starved to death; and meeting two women with six of their Children, and themselves both with Child, they murthered them all, ript open the womens bellies, took out their Children, and threw them into a ditch.

A young *Scottish* Womans Child, they took by the heels, and dasht out its brains against a Tree. The like they did to many other Children.

Anne Hill going with a young Child on her back, and four more by her side, they pulled the Child off her back, trod on it till it dyed, stripped her and the other four Children naked, whereby they dyed of cold.

Some others they met with, hanged them up upon a Windmill, and before they were half dead, cut them in pieces with their Skeins. (87–88)

Mere murder does not suffice to demonize the rebels sufficiently; their crimes must be monstrous, wilfully and shockingly cruel. The succinct summation of fiendishness goes on for twelve pages; substantial quotation is necessary to convey the sense of bludgeoning repetitiveness. The quality and circumstances of the cruelties have reversed since *Acts and Monuments*: whereas the burnings in the earlier work are legalistic inflictions by a tyrannizing hierarchy, in its totalitarian aspiration to crush what Penington called *"the free pure spirit of life,"* the crimes Temple and Fox see are lawless terrorism, the barbaric acts of primitives who ought to be more strictly controlled rather than less. Dehumanizing the Irish into fiends against whom all measures are fair, his work reflects a programmatic desensitization to any pain in Ireland but that of the settlers. Like the most vicious anti-Semitism, *The Irish Rebellion* and *The Arraignment of Popery* stigmatize a people as so vile and degraded that all measures are justified against them and ruthless ones are necessary. Such a one-sided view of Ireland, based on identification with coreligionists and compatriots, forms a standard feature of tracts from the 1640s onward. The xenophobia fed by anti-Papist rhetoric translates across the Irish Sea into a genocidal colonialism.

From a declaration of spiritual emancipation the Protestant cause in Ireland becomes a defense of civilization. Again it assumes the position of sensible moderation against an extremist threat, but this threat comes from the other direction of the dialectic, from barbarism instead of tyranny. The cruelty of legal form, the auto da fes by sinisterly elegant prelates, have turned to baccanals of blood; in discussions of Ireland, Popery is no longer represented as an oppressive order but as a release of disorder. The Anglican pastor Andrew Hamilton recounts a cowboys-and-Indians situation on the Irish frontier. The natives are restless and the settlers nervous about a coming Ghost Dance: "They [the Papists] had Publick Masses through all the North, for the furthering of that which they called *Inteneragh*, that is, a Secret intention. Our Hills were daily covered with Multitudes of them, Arming and Inlisting themselves; and they were quarter'd in our Towns, and in Private Homes."[74] Then comes a (false) rumor of impending massacre, Inniskilling arms, and the main body of the narrative begins, a story strongly resembling the archetype of the Hollywood Western about a beseiged fort. This campaign of national vilification outlived its association with radicalism to justify the long Protestant Ascendancy. Ian Gilmour provides illustrations of Protestant reactions to an uprising in 1798: "'All good Protestants,' wrote Buckingham, believed extermination of the Catholics to be 'the only cure for the present and the only sure preventive for the future.' Another nobleman hoped that a new rising would provide the opportunity to annihilate a million or two of the Catholic inhabitants."[75] It is as well to remember such attitudes, which were by no means new in 1798, when reading Swift's *Modest Proposal*.[76] English willingness to "devour" Ireland reflected in part the simple greed of individual profiteers, but the nation's predators could not have exercised their desires so freely in England's first overseas colony but for a religious ideology that dehumanized Irish Catholics as racial ideologies later deprecated the value of non-European lives.

That George Fox the nonparticipant radical ideologue projects infinitely more horror into his vision than Andrew Hamilton the Anglican eyewitness suggests how Ireland's relation to the Protestant revolution resembles that of another backward western district, the Vendée, to the French Revolution. As Simon Schama has observed of the Vendée, "The exterminations practiced there were, in fact, the logical outcome of an ideology that progressively dehumanized its adversaries and that had become incapable of seeing any middle ground between total triumph and utter eclipse."[77] Radicalism is not always necessarily humanitarian; in the case of Fox and many others, advocacy of the utmost colonialist brutality in Ireland accompanied programs of liberation in England.[78] If Jacob seems unaware that hatred of Catholicism could reflect other sentiments than a highminded subscription to ideals of which he approves, Greaves, while regarding radical republican enmity towards Catholicism as a trivial side issue, also manifests an awareness of its representing an embarrassing blotch on the nobility of the heroism he chronicles:

At root, the radical cause did not die, although some of its more parochial or unenlightened goals – rule by a godly elite and suppression of Catholicism – mercifully

did. But in its broadest principles – government under law, freedom, and toleration – it ultimately triumphed. Viewed in this light, their experience of defeat was
only temporary.[79]

Again, by selecting what is important, the historian imposes his vision on
the past. Rule by cadres and suppression of alien peoples and cultures
become unimportant and long-dead ancillaries to the central triumph of
"law, freedom, and toleration" – as if dominance by elites and metropo-
lises disappeared after the seventeenth century. Protesting trivializations
of the "genuine popular upheaval" of the Popish Plot, Jonathan Scott
tartly observes that "some historians have shown a distinct tendency to
define as popular belief only beliefs of which they themselves approve.
'Radical' views with three followers are dignified as plebeian ideology;
genuinely popular views which are intolerant and unpleasant are dismissed as hysteria."[80] Both Jacob and Greaves are seeking, in Alan Liu's
words, to "restore a past that images (and we at last know it) our best
selves."[81] A simplistic binarism that cheers on "progressive" forebears and
either celebrates or hastily passes over the connection between liberal
ideals and a regimen of genocide reflects an ongoing reproduction of the
cultural amnesia of the liberal state.

v

As Anglican writers regularly reminded the public, Dissenters were not
the only opposers of Popery. It was the task of the Anglican ideologues of
the 1680s to condemn Popery without surrendering to Dissent over church
discipline, to find a "middle ground" in which hierarchy could remain
stable despite the displacement of its papal capstone. Given this project,
too rigorous a logic would have been counterproductive. In a minor classic
of constructively muddled Anglican thinking, Charles Hutchinson argues
in 1687 against the need and possibility of an infallible judge to decide
controversies by begging a series of questions. Replying to Eight Theses
published by a Catholic, he closes with a "Post-Script" of Eight Theses of
his own, five of which demonstrate the incoherence of a church that
asserts its unity while denying any necessity for a mechanism to enforce
that unity. To his opponent's third assertion,

*That the Secular Prince cannot depose or eject . . . Clergy . . . nor introduce others into the Places of
the ejected, without the Consent of the major part of the Clergy.* I say that he talks very
loosely and crudely: For the Prince cannot eject any of the Clergy for doing their
Office as they ought to do it, though he *had the Consent* of the greater part of the
Clergy thereunto . . . But what if *Arianism* prevails in the Majority, both of the *East*

and *West?* Time was, that it did so. Is it more desirable that the Secular Powers should provide for the maintenance of Truth with a few, or help to support Error with the many?[82]

The key words in this passage are "ought," "Truth," and "Error." Unlike the clergy, the author and the "Secular Powers" know what all three terms mean. The same begging of the question recurs in the four points that follow: a "National Synod" may make "Definitions in Matters of Faith" to "reform Errors and Heresies"; better a synod not "free" that "determines against Heresies and Abuses" than one free that "should establish Innovations in the Faith, or Corruptions in the Worship of God"; the majority of the clergy should not rule if the minority is right; nor should laymen obey if clergy are wrong.[83] All these positions assume that right and wrong, or what constitute "Heresies and Abuses," are easily distinguished; that any person seeing the facts will come to the correct conclusion unless led astray by priestly self-interest; that in fact the clergy are less, not more, to be trusted than others as spiritual guides. If the Church hierarchy are not fit to judge, the only alternatives are the "Secular Powers" and the individual conscience: the Church of England represented the former choice, Nonconformism the latter. As a matter of Church governance, the Reformation entailed the subordination of the clergy either to the state or to individuals; Convocation consequently became a marginalized body. The Stuarts were restored in 1660 but not the Ecclesiastical Commission. Particularly after the Glorious Revolution delivered England into the control of an oligarchy that based its claim upon liberty, Dissenters and Whig grandees were thus natural allies against the Church of England, because both sought to repress the Church, the one so that conscience could rule, the other so that they themselves could.

Hutchinson has a precedent more recent than Henry VIII for his unstated assumption that secular power is the best qualification for theological judgment, but it is not one that he would be eager to own. In the official 1643 Parliamentary publication justifying deprivations of ministers, the charges may be generally divided into three categories: that the minister lives licentiously, expresses hostility to the proceedings of Parliament, and "is a great practiser of the late illegal Innovations."[84] Almost every one of the hundred cited ministers is condemned on all three counts, although one who, besides being a royalist, practiced "auricular confession," claimed the power to forgive, and set a "Jesuit badge" over the communion table and a dove over the font, needs no irregularities in his private morals to condemn him (39–40). Typically, however, vice, papistical tendencies, and royalism are inseparable:

Richard Goff . . . is a common haunter of Taverns and Ale-houses, a common swearer of bloudy oathes, and singer of baudy songs and often drunk, and keepeth company with Papists and scandalous persons, and hath confessed, *That he chiefly studied Popish Authors*, highly commended Queen *Maries* time, and disparages Queene *Elizabeths*, as an enemy to learning, and hoped to see the time again that there should be no Bible in mens houses . . . and hath expressed great malignancy against the Parliament, saying that he hoped to see it confounded, and that he cared not a figg for the Parliament. (44)

The similarities among the charges against the hundred ejected ministers suggest that a uniform narrative of turpitude is being imposed on all clergy found obnoxious to Parliament, so that royalism necessarily entails licentious and Catholic tendencies, which are in turn equivalent. Any established church possesses a kingdom that is of this world, and the secular power belongs to whoever holds that power: Hutchinson's sophistry or error is to assume that civil power must always be friendly to his vision of the Church. A Catholic tract of James II's reign with justice sneered at "a Famous *Act of an Infallible* English *Parliament* conven'd at Westminster, and guided by the Holy Spirit of *Shaftsbury*."[85] To satisfy the demands of an Anglican audience whose twin horrors are Popery and disruption of hierarchy, Hutchinson must reconcile support for the "Secular Powers" with, despite the plural of his "Powers," "great malignancy against the [Long] Parliament." Under an Anglican king, a strict royalism readily satisfies both needs, but a Catholic monarch had need be a far subtler trimmer than James II proved.

Before the Glorious Revolution, the Church of England claimed loyalty as its peculiar property, distinguishing it from both seditious Dissenters and fifth-columnist Papists, because the king was its head. *The New Test of the Church of England's Loyalty, Examined by the Old Test of Truth and Honesty*, only one of many Anglican controversial works proclaiming undying fealty to a dynasty about to be discarded, recounts Peter DuMoulin's story of Jesuits' rejoicing at the execution of Charles I (3), the massacres of "*English* in *Ireland*" and "Protestants about *Piedmont*" (6), and at the beginning and end of its ten pages the Anglican "Doctrine of Non-resistance" (1): "we are not for restraining of Princes" (10).[86] To declare loyalty only to an ongoing institutional status quo more important than one Papist king would be incommensurate with the personalizing ecclesiastical discourse of Stuart monarchy, in which the monarch figures as a talismanic origin of authority. After 1688, Defoe derided Anglican claims to a peculiar loyalty, noting their resistance to the Catholic Mary and James II:

The only Error we charge upon the Church of *England*, was setting up pretences of what they really would not practice; crying up themselves for Fools, when we knew thay were Wiser Men, calling themselves humble Slaves, but when the Trial came, proving Stubborn, Refractory, *Liberty Mongers*, even as bad as the worst Whig or Phanatick of them all . . . Pray, Gentlemen, never be imposed upon to pretend to more Loyalty, and more slavish Principles, than you intend to practice . . . Never be ashamed to own, with *your Brethren the Whigs*, that you are willing to Submit to Authority, but that you expect to be govern'd according to the Laws and Statutes of this Realm.[87]

While effective in its observation of Anglican inconsistency, Defoe's satire presumes the self-evidentiality of the nature of law and treats as a joke the genuine dilemma caused by the collision of the two absolutes postulated by the Restoration Church of England, the monarchy and the Church, two absolutes it had presumed identical. Defoe's pamphlet, *The New Test of the Church of England's Loyalty*, has a title nearly identical to that of the earlier Catholic tract to which *The New Test of the Church of England's Loyalty, Examined by the Old Test of Truth and Honesty* was replying; it provides an instance of similarity between Catholic and Nonconformist attacks on the Church of England. As Anglican apologetics claimed, both their enemies did indeed oppose the homology of Church and state in which they gloried. The Church of England had promised the monarchy unqualified support on the tacit assumption that the favor would be returned. When that assumption disintegrated under James, its house divided against itself.

The Church of England, debarred from a publicity of representation by its need to distinguish itself from Catholicism, had come to rely upon the totemic power of the king, a figure divided into the martyred Charles I and his son, Charles II – who was not a tragic tyrant but a divine-comedic fulfiller of the law his father had prophesied. Anglicanism under Charles II had in effect devised a new Trinity: father and son Stuart, a dual Charles who like Jesus had lain dead and was now alive, in a miracle of resurrection validated by and validating its presiding Holy Ghost, the Church of England. Then James threw away this powerful ideological mechanism for the legitimation of an absolutism based, as in Continental despotism (both Catholic and Lutheran), on the two mutually reliant pillars of Church and crown; and into the gap created by the toppling of those two pillars, once James's aggressive Papism drove them apart, thrust Parliament, which made itself the one supreme institution, demoting both the former pillars to props, scaffolding that has slowly fallen away over the centuries since. James's apostasy to Rome destroyed the narrative of theocratic absolutism which the Church had restored under his brother.

Dryden provides an alternative to Defoe's view of the transparency of Parliamentary lawmaking. His last two letters, written to a close kinswoman only weeks before his death, lament the one the House of Commons' "encroaching on the prerogative and the Lords, for they who bear the purse will rule," and the other that "Our Properties are destroyd: and rather than we shoud not perish, they have made a breach in the Magna Charta; for which God forgive them."[88] The second quotation refers to a statute, 11 and 12 William III, which incapacitates Catholics who refuse the oaths of allegiance and supremacy from inheriting or holding property after September 29, 1700. English law proves to consist not in mythical ancient liberties but in the will of Parliament, as it still does today. With the ascendancy of "constitutional" over divine-right monarchy, law resituates from princely decree sacralized by monopolistic state Church to Act of Parliament. The two competing discourses of royal and "popular" – that is, gentry Parliamentary – power, which under Charles II could both assert themselves to be the one true champion against Rome, collapse into a single master discourse of oligarchy, the position of its Jacobite rival permanently undercut after 1688 by the Catholicism of James II and the two Pretenders.

Anglican apologetics had sought to fix a stable and hierarchal Protestantism that could withstand the Catholic charge that "this charge of [Papist] *Novelty*, was nothing but a *strategem* for the introducing of *Novelties*";[89] but when the English state arrived at the stability of the post-1688 settlement it was a stability which tolerated Dissenting, though not Catholic, houses of worship, and in which the Church assumed a subordinate role. The "King's spiritual militia" would not soon again find a settlement of society quite so much to their liking as their exclusive pre-1688 establishment. The Whig ascendancy suited the grandees perfectly, so that the Countess Cowper had reason to celebrate in her diary on the day of the coronation of George I that, "I hope I shall never forget the blessing of seeing our Holy Religion thus preserv'd, as well as our Liberty and Property."[90] Parliament was supreme, and until well into the nineteenth century remained the creature of an hereditary caste, albeit one often of divided opinions.[91] Aristocratic "Liberty and Property" were safe, but many churchmen, such as Jonathan Swift, who split with the Whigs over their Church policy, and the numerous supporters of the Lower House of Convocation and Henry Sacheverell, were less than satisfied with the position of "our Holy Religion."

VI

England under James II presents the remarkable spectacle of a government at war, as one might say, with its own mechanism of legitimation. By claiming in their arguments against Catholicism that the Church of England merely restored Christianity to its primitive constitution, Anglican theologians were undermining their own position, inadvertently preparing the groundwork for the Glorious Revolution, which was similarly claimed to be restoring a primeval constitution, "ancient liberty," in the state. As an established religion, the Church of England acted as an authoritarian institution; as a Protestant religion, it had to justify itself in terms of an individualistic theology. Under James II, the Anglican hierarchy would meet the Catholic challenge to articulate a rationale for the sacralized status quo ante, the Anglican conception of a state consecrated by its state Church, in defiance of a hostile head of Church and state. Michel Serres has noted that, "It is always the center that ... makes enough noise to monopolize noise, that is enough of a parasite to kill off petty parasites, that can tolerate no relations between elements other than those it imposes. This is what is called, modestly enough, the monopoly of legitimate violence."[92] Sometimes, however, the center proves unable to monopolize noise; at that point it ceases to be central. The Church of England sought to maintain a clerical monopoly but was compelled, under James and more lastingly William, to relinquish its former exclusive right to places of worship. Once James permitted Catholic proselytizing, Anglican theology compelled its hierarchy to prepare the logic of their own loss through polemics against equally hierarchal Rome; in the aftermath of the subsequent Glorious Revolution it became an authoritarian institution that was losing its authority. Overcoming the Papist foe but in the process having to cede ground to the opposite challenges of Dissent and skepticism, Anglicanism proved not to be enough of a parasite to preserve an exclusivity of its position at the center. Like the crown, the Church was weakened by the separation of the two institutions.

Narratives of Catholic conspiracy circulated throughout the later seventeenth century. Dissenters pointed to Anglicanism's retention of the Papist traits of establishment, hierarchy, and persecution, and in return the Church of England stressed the exaltation of clerical over secular authority common to Jesuits and fanatics, in contrast to its own "loyalty." By playing on the Anglican motif of a threat to the royal person but detaching that threat from its association with religious independency, to affix it instead solely to Catholicism, the Popish Plot attempted to and for a while did align the Anglican narrative of conspiracy and betrayal with the competing Nonconformist version. On November 18, 1678, "being the Fast day appointed by the King to implore the Mercies of Almighty God in the Protection of his Majesties Sacred Person," the Archbishop of Canterbury preached a warning to the House of Lords that was then published, with numerous other clerical condemnations of Rome.[93] Confronted with the loyalty of Charles II to his brother, however, and the open conversion of anti-Papist agitation into a weapon against the administration, the Church rallied to the counterdiscourse, contrasting its own loyalty to regicidal republicans and religious radicals. Similar patterns of political inconsistency and confused loyalties amid multiple and conflicting dangers characterize the governing stratum of England under Charles II. Competing narratives prevented sustained mobilization of opinion for action at home or abroad, whether the suppression of Dissenters or the championing of the "Protestant interest" on the Continent.

In the Interregnum, the flowering of religious expression had threatened to spill over into threats to property; the succeeding decades' efforts to "settle" the government endeavored to harness popular energies into a usable form that could be directed by instead of against property. "War and war only," however, as Benjamin noted, "can set a goal for mass movements on the largest scale while respecting the traditional property system."[94] The Glorious Revolution, a victory against Popery and Tyranny at home that quickly translated into a generation of nearly constant warfare against Popery and Tyranny abroad, accomplished this ideological consolidation, this mobilization of the populace in the service of the state. Popular animus against hierarchy and ritual remained fixed in the archaic anti-Papist forms of the Reformation, and thus fossilized was amenable to manipulation from above and direction outward against the Catholic Irish and French, then eventually against other external targets as the empire expanded. In the highly politicized form which it attained in England, Protestantism could fulfill the proto-nationalistic function of supplying a mystification underwriting the inauguration of modernity and imperialism, "justify[ing] the ways of God to men."

CHAPTER FOUR

"Reason and religion": the science of Anglicanism

> The philosophy of reason and deduction, of universals – philosophy, ancient and classical, served the king alone. The king and the priest, the two faces of sovereignty.[1]

> Rationality is a social concept, and social divisions in England (and elsewhere) were producing conceptions of what was "rational" which were so different that in the last resort only force could decide between them. The "reasonableness" of the sanctity of private property was imposed by the pikes of the New Model Army and confirmed by Dutch William's mercenaries.[2]

This chapter will examine more closely the short and turbulent reign of James II, and in particular the deployment of a rhetoric of "reason" in Anglican anti-Catholic polemics. In contrast to the Nonconformist–Anglican orientation of the primary religious disputes under Charles II, this reign witnessed an intense propaganda battle between Catholic and Anglican pamphleteers because the former for the first time in over a century were permitted openly to put their case and in response the latter defended their doctrine, and status as the established church, with a new urgency. For the first time, the possibility feared by English Protestants and hoped for by Catholics would be tested, that given encouragement many people would convert to Catholicism, "the most conspicuous deviant element in society"; in the event, unsurprisingly given the brevity of James's rule, both hope and fear proved groundless.[3] In addition to reiterated claims to have scripture and antiquity on their side, apologists for the Church of England offered a third and clinching argument against Catholicism – that reason itself was with them. They saw no contradiction between what Richard Sherlock calls a "scripture-based argumentative framework" and "the priority of natural reason."[4] In *A Rational Account of the Grounds of Protestant Religion*, Edward Stillingfleet developed what would become the predominant Anglican theological case against Catholicism twenty years later, when he endorsed "*the judgement of Sense*" as the means to a *"certainty"* independent of the Papal *"Infallibility"* that "Destroy[s] the *obligation* to *Faith* which ariseth from the *rational evidence of Christian Doctrine.*"[5] Far from mutually exclusive, Protestantism and reason seemed naturally complementary, even identical, to Anglican polemicists: only Popery, in its superstition, idolatry, and implicit faith, was antagonistic to reason.[6] As Richard W. F. Kroll observes, the "defense of contingency, premised on a skeptical empiricism, becomes not the chief discourse of dissent but, again, its opposite: the language of the most visible institutions returned to power after the Restoration."[7] Reason and the Anglican monopoly of worship are consistently identified by Anglican apologists of the 1680s, and Popery threatens both.

What Terry Eagleton has called "the Enlightenment dream of a world entirely transparent to reason, free of the prejudice, superstition and obscurantism of the *ancien regime*" has unacknowledged antecedents in Protestant polemics against "the prejudice, superstition and obscurantism" of Catholicism.[8] This chapter examines the differences between the polemical literatures of the reigns of Charles II and James II, the ways in which "reason" operates as an important force against Catholicism, and the method by which this usage entangles anti-Catholicism in the construction of modern science. In 1685, the year of James's coronation, John Williams argued that religious services ought to be conducted "in a Tongue understood of the people," recommending that "we consult the reason of the thing":[9] reason consists in the Protestant replacement of the spectacle of the Mass with verbalization. In attacking Catholicism, Anglican theologians redefined religion itself as based more on reason than on faith, because Papists could lay equal claim to faith, but only the Church of England possessed reason as they defined it. Stillingfleet's theological career is paradigmatic for Restoration Anglicanism's enlistment of reason in sectarian disputes: his 1662 *Originae Sacrae, or a Rational Account of the Grounds of Christian Faith* defends Christianity as rational, then in 1665 *A Rational Account of the Grounds of Protestant Religion* narrows religious rationality to exclude Catholicism; in the wake of the Exclusion Crisis, the 1681 *The Unreasonableness of Separation* chides Dissenters for being so "unreasonable" as not to conform to the Church of England; and finally in 1687 *The Doctrine of the Trinity and Transubstantiation Compared, as to Scripture, Reason, and Tradition* returns to the subject of *A Rational Account*, tightening its 600 learned pages into colloquial propaganda aimed at lay readers.[10] In the clear light of reason, where the only static – in Michel Serres's sense – is corruption, disagreement (with Anglicanism) becomes impossible.[11] The claim by G. S. Rousseau and Roy Porter that, "Faith in experience and reason as universalizing faculties has been a central plank in the progressive, liberal intellectual tradition, as codified during the Enlightenment, and reaffirmed over the last two centuries" does inadequate credit to the lineage of their subject.[12] Mark Goldie locates the origins of modern skepticism in the very Christian tradition it attacks. Terming Marx's and Engels's *German Ideology* "a manifesto of a new Reformation," Goldie argues that post-Enlightenment secularizing anticlericalism extends the logic of Protestantism's earlier attack on priestcraft.[13] Before becoming defined as the antithesis of religion in general, reason was first defined as antithetical specifically to Catholicism.

Despite, or perhaps because of, the positional turmoil confronting a Church of England compelled to fight a theological war on two fronts, its arguments frequently displayed a conspicuous degree of ideational stasis. Before the Civil War, William Chillingworth had already, in *The Religion of Protestants* – a work published by Oxford University and dedicated to Charles I – proposed reason as an authority superior to papal infallibility. Against a Catholic tract's accusation, "that *if this infallibility be once impeached, every man is given over to his own wit and discourse,*" Chillingworth counters by distinguishing between "*discourse,* not guiding itself by Scripture, but only by principles of nature, or perhaps by prejudices and popular errors" and "discourse, right reason, grounded on Divine revelation and common notions, written by God in the hearts of all men, and deducing, according to the never failing rules of Logick, consequent deductions from them."[14] A final judge of doctrinal differences is unnecessary because "common notions" are "written by God in the hearts of all men," and "Logick" operates according to "never failing rules." Although Chillingworth is arguing specifically only that Protestants may be saved despite Catholic claims of papal infallibility, his emphasis on the perfection of reason, his assertion that "by discourse no man can possibly be led to error," so that any mistakes must necessarily result from defects in "principles" or "error in his discourse" (as if to err were not human), becomes enormously influential in reconciling the contradictory Anglican requirements that thought be free and yet conform.[15] In contrast to Chillingworth's dual emphasis on logic as well as "common notions," however, post-Restoration theologians locate their principal evidence in Stillingfleet's "*judgement of Sense.*"

Anglican pamphleteers cast themselves in Lyotard's terms as "operators of scientific knowledge" at whose hands Catholicism becomes figured as a "traditional knowledge" or "obscurantism" to be dissected by the Protestant rational subject.[16] Michel de Certeau observed that "Modern

Western history essentially begins with differentiation between the present and the past. In this way it is unlike tradition (religious tradition), though it never succeeds in being entirely dissociated from this archaeology, maintaining with it a relation of indebtedness and rejection."[17] The prototype for this "relation of indebtedness and rejection," this Western pattern of dichotomizing the discredited past and the progressive present, is the Reformation.[18] Anglican attacks on Catholic doctrines such as transubstantiation assume for themselves a central subject position of rationality from which they construct the Catholic other as irrational, its "lived body" of traditive accretion "revealed to erudite curiosity through a corpus of texts" as an "exoticism, similar to that which once attracted the ethnologist to the 'savages' of the forest or to French sorcerers."[19] The privileging of reason allows Anglican apologetics to enlist the language of scientific progress and reason, institutionalized by 1685, in their cause. Samuel Johnson expresses confidence that "We are sure a Divine Revelation cannot contradict the Common Sense and Reason of Mankind ... But if this Revelation should contradict the plain Principles of Reason, then it would overthrow the Understanding which we are sure we received from the hands of God."[20] Protestantism assumes a Baconian shape, enlisting the new experimentalism of natural science as axiomatic "plain Principles of Reason" against which the return of open priestcraft under James's patronage is "the return of the repressed, that is, a return of what, at a given moment, has *become* unthinkable in order for a new identity to *become* thinkable."[21] Always figured in these tracts as a medieval relic, in place of the explicitly political aspect it bore under Charles II but that under James is at once unmentionable and obvious, the Catholic has become unthinkable in order for the Protestant to become thinkable. Protestantism, the scientific site of the rational subject, figures as the prototype of the modern.

I

The relation between science, the paradigmatic modern intellectual structure, and theology, the paradigmatic premodern intellectual structure, constitutes the subject of this chapter. Long neglected because the two systems seemed at first natural allies, and then as naturally antithetical, the conjunction of scientific and religious ideologies in the late seventeenth century has only recently begun to receive significant attention. Since the pioneering work of Margaret C. Jacob and James R. Jacob, the intimate relation between these two structures for explaining the world and humanity's place within it, and in particular the pivotal role of the Restoration period, when the two seemed not competing but complementary, has become the subject for considerable discussion. This chapter examines how the immense wave of propagandistic Anglican theologizing under James I I labors to establish the superiority of the Church of England to Rome by re-borrowing the methods and conventions of rationality which scientific experimentalism itself had originally derived from theology. The intensity with which this polemical literature suddenly erupted, and still more suddenly returned to obscurity after James's deposition, reflects its double status. Establishing the concord of Anglicanism and experimentalism as mutually compatible, or even as necessary complements to one another, was fundamental to the metaphysical reordering of political cosmology from a hierarchy culminating in a king or pope, who possessed sole authorizing power, to a republic of observers. There is a catch, however, to the new republic of the mind: in order to qualify as an observer, one must subscribe to the inscription of reason as a discourse of power, and, as a complement, to the exclusion from power of all but the gentry. Religious and scientific epistemologies united in order to supply a rationale for the repudiation of James II and Catholicism as based on essential principles of reason. Because the homology of faith and reason was not quite so perfect as it was convenient to believe, however, just as the rights of the (propertied) subject were not quite so immemorial as in the rhetoric of Parliamentary supremacy, this immense theological literature had to vanish as soon as its delegitimating of the premodern had been fulfilled in the inauguration of the new regime, lest its visible support suggest that that regime required support. What has to be emphasized about Anglican tracts under James II is the degree to which they differ from those before and after because they respond to a different enemy: instead of rebutting "political radicals like the freethinkers" or "religious enthusiasts," these pamphlets have an opposite target, Catholicism.[22]

What Margaret Jacob has called pre-Darwinian "science-supported religion" predates and prepares the way of the Glorious Revolution; far from being "politically ineffectual," as she argues, in the face of the Papist threat the Anglican clergy responded with a vehemence that effectively undercut both Stuart legitimacy and their own continuing professions of dynastic loyalty.[23] The connection between the Williamite settlement and "the Newtonian synthesis" involves less "a tolerant version of Christianity" than one that founds its no-less-real intolerance on "reason" rather than upon argumentatively articulated dogmatic systems.[24] While asserting her difference from "an older genre of writing about science in history

that concentrated exclusively on 'pioneers,' 'achievements,' 'progress,'"
Margaret Jacob nonetheless incorporates much of the narrative of
progress in her contrast between "the cultural rigidity and intolerance
increasingly associated with the absolutist state" and a "liberal Christianity"
whose liberalism consists in its concealment of its mechanisms of domination.[25] Identifying the Restoration as a crucial period in the development
of the scientific ideal of objectivity, Robert Markley has argued that
the "objectivity" of Restoration science "is an ahistorical assumption of
rationality":[26] behind every ahistorical assumption lies an historical
impetus; if rationality is privileged it is for a reason. Markley has since
observed that, with the idea of the "two books" of nature and the Bible,
"the metadiscourse of theology ... relieves [experimental natural
philosophy] from the burden of having to articulate a theory ... to justify
its epistemological procedures and teleological imperatives."[27] If experimental science begins the Restoration dependent on theology to provide it
with a rationale to unite "the homology of royalist politics, experimental
philosophy, and Anglicanism" in the ideology of the Royal Society, however, by the Glorious Revolution Anglican theology is drawing upon
experimentalism to justify itself against the Catholicism of James II without openly denying the royalism central to the founding logic of the
Church of England.[28] This chapter does not attempt to define a single
precise meaning of "science" because clarity, the ostensible goal of
Anglican propagandists, is really antithetical to their purpose, which is to
enlist the intellectual prestige of the new science in the Anglican cause
without subjecting religious principles to too searching a scrutiny. The
"reason" involved must be vague to disguise the elision between the *scientia*
of theology and experimentalism.[29]

By providing an alternative philosophical framework to the scholastic
Aristotelianism that Milton found so irksome, experimental natural
philosophy supplied assumptions distinctively both modern and native
with which to refute Catholic "school-theology," such as demonstrative
principles in science, without having to argue on scholasticism's terms.
Anglican attacks on Popery from the Reformation through the Exclusion
Crisis commonly condemned it on both religious and political grounds as
contrary to scripture and as the perverted and persecuting concoction of
self-interested priests and tyrannical foreigners. Under James, however, it
was impossible to pretend that Catholics were all foreigners and impolitic
to make open accusations of tyranny. With sensationalistic and nationalistic appeals discredited by the Popish Plot and muted by loyalty and fear,
scripture and antiquity were buttressed by a renewed stress on a third

argument – that Catholicism was contrary to reason itself. In these circumstances, and in response to the open circulation of Catholic propaganda, Anglican divines, prominently including the three men who would fill the Archbishopric of Canterbury from 1691 to 1737, produced a flood of tracts defending the established Church.[30] These works represent what may be the most elaborate, or bulky at any rate, justification of the Church of England in print; and by defining Anglicanism they redefine it. Experimentalism, what Robert Boyle calls "the evidence of Sence,"[31] replaces closed logical systems as the primary proof of Christianity, at a stroke delegitimizing centuries of theological and scientific reasoning. Scholastic theology, too, was an Aristotelian system, an elaborate development of logic remote from immediate apprehension, and as embedded in such Catholic doctrines as purgatory and transubstantiation was a popular polemical target. Papal infallibility is an extension of syllogistic logic, premised on the need for a final judge of questions not in themselves open to resolution; Protestant latitudinarian argument becomes probabilistic, denying the necessity of a single ultimate authority to decide what is true.[32] Protestantism, like "Baconianism," is posited as a new beginning, proceeding on first principles disentangled from theoretical encrustations, the "corruptions" and "novelties" of Rome.[33] As Bacon called for a "more perfect use of reason in the investigation of Nature," in place of a logic-chopping "fruitful of controversies and barren of works," so Protestantism would employ a more perfect use of reason in the investigation of God.[34]

Theological debates under James tended to form long chains of thesis and rebuttal between Catholic pamphlets protected from the law by royal patronage and Anglican pamphlets protected from the censor by the power of the Church to license publications. Each pamphlet demonstrated its unassailable triumph over its immediately preceding opponent; none conceded an argument as lost. Numerous Protestant pamphlets went unanswered, however, because they had the weight of numbers on their side. These disputes began when a Catholic defended his church or an Anglican attacked it, but they only had one ending, not logical but chronological. After the Glorious Revolution, the debates cut off, suddenly irrelevant, because their argument acted not as a common construction of an intellectual synthesis but as two clashing justifications of mutually exclusive episcopacies and theologies. One state could not have two established churches. Each side needed to be absolutely right to justify its claim to truth and therefore to power. Once James left, Catholic liberty to print and plausibility as a theological threat to the Church of England left with him, so that one party could not make its case and the other had no continuing need to do so. Prejudice hardened into convention and recurrent occasions such as Gunpowder Day sufficed to remind people that Catholicism was the enemy; to produce elaborate and voluminous rebuttals of arguments no longer heard could only have excited unwanted speculation. A list of 1689 counted 228 Anglican to two Dissenting doctrinal publications during James's reign.[35] The Anglican hierarchy, unlike Dissenters, had the ability to license publications, and some Nonconformists, most notably William Penn, were tempted by James's offer of toleration; but, more importantly, the Church of England had the most justifying to do of the religious status quo because that status quo was their creature. The system James and Rome were threatening was one that had been established for their convenience, not the Dissenters'; to put the matter bluntly, their livings would be the ones lost if Catholicism became established in their stead. The discrepancy also perhaps proves less the greater zealousness against Rome of the established clergy than the crucial need for the Church to prove both to its own members and to hostile Nonconformists that – despite any institutional resemblance to Rome as an episcopal institution supported by laws, property, and tithes – it was a "true religion," a true child of the Reformation. Doctrinal works that under James reassured the Dissenters would irritate them after the Revolution, because they, instead of Rome, would become the party excluded by formulations of doctrine.[36]

II

These voluminous Anglican controversial writings can seem futile in their massive ephemerality. Their thousands of pages (by Macaulay's reckoning, 20,000 pages remained in his time) of painstaking argumentation and vehement abuse were soon left behind by events and have never been reprinted.[37] Nonetheless, they articulate the position of a Church that claims in many tracts to have been stable in its doctrine since its founding and that yet is entering a crucial period of modifying its ideology to deal with the unprecedented situation of opposition from a Catholic king. This asserted stability accompanies reliance on a "commonsense" whose conclusions are both obvious and irrefutable, and this "commonsense" in turn claims experimentalism as the origin of its authority.[38] The tracts' claim to historical significance is that they illuminate a process of development that would otherwise remain obscure, but it also accounts for their neglect: the rationale of spiritual governance they preface, like that which they are disengaging themselves from (while denying doing any such thing), requires that its truth be transhistorically self-evident, not dependent on contingencies. An eternal truth embedded in Foxe's *Book of Martyrs,* that kings are the salvation of the true church against Antichrist's impostures, must yield to another eternal truth, the supremacy of Protestant reason. By adhering to their doctrinal system, Anglican theologians are able to avoid endorsing the toleration of Dissent embraced by both the government and its secular opposition. In *A Letter to a Dissenter*, Halifax cautions Dissenters against heeding the royal offer of toleration:

This Alliance, between *Liberty* and *Infallibility*, is bringing together the Two most contrary things that are in the World. The Church of *Rome* doth not only dislike the allowing Liberty, but by its Principles it cannot do it . . . you Act very unskilfully against your visible Interest, if you throw away the advantages, of which you can hardly fail in the next probable Revolution . . . .The *Church* of *England* convinced of its Errour in being Severe to you; the Parliament, when ever it meeteth, sure to be Gentle to you; the next Heir bred in the Country which you have so often Quoted for a Pattern of Indulgence; a general Agreement of all thinking Men, that we must no more cut our selves off from the Protestants abroad . . . Our Dis-union is not only a Reproach, but a Danger to us.[39]

The politician is already, in 1687, looking forward to "the next probable Revolution"; James will soon be gone, but the Dissenters will still have to deal with the consequences of this Catholic–Dissenter misalliance. Halifax is also attacking the paradox of a situation in which the aspiring autocrat was receiving support from religious radicals such as William Penn, who were willing to accept toleration from anyone. After noting that "the Promises made to induce the late Kings [Charles II] Restoration" were broken, Penn observes that toleration "is not Introducing Idolatry (taking for granted that Popery is so) but saving the People from being Destroy'd that profess that Religion . . . *Idolators* are to be *Enlighten'd* and *Perswaded*, as St. Paul did the *Athenians* and *Romans*, and not *knockd on the Head*, which mends no body."[40] Penn looks at Catholics and sees an oppressed sect like his own Friends. Neither Halifax's realpolitik nor Penn's gospel of toleration without limit suits the needs of a Church intent on defending its interests.

Penn's position seems so commonplace today that it is worth pausing a moment to stress how unusual it was in its time. His cheerful acceptance of Catholic proselytizing – "What they convert upon the Square, *Perswasion* I mean, is their own and much good may it do them"[41] – may be contrasted to Richard Baxter's *Fair-Warning: or, XXV Reasons Against Toleration and Indulgence of Popery*. Although this latter work dates from a Presbyterian of a generation earlier, before James even converted to Catholicism, its charges had been circulating for much longer and would continue to do so. Popery "is not to be tollerated" because it "persuades men to believe and live by the traditions of men, and to make the word of God of none effect" (2), and "rather [to] obey a foreign power, then submit to our lawes" (17). "Popery destroyeth your government" (14), so that toleration is "more then *Protestants may with safety grant*" (19). Popery is both morally wrong and politically dangerous (the two are indissolubly connected), and the first and worst of its heresies is "That the word of God (I tremble to write it) is obscure, imperfect, and insufficient to lead us all to truth" (14).[42] The biblical text must be at once sufficient and transparent to justify the logic shared by Presbyterianism and Anglicanism, as churches that aspire to inclusiveness but base their theology on the revolt against Rome, that agreement about doctrine is essential but requires no official mechanism of interpretation, such as Catholicism's councils and Papal decrees. This fantasy of spontaneous universal agreement remained as vulnerable to skepticism as it had been when Milton concluded that "*New Presbyter* is but *Old Priest* writ Large";[43] Matthew Tindal uses Milton's comparison in reverse to mock High Church pretensions to independence of governmental control in his 1709 *New High-Church Turn'd Old Presbyterian*. Tindal contrasts the Presbyterian doctrine that upheld clerical independence of the state in "Church Matters" to the Anglican reliance on the civil power, and mockingly observes that "But now, ever since the Revolution, the Scene is quite alter'd."[44] Prior to 1689, the royal supremacy provided the Church of England with a clear legal mandate for exclusive predominance; as Penn reminds Dissenters, "if the Laws are not repealed, there wants no new ones to Destroy you, of the Papists making."[45] The Anglican pamphlets of James's reign, then, have the double burden of defending a national church against a rival universalizing church while upholding the idea of such universality *within* the nation.

That the Church of England's aspiration to rule parallels Rome's becomes again an accusation in the High Church controversy of the early eighteenth century. In 1718, *An Essay upon the Nature of a Church and the Extent of Ecclesiastical Authority* asserts that any church that practices "*the Damnable Doctrine of Persecution*" is no church at all, and laments that "Millions and Millions have been sacrificed *to this Idol of Ecclesiastical Authority.*"[46] This pamphlet is characteristic of Dissenting rhetoric, such as Milton's *Of True Religion* forty-five years before, in its elision of Anglican intolerance into the long tradition of Catholic horrors. (The title page asserts that the *Essay* is "By a Lay-man of the Church of England," but such an ascription proves only that the author wished not to be identified with the Dissenters and knew that he would be.) This pamphlet also makes the classic Protestant assertion that Catholicism is a bad-faith ideology, an evil conspiracy:

the Tribe of Hereticks and Schismatics who adhere to the Pope of *Rome*, and commonly go by the name of the *Church of Rome*, are in Reality, and in strict and proper speaking no *Church* at all ... the distinguishing Doctrines of that *pretended Church* are such an abominable Mass of Impiety, Absurdity, and Nonsense ... it was Originally contrived, has been, and is at this Day, supported wittingly and knowingly in direct Opposition to all the Ends of the Gospel, and that by the most inhuman Cruelties that the Will of Man, help'd and assisted by the Cunning and Contrivance of the Devil, could invent: so that the Name Church may with as much Propriety be extended to a *Den of Thieves*, or a *Nest of Pirates*, only with this woeful Disadvantage to *the pretended Church of Rome*, that she fathers her Villainies upon *God Almighty* himself, and is guilty of carrying on the *most hellish Designs*, under the Pretence of his Authority, and the Colour of Religion, and therefore must appear more odious and abominable in the Eyes of God, than Robbers and Pirates, or the greatest Villains upon Earth besides. (5–6)

We are back in the central trope of Foxe's *Book of Martyrs*: Rome is the kingdom of Antichrist. Upon that all Protestants could agree, the Nonjuring archbishop Sancroft and zealous Whig Gilbert Burnet with Henry Stubbe and Milton. If Catholicism is a monstrous fraud which any honest external observer must be able to see through, then the agreement of such observers may be emphasized, instead of their differences, to create an impression of consistency. One Catholic pamphlet of 1687, *Reason and Authority*, satirically observes that "I began to make up my *account*, and drew a *Scheme* of Divinity ... However, being taught by your selves to suspect General Councils; to Judge the Works of the *Fathers*, whether they were *genuine*, or *suppositious*; and of the *truest*, to interpret them according to our own *private Opinion*, or condemn them, as *erroneous*, when they differ'd from our Sentiments; I stuck close to my Reason, finisht my Scheme, and my Reason subscrib'd to it."[47] But sadly it differed from all extant sects, so for the sake of "temporal Peace" he decided not "to set up for a Heresiarch."[48] This tract suggests that the proper interpretation of Christianity is indeed, in Richard Baxter's words, a question "obscure, imperfect, and insufficient to lead us all to truth." It is against such a skeptical conception of reason that Anglicanism recruits experimental science's emphasis on witnesses.

Anglican ideologists had to resist the tendency of freedom of thought to result in freethinking, to produce an anarchy of opinions inconsistent with the Church's hierarchal structure and purpose. In their attempt to strike a balance between Dissenting individual interpretation and

Catholic coerciveness, Anglican theologians relied heavily on the superior rationality of their church. Their insistence on the centrality of rationalistic discourse informs their articulation of the traditional Protestant hostility toward images and idolatry. William Sherlock asserts that "a Picture informs a man of nothing, but what he was informed of before. The Picture of a Crucifix may put a Man in mind of what he has heard or read of Christs dying upon the Cross; but if he knows nothing of the History of Christs Sufferings, the bare seeing a Crucifix can teach him nothing. Children may be taught by Pictures, which make a more strong impression on their fancies than Words; but a Picture cannot teach; and at best this is but a very childish way of learning."[49] All that can be learned is reason; "fancies" are childish, unworthy of divinity. What Sherlock omits to say is that a picture in its indeterminacy incites the viewer to independent speculation; what he values are words whose "teaching" consists in their imposition of a single meaning. Like Baxter, he defines language to be transparent, absolutely controlled by a fixed reason antithetical to ambiguity.

The Church of England, though, could be embarrassed by contrasting the contradictory positions it was at various times obliged to support as an institution complicit in governing.[50] Comparing Anglican arguments against Dissenters and Catholics, John Gother argues that the Anglican case against Dissenters is approved by Catholics as sound doctrine and can be applied to its own disagreement with Rome.[51] John Williams angrily denies Gother's parallel of the Anglican position against Dissent and the Catholic position against Anglicanism; the difference, he argues, lies in the superior loyalty of the Church of England. Writing in 1688, the year of the Glorious Revolution, he dares Catholic writers to "challenge the [Anglican] Sermons with Principles of Disloyalty to their Prince ... Do they find there the [putatively Catholic] Doctrines of the People's Power over Princes, of the Lawfulness of Resisting, or of a foreign Jurisdiction over their Soveraign?"[52] It may be noted that Gother's pamphlets tend more toward satire than the bludgeonings of doctrinal argumentation; his answerers took offense at his flippant attitude and imaginative approach in sacred disputation. The burlesque indictment of the Church of England by "Zealous Brother" in the *Amicable Accommodation* and the imagined distant Papist preacher attacking Protestants with their own texts in *A Reply to the Answer* are both making the serious point that Papists ought not to be treated as if inhuman.[53] Gother is not always mocking: "I know 'tis thought necessary for the Establishment and Security of the Protestant Religion, that the People should be Preach'd into a dread of Popery: but let it be so; is it a Christian method to make use of Artifices to encrease the horror? Why should every thing the Papists do, be stretch'd and strain'd, and forc'd, to make it ugly?"[54] William Wake complains of *"mean Reflections,* and *trivial Jestings,"* of *"lightness* and *scurrility,* as if their Zeal for their Church had made them forget *that Religion is the Subject, and Christians and Scholars,* to say no more of them, *their Antagonists."*[55] Wake's outrage that the motives of Anglican clergy could possibly be suspected contrasts markedly, however, with the routine Protestant assumption that the designs of Catholic churchmen are always dishonest. To call Papists monsters is only just, but *"lightness* and *scurrility"* about the established Church is intolerable. Wake's thin-skinned institutional loyalty resembles that of Jeremy Collier's *A Short View of the Immorality and Profaneness of the English Stage* a decade later, which most strongly condemns the theater for its lack of respect for clerical dignity.[56] Imagination leads to superstition and immorality; reason is the sure guide to Anglican truth.[57]

Anglican theology under James can be startlingly literal-minded. Sherlock replies to Gother's "Zealous Brother" (who in a fantastic strain rephrases Anglican charges against Rome as they might be applied by a sectarian against the Church of England) without betraying any awareness that humor could be intended, and denies Anglican persecution: "The [churches] all judg for themselves ... only with this difference, that being established by Law, her [Anglican] Communion and Government is enforced by Laws. And what a mighty Absurdity and Contradiction is this, that men should be taught to use their own Reason and Judgment in Religion, and yet required to submit and conform to a Church, whose Faith and Worship is consonant to Scripture and Reason."[58] Although the blindness of this statement may seem to approach self-satire, it follows logically from the opinion which Baxter implies by stating that he trembles to write that Rome disagrees with it: that religious truth is simple and easily apprehended with clarity. Baxter and Sherlock know exactly what scripture means and what conclusions "reason" can draw from it. This is a claim that both Presbyterians and Anglicans of the seventeenth century have to make to be able to aspire to a clerical monopoly in a Protestant country where the Bible is open for all to read and interpret. In the absence of sin, controversy is unnecessary, as the future archbishop Tenison observed:

If the Lusts and Passions of Men were Mortified; all Christians agreeing in the certainty of the Scriptures, though not of any Living Guide; and the words of the one being as intelligible as those of the other: All might agree in one Creed, and put an end to those unnecessary Controversies which entangle Truth, and extinguish Charity.[59]

Despite the evidence of the Interregnum and persisting Dissent, the Church of England can be completely national if every reasonable individual who examines scripture will come to a similar conclusion; at least, it can claim to be completely inclusive so long as it can assert the possibility of unanimity. In the absence of mechanisms of authority such as Catholicism's councils and popes, conformity demands that reason itself must be uniform. With similar literal-mindedness, Sherlock demands in another tract, "whether there be any such thing as External and Visible Idolatry? If there be, it must consist in External and Visible Actions, for we can never know what mens intentions are, but by their Actions; and then if men do such Actions as are Idolatrous, how can the intention excuse them from Idolatry?"[60] The inward state has an unmistakable outward sign.

This insistence on clarity, paradoxically, feeds paranoia. If truth is readily apprehensible and comprehensible, disagreement cannot result from a sincere difference of opinions, but must have been planted deliberately; a villain is thus necessary to make the mischief. The one available since the Reformation still serves: "While these Gentlemen lay behind the Curtain, and acted the part of a *Zealous Brother* under several disguises, there was much more danger of them, than now."[61] Sherlock perpetuates the legend of Papist infiltration and encouragement of Nonconformity, a myth so agreeable to Anglican clergy in its union of their enemies to both sides that Swift revives it a generation later in *Examiner* 39.[62] As the meaning of the Bible is obvious, so is the relative morality of Protestants and Catholics. In *A Second Defense* William Wake charges against Roman controvertists, "with what Industry they conceal the Real *Doctrine* of their *Church*, and by complaining loudly against others for *Misrepresenting* their Opinions, endeavor to keep men from suspecting that the *Juggle* indeed lies at their own Doors. I cannot but call to mind the Complaint of an *ancient Father* against the *Heathen Philosophers* ... 'But what can be done to Men that are obstinately bent *to serve a Cause*?' – Ye know that ye maintain an *ill Cause*."[63] Such accusations of Catholic bad faith, as has been mentioned, are standard Protestant charges, and indeed result logically, inevitably, from the presumption that Catholicism is so patently monstrous a system as to be able to survive only by gross ignorance among the laity, savage persecution of heretics, and a corrupt and ruthless hypocrisy among the clergy.

Wake's repetition of such charges coexists with his indignant rejection of the thought that their like could be levelled at Anglican clergy.[64] To suggest that the clergy of an established church have an interest in the well-being of their institution in this case becomes an outrage: "That is, in other Words, that those of the *Church of England*, who oppose your *Designs*, are all of them a pack of *Atheists* and *Hypocrites*; who value nothing but their *Temporal Interests*; and therefore seem resolved *at any rate* to run down *Popery*, *least they should suffer prejudice by its increase*. A *Character* so Vile and Scandalous; so void of all appearance of *Truth* as well as of *Modesty*."[65] Nonconformists had long made precisely such charges against the Church of England, of course, most familiarly in the denunciation by "The Pilot of the *Galilean* Lake" of "Blind mouths!" in Milton's "Lycidas."[66] A condemnation of the executed Archbishop Laud, "Published according to Order" for the Long Parliament, describes him as precisely such a monster as Wake asserts no Anglican could be:

This is that Canterburian Arch Prelate, in his life time heir-apparant to the Pope-dome, subtile, false, treacherous, cruel, carrying two faces under one hood, Sathans second childe, who ever is the first, as hard to speake truthe, as to do good, or to repent of any evill, as his Father the Devill, an inveterate adversary to Christ, and all true Christians, an underminer of the Civill State, a Traitor to his Countrey, wilfully damning his owne soul, to save the credite of his cursed cause, sealing with his blood the Kings part, with Romes, to be righteous, and the Parliaments odious, that so he might be as unlike Sampson, as possible, to do as much (if not more) mischiefe to his native countrey at his death, as he had done in his life; and therefore worthy to have dyed the ancient death of parricides, or Traytors to their Countrey, which the ancient Romans used, to be sowed up in a Culleus or leather sacke, and cast into the warer [sic], and there to perish, as unworthy to touch either earth, or water, or ayre, as Natures out-cast.[67]

The rhetorical strategy of this pamphlet, as so often in Dissenting attacks (including Milton's) on the Church of England, is to make Laud a Catholic. For Anglicans to admit such a parallel between their church and that of Rome would be to undermine the Anglican claim to a national universality as a "true Protestant" religion; it would confess the anti-episcopal campaigners of the 1640s to have been correct. The Church of England wished to defeat Rome, but not at the price of losing the Civil War once more. The Pope must be cast down, but not bishops. To perform this maneuver it had carefully to delimit and define the field of ideational combat.

III

One pamphlet that undertakes this task is Sherlock's *A Vindication of Protestant Principles of Church-Unity and Church-Communion, From the Charge of Agreement with the Church of Rome*, which distinguishes Anglicanism from both Catholicism and Dissent. The central distinction lies between the legitimate authority of bishops and the illegitimacy of any higher ecclesiastical authority, whether council or pope: if episcopal rule lacks authority, then the Church of England must surrender to the Dissenters; if councils or popes have authority, it must surrender to the Papists. This distinction necessarily involves a definition of legitimacy: "The Church of *England* Reformers never made a mere Opposition to the Church of *Rome*, the Rule of their Reformation; but Reformed only those abuses of the Church of Rome which needed a Reformation."[68] That Anglicanism differs from Rome does not suffice to guarantee the adequacy of a doctrine; nonetheless, there is a method to determine its truth, and the elaboration of this method represents the chief business of the tract. The method relies on a sophistry, however, grounded in a fantasy of apprehensible truth and a golden age of church concord. If truth is obvious, then any viewpoint contrary to that truth is equally obviously false, so that theology ceases to become an uncertain realm of individual inspiration and institutionalized doctrine and instead becomes a matter of manifest and reproducible results upon which all observers can agree.

Sherlock is attempting to extricate his writings against Dissenters from allegations of proto-papism. His "defense of Dr. *Stillingfleet*'s unreasonableness of Separation" does assert that "*the National and Universal Church consists in one Communion,*" but also "That their Unity consists only in consent, not in any superior Governing Ecclesiastical Power on Earth."[69] The Church is united, but needs no mechanism to remain so: "[N]o Bishops either single or united have any direct Authority or Superiority over each other."[70] He admits that he allowed Councils "an Authority of censuring Heretical and Schismatical Bishops," because "Hereticks and Schismatics, wicked and profligate persons, may be flung out of the Church" (26), but who is to do the flinging remains as yet unstated.

And therefore this is no usurpation upon the Episcopal Power and Government; it is not imposing Laws and Rules on a Bishop for the Government of his Church without his consent, which is an Usurpation upon the Episcopal Authority; but it is only judging him unworthy to be a Bishop, and committing the care of his Flock to some more fit person . . . For these are two very different things, To have Authority to compel a Bishop to govern his Church by such Laws as he himself in his conscience does not approve, and to have Authority to fling a notorious Heretical or Schismatical Bishop out of their Communion, and to command and exhort his Presbyters and People not to own him. (26, 27)

The flaw in his argument is that the power to decide who is fit to be a bishop is in effect the power of control over that bishop; to have the power of deprivation approaches a power of appointment and implies superiority. By Sherlock's logic, a council could declare anyone, for instance the Archbishop of Canterbury, "a notorious Heretical or Schismatical Bishop," and deprive him of his see. A bishop could defy "such Laws as he himself in his conscience does not approve," but conscience is not in itself, by Sherlock's own statement, an adequate defense. To refute the charge of having persecuted Dissenters, Sherlock earlier asserts that "every man who suffers for following his Conscience, is not therefore persecuted; but he who suffers for being in the right" (6). As the Church of England is "in the right," any "who suffers for following his conscience" contrary to its teachings "is not therefore persecuted." Any Romist who thinks himself right and the Church of England wrong – who does not, that is, as Wake put it, "know that [h]e maintain[s] an *ill Cause*" – could, however, apply Sherlock's argument against "the Anglican heresy."[71]

The omitted element in Sherlock's presentation of the question of authority is how it is to be defined and enforced; he can ignore mechanism because, for the Church of England, church governance is only a department of civil governance. A council's "authority to censure Heresie and Schism, and to preserve the Communion of the Church pure" (28) might, in the absence of a strong civil authority such as Sherlock assumes, be apt over centuries to drift toward a coercive power. Sherlock scorns "how he [Gother, in *An Agreement between the Church of England and the Church of Rome*] turns the power of deposing, and censuring heretical Bishops into a power of declaring Heresy" (29), but he omits to explain how one can depose a heretical bishop without having decided what heresy is. How councils arrive at their opinions is irrelevant because their opinions are not the one that counts: "that Opinion, which People have of them [bishops]" (30) is the final judge.

For who ever pronounces the Sentence, (excepting the interposing of Secular power) the People must execute it, and if they will still adhere to their Bishop, he may defie his Deposers, and all their power: As the *English* Bishops and People do all the *Anathemas* of the Church of *Rome* . . . As to whether they do right or wrong in this, their own Consciences must judg in this world, and God will judg in the next: This is all that can be said or done in such a broken and divided state of the Church, as we now see. When nothing was called Heresie but the denial of some plain and acknowledged Article of the Christian Faith, while there was no dispute, who were Hereticks, the power of deposing Hereticks was sacred and venerable; but since what is Heresie is the Controversie, and the world is divided about it, tho the power remains still, the exercise of it grows very contemptible, when a Church first coyns new Articles of Faith, and then Excommunicates, Censures, Deposes those for Hereticks, who will not believe them. (30–31)

To justify the defiance of Rome by the Church of England, Sherlock must abandon legitimist, hierarchal theoretics for a position that approaches democratic theory. A Bishop rules by the approbation of his flock, by the consent of the governed, not because he has an indefeasible hereditary right by apostolic succession. Conscience again is the final judge when confronting the claims of Rome, and the necessity of stressing the freedom of conscience of bishops comports ill with denying that freedom to Dissenters. Catholic pressure is impelling a resisting Anglican theology away from its secure theocratic monarchism under the Charleses. "[T]he interposing of Secular power" resolved the contradictions of a church at once established and insurrectionary, but only if the monarch were of the fold. With a Papist on the throne, the twin loyalties to king and Church could not so easily be equated. The golden age of concord Sherlock projects onto the primitive Church, despite its history of being racked by a succession of desperate doctrinal divisions – that the Arians, Pelasgians, Manichaeans, et al. agreed that they were themselves heretics seems unlikely – is an idealizing projection of national unanimity of purpose to be achieved by melding nationalistic and religious passions. Its symbols are Queen Bess and the Armada. Sherlock's argument rests on an unspoken analogy between the pastor and the squire, the lords bishop and lords temporal: the clergy need no divinely appointed pope to rule souls any more than the gentry need a divinely appointed king to rule bodies. The "People" who have the right to control religion are the same propertied "People" who control Parliament.

In negotiating his middle path between Nonconformists and Papists, Sherlock signals the unique position of his institution. He derives Gother's argument from "an Independent Protestant" tract, *The Catholick Hierarchie* (1681), which in "*a Digression concerning the Subordination of Pastors*" argues that "*Subordination of Pastors*" implies "*the Supremacy of an Oecumenical or Universal Pastor.*"[72] Making the customary riposte to "Independent Protestant" charges that the Church of England is Papistic, he parallels Dissenting and Catholic positions, a parallel that survives in Swift's observation upon Jack's tattered coat in *A Tale of a Tub* that "it is the nature of rags to bear a kind of mock resemblance to finery."[73] What Swift does not retain is Sherlock's acknowledgement that Anglican doctrine differs from those of both Dissenters and Rome in that "the Church is Incorporated into the State," so that its archbishops possess "a mixed Authority derived from the Civil Powers, and this may be greater or less, as the Civil Powers please. All compulsory jurisdiction must be derived from the Civil Powers, because the Church has none of her own" (72, 73). This doctrine became less comforting once "the Civil Powers" had reduced the "compulsory jurisdiction" of the Church by introducing toleration after the Glorious Revolution. Sherlock's positioning of the Church of England at a pole opposite to both Dissidents and Papists is reiterated also in the nonjuror Charles Leslie's reminder to Dissenters that "*Episcopacy* has none so great an Enemy as the *Papacy*; which would Engross the whole *Episcopal* Power, into the single *See* of *Rome*; by making all other Bishops absolutely dependent upon that, which only they call the *Apostolical* Chair." In Leslie's presentation, however, the episcopacy becomes a kind of House of Lords pitted against the monarchical power of the Pope – and against the "vast number of *Presbyterian* Priests, that is, the *Regulars*," whom the Pope employed "to carry his Cause against *Episcopacy* in the Council of *Trent*."[74] As Milton and other Dissenters earlier gave an anti-Papist rationale to their arguments against episcopacy, so Leslie uses the same ploy in its support, but he is also suggesting to the aristocracy that his cause is theirs. Supporting episcopacy alongside an undiluted view of the rights of hereditary succession in the Stuarts, he softens the threatening aspect of his Jacobitism by his casting of episcopacy as a diet of nobles.

The Church of England becomes in Sherlock's logic a uniquely this-worldly religion because of its "mixed Authority." It is by such a distinction that the veiled coercion of Gilbert Burnet's *Pastoral Letter* about the oaths of allegiance and supremacy can be distinguished from the equally coercive *Pastoral Letter* of Bossuet to the "New Catholics of his Diocess" after the revocation of the Edict of Nantes. After 1685, Protestantism ceases to be tolerated in France, and a few years later, after the Glorious Revolution, support for the Stuarts is no longer tolerated in England; still, there is a difference between prohibition of worship and deprivation of a benefice. In fairness to Burnet and his cause, Bossuet's masquerading of power as tenderness possesses a sinister suggestiveness different in kind from Burnet's straightforward partisanship: "Such an unexpected Change as this in the whole Kingdom, has too much the Hand of God in it, not to be maintained; and the piety of the King, who is visibly protected by God, will put an end to this great Work."[75] The Gallic Church is also reliant upon the civil power for "compulsory jurisdiction," but by its own fiction of independence must pretend that the compulsion is voluntary. In contrast to Bossuet's insinuation that one must learn to love Big Brother, Burnet is merely self-congratulatory and xenophobic in his celebration of "the present Settlement of the Nation" that "gives us all the security that, humanely speaking, we can look for, both for the Protestant Religion, and for Civil Liberty" against "*Popish Tyranny, an Irish Conquest and Massacre*, and

French Barbarity and Cruelty."[76] Where Bossuet demands an internalization of doctrinal consent, Burnet settles for an outward assent justified by external enemies. In France, the secular power enforces the dictates of the spiritual; in England, the spiritual power enforces the dictates of the secular. The only conversion Burnet requires is that the loyal subject-clergy of James II become equally loyal supporters of William III.

IV

As Burnet demands only external assent, so, under James II, Anglican clergy attack Catholic doctrine, and transubstantiation in particular as the most hateful and absurd part of that doctrine by demanding that all evidences must be external, measurable, witnessed. Sherlock's assertion in *A Papist not Misrepresented by Protestants* that there is such a thing as "External and Visible Idolatry" represents a shift from his earlier view that "the Bread according to the Doctrine of the Church of *England* is no Representative Object of Worship, and therefore we neither Bow *To*, nor *before*, nor *in Presence* of the Bread, as a Representative Object; therefore the Answer that Author [Stillingfleet] gave, that we do not Kneel to the Sacrament, but receive it Kneeling, is a very good Answer still."[77] While he refuses to retract what he had written earlier against Dissent, a different enemy requires a different emphasis. Against Dissent, Sherlock argued a distinction between form and substance; later, opposing Catholicism, he urges the irrelevance of such a distinction. Substance is a demonstratively irrefutable fact.

A similar evolution occurs between Robert Boyle's *The Excellence of Theology* and *Reasons Why a Protestant Should not Turn Papist*. In *The Excellence of Theology*, Boyle is arguing against religious unbelief in "Modern Naturalists."[78] Admitting "And if there be any Articles of Religon, for which a Rational and Cogent Proof cannot be brought, I shall for that very reason conclude, that such Articles are not absolutely Necessary to be believ'd" (139), he nonetheless denies that demonstrative proof is the only or highest sort:

as a Moral certainty (such as we may attain about the Fundamentals of Religion) is enough in many cases for a wise man, and even a *Philosopher* to acquiesce in; *so* that Physical Certainty, which is pretended for the Truths demonstrated by Naturalists, is, even where 'tis rightfully claim'd, but an inferiour kind or degree of certainty, as Moral certainty also is. For even Physical Demonstrations can beget but a Physical Certainty (that is, a Certainty the thing believ'd should be other than true). (140)

Boyle subordinates the physical, like the moral, to the metaphysical; later, in *Of the High Veneration Man's Intellect Owes to God*, he urges "the contemplation of his works, and the study of his word" and condemns "presumptuous discourse, as if the nature and perfections of that unparalleled Being were objects, that their intellects can grasp."[79] What is presumptuous is a rationalism that places itself above God:

> For though we grant, that physically speaking, it is false, that a virgin can bring forth a child; yet that signifies no more, than that, according to the course of nature, such a thing cannot come to pass; but speaking absolutely and indefinitely, without confining the effect to mere physical agents, it may safely be denied, that philosophy pronounces it impossible, that a virgin should be a mother. For why should the author of nature be confined to the ways of working of dependent and finite agents?[80]

As Anglican divines argue against the presumption of enthusiasm that places its inner light above Church teachings, so Boyle condemns a reason that presumes to subject God to its own measure. The individual must respect the superior wisdom of God and His institution. God's ability to violate ordinary causality is His ability to create miracles, however, and as such is much fitter to emphasize when arguing against atheism than when Catholicism is the subject. Like Anglican clergymen turning from Dissent to Papism, Boyle has to reorient his arguments in the face of a new opponent; under James II, it is no longer rhetorically appropriate to quote "that strict philosopher *Des Cartes*," who "was so far from thinking, that what was impossible to them ["matter and motion"] must be so to God too."[81] Instead of the presumptuousness of individual insight, the danger becomes the institutionalized presumptuousness of Catholic denial of a consensual standard of truth. Both deviate from an Anglican norm that is being assimilated to an experimentalist logic.

What is dangerous to order depends on how order is constructed. When Steven Shapin and Simon Schaffer observe that "Hobbes as a *natural philosopher* has disappeared from the literature" because, they argue, "Within the tradition of 'Whig' history, losing sides have little interest," their statement is more literally true than they intend.[82] Not only "Whig" history in the general sense of history written by the victors, but Whig history without quotation marks contributes to the de-emphasis of Hobbes's plenum. In shifting the paradigm of scientific knowledge from demonstrative to experimental logic, Boyle is participating in a wider rejection of ideals of plenums of state power and ecclesiastical comprehension. Theological absolutes themselves were in flux. Boyle asserts in his 1675 *Some Considerations about the Reconcileableness of Reason and Religion* that

"'I do not think, that a Christian, to be truly so, is obliged to forego his reason; either by denying the dictates of reason, or by laying aside the use of it'":[83] his argument echoes the insistent Protestant claim that their faith is consistent with reason, but that Catholicism demands that a believer "forego his reason." William Clagett's *The School of the Eucharist* is devoted entirely to ridiculing "the later Miracles" (but not "The old ones," that is, biblical miracles); another work published with it as its "Appendix," Samuel Johnson's *Purgatory Prov'd by Miracles*, similarly mocks "Forgeries" and "Cheats of Priests": the age of reason that scorns the gothic began with the Reformation.[84]

More commonly, however, the issue seems too serious to pass off with a jest: asking readers to "consider with what strategems of force and fraud this Church hath laboured to keep the People in ignorance for the sake of her New Doctrines," John Hartcliffe confesses, "And to speak the truth, I do not understand that there is any Religion farther than that which is owned among Protestants: what more is to be found among the Papists, is accommodated to serve some bye-ends and purposes."[85] We have returned to the realm of discourse of Marvell's dismissal of Catholicism as "the bold imposture of priests under the name of Christianity,"[86] but with James already on the throne something more must be said beyond "the Laws of the Roman Religion, that are written in Bloud." Hartcliffe praises the Church of England "that doth not enjoin an implicit Faith, or blind obedience, but allows to every Christian a judgment *of Discretion*, who keeps within the bounds of due obedience and submission to his lawfull Superiors."[87] As in Burnet's *Pastoral Letter* and Sherlock's *Answer to an Amiable Accommodation*, what is required is obedience, not agreement. Tract after tract organizes its attack on Rome into three headings: that it is contrary to scripture, to antiquity or the primitive Church, and to reason. Repeatedly, this order of these three topoi recurs – Scripture, history, and reason – although the latter two occasionally switch places. The book of God, the book of nature, and inward guidance formed a conventional rhetoric of Anglican apologetic. Papism is "implicit Faith, or blind obedience" regardless of or even contrary to reason; only Protestantism is true religion, and reason is testimony to that truth. Yet in their very conformity to a set pattern of argumentation, these pamphlets suggest the degree to which their endorsement of "reason" presupposes reason to be normative, a system of control, not liberation.

What constitutes reason has been simplified as well. Rome is so corrupt as to be upheld only by lay ignorance and "Cheats of Priests," but its most monstrous doctrine is transubstantiation because it routinizes miracles.

William Payne complains that "there is nothing can expose such a doctrine, for nothing can be more uncouth and extravagant than itself, it not only takes away all evidence of sense upon which all truth of miracles, and so of all Revelation does depend, but it destroys all manner of certainty, and all the principles of truth and knowledge."[88] Metaphysical and moral certainties have been forgotten with distinctions between kneeling before or in the presence of the host. Revelation depends only on miracles, and miracles only on what is no longer "an inferiour kind or degree of certainty," the "evidence of sense." Boyle himself joins the movement of opinion in *Reasons Why a Protestant Should not Turn Papist*, in which he too emphasizes the primacy of "the evidence of Sence, *Touch and feel*."[89] What is remarkable about Boyle's argument is how unremarkable it is; he covers the same ground in the same terms as his clerical fellow Anglicans. The table of contents features a familiar cast, beginning with an assertion that Rome is "*neither Catholick nor Infallible*," continuing that Protestants are not in "*Schism, Heresie, or Apostacy*," that Infallibility is a snare and a delusion, part of Rome's "*Novelty*," and that "*Transubstantiation strikes at the Foundation of the Christian Religion*" and was "*unknown to the primitive Church*" (n.p.). Not one topos is new. That "her Transubstantiation I could never believe, and if I did, I should soon doubt of the confessed Fundamentals of the Christian religion" (22) echoes the logic already repeatedly expressed by such as Payne. Reality must be palpable; Boyle's pamphlet voiced the common-sensical refutation typical of short Anglican tracts in a popular style, such as John Williams's round sneer that "It's impossible to convince a man that has Sense and Reason that he must not use them."[90] Yet it was not possible for so many scholars to comment on "Sense and Reason" without making attempts to define what "the first principles of reason" might be beyond "the universal sense of mankind."[91]

Certainty is essential, yet most polemicists suppress the cause of the anxiety to secure "certainty" in their chain of reasoning. In one tract, *Of the Incurable Skepticism of the Church of Rome*, Jean de La Placette alleges that "all things are there doubtful, all uncertain, and nothing firm," that "their Divines in teaching that the very Existence of God is not so much known as believed, manifestly betray to Atheists the Cause of Religion."[92] The same author elsewhere demonstrates "That Transubstantiation establishes Skepticism; and absolutely destroys the certainty of First Principles."[93] What is known is only what is manifest to sense; First Principles, like the operation of an air-pump, are subject to demonstration. In a more idealizing strain, Henry More concludes his condemnation of the real presence by terming it contrary to "the *indelible Principles* of *sound Reason*, those immutable *Common Notions* which the Eternal *Logos* has essentially ingrafted in our Souls, and without which neither *Certainty* or *Faith* can consist, nor any assured sense of either the Holy Scriptures or any Writing elsewhere can be found out or understood."[94] William Payne dismissed transubstantiation by lamenting "that humane reason should be so decayed and besotted, as to believe and defend such palpable Absurdities!"[95] If the sermons of this transitional generation of Church of England clerics seemed to later Anglicans into the nineteenth century to possess a "lasting importance," as Gerard Reedy observes, it is because they adapt doctrine to conform to the post-1688 regime; the Anglican controversial divinity of the reign of James II was not reprinted, not included in that continuing influence, because it presents the Church of England in a state of institutional anxiety.[96] As Boyle's *Reasons Why a Protestant Should Not Turn Papist* does not appear in eighteenth-century editions of his works, that the new order could have been insecure at one time is effaced in Anglican theology to reinforce the effect of its self-evidentiality.

A six-page Catholic leaflet started one episode in the vast tract war over transubstantiation. *A Dialogue Between a New Catholic Convert and a Protestant* sums up its arguments as,

First, the Tradition of one Doctrin cannot be stronger than another, where both have been at least equally question'd. Secondly, 'Tis as reasonable to take *This is my Body* literally, as it is to take these Texts *I and my Father are one God over all blessed for ever*, and *By him all things were made*, without reference to other Scriptures, and a Figurative Interpretation. And lastly, I think to Human Reason 'tis as equally unreasonable, and as seemingly repugnant, to say One is Three, as to say a Body is not what it appears.[97]

This booklet excited over 100 pages of Anglican confutation by two bishops and a dean. Richard Kidder states that "this Doctrine [transubstantiation] destroys the evidence of Sense, and consequently subverts our whole Religion"; only senses attested to Christ's miracles and Resurrection, so to deny the reliability of senses would "leave nothing certain or true but itself; nor leave us any evidence that itself is true."[98] The Catholic claim that the Trinity might be excepted against as easily as transubstantiation as absurd meets with this distinction by Sherlock: "Thus the Doctrine of the Trinity, tho it be above the comprehension of our finite minds, as every thing must be, which is infinite, yet it does not contradict any necesary Principle of Reason, as *Transubstantiation* does, which is contrary to Sense and Reason. Whether any Body be Bread or Flesh, fall under the notice of Sense, and therefore our Senses must judge of it . . . It is essential to the same Body to be but in one place at a time, and yet all confess that the Body of Christ is whole and intire in Heaven."[99] Distinguishing between the Trinity and transubstantiation becomes a crucial instance of the appropriation by Anglican theology of scientific experimentalism: no one can see God, so whether He is triune cannot be tested by the senses, whereas any witness can see that bread and wine are only bread and wine. In his contribution to the same controversy, Stillingfleet takes this argument its final step: "And methinks, for the sake of our common Christianity, you should no more venture upon such bold and unreasonable Comparisons ... For upon the very same Grounds, we may expect another Parallel between the *belief of God* and *Transubstantiation*; the effect of which will be, the exposing of all Religion."[100] To question reason is to question God.

To attack transubstantiation, Anglican polemics redefine it from a question of doctrine, where one claim may be as good as another, as all rest upon belief, into a matter of experimentally verifiable fact. John Patrick condemns transubstantiation by stating that "when the *Question is, whether Bodies can be so present after the manner of Spirits, as to lose all the natural properties of Bodies, and a material substance lost under the Accidents proper to it*, it's to be hoped our Senses may be proper *Judges of the one* by the *other*."[101] Samuel Johnson gives perhaps the clearest exposition of this distinction, stating that "it has always been held, That the Essential Properties and Affections of a Body, such as Quantity, Figure, and its relation to Place, *&c*. are the Proper Subject of Demonstration. And let me here add, That such a Doctrine as Transubstantiation, neither is, nor can be, a Matter of Revelation."[102] It is no more credible than "That the Duration of 24 Hours is the Duration of 1688 Years. That a Miles Distance, and the Distance of 10000 Miles is Equal. That the same thing may Exist and not Exist at once ... We are sure that a Divine Revelation cannot contradict the Common Sense and Reason of Mankind" (iii). In effect, man is the measure of all things. He explicitly attacks Descartes's position

"That we must fix this in our minds as the chief and principal Rule, That those things which are revealed to us by God, are to be believed as the most certain of all others: And altho perchance the most clear and evident Light of Reason that can be, should seem to suggest to us the contrary, yet we must believe Divine Authority alone, rather than our own Judgment." Now this I say is an impossible Case; for we have not a more clear and evident proof, than the most clear and evident Light of Reason that can be, Either that God has revealed any one doctrine in particular, Or made any Revelation at all, Or that there is a God. (iv)

Reason is the test of revelation, even of the existence of God; what Johnson avoids conceding is that perhaps reason "persuades us that there is a God" (vi), but perhaps it does not. At once the strength and weakness of the Church of England lay in its careful evasion of paradox: if a common-sensical reason is supreme, then both the inner light of enthusiasts and the subtleties of the Schools may be dismissed as errors, and, if this reason finds belief in God as self-evident as that one mile is not 10,000 miles, then that reason poses no threat to the Establishment. A disinclination to look beyond the obvious becomes a duty. In its pamphlet war with the Papists, the Church of England at once exalts reason as the arbiter of disputes and defines its own doctrines as "obviously" reasonable. This privileging of the status quo recapitulates into doctrinal form a pragmatism cognate with the demotion of the crown within the polity.

v

In a 1690 pamphlet, Boyle returns to cautioning scientific skepticism against extending to things divine. *The Christian Virtuoso* warns of "the dimness and other imperfections of the human understanding," and the *Reflections upon a Theological Distinction. According to which it is said, That some Articles of Faith are above Reason, but not against Reason* "subjoined" to it urges that "there are divers truths in the Christian religion, that reason, left to itself, would never have been able to find out, nor perhaps to have so much as dreamed of."[103] Such "truths" include free will, the creation of the world in six days, the virgin birth, and the union of the divine and human in Christ.[104] If *The Christian Virtuoso* returns to warning scientific pride from presuming to outreach God, *Reflections upon a Theological Distinction* pronounces a last word on the transubstantiation controversy, without admitting that it is doing so. *Reflections* argues that the difference between a thing's being above and against reason "is not an arbitrary or illusory distinction, but grounded upon the nature of things." As an example, he suggests that we cannot see the bottom of the ocean, but can perceive that a pearl brought to the surface is not as "large as a tennis ball."[105] The example he refrains from mentioning is transubstantiation, which according to his schematic is not above reason, like the virgin birth, but against it, like a claim that pearls are as large as tennis balls. This brief essay appended to the much longer *Christian Virtuoso* attempts to reconcile Boyle's principal self-appointed task of taming scientific doubt to the condemnation of the real presence of Christ in the host in which he along with many others had recently been engaged. With James gone, however, he refuses to state explicitly the context of his endeavor; there is no longer any need to admit the possibility of any alternative to the Church of England even by open condemnation of that alternative. Silence is more effective than argument.

If experimental science in the late seventeenth century is deliberately incomplete in its assumptions, it parallels developing theological and political structures of thought confronted by the alarming demand that they construct a logic, whether of reason, spirituality, or government, deprived of former hierarchal absolutes. Foxe's union of true king and true Church is disintegrating. The all-encompassing plenum and monarchy by divine right become discredited together, following the infallible Pope before them. The "defense of contingency," in Kroll's words, becomes a defense of authority. The Church of England inherited a centralized episcopal model of church government, albeit one weakened like the crown by the partial loss of its pre-Civil War coercive powers, but could not maintain its exclusive authority of interpretation when in theory everyone had an equal right to read scripture, as in theory the consent of the governed governed England. The open authoritarianism of the Catholic position, that doctrine is decided at the top, becomes replaced by a liberty in which everyone is free to decide for himself (women were hardly entitled to an opinion; the presumed audience in all but the very few pious works specifically, and condescendingly, directed toward women is male), but must agree unless he is possessed of a perverted reason, like dishonest Papists. Anglicanism could no longer function as the auxiliary of an independent crown, but if it endorsed hierarchy over collaborative authority would only be undercutting a triumphantly emerging oligarchy with little more taste for centralized authority in Church than in state. The hostility between the Whig and High Church parties arose because the one relied on a rhetoric of liberty that effectively meant the freedom of local elites to run their neighborhoods and inferiors with little less encumbrance than they ran their estates, and the other sought a rhetoric of absolute truth to justify their being more than just another sect. In time, the clergy became satisfied with the same de facto power as their lay counterparts; eventually, they became prime allies of the state once more when another ideologically charged enemy arose, the French Revolution.

The equivalence of reason and Protestantism remains an ongoing theme, although one that loses its urgency as the Catholic threat fades. More than thirty years after the flight of James II, *Cato's Letters* interrupt their tirades against tyranny, paeans to "old *English* Liberty," and observations "*That the two great Parties in* England *do not differ so much as they think in Principles of Politicks,*" to devote three numbers (77–79) to "*superstitious Fears.*"[106] The connection between praise for "mixed Forms of Government" (3.13) and refutation of "*the vulgar Absurdities about Ghosts and Witches*" (3.108) may seem a remote one today, but it was so automatic then that when number

69, "An Address to the Freeholders, &c. about the Choice of their Representatives," warns against voting for corrupt M.P.s, it cautions that: "Exorbitant Taxes, Want of Trade, Decay of Manufactures, Discouragement of Industry, Insolence and Oppression of Soldiers, Exactions of Civil Officers, Ignorance, Superstition, and Bigotry, are all the constant Concomitants of Tyranny, always produce it, and are produced by it" (3.8–9). "Superstition, and Bigotry" are the spiritual part of a system whose temporal dimension is the abuses (detrimental to commerce) of Continental absolutism. The series of three essays against belief in spirits culminates in the claim that such entities abound more in Popish than in Protestant countries, "and there are more of them in ignorant Popish Countries than in knowing ones, in poor than in rich ones; and they appear oftener in arbitrary Governments than in free States" (3.117). Only Holland has fewer than England. "[T]rue Religion is so well supported by Reason and Revelation, that there is no Necessity of telling Lyes in its Defense, and putting it upon the same Bottom with the Heathen Superstitions, and the Popish Forgeries and Impostures" (3.117–18). "Reason and Revelation" stand firmly together in support of "true Religion" (synonymous, as ever, with Protestantism) against "Popish Forgeries and Impostures." *Cato's Letters* communicate no urgency in a struggle against Catholicism; instead, the tone is one of consolidation and confirmation of a victory already won.

CHAPTER FIVE

Polemic and silence: Jeremy Collier, Elkanah Settle, and the ideological appropriation of morality

> The concept of the historical progress of mankind cannot be sun-
> dered from the concept of its progression through a homogeneous,
> empty time. A critique of the concept of such a progression must be
> the basis of any criticism of the concept of progress itself.[1]

If individual thought rather than a body of doctrine is the basis of authority, if "Reason and Revelation" are coextensive, then reason itself must become subject to authority if it is not to endanger that authority. If one wishes to name necessarily arbitrary dates for such things, the stage-reform debate that began in 1698 may be said to mark the inauguration of the Foucaultian regime of internalized repression. In response to the combination of proclaimed liberty at home and sustained war abroad that marked the reign of William III, the stage needed to be incorporated into an increasingly integrated economy of market and military exploitation. In place of the antagonism between "city" and "court" that marked the Stuart years, financial and governmental power became progressively consolidated in a more unified social stratum, Disraeli's "Venetian oligarchy," in the decades following the Glorious Revolution. The campaign to "reform" the stage got underway, not coincidentally, several years into England's engagement in its most large-scale and protracted Continental war since the Hundred Years War. For such a struggle, the government sought not merely to command but to motivate the population. The subject of this chapter is the impressing of the theater into the moral economy of war through a discourse of stage reform; reform becomes a pretext for enlisting the stage as a mechanism of ideological mobilization. This mobilization, moreover, has had a lasting impact; Brian Corman notes the long-time exclusion of Restoration drama from the canon on "moral grounds" and "political grounds," and also because it has not seemed "useful," " 'to be us,' " like Shakespeare, but he does not articulate the interrelation of the three elements.[2] Identity and morality, though, are political, or to put it another way political morality is a question of identity, of self-creation.

Charles II was able to return to his father's throne because, after the collapse of Cromwell's Protectorate, he seemed the only alternative to military rule or a resumption of civil war. In an anonymous 1661 pamphlet, *The English Prelates Practizing the Methods and Rules of the Jesuits*, the seventh Jesuitical rule which the Church of England is alleged to follow, in a design of "*Reducing the People to Popery,*" is that it forbids all private conventicles: "men may meet together at Cock-fighting, Hourse-coursing, Stage-playes, to swear, and bee drunk, and unclean; but they must not meet to pray and confer together of the Scriptures, no, not in those places and Parishes where the Ministers are no better than dumb Idols."[3] As a place "to swear, and bee drunk, and unclean," the stage was no better than "Cock-fighting, Hourse-coursing," a purely destructive social site, in contrast to the purely positive devotional space. On the other side, 1660s anti-Roundhead stage comedies inverted the pattern, constructing the theater as a civilizational savior against destructive fanaticism. Both stances posited theatricality and piety as mutually exclusive absolutes. The pragmatic accommodationism of the post-1688 regime aimed to mediate between the hostility of the Clarendon code toward Nonconformist worship and the Interregnum's prohibition of the theater in order to neutralize both as sources of potential destabilization. Dissent, in the religious sense, was permitted if it did not threaten the state, and drama was permitted if it could equally be made harmless. Regulation became informal, more a matter of a commonsensical propriety than a formal institution, the business of a *Spectator*, not a censor. As the mechanism of cultural control became less obtrusive, as instanced by the lapse of the Licensing Act in 1695, it became coded in a *prima facie* morality. The moral policing practiced by the Church of England before the Civil War diminished to Roger L'Estrange's civil censorship after the Restoration, then after 1695 lost distinct institutional embodiment – yet restraints on publication persisted, despite their apparent disappearance.[4] As reason was enlisted to support a theology decentering the king in favor of the gentry and their "*Infallible* Parliament," so moral legislation became now vested in the more diffuse, less visible, but for those reasons more all-encompassing spectatorial regime of the bourgeois public sphere. This chapter, then, could be said to negotiate the customary critical disjunction between discussions of court-centered Renaissance censorship, exemplified by Annabel Patterson and recently challenged by Richard Burt, and the more institutionally diffuse Foucaultian conception of socially constructed censorship in the eighteenth century that is marked by no identifiable process of initiation.[5] The stage-reform controversy suggests how subtler mutilations replace the shearing of ears.

Patterson's oppositional model, in which censorship figures as only the legally instituted variety, becomes in Burt a discourse of discourses wherein censuring and censoring become mutually implicated. What is distinctive about Stuart censorship, however, in contrast to subsequently emerging practices in Britain and America, is precisely the extent to which a formal, state-sponsored censorship participates in a critical process that has since become more indirect in its restrictions. The institutional discontinuity within English departments between "Renaissance" and "eighteenth century" has conspired to obscure the continuity between the premodern regime of formal censorship and the modern one of normative moral criticism.[6] As we saw with the civic pageants of Middleton, an alternative patronage to that of the court was available even before the Civil War. This incipient shadow government, as it might almost if not quite be called, took power after 1688; impulses that militated opposition against the Stuarts became justifications of the Hanoverian establishment. The significance of the stage-reform controversy at the turn of the century is that it specifically situates the historical continuity within the apparent discontinuity in modes of censorship. In place of the juridicial processes of the Tudors and Stuarts, a government that bases its legitimacy on an identification with the "public," which is to say the moneyed and literate urban bourgeoisie, delegates the function of censorship to that public instead of a court-appointed administrator.[7] A system of invisible authority, Protestant liberty and morality, constructs itself as liberation against the visible authority of Catholicism or censorship.

The principal attempt to bridge the gap between Renaissance and eighteenth-century critical regimes has been made by Marxist criticism. In its investment in a revolutionary model, however, this criticism can become implicated in a dynamic that reproduces that of bourgeois Enlightenment. Terry Eagleton has argued that "Modern European criticism was born of a struggle against the absolutist state"; the book that so begins also ends with precisely the same sentence, with this addition: "unless its future is now defined as a struggle against the bourgeois state, it might have no future at all."[8] Eagleton's critical strategy is necessitated by his attempt to coerce the complexities of social development into the Marxist metanarrative of revolution, which itself updates the bourgeois one of progress. Following Habermas in rejecting "Frankfurtian defeatism," Eagleton presumes that historical movement must be ascension, that the future improves upon the past.[9] When "Authoritarian, aristocratic art judgments were replaced by a discourse among educated laymen," however, the result was less Eagleton's "certain historical emancipation"[10] than an emergence into the modern condition in which, in Umberto Eco's formulation, "power is not something unitary that exists outside us"[11] but nonetheless it remains coercive. The form of censorship, what Burt calls "the administration of aesthetics," has altered, but its effects remain.[12] This change in form, moreover, parallels that in the polity, from a confessedly authoritarian divine kingship to a constitutionalism that functions as a disguise for oligarchy; and both these new censorial and governmental regimes found their legitimacy on their self-differentiation from an absolutism discredited by its association with Catholicism. The ultimately successful struggle for emancipation from the Catholic menace presages not a totalizing liberation but what Jane Eyre calls "'a new servitude.'"[13] Her desire for change from an authoritarian institutional regimentation leads within a few pages to her introduction into the domestic economy of Thornfield, home of Gilbert and Gubar's madwoman in the attic. "The classical public sphere," described by Eagleton as a "discursive reorganization of social power, redrawing the boundaries between social classes as divisions between those who engage in rational argument, and those who do not,"[14] excludes as irrational, as we saw in the preceding chapter, the Catholic, who has abandoned his reason into the charge of a corrupt church. The same logic of exclusion could be, and was, extended to others.[15] As Alexis de Tocqueville long ago observed:

Fetters and headsmen were the coarse instruments that tyranny formerly employed; but the civilization of our age has perfected despotism itself, though it seemed to have nothing to learn. Monarchs had, so to speak, materialized oppression: the democratic republics of the present day have rendered it as entirely an affair of the mind as the will which it is intended to coerce. Under the absolute sway of one man, the body was attacked in order to subdue the soul ... Such is not the course adopted by tyranny in democratic republics; there the body is left free, and the soul is enslaved.[16]

As the pioneer in both nationalism and enlightenment, England was the first such "democratic republic" in which "the body is left free."[17]

I

Subsequent centuries decanonized "immoral" Restoration drama to marginalize its destabilizing potentialities. In *A Short View of the Immorality and Profaneness of the English Stage*, Jeremy Collier makes explicit his concern that a licentious stage endangers not only morals but patriarchy. As the official censor metamorphoses into standards of morality and taste, his successors at policing the stage elide the political entirely into the moral;

the cynical rake transmogrifies into the sentimental hero. By the time Macaulay writes his dismissal of Restoration comedy, the entire period has sunk into a notoriety phrased in purely moral terms; political repression has become sexual fetishization. This chapter undertakes the excavation of the nearly forgotten Elkanah Settle, a then-prominent practitioner of theatrical spectacle, an anti-Catholic political pamphleteer and playwright, and the most cogent defender of the liberty of the stage against encroaching censorship at century's end. A specialist in elaborate stagings, authoring operas, the "masque-like"[18] *Cambyses*, the first illustrated English play, *The Empress of Morocco*, the last civic festivals for the Lord Mayor's Day, accounts of vast mob demonstrations during the Exclusion Crisis, and finally a Bartholomew Fair show, he has been regarded as the antithesis of the "literary" and in consequence neglected. In the words of Michael D. Bristol, Settle's popular stagecraft is a theater of "plebeian culture," "the 'other' form of knowledge, a comprehensive 'art and science' of social and collective life" that challenges "The monopoly of knowledge retrospectively claimed for education and 'the educated.'"[19] As the matter would once have been put, he is "common." Robert D. Hume says of *The World in the Moon* that "As literature, the piece has few merits," then calls it "a unique and fascinating experiment."[20] Similarly, Settle the polemicist and countertraditional playwright has gone unread for 300 years because, however "unique and fascinating," his works were not considered "literature." They do, however, supply an opportunity to observe the interactions of political, theatrical, and moral discourses in the framing of a single career. The significance of Elkanah Settle lies in what his continuing defense of freedom – resituated from religious politics to the theater – reveals about the persistence of censorship after the proclaimed emancipation of the Glorious Revolution. Freedom from Popery and tyranny evolves into the ratification of what Lisa Moore has called "the naturalizing narratives of bourgeois culture."[21] As a defender of Bowdler's *Family Shakespeare* observed, "it is taste, too, that seduces us to read Dryden, and send Marvel and Elkanah Settle to the pastry-cook."[22]

This chapter covers a crucial phase in the evolution of what might be called the literature of propaganda, the reformulation of an ideology of liberation into one of a silencing morality. Before the Glorious Revolution, a compound of religious sentiments bound up with property interests had alienated significant segments of the "natural rulers" from the Stuarts, with the Catholicism suspected in Charles II's court and fully manifested in James II embodying the premodern hierarchy that placed status above contract, rule above property. Feudal tenures were gone forever, and the gentry's plunder from the Church had become inalienable at law, but what if the law and lawmakers should change under a Papist prince out to win the same independence as Continental monarchs? After 1688, there remained only the task of ratifying the reconciliation of property and the governmental structure, of retracting any embarrassing liberty of specu-lation that had grown up in the embittered estrangement between the executive and the legislature that had now absorbed it. The moral reform movement of the 1690s and after resulted. This moral crusade's pretense of disinterestedness was accepted into our own time, yet the original crusader, Collier, himself openly avowed his political agenda.[23] Peter Stallybrass and Allon White argue that the elimination of the Bakhtinian grotesque by the classical assumes topographic specificity in the withdrawal of "the middling sort" from the sites of popular festivals, the domain of the "Smithfield Muse" of Pope's *Dunciad*, fairs, and Lord Mayor's Day pageants.[24] As Stallybrass and White conclude, "For bourgeois democracy emerged with a class which, whilst indeed progressive in its best political aspirations, had encoded in its manners, morals and imaginative writings, in its body, bearing and taste, a subliminal elitism which was constitutive of its historical being. Whatever the radical nature of its 'universal' democratic demand, it had engraved in its subjective identity all the marks by which it felt itself to be a different, distinctive, and superior class."[25] Settle vanishes because he did not participate in this "subliminal elitism" that ratifies the propertied as heirs to kingly power. His is a "Smithfield Muse."

The crisis of England's Restoration settlement, the Glorious Revolution of 1688 supplanted the halfway house of the 1660 settlement, half monarchy, half aristocratic commonwealth, with a more cohesive oligarchism. This decisive event had forerunners and aftershocks. A principal forerunner was the Exclusion Crisis; one aftershock was the stage reform controversy, which was ostensibly about morality but also consolidated on the literary front the victory already won on the political. Elkanah Settle, a man then so notorious that he had to resort to disguise and anonymity in his publications but now all but forgotten, took a leading part in both of these controversies. In 1698 Collier published *A Short View of the Immorality and Profaneness of the English Stage*, beginning a long campaign to "purify" the theater. The first extended reply to it, Settle's *A Defense of Dramatick Poetry* and *A Farther Defense*, responded to this totalizing attack by denying its premises, unlike James Drake's *The Ancient and Modern Stages Surveyed* or William Congreve's *Amendments*. Unlike Congreve, Collier's more famous respondent, or the more pedantic Drake, Settle was uniquely well-placed to be sensitive to the nature of Collier's attack. Experienced in pamphlet warfare both literary and political, a Whig turned Tory turned pariah, a man of letters who had witnessed every quarrel in the interlocking circles of literary and political London, and taken part in more than his share of them, for thirty years, he had won his first battle, against no less an adversary than Dryden, when Congreve was a child.[26] If Congreve, inexperienced in controversial writing, was, in Bonamy Dobree's phrase, "not the man to take an effective part in this sort of literary fisticuffs," Settle was, precisely because he recognized the continuity between politics and literature.[27] Yet, undiscussed, he has been assumed to be not worth discussion; his obscurity has seemed to justify itself.

As Settle opposed a popular conception of the theater to one subservient to the upper classes, so he opposed to the emerging paradigm of an ecumenical morality in the service of oligarchism the religious sectarianism which had fractured English politics for the previous century, enabling the execution of Charles I and dethronement of James II. Despite his Jacobitism, Collier's assertion of an uninstitutionalized moral authority contradicted the vision of an authoritarian unity of Church and state that underlay High Church resistance to the Revolution, a unity of two institutions that under the Stuarts both claimed prescriptive rights, of apostolic succession and indefeasible hereditary right, independent of property rights and at times superior to them.[28] Although Collier oppposed Parliament's selection of a new king, still worse would be a progressive dissolution of authority in a repetition of the Civil War. J. Douglas Canfield dismisses Settle's *The Female Prelate* as "anti-Catholic propaganda," as Janet Clare asserts that "as serious political drama it has nothing to commend it," but both claims rest on an implicit devaluation of religion as a political criterion.[29] This study aims to overcome the radical disjunction of propaganda and literature because it forms part of the same logic of suppression as that which has erased the formative role of anti-Catholic rhetoric in the institution of the modern state in order to place the legitimacy of that state beyond question.

II

From his youthful triumphant debut with *Cambyses* (not later than 1671) to a lost tragedy on *The Expulsion of the Danes from Britain* that was never acted or printed because his death in 1724 intervened, Settle's career as a dramatist spanned over half a century. His reputation, though, had decayed long before he died.[30] The most immediate and violent cause of disfavor was his extremely prominent and incautious part in the Exclusion Crisis. He wrote *The Character of a Popish Successour* and other pamphlets against James's succession, as well as *The Female Prelate*, an undisguisedly and exuberantly anti-Catholic tragedy, and served as the master of ceremonies at London's Pope-burning ceremonies. Then, after Shaftsbury's fall, he wrote for the Tories a refutation of his previous work, *A Narrative* exposing Titus Oates, and a panegyric to Judge Jeffries. So visible and unambiguous a volte face could make few friends and many enemies. Settle's political evolution, or opportunism, was hardly peculiar to him, but an artist who sticks to fictional forms may escape the worst fury of partisan controversy, since with a minimum of prudence such forms allow an element of ambiguity, of deniability. Addison's *Cato*, patronized by both parties at its 1713 debut, is the best-remembered example of such temporizing, or broad, "aesthetic" appeal. Similarly, Nathaniel Lee's *The Massacre of Paris* seems a Whig play to Susan Staves and a royalist one to J. Douglas Canfield.[31] A case can be and has been made on either side about its politics; and if the party it supports, or whether it clearly supports either party at all – which Richard E. Brown denies – is still uncertain today, one may suspect that contemporaries may not have been positive either.[32] In 1680, Settle's Catholic-bashing play about Pope Joan, dedicated to the Earl of Shaftesbury, however, could have left few guessing. As he remarks in his dedication, "I believe this plain dealing may have gain'd me a great many Enemies."[33]

His dealing was not only plain but forceful. His *Character of a Popish Successor* was, with Oates's *Narrative*, one of the two most frequently answered controversial pamphlets of the period, and was regarded by Whigs as "unanswerable."[34] A look at this document indicates that they had reason for that opinion. It is cast in the form of questions and answers, each question expressing skepticism about the dangers of a Catholic's becoming king only to be refuted. In contrast to the many Exclusion Crisis pamphlets that appeal only to emotion, the chain of reasoning is cogent, although ably supported by emotional appeals to the dread of Catholicism and despotism already strongly present in the English public mind. The specifics of the *Character* were also vindicated by the events of the years following. It first traps those who claim a Catholic king may "uphold the Protestant Interest" in the contradictions of their own logic.

[H]e must confer his Favours and Smiles on those very Men, whom . . . he cordially believes do preach and teach, and lead his Subjects in the direct way to Hell: . . . he must not only punish and persecute but perhaps imprison and hang those very only Righteous Men, whom from the bottom of his Soul he believes can onely open them the Gates of Paradise . . . A very pretty *Chimaera!* Which is as much as to make this Popish King the greatest Barbarian in the Creation ... the basest of Men, and little less than a Monster ... a Coward so abject, that he dares not be a Champion even for his God.[35]

Settle then wonders, with some justice, how desirable or likely such a king is. On the other hand, he supposes, James may overflow with virtues: so much the worse. "If he's a Bigot in Religion, all his Morals are Slaves to his Zeal. Nay, grant him to be the most absolute Master of all the *Cardinal Vertues*, there's not one of them that shall not be a particular Instrument for our Destruction" (*Character*, 4). Fortitude will make him bolder for Rome; in pure justice "he'll certainly judge the *Popes* Restoration as great a piece of Justice, as his own Coronation"; temperance will make him steadfast and diligent in his purposes, like Philip of Spain; and, "If he has Prudence, that's worst of all. That's his only winning Card," for only so will he be able to carry his plans into effect (*Character*, 4). The portrait in advance of James's character as a monarch is remarkably accurate, except that he lacked that "winning Card" of prudence. Philip of Spain is as deliberate an example as those of Queen Mary on the next page, and Louis XIV on the following, as instances of how Catholics think nothing of breaking their word in the service of their faith. These monarchs were the stock bogeymen of English Protestantism, figures emblematic of sanguinary Catholic tyranny past and present. The projection of what means James would employ to introduce absolutism proved similarly shrewd: patronage, the royal revenues not dependent on Parliament, which, he twice observes, had tripled under Charles, and a standing army (*Character*, 8–9). In his projection of James's policies, Settle's only significant mistakes are to imagine a war scare to raise the money for the army of domestic occupation and not to think of packing of corporations. Nor is Settle above mingling plausible arguments with disingenuous appeals such as laments that James is dishonoring his Protestant martyr father and injuring his beloved brother. The pamphlet concludes that the only alternatives to a change of succession are either "to put the executive power of the Laws into the hands of the People" (*Character*, 13) or that "Popery must and shall come in, (as by Law it cannot) and consequently must be restored by Arbitrary Power ..." (*Character*, 21). Settle asserts, that is, that a Catholic succession would break apart the Restoration settlement, and ensure supremacy of either crown or Parliament. His case is strong, as subsequent history testified, and strongly put.

But it could as little endear him to royalists as *A Narrative*, written only two years later, could please Whigs; and, unluckily for him, the side he abandoned was the one that ultimately prevailed. Settle's *Narrative* has the same title as Oates's account of the alleged Popish Plot, and is a methodical exposure of his extravagant and contradictory impostures.

For let the Whiggs take it as they please, they cannot be divided but into two Classes. They amongst them that are so shallow as to believe a hotch potch of Incongruity and Contradiction for Truth are Fools; and the greater and Wiser Men amongst them that I am sure have better Intellects, and yet notwithstanding by all the Arts, and Study endeavor to impose that upon weaker understandings, what they do not believe themselves, are Villains, and whilst they make it their business to uphold Lies and Shame, are so far from what they pretend them-selves[,] Patriots, that they are nothing but Incendiaries, whilst the National Service is but the pretence and their own Revenge or sinister Interests the great end they drive at.[36]

So *A Narrative*, at once logical and demagogic, climaxes. Although it is textual criticism of the fault-finding sort rather than a jeremiad like *The Character of a Popish Successor*, Settle's rhetorical strategies have changed less than his politics. The two modes of writings are combined in Settle's response to Collier. Their author is not a man likely to be afraid of a bold, or an unscrupulous, response, and he has shown himself acutely aware of political nuance.

Like Collier, Settle writes as a controversialist in the no-holds-barred, slash-and-burn tradition of the seventeenth century, in the same un-compromising tones he uses in his 1683 "Remarks on Algernon Sidney's Paper, Delivered to the Sherriffs at his Execution": "This dying speech was calculated for the understanding of the Rabble; and Reason or Truth is no part of the Fuell, where the Crowd is to be inflamed. Calumny sticks with them."[37] Following 1688, however, after the bitter division between Whigs and Tories, England was re-entering what Michael McKeon has called "that stable state of affairs, in which ... hegemony incorporates all potential negations, and all anomalies seem tautologically to confirm the reigning paradigm."[38] The open wound of the seventeenth century had produced its open mind, and both were together beginning to shut. The competition in the Collier controversy was for the successful identification of one's side with that one paradigm; dramatists and moralists alike had to prove that their position was the one more conducive to the legitimation of the regime.

III

In *A Short View of the Immorality, and Profaneness of the English Stage* Collier is unambiguous about what is at issue. He opposes verbal license because it encourages social license. He was, after all, no remote philosopher elevated above mundane affairs but rather, in Pope's phrase, a *"profound, dark,* and *dirty Party-writer."*[39] One of the most noted nonjuring divines, he was a prolific Jacobite pamphleteer; most of his works published in the 1690s were political polemics. The failure to take this political dimension of *A Short View* into account is the flaw of such formal approaches as Aubrey Williams's. Having shown how distorted, sensationalistic, and well-answered Collier was, Williams "wonder[s] . . . that so many ever since have considered it a just piece of criticism and also the triumphant document in the controversy it generated."[40] The triumph is a wonder only if the issue is considered on purely formal grounds, but Collier's agenda was far from pure. In his "Preface" he observes that "As *Good* and *Evil* are *different* in *Themselves,* so they ought to be *differently Mark'd.* To *confound* them in *Speech,* is the way to *confound* them in *Practise* . . . Indeed *Things* are in a great measure *Govern'd* by *Words."*[41] His concern, however, is not with any abstract, absolute conception of virtue. His rage is not a Platonist's against the Aristotelian stage on which, in Congreve's words, "Comick Poets are oblig'd . . . to represent vicious and foolish Characters"; his grievances are more concrete.[42] He declares what he terms obscenity to be not merely wrong but politically dangerous.

Smuttiness is a Fault in Behaviour as well as in Religion. 'Tis a very Coarse Diversion, the Entertainment of those who are generally least both in Sense, and Station. The looser part of the *Mob,* have no true relish of Decency and Honour, and want Education and Thought, to furnish out a gentile Conversation . . . The modern Poets seem to use *Smut* as the Old Ones did *Machines,* to relieve a fainting invention. (*Short View,* 6)

He identifies morality with elite behavior, and his object is less to promote virtue than to reinforce class divisions. That the stage "stud[ies] to outrage *Quality* and Virtue" (*Short View,* 13) is its real crime – and the italicized word of the two is *"Quality,"* not "Virtue." Praising the ancient theater at the expense of the modern, he observes that in Plautus, "The Men who talk intemperately are generally *Slaves,"* and, on the only four instances they do so before women, two of the women are slaves as well, and a third is a "Wench" (*Short View,* 16–17). That women are portrayed by Restoration dramatists as immodest disturbs him less than that the women so portrayed are upper-class. Three of the four women, all of good family, in Congreve's *Double-Dealer* are "Whores": "A Great Compliment to Quality to tell them there is not above a quarter of them Honest! This was not the Roman Breeding. *Terence* and *Plautus* his strumpets were little people" (*Short View,* 12). Immorality on the stage seemed less pernicious to Collier than the fact that this immorality appeared in the persons of the great and therefore lessened respect for them and subverted the structure of society. Opposed to the present government of England as he might be, he hardly desired an eruption from below; he thought the social hierarchy wanted a stronger crown to secure it, not a general discrediting and, things being governed by words, consequent weakening. Since both Whig and Tory dreaded the prospect of an upheaval such as that of the 1640s, if his definition of the situation, that theatrical immorality threatened social order, were allowed to stand, his victory would be inevitable.

As the best known of the replies to Collier, and the one by the most famous hand, consider Congreve's approach in his *Amendments of Mr. Collier's False and Imperfect Citations*. The title promises a close attention to detail. Congreve declares on the first page that

> I have no intention to examine all the Absurdities and Falshoods in Mr. *Collier*'s Book ... My Detection of his Malice and Ignorance, of his Sophistry and vast Assurance, will lie within a narrow Compass, and only bear a Proportion to so much of his Book as concerns my self.
>
> Least of all, would I undertake to defend the Corruptions of the Stage; indeed if I were so inclin'd, Mr. *Collier* has given me no occasion; for the greater part of those Examples which he has produc'd, are only Demonstrations of his own Impurity, they only savour of his Utterance, and were sweet enough till tainted by his Breath.
>
> I will not justifie any of my own Errors; I am sensible of many; and if Mr. *Collier* has by any Accident stumbled on one or two, I will freely give them up to him ... [43]

Instead of considering Collier's attack as a whole, he restricts himself to point defense of particular passages: he thus voluntarily forsakes the opportunity to question Collier's thesis. He appears unwilling to challenge Collier's overall assertion that stage portrayal of elite immorality weakens the social fabric, and is thus reduced to pouncing on particular points. Instead of defending what Collier deems "Errors" and "Corruptions of the Stage" in themselves, he protests that the blight is in the eye of the beholder, and that the stage is already as respectable as Collier could wish. He thus abandons to his opponent's mercy any passage that Collier can prove improper by his own standard of authoritarian morality, because Congreve proposes no alternative standard. Indeed, when he finds himself in the wrong by a moralistic measure identical to Collier's, only less industrious in discovering offenses, he simply apologizes, as when he admits his guilt in Lady Plyant's saying "Jesu" in *The Double-Dealer* (*Amendments*, 183).

Congreve's whole defense is that "Mr. Collier ... first commits a Rape

upon my Words, and then arraigns 'em of Immodesty" (*Amendments*, 172).
He lays down four premises: first, that comedy is, according to Aristotle,
"an imitation of the worse sort of people"; second, that characters' words
should not be imputed to the author; third, that passages must be looked at
in context; and, fourth, that words should only be applied to sacred things
if they are so intended.[44] Only the first premise addresses an issue broader
than what exactly particular expressions mean, and that premise, with its
appeal to the authority of Aristotle and sedulous ignoring of the political
dimension of Collier's attack, betrays Congreve's inability or unwillingness to engage his opponent on fundamentals. The rest of Congreve's
Amendments toils through his dramatic corpus, citation by citation, nitpick-
ing over words, exulting that Collier has written "*Learning* a Spaniel to set"
instead of "teaching a Spaniel to set" (*Amendments*, 179), and "shew[ing]
that Mr. *Collier* himself, when he is in the Humour, will allow of the
Distinction betwixt the *Man* and the *Priest*, the Person and the Function"
(*Amendments*, 195). The method is tedious and unconvincing; if he is right
about ninety-nine particulars, because he makes no effort to relate them in
a general proposition he has still proved nothing about a hundredth. As
Samuel Johnson observed, "His chief artifice of controversy is to retort
upon his adversary his own words," but it fails, not because "The cause of
Congreve was not tenable,"[45] but because his method of argumentation
does not address the underlying issue of whether the purpose of the stage
is to endorse the political status quo. He simply uses the terms and follows
the agenda his opponent had set, not once engaging and refuting the ideas
behind the mass of minutiae.

An example of his technique is his response to Collier's charge that
three of the four women in *The Double Dealer* are "Whores." He begins by
trifling:

> There are but four Ladies in this Play, and three of the biggest of them are Whores. These are
> very *big* Words; very much too *big* for the Sense, for to say *three of the biggest*, when
> there are but four in Number, is stark Nonsense. Whatever the *Matter* may be in this
> Gentleman's Book, I perceive his *Stile* at least is admirable. (*Amendments*, 175)

After more jesting at the expense of "big" and "biggest," he denies a strict
arithmetic correspondence between the numbers of immoral women on
stage and those in life:

> . . . if four Women are shewn upon the Stage, and three of them are vicious, it is as
> much as to say, that three parts in four of the whole Sex are stark naught . . . It was
> a mercy that all the four Women were not naught; for that had been maintaining
> that there was not one Woman of Quality honest. (*Amendments*, 175)

He then observes that Virgil's bad women outnumber his good, and concludes that

This is *Bossus's* Remark, and he says that *Virgil* in the Characters of the Sex, has closely observed the Rule of *Aristotle*, who in his Treatise of Poetry has ventured to affirm, That there are more bad than good Women in the World; and that they do more harm than good. (*Amendments*, 176)

Congreve first ridicules his opponent's style as low, implicitly exalting in contrast his own gentility, then to similar effect chastises Collier's vulgar literalness of interpretation, and ends with authorities that prove his own learning, correctness, and impeccable contempt for women. The snobbishness that would later lead him to style himself a gentleman rather than an author to the visiting Voltaire is abundantly evident; what is not is a substantive rebuttal of Collier's charge that the representation of the upper classes as immoral is likely to weaken respect for them and thus the integrity of hierarchical subordination. Because he was as authoritarian as Collier, Congreve was unwilling to challenge his antagonist in essentials.[46] But his was not the only voice in the controversy that rebutted Collier.

Another of the numerous answers to Collier, James Drake's 1699 *The Ancient and Modern Stages surveyed*, takes a more learned approach. Although, unlike Congreve, he has no works of his own to vindicate, he declares that he, too, will restrict his attentions to correcting errors and drawing a more proper parallel between ancients and moderns. The several hundred pages of the body of his work follow this agenda, finding the "Moral of the Fable defective" in *Oedipus* and "*Prometheus* immoral" and praising the "Advantages of the Moderns over the Antients in the Morals of their Fables": moderns "don't interest Providence in promoting Villainy; as the Antients have notoriously done in many of their plays."[47] Drake asserts in his first sentence a program as focused on morality as Collier's own: "The aim of all Writers is, or ought to be, to maintain or propagate *Truth*, to inform the *Judgment*, improve the *Understanding*, and rectifie the *Mistakes* of others" (1). He agrees with Collier that truth is definite, knowable, and unitary, and also that morality and hierarchy are complementary. He remarks that in Roman comedy "The Slaves are so familiar with their Masters," and that the slave "generally appears to have more wit than his Master" (321). The modern stage becomes in Drake's view a model of social subordination in comparison to the pagan and disreputable ancients. His Epistle Dedicatory to the Earl of Dorset (who as Chamberlain ejected Dryden from the Laureateship) protests that "Immorality and Profaneness are things so justly abhorrd" and echoes Congreve in asserting that Collier "tortures Expressions, to extort a Confession from 'em of things to which they are absolute Strangers" (n.p.). For Drake, the modern stage and contemporary political settlement are alike ideal; but, by agreeing with Collier that servility is the highest of dramatic values, like Congreve he voluntarily subjects the stage to whoever can control it most strictly.

Drake makes one argument missing from Congreve's *Amendments*. He compares his own high view of the Church – "Our Clergy deservedly have both at home and abroad the reputation of the most learned Clergy in the World, and I shall venture to affirm, that they are the Best in the World" (n.p.) – to Collier's Jacobitism: "For to extend the Power and Authority of the Priest, he curtails the Articles of the Church, and denies the King's Supremacy" (n.p.). Drake here ventures briefly to undercut Collier's standing as a champion of the Revolution settlement, but does not develop the hint. Nonetheless, his connecting the stage reform controversy to a political agenda stands in marked contrast to Congreve, whose principal career, in number of years, was not writing plays at all but being an ex-playwright "gentleman" above partisan politics and enjoying veneration and patronage from both Whig and Tory authors and politicians. If Congreve's approach formed a deliberate strategy, it was one that repaid him handsomely in material and social compensations, but did nothing either to protect the liberty of the stage or to keep himself employed as an active playwright after 1700. Beyond the one momentary mention, Drake's demonstrations of the depravity of the ancients evade, like Congreve, engaging the main points of Collier's attack; but he is not the first of Collier's answerers to detect "a Snake in the Grass" (n.p.). It is Settle who addresses the political dimension from which Drake and Congreve shrink.

IV

Settle wrote an earlier reply to *A Short View*, the first above thirty pages, *A Defense of Dramatick Poetry*, followed a few weeks later by *A Farther Defense of Dramatick Poetry*.[48] These two pamphlets, the first 118 pages, the second 72, constitute, as the preface to *A Farther Defense* explains, a single work divided by "my *Bookseller's* over-hasty Publication of my former Discourse."[49] This double treatise, unlike Drake's or Congreve's, shows a combination of practical theatrical knowledge and ferocious political invective unafraid to argue fundamentals. *A Defense* opens aggressively; rather than merely chide a dirty-minded clergyman for reading in meanings that innocent poets never intended, he charges

That all this Labour'd Pile of Stage-Reformation is only the Product of Idleness and Abdication. He takes up the Whip for the Play-house, as Dionysius the Tyrant did the School-birch, when he had lost the Scepter . . . The Theatre was then [in "Mr. *Collier's* smiling Days"] too much the Minion of his old *Great Master* and *Mistress,* and Mr. *Collier,* we all very well know, was more the Courtier, under the Blessings of that warm Sun, then to rally either This or any other Darling of Power.[50]

The argument of Collier's unfitness to pose as a guardian of morality in light of his position on the losing side of the Stuart–Williamite divide that Drake mentions and hastily drops becomes developed at length. Nor is this the only place where Settle recalls his past as a pamphleteer and deals out the most violent, and politically loaded, condemnations. Besides such a throwaway line as "Well, here's one positive Bill of Exclusion,"[51] the climax to his peroration, at the end of *A Farther Defense,* is

pious Craft in all Religions is much the same; and *Legends* will creep into all *Churchs* . . . I acknowledge his view has some matter of Truth in it; but at the same time its Veracity a little agrees with the Description of Dr. *Oates* his Plot, in *Absalom and Achitophel.*

> Some Truth there was, but brew'd and dasht with Lies,
> To Please the Fools, and puzle all the Wise.

And here I must give Mr. *Collier* the Honour of leading a small Squadron of *Truths* to attack the Stage; but like Dr. *Oats* too, with a whole Legion of Pilgrims and Black Bills to back them. (*Farther Defense,* 71–72)

Settle, who had burned the Pope in effigy twenty years before and then written *A Narrative,* was familiar with the madness of crowds. Opposite in his personal situation to Congreve, that "very young man, elated with success, and impatient of censure,"[52] he was better able to see the contest for political legitimacy underlying the controversy. Marginalized from literary culture since his treacheries of the 1680s, he did not need to cultivate blindness in the ideological spectrum. Instead of agreeing with Collier, like Congreve and Drake, that the theater must deny the possibility of disagreement, he attempts to assimilate the discourse of stage morality to the discourse of sectarian politics that had prevented the consolidation of absolutism under the Stuarts.

Considered as a single work, *A Defense of Dramatick Poetry* and *A Farther Defense* comprise an extended rebuttal of Collier's *A Short View* that concedes to its opponent only the charge of lewdness, a concession confined to a single page and buried well to the rear. More than half of *A Defense* is devoted to a laborious and, for the most part, effective refutation of Collier's appeals to legal, philosophic, literary, and religious authorities to support his case against the stage. Settle begins with law, the knitter of the social fabric, and cites black-letter statutes until he leaves Collier with no support but Sparta and those to whom "A profane *Comedy* or *Tragedy*, were all Heathen and Antichristian, but Pious *Regicide* and *Rebellion*, were Religion and Sanctity" (*Defense*, 13). Collier's only allies in law are reduced to those who overthrew law: Settle imposes this last ally upon Collier. As a Jacobite, Collier might seem an odd person to equate with Roundheads, but Settle is beginning to make his case that the Jacobite, for all his superficial political antagonism to the Puritans, is now what they were before, the real threat to society. Settle posits his own position as central, like the Church of England with Dissenters to one side and Catholics to the other; after 1688, it is Jacobites, not Nonconformists, who deny the crown's title.

Next Settle refutes Collier's philosophical sources. This section is promiscuous, drawing distinctions when distinctions exist to be drawn and doing without them when they do not. His object is to show that the theater was endorsed by both pagan and Christian ancients, to deny Collier their support, and he is not too particular about his argumentation. Ovid and "the Author of the *Plain Dealer*" mention playhouses only as places of public resort where a man may "pick up a Wench" (*Defense*, 29), a purpose for which a park or church would do as well; and a long quotation from one of Collier's nonjuring tracts gives a weightier reason to avoid church: " 'Does the Being of a Church consist in Brick and Stone? What would you do if *Jupiter* was worshipped there? . . . *Better be alone than in ill company*' " (*Defense*, 31). Again, Collier the Jacobite, like Collier the new Prynne, is the disrupter, the danger. Subsequently, thirty pages of patristic argumentation appeal to the silence of scripture about the theater, the sufferance of the Christianized empire, and the fact that it was a heathen stage to which some Fathers objected (*A Defense*, 34–67).[53] In the middle of this religious discussion, Settle interrupts his argument to observe the absurdity of Collier's both asserting the purity of the ancient stage and quoting denouncers of that stage's wickedness (*Defense*, 47–54). What all these discussions of various authorities have in common is the aim of isolating Collier from the socially sanctioned supports he claims. Collier alone can be described as an intruder on the stage and a threat to social order; Collier with Christianity, law, and the classics central to aristocratic culture behind him cannot.

The remainder of *A Defense* is divided between a justification of the stage's raising passions and a defense of *Amphitryon* and *King Arthur* against charges of profaneness and blasphemy. Collier contradicts himself, Settle claims, in finding Jupiter in *Amphitryon* at once too like God and not sufficiently godlike (*Defense*, 114). To justify the stage's raising of passions, Settle defends tragedy on the grounds that "Pity is a little Kin to Love" (*Defense*, 72) and that tragedy extols not evil but good, not vicious but exalted love (*Defense*, 79). If the stage represents revenge, what is the entire legal system but systemized revenge? "Nay here's the very Law it self Arraign'd, as little less then Antichristian for punishing that Injury, which the express Law of God, even seventy seven times over, obliges us to forgive" (*Defense*, 95–96). Similarly, Settle argues, if the stage is vain, so is every shop that sells luxuries, but to close them would make many beggars (*Defense*, 97–98). Thus the reformer, not the stage, is again the threat, this time to the prosperity of commercial society. The stage has not corrupted society: on the contrary, when he at last briefly admits corruption has existed, Settle is "sorry that the *Age* has corrupted the *Stage*" (*Farther Defense*, 63). The age he names as the corrupter, by no coincidence, is the reigns of the last two Stuarts. Stage libertines are gentry because "we must not lash the Vices at *Wapping* to mend the Faults at *Westminster*"(*Defense*, 89), and they are not obvious monsters because "every Fool would run from a Devil with a visible Cloven-foot" (*Defense*, 90). A moral use is found even for cuckoldry: Isaac Fondlewife warns "Reverend City Sixty . . . against the Marrying to Sixteen" (*Defense*, 88). Cuckoldry thus becomes positioned as a corrective to abuse of social and financial power for purposes of sexual oppression; it is a release from tyranny, like the Glorious Revolution itself.

For Settle, dealing with Collier's "Diviner Qualification, as the *Churchman* and *Philosopher*," with "Moral and Religious Objections against the Stage," serves only as preparation for the climax of his response: an examination of his opponent's "Humane Capacity . . . not only as a Church-Champion, but that Humbler Stage-Combatant, a *Critick*" (*Farther Defense*, 1). If *A Defense* is rarely more than a defense, a more comprehensive one than Congreve's, but still not carrying the fight to the enemy in more than isolated sallies, *A Farther Defense* goes further. Having defended the stage in detail against Collier the social philosopher and stripped him of his claim to moral authority, Settle is now free to go on the offensive. Where Collier condemns the protean dynamism of the stage as subversive of social stability, Congreve quibbles, and Drake simply endorses the status quo as admirable in every respect, Settle insists that the legitimist tendency of Collier's stance, implicitly endorsing absolutism and discrediting the Glorious Revolution, remains, as in the Exclusion Crisis, the true threat.

As in *A Defense*, the longest section of *A Farther Defense*, and the one most filled with citations of texts, is the first. Only one text, however, is examined, Vanbrugh's *Relapse*. The examen follows a preface that concludes

that there seems to be no truly general *Privilege of Lying,* but in God's Name . . . when a single private Hand sets up for a *Public Reformation* . . . suspect either the *Enthusiast* or the *Hypocrite, viz.* That either the *Mad* Zeal or the *Pretended* One sets Pen to Paper. (*Farther Defense,* n.p.)

The alternatives of madman and hypocrite echo the choice of characters permitted the Whigs – fools or villains – in Settle's *Narrative*. Vanbrugh's own *A Short Vindication of the Relapse and the Provok'd Wife*[54] appeared in the brief interval between the publication of *A Defense* and that of *A Farther Defense*, which gives Settle the opportunity to say that, as "the Ingenious Author of the Relapse" has already answered those charges of immorality and profaneness, this treatise will "only make some general Observations of that part of Mr. *Colliers* Remarks" (*Farther Defense,* 39–40). By this device, Settle is freed from the necessity of rebutting Collier in detail, the procedure which bogged down both Congreve's *Amendments* and his own discussion of Dryden's *King Arthur* and *Amphitryon* in *A Defense*. Given the use he makes of this opportunity, his choice seems deliberate to use as the text for his defense of playwriting the only play that had already been defended at length.[55]

The account of *The Relapse* that ostensibly fills most of *A Farther Defense* begins with an extended, and rather plodding, examination of Collier's charges, both moral and literary, against the plot and characters of the play. Of Settle's two principal arguments, the defense of the plausibility of the plot is irrelevant to the issue of morality; the other vindicates the play as a moral whole. Young Fashion is not a libertine but has only been extravagant in a small way, and that too in a good cause, not any "Brutal Prodigality" but "Travel that has been accounted the most Honourable Improvement of a Gentleman; a great part of this Extravagance occasion'd possibly to bear up the Port of his Birth, and the Honour of his Family" (*Farther Defense,* 7). Further, Younger Fashion tricked his brother only after his appeal for aid was refused, an appeal particularly justifiable in light of the hard "Paternal Provision" (*Farther Defense,* 11) that left the elder brother £5,000 a year, and the younger only a £200 annuity. Sir Tunbelly too is so "sordid and avaricious a Character, so over-cautious a Coxcomb" (*Farther Defense,* 12), that "an honest Dramatick over-reach . . . not by any ignoble rascally Impostor, but a Young Gentleman, at least of equal Birth and Quality" with Sir Tunbelly's daughter, is fair play. As when he found a moral value in cuckoldry in *A Defense*, Settle does not accept Collier's absolutist stance in favor of patriarchal authority. Settle is defending not any absolute pleasure, though, of radicalism or licentiousness, but, as the remark above about "Birth and Quality" indicates, the *Relapse* as sound Whig moderatism. An unlimited right in fathers and older brothers would be of a piece with an unlimited right of kings; as the king should in justice share power with the gentry (but not "ignoble rascally Impostors"), so should the overendowed Lord Foppington share with the underendowed Young Fashion. They are family.

After the defense of Vanbrugh's play, *A Farther Defense* becomes more wide-ranging in its discussion, while continuing at times to allude to the *Relapse* as an example. Its first object is a defense of the English stage against the doctrine of the three unities, "French Slavery to our English Liberty" (*Farther Defense*, 28). The phrasing has obvious echoes beyond the playhouse. The unity of time Settle allows to be desirable, so long as it remains not an end in itself but "*Handmaid* to our Delight" (*Farther Defense*, 31), since "Delight is the great End of Playing" (33). The unity of place he briefly dismisses as wrongheaded because "our Audience expect a little Variety . . . To continue it all on one spot of Ground, in one Chamber or Room . . . only labours to be dull; and deserves a success accordingly"(35). The unity of action too is "seriously impertinent"(36), because it "is so nauseous to an *English* Audience, that they have almost peuk'd at a very good Dish for no other Fault . . . On the contrary here must be Under-plots, and considerable ones too, possibly big enough to justle the Upper-plot, to support a good *English* Play" (37). Throughout this part of the essay, Settle speaks as a pragmatic theater veteran, nor does he scruple to appeal to jingoism. His business is to please not just any audience but an English one, which is distinct from a French, who are "the dullest of Mankind at their Play-houses; can be contented to hear a Play made up of a short-winded Plot, and a few long-winded Speeches, much about enough for the Argument of one of our *Acts*" (28–29). The English theater is part of English freedom, as French criticism is an aspect of French tyranny, that is, of absolute monarchy, with which Settle once more reminds his readers the Jacobite Collier is associated. After dealing with the unities, he turns to the charge of blasphemy, and anticipates Congreve, urging the moral utility of "the publick exposure of Debauchery," and protesting that "the Language of the Libertine Characters" ought not to be "charged as the private Sense of the Author" (40). Then, "granting the Poets have Launch'd a little too boldly"(41), he contends, again like Congreve, that Collier's "Work is not so much to *find* the Devils upon the Stage, as to *raise* 'em there"(42). Settle calls "above two thirds" of the instances in Collier's "Spiritual Cant" false, and, to show "how easy 'tis to extract Blasphemy from Mr. *Collier*'s Limbeck"(49), burlesques the divine's method for a half-dozen pages. He also observes that the stage uses "the old Heathen Mythology . . . on purpose to give no shadow of Offence to the Christian Religion" (51). These two sections of *A Farther Defense* treat of subjects applicable to the theater as a whole, not just particular plays, and the climaxing and concluding parts that follow carry this process of generalization to its end, the transfer of the onus of being a social menace from the theater to its critic.

Settle first quotes Collier as terming Cervantes a " 'Gyant,' " and

fanc[ies] Mr. *Collier* will assent with me; That both *History* and *Romance* are lawful to be read . . . What is *History* or *Romance* but the Relation of Human *Action*, *Passions*, and *Conversation*? And that Relation *Narratively*, or *Dramatically* set forth, differs only in the *Modus* or *Form*, not *Substance* . . . Nay, *Reading* it self gives us a kind of *Theatrical Representaion* of the whole subject we read . . . So that . . . *Reading of Books*, as 'tis plain, [is] equally, or rather more dangerous, than *Acting of Plays*. (52–53, 56)

Following this exercise in pinning reductive logic onto Collier, Settle justifies swearing and cursing on stage as legal, since only swearing by or jesting with the Trinity is fined by the statute Collier cites (57–58). It is also gentlemanly, because a "*Lover*'s Oath," the kind commonest onstage, is not so terrible to women as a "*Soldierly* Oath" (59). He wonders at Collier's finding that the "greatest Transgression of the Stage, is, the Abuse of the Clergy" (60), since "the Author of the *Persuasive to Consideration*," a non-juring tract, "falls himself so heavy, both upon the *Head* and *Body* of the *Church*" (61). Additionally, Collier "himself has furnish'd it with one of the most Divertive *Characters* for a *Comedy* . . . *The Parson turn'd Critick*"(62). Collier is both ridiculous and, again, a greater threat to the regime than the theater. Following this mockery, Settle apologizes in once sentence for the "Immoralities and Licentiousness of the Stage," which he attributes to the fact that "the *Effeminacy* of the two last Reigns has both furnish'd the Stage with so many *Libertine Pictures*, and indulg'd their Reception" (63). Again the morality of the stage is politicized; Collier the stage-moralist is portrayed as the alter ego of Collier the Jacobite, promising order but secretly promoting the return of the Stuarts. The stage has been at fault, but the nostrum Collier promotes is in disguise the despotism that caused that fault; Settle's apology is briefly given and swiftly negated. Although agreeing that the stage should represent more innocent characters, Settle hopes that

> Mr. *Collier* does not expect that *All* the Characters in the Comedy should be Virtuous; A Composition of that kind cannot well be made; nor would such a Composition truly reach the whole Instructive Ends of the Drama . . . *The Foyl sets off the Diamond* . . . 'Tis not supposed therefore that the Dramatick Poet must be oblig'd to borrow his Characters of Virtue from Lazy Cells, and Melancholy Cloysters; a Copy from a *Hermit*, or an *Anchoret*. No; his Characters of Virtue must come forth into the gay World, with Levity, Vanity, nay, Temptation it self, all round them. They must go to the Court, the Ball, the Masque, the Musick-Houses, the Dancing-Schools, nay, to the very Prophane Play-Houses themselves, (to speak in Mr *Collier's* Dialect;) and yet come off unconquered. (64–65)

"Hermits" and "Lazy Cells" might suggest a thrilling medievalism to Catherine Morland in Austen's *Northanger Abbey* a century later, but in 1698 they were part of the absolutist, Catholic worldview that had been defeated in England only ten years before. The finality of this defeat was not yet certain, for James and Louis yet lived abroad, and their partisans such as Collier at home. The conclusion, a bitter personal assault on Collier, follows; Settle charges that his adversary wrote for fifty pounds, not for conscience: "the *Fee* was large and *Pleadings* must deserve it . . . nothing but a total Overthrow of the Stage could make it so selling a Copy . . . Thus Fasehood employ'd the Workman. Falsehood found the Materials. Falsehood raised the Structure, and Falsehood upholds it" (*Farther Defense*, 69–70). The comparison of Collier to Oates comes next, and ends the tract. Settle has reversed Collier's logic: it is the stage that is moral, its attacker who is immoral. It is Collier, not the stage, who seeks an "Overthrow." The repeated political slurs have the double function of discrediting Collier by emphasizing his political alienation from the regime and by indicating the trustworthiness of the stage now that its corrupters "of the last two Reigns," that is, those of Charles II and James II, are gone.

Yet Settle lacks an alternative to the bipolar political model that had caused England to teeter alternately on the verges of absolutism and anarchy throughout the seventeenth century. He is willing to see the constructive side of even cuckoldry, which threatens to throw property relations into disorder by rendering succession suspect; a similar anxiety about legitimacy, however, on the national scale is precisely what underwrote the Stuart doctrine of indefeasible hereditary right. Settle's boldness in daring to permit the inferring of such a parallel indicates his estrangement from the strategy of conservative reformism that distinguished the Revolution from the Civil War – a conservatism disguised by the Revolution's rhetoric of religious emancipation, an emancipation that resided principally in the ratification of the long-since completed Reformation. He attempts to align Collier with "his old *Great Master*," but fails to reckon on the alteration in priorities between an insurgent Whiggism endeavoring to overcome Stuart legitimism with fear of Popery and the post-1688 regime; he remains oppositional, failing to recognize the great difference between being Out and In. The only polarization in demand in 1698 was such as would encourage not internal divisions but a national mobilization against external enemies. Like many later writers, he envisioned a more emancipatory Revolution than in the event occurred.

v

Settle, however, had not yet finished his part in the stage-reform controversy. In 1711 he published a further reply to Collier in the form of a satire on stage reformers, *City-Ramble*. This play remains significantly uncompromising still for one appearing so late in the reform controversy. The address "To the Reader" presents a paranoid picture of a man alone and beleaguered by enemies:

> Of all Oppressions those from *Prejudice* and *Prepossession* are the severest. Let Merit and Reason in this Case be never so strong on the suffering Side, however neither Plaint nor Plea shall be ever permitted to speak in their Behalf, as falling into those merciless Hands where they are certain of lying under irrevocable Condemnation, and that too of all Sentences the hardest, *untried* and *unheard* . . . Having now by me some finish'd Pieces that have long lay dead upon my Hands, through my Exclusion from the Stage: I resolved to write this with that Silence and Secrecy, as to be able to surmount all Opposition, by bringing it into Light by an adopted Father's Hand. But so it hapned, that the Secret took Air, insomuch that hopeless of stemming the common Torrent against me, I was reduced to the Necessity of bringing it in in the long Vacation, and consequently with a very narrow Expectation of Profit . . . [56]

The play itself is more a tragicomedy, an outmoded form by 1711, as J. Douglas Canfield has observed, in mixed blank verse and prose, than a straight comedy.[57] Its relevance to the controversy over stage reform lies in the device, borrowed from *Knight of the Burning Pestle*, of a framing subplot consisting of putative members of the audience who comment on and interact with the main action. These members are a Common Councilman, a great enemy to the stage and an equally great fool, his sensible wife, and their daughter. Early in the play, the daughter, with her mother's connivance, goes in disguise onstage to play a shepherdess, as a ruse to get her father to bless unaware her wedding to a young gentleman playing the shepherd in love with her. He has £1,000 a year, a great fortune, though only a third as much as the old alderman her father has selected for her; he is also of good family, but her father is incensed against him because as a lark he has sometimes acted. The father begins with the view that "since my Wife has dragged me hither amongst you, I am resolv'd to make a little Reformation-work among you" (2), and throughout the play denounces its portrayal of the "Iniquity" of "Rakes and Scoundrels!" (26). In the last act he is still exclaiming that

the Reprobate Scriblers of this Age are such a senseless Pack of Rogues, that they bewray their own Nests, stuff so many villainous lewd Characters into their Plays, 'till they have almost undone the very Stage they live by. (58)

But what the Councilman is denouncing in this last instance is his own disguised daughter's stated disinclination, in her role as a jilt, to matrimony as a "Jayl" (56) and reluctance to follow through on a promise of marriage. He insists that she honor her word, and she takes this as consent and runs off to wed her lover. When they return, married, at the end of the play, he confesses his error.

Well, Wife, thou hast conquer'd and convin'd me; and instead of reforming the Stage the Stage has reformed me, made me marry my Daughter to a brisk young Fellow that deserves her; and so bless you together. (71)

The reformer is reformed; the Councilman who had insisted that his daughter "marr[y] where I please" (9) is brought by a little judicious intrigue to admit of a less absolute conception of his power. As the prologue explains, merchant and gentry are reconciled in a quintessentially Whiggish wedding of town and country. "While mutually each others Help we need, / We gild your Honour, and you mend our Breed" (1). While the reformer is mocked, and his absolutist, patriarchalist pretensions disallowed, Settle is careful to show that this process implies no confounding of society. He wants his attack to be effective, and to be so it has to position itself at the sociopolitical center; *City-Ramble* posits itself as the moral norm and its target, Collier-like reactionary intransigence, as deviant. The theater again is presented as Whiggish in principles, and its reformer as an overrigid promiser of order whose stage criticism is as uncomprehendingly unbending as Jacobitism.

By 1698, Settle had thirty years of experience as a professional playwright, and twenty as a pamphleteer on both sides of the great divide of English politics. Congreve became an adult after the battle of the age had been decided, and had been a social insider in both the literary and political spheres from earliest youth. In Bunyan's language, he had only walked with Whiggism when the sun shone and it wore its silver slippers. He could not articulate any coherent philosophy to oppose to Collier's because to admit of alternative values would have required an awareness of multiple possibilities, and, situated as and when he was, he had neither need nor desire to explore any possibilities other than the, for him, comfortable fact of the new order. Settle was a survivor of an earlier, more cynical generation, a veteran of both sides of its most desperate struggle. As such, he had a better notion of what was at stake and how to fight those who, with his Common Councilman, said,

if these Libertine Scriblers, and you Libertine Players too, don't mend your Manners, and that very quickly, if I live to get a Foot of Authority into the Government, as I hope I soon shall, I shall have a kick at both your Theatres. (59)

Settle, unlike Congreve, knew the necessity of kicking against such kickers. By the time he comes to write *City-Ramble*, Settle has more smoothly integrated his project of defending the stage with the political necessity that the result seems unthreatening; the consolidation of mercantile elite and gentry in the conclusion of the play represents the theater as participating in the Whig ideal of social harmony.

VI

Returning to earlier in Settle's career, I conclude by considering a drama of his that is antithetical to Collier's program of a censoring reformism. As a deeply politically committed piece of antinomian agitprop dominated by a dynamic and immoral woman, *The Female Prelate* is the very type of what Collier wanted censored. Collier observes that in *An Essay of Dramatic Poesy*, Dryden

Censures the *Romans* for making *Mutes* of their single Women. This he calls the *Breeding of the Old* Elizabeth *way, which was for Maids to be seen, and not to be heard*. Under Favour the old Discipline would be very serviceable upon the Stage. As Matters go, the *Mutes* are much too few. For certainly 'tis better to say nothing, than talk out of Character, and to ill purpose ... Modesty is the distinguishing Virtue of that Sex, and serves both for Ornament and Defense. (*Short View*, 21, 11)

Settle's Pope Joan lies at the furthest remove from Collier's "muting" of women. A horror tragedy in which the horror lies in inversion of sex roles and transsexualism symbolizes Catholicism, *The Female Prelate* debuted with great, and highly partisan, success in 1679, and was reprinted three times in 1689, immediately after the Glorious Revolution, then never again. While the hero, the Duke of Saxony, orates bombastically and futilely, "a-cursing like a very drab, / A stallion,"[58] the action and interest center in the schemings of the villainess, the legendary Pope Joan. By portraying a male hero undone by a female Papist priest-machiavel, Settle plays upon the legend of Papistical duplicity and cunning, as well as recurrent Protestant uneasiness at the demasculinizing celibacy of the Catholic priesthood. By abstaining from sexual bipolarity, this priesthood represents like homosexuals a subversion of the binary economy, an obstacle to bourgeois domesticity.[59] As a matter of practical theatrics, Settle is also returning to the theme of his greatest success, *The Empress of Morocco.*[60] Whereas that play's Empress betrays her son to her lover, however, and is in turn betrayed by him once he holds power, Pope Joan in her own person seizes the highest ecclesiastical position in Christendom, a position that in Rome is the highest temporal one as well. Unlike the victim-heroines of "she-tragedy," she anticipates the link between Catholicism and immoral female independence portrayed in such nineteenth-century novels as Walter Scott's *Waverley*, Thackeray's *Henry Esmond*, and Tolstoy's *War and Peace*. Her female usurpation of divinely sanctioned male domination parallels Rome's usurpation of divinely sanctioned secular kingship.

Joan feels acutely conscious of the anomalousness of her aquisition of male role and power. Amiran, a woman who attends her in the guise of a page, asks why, after being sexually betrayed in her youth by the father of the hero, the Duke of Saxony, she turned priest:

> But why a Monk? Why not t'a Nunnery?
> That last retreat of all distressed Sinners
> Where the poor Nymph flies her false Shepherd's Arms,
> Mourns her neglected Sighs, and fading Charms.
> To a Church-Anthem tunes her tender Cries;
> Whilst like th'expiring Swan she sings and dies?
> *Lor* [-enzo, Joan's confidant]. Yes, Madam, why not to a Nunnery?
> *Pope*. No; that had been t'have published my despair,
> And given th'insulting Duke too great a Triumph.
> Besides [playing] a Priest was th'Engine for my Vengeance.[61]

Unless she unsexes herself, Joan can only be passive, reduced to "Mourn[ing] her neglected Sighs, and fading Charms." She refuses to conform to the social script of passivity and helplessness for a wronged woman. This script continued to be available in the Restoration, as it was before and after; what is remarkable about the period is that any alternative to it is portrayed at all. In Etherege's 1676 *The Man of Mode*, in contrast, the neglected Mrs. Loveit can take no action more effectual than tearing her fans and raving "Lightning blast him" and other vocative pleadings that another power besides herself avenge her injuries.[62] When Belinda rouses Loveit's jealous rage to provoke her to a quarrel, four of Loveit's last five utterances before the Page announces Dorimant's arrival are couched as subjunctive requests:

Shame and confusion be ever in her face when she shows it . . . I will tear him from mine, or die i'the attempt . . . Would I had Daggers, Darts, or poyson'd Arrows in my Breast, so I cou'd but remove the thoughts of him from thence . . . Who e're she be, all the harm I wish her is, may she love him as well as I do, and may he give her as much cause to hate him . . . May all the passions that are rais'd by neglected Love, Jealousy, Indignation, Spite, and Thirst of Revenge, eternally rage in her Soul, as they do now in mine.[63]

She implores some indefinite, in fact nonexistent, agency to conduct her vengeance on her behalf, like the male relative whom she apparently lacks or cannot appeal to because of her own loss of reputation. Without male agency, she assumes herself incapable of activity. The only actions she can conceive herself taking are ceasing to love and dying; both are intransitive, without effect beyond herself, and without a man's love futile. By assuming the masculine role of a priest, however, Joan becomes the old Duke's confessor, and, prior to the play's beginning, poisons him. Unlike Loveit or the lovely woman who stoops to folly of Goldsmith's song, neither of whom can imagine a more active vengeance than wishing or dying, she actively avenges her lost honor. Instead of a cast mistress of intrigue comedy or a sentimental heroine, a figure for contemptuous laughter or pitying tears, she acts as a female Vindice, as a subject, not an object. Pope Joan is not the only vengeful woman in Restoration tragedies, but the type, born after 1660, quietly expired in the reorientation of English drama toward the moral, the sentimental, and the domestic in the eighteenth century. Like its spearhead Collier, the reform movement continued to value "the Reservedness of a Maiden-Character" (*Short View*, 20). Moreover, Joan's vengeance predates the action; during the play itself it is the Duke who assumes the role of would-be avenger, a role at which he, unlike her, fails ignominiously.

Besides acting as the moving force in everything that happens in the play that bears her name, she possesses the two traditionally male attributes of intelligence and libertinism. Her account of her youth casts her as a universal genius like Marlowe's Faust:

As many Languages as *Romes* proud Hills
My Virgin Nonage spoke. As many Arts and Sciences
As the famed Stagyrite studied to inspire
The Conqueror of the Universe, were mine . . .
Could give the Earth and the Heavens first Foundation
To Nature, or to Natures God at pleasure:
Dispute on both sides, and on both sides vanquish . . .
But 'twas my Pride preserved my guarded Innocence.
Who yields to Love, makes but vain man her Lord:
And I who had studied all the greater Globe,
Scorn'd to be vassal to the lesser World.

(Female Prelate, 23)

Exulting in her ingenious villainies, she asks, "Why was not I the first created Woman? / 'Sdeath, I'd have met the subtle plotting Serpent, / And by my Arts blown up the shallow Fiend" (*Female Prelate,* 8). Like the nuns in Marvell's "Upon Appleton House," she "Scorn'd to be vassal." In her pleasures as well, she takes the part not of victim but of rake hero. She falls in love with the son as she had earlier with the father, contrives how she and her parasite and sometime paramour, Lorenzo, may respectively enjoy the Duke and his new bride, and avows herself entitled to sexual liberty:

Why should we
Who've loved and loved till we have pall'd our Appetites,
Drawn off Love's Nectar to the dregs, be Slaves
To senseless Constancy? Give me a loose
In Pleasures uncontrouled, unlimited
As Ocean Tides, whose wanton Billows roar,
Rove, and roll on to the Worl'ds [sic] utmost Shore.
These, these are my Principles . . .
In our delights let old *Romes* Glory shine,
Thou the brisk Tarquin, I the wanton Messaline.

(Female Prelate, 34)

For a woman to be a sexual aggressor, like the infamous Messaline, is at least as monstrous as for a man to be a rapist like Tarquin; she is not only aggressive, however, but ruthless and able to put interest above passion. Where Amiran shrinks from serving her mistress in what Auden called "the necessary murder,"[64] crying "but oh, there's something / In Murder so beyond a Female Villain" (*Female Prelate,* 48), Joan need only reason with herself to find resolve: " 'Tis very hard to kill the man I love; / But if he keeps a tongue, I lose a head . . . / Oh, I must send thee to thy Father's

Grave: / For know my Love must be my glories slave" (*Female Prelate*, 46). Her final unsexing (more successful than Lady Macbeth's), by assuming a man's murderousness, like her first in assuming his garb and role, results from a refusal to permit her destiny to be controlled by her reproductive apparatus. Nature, however, proves too strong. Crafting an expedient to counter every crisis, she progresses from crime to crime successfully, until the final intervention of biology: on the last page cardinals enter and scandalizedly announce that she dropped a child during a procession (the legendary end of Pope Joan). An offstage fall on the last page, though, hardly outweighs the phenomenal energy of her previous career.

In reaction to the scandal, the cardinals resolve to inspect the genitals of new Popes, and the play concludes: "Now Devils we defie your utmost power / *Romes* awful throne shall be profan'd no more. / Put Whores and Bawds upon us, if you can, / *Romes* Mitred Head henceforth shall be a man" (*Female Prelate*, 60). By this farcical conclusion, none of the systemic corruption portrayed has been redressed: persecution, "*The Scene a Prison, which opening, discovers variety of Heretics in several Tortures*" (*Female Prelate*, 35); the gross superstition of the "Rabble," who in the only prose scene talk of buying their way out of Purgatory (*Female Prelate*, 55); the cardinals' own approval of poisoning a heretic king, so that the Duke's accusation of Joan becomes the cause of her elevation to the Holy See (*Female Prelate*, 15). Abundance of occasions for anti-Papist speeches occur. The Duke declaims that "The blind Idolaters that kneel'd and yraye'd [sic] / To their deaf, senseless, molten Gods, were Saints / To this Church-Spawn; this Nest of Scarlet Tyrants" (*Female Prelate*, 17), and his Duchess observes upon "several Cardinals, crossing the Stage," that

> Now were I Confessor to these grave Lords,
> I would lay odds, there's not that Priest amonst 'em
> But has so great an Itch to be a Pope
> That on my Conscience he'd shake hands with Heaven
> And fairly quit his hopes of Crowns above,
> Proudly to lord it over Kings below.
>
> (*Female Prelate*, 3)

Settle stresses the overweening temporal ambition of the Church, its "lord[ing] it over Kings" to indicate that the proposed Exclusion Bill to deny James Stuart the throne is not an attack on monarchy as such. In his portrayal, the Church constitutes the threat; upon his arrest, the Duke says, "If I have done ill, I am a Sovereign Prince; / And faults of Princes stand accountable / Only to heaven; and that too not till Death: / But *Rome* can both depose and murder Kings" (*Female Prelate*, 19). Deposing and murdering kings, the crime of the Commonwealth, with which royalist propagandists such as Behn and Dryden repeatedly tried to equate the Whig opposition, is displaced onto Catholicism.

Protestant polemics since before Foxe frequently condemned the Pope's assumption of temporal authority as the original sin from which all the evils of Catholicism flowed. During the Exclusion Crisis, to avoid accusations that they were trying to reintroduce the social and political turmoil of the Interregnum, even the writers most hostile to the government professed their undying loyalty to Charles II, despite a deep anxiety about Papist machinations and the Duke of York. The combination of this variation on the old theme that the king can do no wrong with excoriation of the "Papal monarchy" resulted in a paradoxical situation in which every monarch's authority was divine except the one monarch whose succession was professedly apostolic. In *The Female Prelate*, Pope Joan and her persecuting yet amoral Church are equally contrary to nature. Though it has no direct agency in the plot, nothing actually to do, the supernatural enters, providing the audience with both spectacle and a visible spiritual sanction for their prejudices: "*Here the Ghost* [of the old Duke] *with his Taper touches a train of fire above him, which immediately writes upon the Wall, in Capital letters in a bloudy fire, the word MURDER; which continues burning some time*" (*Female Prelate*, 43). In its uniting of supernatural horror and a demonically feminized vision of Catholicism, *The Female Prelate* represents the shaping prehistory of the horror genre, which, as Maurice Levy has hypothesized, has a more intimate connection with the Glorious Revolution of 1688 than with the French Revolution.[65] At the heart of the gothic lies the irruption of the past into the present and the threatening isolation of the individual conscience in an alien environment. As English culture constructs the Catholic as the other par excellence, the sinister soul-devouring engine of Continental aggression against which the national identity defined itself, the position of the Duke of Saxony in the dungeons of Rome becomes paradigmatic of that of the gothic hero.[66] As in *Melmoth the Wanderer*, the antithesis of hope is to be "*in the prison of the Inquisition.*"[67] An upstart ruler like Tamburlaine, a great scholar like Faust, a machiavellian contriver like Barabas, Joan is a compound of triumphant Marlovian overreaching in a female form, as the Papacy itself overreaches in extending the spiritual dominion of the clergy into temporal power. Women and churches should be passive, the play overtly teaches, yet while embuing its villainess with such dynamism as to undercut the purported message.

The Female Prelate certainly does not portray clerical characters, as

Collier wished, in a favorable light. More fundamentally, its portrait of a deeply corrupt society in which authority is illegitimate and tyrannical corrodes assumptions of social deference. The term "subversive," though sometimes promiscuously used, is here appropriate. Violent, extravagant, and spectacular, *The Female Prelate* is exhuberantly (rabble)rousing popular entertainment, as befits a playwright who would go on to set up shop at Bartholomew Fair. If *City-Ramble* is a tragicomedy, *Pope Joan* is, like Thomas Shadwell's *The Libertine*, a black comedy, a blood and thunder farce-tragedy, and in its raucous ungentility antithetical to Collier's gentrification project for the stage. Settle riots in the failings of the "better sort," which Collier would have concealed lest they breed disrespect in their inferiors. There is one inherent limit, however, to Settle's radicalism. Like Webster and Ford in their Italianate tragedies before him, Settle, by placing his action at the heart of the notoriously decadent realm of the Papist Antichrist, of "the Kingdome of Darkness" in Hobbes's phrase, gains the freedom to depict limitless depravity because he can always profess that of course the English are not like that.[68] The price of that liberty, though, is that, by directing indignation against a foreign and heretical enemy, Settle opens his subversion of the Stuarts to cooptation by a strenuously Protestant English government which will assume the sacred role of national crusader against the Popish demon. Anti-Papism served as a potent mobilizing tool against the Stuarts, but thereafter, once the Glorious Revolution instituted precisely such a crusading regime, it served rather to legitimate than undercut the status quo, as the multiple 1689 editions of *Pope Joan* indicate. Like Middleton before him, but far more explicitly because of the rise of party politics, Settle was working for the opposition, and, when that opposition came to power, his critique of kingly power metamorphosed into an instrument of Parliamentary sovereignty. As a principal provocateur for the Whigs against the independent executive of the Stuarts, Settle was unknowingly preparing for his own exile to Bartholomew Fair, and neither the *Defense* nor *Farther Defense* could save him, the liberty of the stage, or ultimately even the fairgrounds to which he was driven in exile from the playhouses under a reconsolidated, resurgent, and silencing hegemony.

CHAPTER SIX

"Politeness *and* politics": *the literature of exclusion and the "true protestant heart"*

> By public police and economy I mean the due regulation and domestic order of the Kingdom, whereby the individuals of the state, like members of a well-regulated family, are bound to conform their general behavior to the rule of propriety, good neighborhood and good manners; to be decent, industrious in their respective stations.[1]

This study has been drawing connections among religion, literature, and the development of English and British – which are not the same thing – nationalisms. To speak largely, positing a hypothesis which need not be absolutized, the seventeenth-century pattern of Anglican hegemony and Dissenting resistance may be said in a sense to invert after the Glorious Revolution into a fusion of Protestant and nationalistic triumphalism on the one hand and the ambiguous alienation traditionally denominated "Tory satire" on the other.[2] Such a pattern, if given without qualification, is confessedly simplistic; Rose A. Zimbardo's contrast of the "deconstructive process" of Restoration satire to the promotion of "institutional stability, social cohesion, and nationalism" by "latitudinarian mimetic discourse" locates alienation already in court wits even before the Glorious Revolution.[3] In the following century, however, Swift's estrangement from the new establishment in religion leads directly to his embrace of the cause of England's first overseas colony, his native Ireland; he turns Irish patriot only after failing as an English statesman. As Islamic and Hindu fundamentalisms and the former Yugoslavia, not to mention Ireland itself, are demonstrating today, the origins of modern postcolonial nationalism can derive from a religious self-definition frequently deprecated as premodern. It is no longer easy to be confident that we know exactly what constitutes progress. Lyotard's observation of the continuity between "progress" and "development" finds striking exemplification in Defoe's *A Tour Through the Whole Island of Great Britain*, with its lumber-company view of trees as no more than "an inexhaustible store-house of timber."[4] Further, the narrative of progress is implicated not only in liberal capitalism, the "commercial republic" as the eighteenth century called it, but also in colonialism; Richard Steele accuses the *Examiner* of being "pleased to insinuate, that the Kingdom of *Ireland* is a Province under a Viceroy, and without taking notice that the Protestants of *Ireland* are our selves transplanted from *Great Britain*."[5] Catholic Irish go unmentioned in the context of rights because it goes without saying that as Papist foreigners they have none, just as James II "being Popish had no right to rule."[6] Gary Hentzi observes that Defoe's novels "reflect some of the most expansive and liberating impulses in eighteenth-century English culture, and simultaneously link those impulses to the culture's worst abuses."[7] Ines G. Zupanov notes that in colonial India, as in the New World, it was precisely the villains of the Whig narrative of progress, aristocrats secure in their own social position, who were willing to view non-European cultures with more sympathy than those who compensated for their fears of inferiority within their own society by projecting a corresponding inferiority onto other societies.[8] In its quintessentially modern erasure of local particulars in favor of universalizing principles defined by the metropolis, revolution can itself be an imperial idea.

Two competing visions of loyalty and national identity, dynastic and religious, struggle throughout the century between the Civil War and the final Jacobite challenge of 1745, and both assert their exclusive legitimacy. This chapter investigates some of the most politically active writers of the early eighteenth century, Swift, Addison, Defoe, and Fielding – two of whom, Defoe and Swift, define themselves primarily in religious terms, and all of whom have to deal with the chasm between English, loyal Protestantism and foreign, seditious Catholicism – to explore the definition and redefinition of politeness and literature, loyalty and disaffection, in a crucial period of transition for English politics and letters. Swift's *A Tale of a Tub*, for instance, and Defoe's *Religious Courtship* may be read against each other as alternative histories of legacy and legitimacy: male heirs of doctrine versus female heirs of conduct, an Anglican patrimonial coat versus a Dissenting matrimonial code. Consider three of Swift's works. *A Tale of a Tub* gives a genealogy of Christian sectarian divisions; *The Conduct of the Allies* analyzes a state at war; *A Complete Collection of Genteel and Ingenious Conversation* presents a chamber play in which nothing happens or is said. Except for the self-aggrandizing narrators of the first and last, these works might seem to have little in common besides their author. When placed together as a three-act suite, however, in their order of composition, they suggest a progressive evacuation of historical meaning. The *Tale* enacts a struggle between the dense past of its historical and theological references and the convoluted present of its text; the *Conduct* constructs a decontextualized present, a present whose authorship it ascribes to the socially destructive effects of generation-long warfare, as an economically defined alternative to the overpowering past of the *Tale*; and *Genteel and Ingenious Conversation* presents the consequence, a discourse of inanity and paralysis. Popery is at first the lesser of two religious enemies in a doctrinal enmity grown stale and farcical, then an irrelevance in the crisp computations of realpolitik, and at last an idea inconceivable in a hermetic isolation where ideas, imagination, and thought cannot intrude. It is Swift as a polemicist who explains the transition between the early and late "imaginative" works, and my examination of Swift consequently concentrates on his controversial writings.

I

A priest his whole adult life, Swift undertakes to defend his institution from its enemies, who seem more threateningly those who directly defy the Church's lingering aspirations to monopoly of worship than the proscribed Catholics. His position thus continues that of the Church of England under Charles II, as Irvin Ehrenpreis argues, but this High Church continuation after the Glorious Revolution becomes complicated by the problematic position of a Church designed as a ruling institution that is regarded with suspicion by a regime whose legitimacy is grounded in the repudiation of Restoration legitimism in favor of the Lockean social contract.[9] In *A Tale of a Tub*, Swift's formally evenhanded recognition of the equal deviance of Rome and "enthusiasm" from the true Anglican mean, but effectively greater concentration upon Jack as the ongoing threat, rather than the errors of Peter, reproduces the Anglican position of nearly any period of the seventeenth century except the reign of James II. His later works do not even attempt *A Tale*'s gesture toward balance; thus George Orwell's accusation, in an essay written shortly after the end of World War Two, that "there is a touch of quislingism in his [Swift's] attitude."[10] British patriotism defined itself originally against Papism, so that to be more concerned with internal struggles than with union against the Romish other is to call one's patriotism into question. Swift's stance, however, is best understood not as politically reactionary but as a defense of the institution to which he devoted his professional life; he de-emphasized Popery as an issue because fear of it was the principal weapon of adversaries of the High Church conception of the Church of England.[11]

For more than a century after his death Swift possessed the anomalous position of being an indisputably canonical author and yet a sinister, discomfiting figure. For Johnson, he was perverse and disagreeable in his habits of thinking, commonplace in style, and as a poet less worthy of commentary than Broome. In *The English Humorists*, Thackeray exaggerated this portrait into a grotesque of a miraculous ogre, the original yahoo, a genius to be sure but one whom nobody would wish to meet or still less resemble, the "moral" of *Gulliver's Travels* "horrible, shameful, unmanly, blasphemous."[12] Recently, the qualities that once made Swift suspect have attracted a more favorable notice, as critics have found a potentiality for resistance against strategies of domination in his "unmanly" refusal to underwrite oppression with mystification. The dimension I wish to add to this discussion is to examine Swift as simultaneously and successively an English resister of a nationalism harnessed to a party within his own (English) people and the first Irish writer to stir his (Irish) people to a national resistance against England's oldest overseas colonization project.[13] Whether as High Church Tory propagandist, Dean-Drapier demagogue, or pioneering novelist of the anti-novel, Swift evades linear logics of dominance and submission, narrative and convention, metropolis and colony. As Laura Brown observes, "Swift's travesty of true consciousness is the true radical political criticism"; but just as she finds his misogyny central to his critique of racism, so my examination argues that his resistance to imperialism has its origin not in any "progressive" impulse but in his hieraticism.[14]

With the fading of the inevitability of Whig order, what Ricardo Quintana called a number of years ago the "absurdly false view" of Swift as "irresistibly evil" can be joined in questionableness by the view of him as imbalanced.[15] When John Traugott writes, "Had he been a saner man, a Burnet or an Addison," he seems oblivious to what contemporaries would have noticed immediately as the obvious difference between him and them: that he was a Tory propagandist and they were Whig ones.[16] In a similar vein, F. P. Lock has observed that "Swift had the misfortune to be a 'natural' Tory who held certain moderate 'Whig' intellectual convictions ... Temperament would finally triumph over intellectual conviction."[17] This late in the twentieth century, it is no longer enough to equate a "moderate," central Whiggism with sanity and intellectual conviction in opposition to a marginalized Toryism virtually senseless in its effeminate passion. The classic instance of such a marginalizing strategy remains Macaulay's essays on Samuel Johnson, but it has its origins in an earlier political rhetoric that positioned power as the self-evident "sense of the nation" and opposition as sedition. If historical meaning is, in Swift's view, evacuated from the rationalistic Whig world, the reason for that view lies, not in his being irrational, but in the dispossession of the Anglican clergy from their monopoly as an organ of interpreting and thereby creating meaning.

An ability to ensure stability is the prime requisite of any government. Throughout the late seventeenth and early eighteenth centuries, an absence of consensus upon legitimacy, in the conflict between monarchical and religious principles, "divine right" versus "true religion," recurrently climaxes in crises which undermine and sometimes overthrow regimes. In the resulting unsettled atmosphere, governments from Charles II to George I all sustained their power by frequent invocations of subversive conspiracies. Joyce Lee Malcolm writes how "Endless alarms of plots" were used after the Restoration to keep "militia on a war footing" and arms restricted;[18] Joseph McMinn notes that Swift's "favorite tactic" in the *Examiner* "is to characterize all critics as conspirators";[19] and Paul S. Fritz has observed how Whig ministers after 1715 felt, besides "genuine fears, an acute awareness of the political advantages to be gained from a careful exploitation of such fears."[20] In *The Vindication of the Duke of Guise*, Dryden asserts that "Our Liberties and our Religion both are safe, they are secur'd to us by the Laws, and those Laws are executed under an establish'd Government, by a Lawful King. The Defender of our Faith, is the Defender of our Common Freedom ... the Sorbonists were the Original, and our Schismatiques in England were Copiers of Rebellion."[21] Equating opposition with subversion and Dissent with Catholicism, Dryden makes the fate of France's Henry IV the model for that of Charles I, and extends the parallel to the Popish Plot, observing that "there is a *Faction here*, which is like that other that was in *France*."[22] The most vehement denouncers of Popery are revealed to be equivalent to Papists in their disloyalty. Dryden has on his side the great fact of possession, enabling him to assert that by not "altering the *Succession*" Charles II "not only preserv'd our present quiet, but secur'd the Peace of our Posterity."[23] After the "abdication," as it was called, of James II, the Tories cease to be the party of the status quo, and after the accession of George I a pamphlet, possibly by Defoe, can argue that the Whigs are the only party the monarch can trust.[24] Nor was this pamphleteer the only person to hold such an opinion; for half a century, George I and II followed his prescription.[25]

As Roger Schmidt has recently observed, Jacobitism has moved from a peripheral to a central position in eighteenth-century studies.[26] The fiction of James II's abdication provided a convenient rationale for those who wished to deny that any change of loyalties had occurred between

1688 and 1689 besides the normal succession of one ruler to another. If William III were nominated to a throne vacated by James's flight, then one could support hierarchal stability and deference but also the Glorious Revolution. As well as being generally useful for preserving the mystique of power, this reasoning, the one officially adopted at the beginning of William's reign, was particularly convenient for persons who had publicly supported James until his fall. Such persons abounded in the Church of England, not because the clergy were necessarily more duplicitous than others but because it was an integral aspect of their function to propagandize in pulpit and in print for whoever held power. To use the words of Dr. Archibald Cameron, the last Jacobite to be executed, in 1753, for his beliefs, "the principles of Christian loyalty" needed to be shown adaptable to non-Stuarts to maintain the illusion of a divine sanction for earthly social arrangements.[27] Ian Gilmour observes that the Whigs adopted the view of the Tory Bishop who said in the debate on the impeachment of Sacheverell that "the legality of resistance in some extraordinary cases . . . 'ought to be kept from the knowledge of the people, who are naturally too apt to resist.'"[28] To deny all resistance would be to deny the "revolution settlement," which would be treasonous, but to support resistance as an ongoing possibility would encourage popular discontents.

Gilbert Burnet supplies an example of a churchman who had written in support of the Stuarts and then of their successors. In his "Gunpowder-treason Day" (November 5) sermon of 1710, the year of the Sacheverell trial and riots, he justifies his consistency and integrity. After condemning Guy Fawkes for "so diabolical a Plot" inspired by "the restless Spirit of Popery," Burnet condemns James as intent like Fawkes on "Subversion of our Constitution . . . He put Judges, Sheriffs, and Magistrates, who were under legal Incapacities, into all Imployments; all their Proceedings were so many Nullities: So the whole Justice and Government of the Land was broke into, and even the calling a legal Parliament to redress all was impossible; all Returns made by such Officers were null and void."[29] As Burnet's purpose is not to excite hostility to Papism so much as to supply a legalistic defense of the Revolution and his own consistency – not to excite at all but to lull the audience – he stresses the fact of the disability and passes over its consisting in the Catholicism of those officers. After expressing a due horror of "*Usurpers*" (10), he continues that "a Prince who supercedes the Law, and acts in Defiance to it, becomes plainly a Usurper," and thus his "*withdrawing himself* . . . after a Course of illegal Government" is "Abdication" (11) – unlike the flight of Charles II, who had made no "illegal Pretension to be above the Law" (12). James, not

William, is the usurper. To avoid a parallel with the Long Parliament, Burnet omits mention of Charles I, the "royal martyr," who nonetheless was charged with "illegal Pretension" similar to that of James. Burnet concludes his defense of the alteration in regimes by asserting that "the Revolution" is "a continued Usurpation to this Day, if these Principles are not true: All the Oaths taken to support it are so many solemn Perjuries" (12); in other words, to differ from him is to incite rebellion and commit treason. He then moves from the general case to a defense of himself in particular. "About forty Years ago," writing against Dissenters,

I made this the main Subject of the Debate, That a Magistrate governing by Law was not to be resisted upon the Account of Religion: And being at that Time of the same Perswasion that I continue in to this Day, I did in plain Terms express it, (p. 16) *In case the Magistrate be Furious, or desert his Right, or expose his Kingdom to the Fury of others, the Laws and Sense of all Nations agree, that the States of the Land are to be the Administrators of the Power.* And (p. 17) *The Case varies very much when the Abuse is such, that it tends to a total Subversion; which may be justly called a Phrenzy, since no Man is capable of it till he is under some Lision of his Mind; in which Case the Power is to be administer'd by others, for the Prince and his People's Safety.* (12–13)

His quotations from himself address more a case of royal madness than a difference between the executive and legislature – George III, not James II – but simply to admit that he had been wrong or hypocritical would compromise not only his own integrity but the claim of English institutions to the legitimacy granted by continuity, despite the Glorious Revolution. The oppositional Whiggism of the Stuart period has become concerned with proving its pedigree, but Burnet is also expressing an ongoing commitment to the Church to which he has devoted his life. The second of the *Two Sermons* in his pamphlet endorses the war party's object of conquering Spain as part of a Protestant crusade, but begins its concluding paragraph with the double wish that "May the Protestant Religion and the Protestant Succession be for ever Secured! And may *the Church of England by Law established ever continue and flourish among us!*" (32, emphasis in original). The function of the Church of England as an upholder of the government, any government – with the proviso that it be Protestant added after 1688 – made for many a Vicar of Bray in the seventeenth century.

II

Swift's assertion that his zealousness for the Church is what alienated him from the Whigs thus deserves to be considered more seriously than it has been. It is this distinction between secular and religious politics that makes possible the radical divergence in the views of him by F. P. Lock and Perry Anderson on the one side and Carole Fabricant and Ellen Pollak on the other. Lock calls Swift a "crypto-Jacobite" and deems him "conservative, even reactionary" in favoring an "alliance of church and state"[30] where Pollak sees in Swift a "place to stand for leverage (however precarious that place may be), in the ongoing project of unraveling – and undoing – the ideological grounds of patriarchy as we know it in the West."[31] Carole Fabricant argues,

I can't help thinking that Swift, were he alive today, would readily find his bearings in many of the debates about modernism and postmodernism, in the *New Left Review,* and would be able to contribute to them in ways that would perhaps surprise Perry Anderson not a little, forcing him to recant his identification of Swift with a Tory reactionism that "meant the triumph of bigotry, hierarchy, authority, [and] legitimacy in early 18th-century England."[32]

Where the two men read Swift's clerical politics and see that, with most Anglican clergy, he longed for a strengthening of the church, the two women, like Brown, perceive his discontent and contradictory ideological position. The "Bangorian Controversy" in 1717 resulted in the suppression of Convocation until 1852, a suppression almost as long as that of the Estates General of France before 1789, and one with the same purpose: to silence an institution deemed threatening to the government.[33] The High Church position, although reactionary and authoritarian, seemed dangerous because it suggested the potential for an independent power in the state. It is because of his grounding in this alternative power structure that Swift is able to make what Fabricant calls his "often incisive critique of the country house ideal" of "'power houses – the houses of a ruling class'"; he appears to "stand as a witness to the radically provisional nature of all human structures, creations, and would-be solutions" because he speaks from the vantage of a defeated "human structure," the Church, and against the "would-be solutions" of those who had defeated it.[34] The contemporary battle of the ancients and moderns over Swift, where Fabricant's postmodernist contends with Will Brantley's "reactionary in more ways than one," results from partial readings that may be reconciled.[35] Swift is a radical *because* he is a reactionary.[36]

The relevance of Popery to all these intra-Protestant disputes is that the Catholic Church provided both a pre-eminent example of a church independent of the state and a limit for debate, a boundary beyond which no argument could penetrate. Papistical tendencies re-emerged obsessively as the ultimate insult and sanction; if an argument or doctrine could be persuasively identified as tainted with Catholicism it was discredited.

When the immediate threat of James II had passed, the old feud between high and low church factions resumed, but with the balance of power decisively altered. The anti-sacerdotalism of Benjamin Hoadly, the Bishop of Bangor, caused an uproar not because it had never been heard of but precisely because it was an all too familiar Dissenting argument against the Church of England – only now a bishop was voicing it, with the full backing of the government. It is, indeed, Milton's case in *Of True Religion* translated to a cathedral: "When you are secure of your integrity before God, and of your sincere disposition to search after His will, and to receive the truth in the love of truth, whensoever and from whomsoever it is offered, this will, I confess, lead you, as it ought all of us, not to be afraid of the terrors of man, or the vain words of regular and uninterrupted succession."[37] Hoadly transforms religion from a doctrinal matter suitable for clerical formulation, and dissemination to believers, to a matter of individual choice, "whensoever and from whomsoever it is offered," implicitly denying the clergy any special role. Whereas under Charles I such a dissolution of doctrine undermined the basis of a confessional state, however, when Hoadly wrote the church he undercut was a bulwark of opposition to the regime. Toleration is being preached, but by authority, and when lesser clergy object the government takes punitive action. The very title of Hoadly's 1716 tract, *Preservative against the Principles and Practices of the Non-jurors, both in Church and State; or, an Appeal to the Conscience and Common-sense of the Christian Laity*, echoes those of Anglican anti-Papist pamphlets such as William Sherlock's 1688 *A Preservative against Popery* and a 1715 publication of similar title.[38] In response, Andrew Snape, one of the High Church attackers of Hoadly, revives the old charge of Jesuits in disguise:

> Before you are so free then, in casting Reproaches on others as *Popishly* affected; you would do well to put away the *Jesuit* whom you entertain in your Family . . . His putting on the Air of a *Free-Thinker*, is so far from being a Proof of his Conversion, that it is to me a sure Evidence of the contrary, and gives me the same Impression, as if I saw him officiating at *High-Mass*.
>
> 'Tis one of the known and stale Artifices of that Politick Fraternity, to personate all Characters, to appear in every Shape and Dress, in order to promote their main Design, the Subversion of the Church of *England*: Which they have always felt to be the Grand Bulwark of the *Reformation*, and the Mound that keeps out the Inundation of *Popery* from once more overflowing all Europe.[39]

Popery was a charge that anyone could make, but not everyone could equally make it stick. As both Monmouth's Rebellion in 1685 and the Gordon Riots in 1780 were able to mobilize the population by appeals to fears of Catholicism, Gilmour reports "inappropriate shouts of 'No Popery'" from 1710 "'Church and King'" rioters.[40] What made those shouts "inappropriate," though, was the improbability of associating the Whigs, with their fervent Protestant and patriotic rhetoric, with Popery. High Church Tories, on the other hand, since the Glorious Revolution had become doubly vulnerable to both accusations of "crypto-Jacobitism" and the older Puritan suspicion of crypto-Papism.[41]

Snape attempts to revive the old royalist riposte that those cunning Jesuits hide most where most incongruous, but as a bishop and governmental pamphleteer Hoadly was far less vulnerable to allegations of subversiveness than the opposition writers whom Dryden compared to partisans of the good old cause. Snape resurrects the Anglican association of disaffection toward the Church of England with Jesuit intrigues; instead of being able to count on governmental support, however, Snape lost his position as Chaplain in Ordinary to His Majesty for his opposition to Hoadly, who went on to further promotion in the Church. High Church sentiments were no longer synonymous with but antagonistic to "loyalty" to a crown defined by Protestantism after 1688. Snape's attempts to turn the Popery charge onto his opponent, maintaining the argument on seventeenth-century sectarian grounds, then, fail because the Whig union of patriotism and Protestantism at that century's end enables Hoadly to consolidate issues of national and religious loyalty. The Bangorian controversy demonstrates how politically marginalized the High Church cause is after 1715. In his pamphleteering for the Tory ministry of Oxford and Bolingbroke late in Anne's reign, Swift abandons the traditional Anglican parallel of Nonconformists and Papists as equally contradictory to the unique loyalty of the Church of England, based on its subservience to the state, changing the terms of the debate to the economics of war. He attempts to relocate the argument in response to a situation where the opposition is as likely to occupy an archbishopric, as in the Convocation controversy at the start of the century, as a Dissenting chapel. Nonetheless, for all the effectiveness of his polemic, his critique of the Whigs does not entirely escape the necessity of an anchoring, like Snape's, in the fact of possession. Like Dryden after 1688, Swift after 1715 can no longer articulate a counter-rationale of rule in opposition to the Whig machine, but, unlike Dryden, he does begin to articulate a strategy of resistance.

In his writings for the Tories, Swift develops a sophisticated argument to discredit Whig imperialistic ideology, but it has the weakness of requiring an insider position, that like Dryden in *The Vindication of the Duke of Guise* he speak on behalf of the crown; after the Hanoverian succession, this weakness proved fatal.[42] This insistence on his loyalty, and insinuation that the opposition is disloyal, was the staple of Restoration royalist logic, but after 1688 it had the weakness that whoever captured the throne could then make the same point, as indeed, after the death of Anne, Addison did in the *Freeholder* – as well as the Parliamentary Whigs with their treason inquests. To the extent that his argument is inherited and unoriginal it is imperilled. What is new in Tory argument after a generation of Whig rule is the attack on corruption, which would remain a recurrent theme in eighteenth-century England, ruled as it was by the bribery-driven system of aristocratic despotism under the form of Parliamentary democracy that would come to be called Old Corruption. By attacking the "moneyed interest," the financial-military complex as it were, in the name of both loyalty and the landed interest, Swift is drawing upon the rationales of both seventeenth-century Stuart royalists and eighteenth-century oppositions.

In Swift's period as a governmental propagandist, *The Examiner, The Conduct of the Allies*, and other tracts from early in the Tory administration buoyantly assume that public and power are with him. Only slightly later, *The History of the Four Last Years of the Queen* attempts to present a polemical history of 1712–13, but first the ministry and later, in the 1720s and 1730s, English friends discourage its appearance, thinking the sentiments imprudent, so that it did not appear until more than a decade after his death. His engagement in pamphlet warfare continues into the latter period of the Tory administration, after he went to occupy his Deanship of St. Patrick's, only to be recalled in weeks to assist the government. Except for "The Importance of the Guardian," the later pieces have a defensive tone and lack the high-spirited exaltation of the earlier; the last are largely devoted to justifications of the policy of a ministry already wobbling or fallen. Thereafter Swift's openly political publications deal with Irish topics. Collectively these works enact a rhetoric of mastery, witness its wavering and collapse, then set out to reconstruct it into one of resistance. He is in his element on the attack. After aspiring to restore Toryism as the natural party of government following what the *Examiner* represents as a twenty-year interregnum of Whig power founded on perpetual warfare (like the earlier Commonwealth), Swift concedes the metropolis to the "moneyed interest" he had decried and settles for defending Ireland from its depredations.

The first *Examiner* to be written by Swift, issue 13, quotes the same two lines from Lucan's *Pharsalia* as Francis Bacon's essay, "Of Seditions and Troubles," and provides a translation as well into contemporary fiscal

jargon. *"Hinc usura Vorax, avidumque in temore foenus, Hinc concussa fides, &*
multis utile bellum" becomes *"Hence are derived those exorbitant Interests and*
Annuities; hence those large Discounts for Advances and prompt Payment; hence publick
Credit is shaken, and hence great Numbers find their Profit in prolonging the War."[43]
The quotation appears early in Bacon's essay, which is with "Of True
Greatness of Kingdoms and Estates" and "Of Gardens" one of his three
longest, to illustrate a discussion of "the materials of seditions ... The
matter of seditions is of two kinds, much poverty and much discontent-
ment. It is certain, so many overthrown estates, so many votes for troubles
... This same *multis utile bellum* is an assured and infallible sign of a state
disposed to seditions and troubles."[44] The purpose of *The Examiner* was to
persuade the nation to quit a successful but long and expensive war, and in
his first issue Swift sets forth the overarching rationale of the case for peace
– that the war has been both ruinous to the nation and profitable to great
numbers, who are prolonging it for their own purposes. Whereas the
Glorious Revolution broke the power of the crown by uniting the nation
against Popery and tyranny, Swift attempts to free the crown of Whig
domination by dividing this alliance, distinguishing the interest of landholders from that of commercial elements, whom he characterizes as war
profiteers: "for it is a desperate case, if those that hold with the proceeding
of the state be full of discord and faction, and those that are against it be
entire and united," as Bacon noted.[45] The true tyranny under which
England is suffering, Swift argues, is one not of Papists but of Whig
swindlers. Swift's division between virtuous landholders and a corrupt
clique reproduces in reversed form the opposition's logic of the Exclusion
Crisis, when, as Richard Ashcraft notes, "Whig election propaganda ...
appeal[led] to the nation to support 'the industrious' rather than the 'court
parasites' or 'pensioners.'"[46] In Swift's account, "'the industrious'" have
become the "'parasites.'"

Examiner 13 begins by announcing its author's largeminded practice of
"convers[ing] in equal Freedom with the deserving Men of both Parties."
It then grieves that he has been forced to suspend this impartiality because
"several of my Acquaintance, among the declining Party, are grown so
insufferably Peevish and Splenetick" that, "instead of hearkning to further
Complaints, [he will] employ some Part of this Paper for the future, in
letting such Men see, that their natural or acquired Fears are ill-grounded,
and their artificial ones as ill-intended" (*Works*, 3.3). As his argument
develops, this division of fears into different kinds divides Whigs into the
naive or deceived and the dishonest, so that an honest Whig is "a fool
among knaves."[47] The specifics follow of "some specious Objections,

which I have heard repeated by well-meaning Men, just as they had taken them up on the Credit of others, who have worse Designs": changing the ministry in time of war, offending a victorious general, "spiriting the *French*," injuring credit and stocks, with, "lastly, That, all this naturally tends to break the Settlement of the Crown, and call over the *Pretender*" (*Works*, 3.4). At this point, having summarized the opposition's argument, he quotes Lucan about how *"great Numbers find their Profit in prolonging the War,"* thereby at once identifying himself as learned and them as dissentious, then explains the averseness of the previous administration to peace by suggesting:

Let any Man observe the Equipages in this Town; he shall find the greater Number of those who make a Figure, to be a Species of Men quite different from any that were ever known before the Revolution; consisting either of Generals and Colonels, or of such whose whole Fortunes lie in Funds and Stocks: So that *Power*, which according to the old Maxim, was used to follow *Land*, is now gone over to *Money*; and the Country Gentleman is in the Condition of a young Heir, out of whose Estate a Scrivener receives half the Rents for Interest, and hath a Mortgage on the Whole; and is therefore always ready to feed his Vices and Extravagancies while there is any Thing left. (*Works*, 3.5)

In an argument that anticipates such American critics of military spending as Noam Chomsky, Swift maintains that war is not an ideological crusade or a display of national glory but a business, lucrative to an inner circle but destructive to national prosperity. Swift reviews recent history "as high as the Revolution" (*Works*, 3.5), which he approves as a "Necessity," but which was followed by "an under Sett of men" who "found means to whisper in the King's Ear" against the Church of England and for running up debts. Swift shifts the terms of debate from the inspiring declared ends of the war policy to its immediate effects, placed of course in the most invidious light. The remainder of the essay develops the idea that the war has been pursued and protracted solely as "a Complication of Knavery and Couzenage" (*Works*, 3.7). The Whigs would devour England's landholders as England would Ireland in *A Modest Proposal*.

It is impossible to give a single character to all the succeeding *Examiners*, because they respond to the shifting demands of the political moment, but excoriation of the preceding ministry as a corrupt and disaffected faction, praise of the present ministry as selfless patriots, and contrasts of lying opponent scribblers to his own integrity recur as the chief themes. As much might be said of nearly any governmental gazetteer; differences lie in details, but nonetheless the effect rarely goes beyond what a journeyman of controversy might produce. For a clerical pamphleteer, Swift is relatively sparing of religious discussions, and when he does address such issues the result seems at first studiedly conventional. Only two numbers focus on religion. *Examiner* 21 condemns "that Inundation of Atheism, Infidelity, Prophaneness, and Licentiousness which were like to overwhelm us" only to celebrate "how the People joined with the Q∪EEN's Endeavours to divert this Flood" (*Works*, 3.49), and number 42 praises how, in contrast to "when every Session of Parliament was like a Cloud hanging over their [clerics'] Heads" the present Parliament has ordered fifty churches built, for "somewhat *under* the Price of a *Subject's Palace*" (*Works*, 3.158–59) – that is, Marlborough's Blenheim. As in the secular papers, "the *Ruined Party*" (*Works*, 3.64, *Examiner* 24) is a scheming gang of plunderers. Both condemnation of irreligion and praise of churchbuilding are as inoffensive to a general audience as clerical issues could well be: Swift is being carefully competent, not aggressively slashing as on secular issues. Because religious issues are so sensitive, aggression would be dangerous, possibly offending more than persuading.

Although only the two issues center on religion, the subject crops up briefly with increasing frequency in the course of rebutting Whig assertions "that the Design of the present Parliament and Ministry, was to bring in *Popery, Arbitrary Power*, and the *Pretender.*" *Examiner* 25 mentions the accusations only to ridicule them as less likely than "that some late Men had strong Views towards a *Commonwealth*, and the Alteration of the *Church*" (*Works*, 3.69, *Examiner* 25), propositions which the rest of the paper fancifully elaborates, but with much more heed to political issues than to ecclesiastical. As Popery had become less a religious antagonist than a codeword for Continental despotism in Restoration anti-royalist pamphlets, Swift is maintaining the discussion at the same secularized level, but attempting to turn its point.

[T]hat baffled Question, *Why was the late Ministry changed?* . . . [is] as trifling as that of the Papists, when they ask us, *Where was our Religion before* Luther? And indeed, the Ministry was changed for the same Reason that Religion was reformed; because a thousand Corruptions had crept into the *Discipline* and *Doctrine* of the *State*, by the Pride, the Avarice, the Fraud, and the Ambition of those *who administered to us in Secular Affairs.* (*Works*, 3.95, *Examiner* 29)

By analogizing the contemporary political situation with the Reformation, by applying the logic and terms of Protestant attacks on Catholic corruption to secular corruption, Swift historicizes English religion in a manner antithetical to the transhistorical teleologizing of the present in Foxe's *Acts and Monuments* and its successors in Protestant polemic. Catholicism remains unmitigatedly evil, but in a way no different from an evil much closer and more familiar, the late ministry, rather than being uniquely and radically depraved. In Swift's writings, Catholicism is an historical actor like any other. Similarly, in the next number differences among "those who wish well to the Publick" are fomented by "our Men of *incensed Moderation*," "which, although it be an old Practice, hath been much improved in the Schools of the *Jesuits*; who when they despaired of perverting this Nation to *Popery*, by Arguments or Plots against the State, sent their Emissaries to subdivide us into Schisms" (*Works*, 3.98, 3.97, *Examiner* 30). From adapting an argument of the Reformation to present purposes, Swift moves to employ one of the Restoration, the royalist allegation that Jesuits encouraged the multiplication of sects, though he drops the colorful addition of a Jesuit's implication in the beheading of Charles I. The work of a religious policy void of integrity becomes that of a political one equally abandoned.

Further essays continue the equation of Whig and Papist machinations. In *Examiner* 32, Swift has the opportunity to react to an event that can hardly help but create sympathy for the government, an attempted assassination of Robert Harley "in the Execution of his Office, by the Hand of a *French Papist*, then under Examination for High Treason" (*Works*, 3.106). A treasonous French Papist is the ideal villain, of course, because a French Papist is doubly an hereditary enemy, and if a traitor is trebly abominable: the target of such a fiend must be a patriot. Swift summarily sketches a history of assassinations, then quickly proceeds to observe, "Had such an Accident happened under that [the previous] Ministry . . . This would have been styled a *High-Church Principle*; the Clergy would have been accused as Promoters and Abettors of the Fact . . . But, the present Men in Power hate and despise all such detestable Arts"; despite this disclaimer, though, he ends up noting how "the *High-flying Whigs*, and the Friends of *France* . . . join in [seeking] the Destruction of the same Man" (*Works*, 3.108–9). Although the Whigs are not in actual league with France or Papists, a charge that would be extremely difficult to make stick against the Low Church war party, they are becoming indistinguisable from them.

In a like manner, *Examiner* 39 investigates Whig allegations of "our endeavouring to introduce *Popery*, *Arbitrary Power*, and the *Pretender* . . . As to *Popery*, which is the first of these; to deal plainly, I can hardly think there is any Sett of Men among us, except the Professors of it, who have any direct Intention to introduce it here: But the Question is, whether the Principles and Practices of us, or the *Whigs*, be most likely to make Way for it?" (*Works*, 3.143, *Examiner* 39). By 1711, James II has been gone for a generation, and Catholics have long been a proscribed and powerless minority, as Swift several times observes, so that he can plausibly assert that suspicion of Popery is no longer relevant to the political situation as it actually exists. He then again parallels Jesuit attempts to multiply sects with Whig attacks on "*the Church Established* . . . As if Places would go a begging, unless *Brownists, Familists, Sweet-Singers, Quakers, Anabaptists* and *Muggletonians*, would take them off our Hands." Whig "*Liberty of Conscience*" is "the very Counter-part of the late King *James's* Design"; if the Whigs exclude Papists they outdo James in allowing freethinkers, and "it is agreed by the Learned, that there is but a very narrow Step from *Atheism*, to the other Extream, *Superstition*" (*Works*, 3.143–44, *Examiner* 39). The argument here is the same as the one climaxing the 1708 *Argument against Abolishing Christianity*: "the abolishment of the Christian religion will be the readiest course we can take to introduce popery."[48] As in that piece, Swift is neither speaking entirely seriously nor expecting to be regarded as doing so. While he is earnest in defending the Church, to deflect Whig appeals to Protestant chauvinism it is necessary that the menace of Popery be made to seem less urgent, though in the ministerial periodical it is not the joke it became in the *Argument*. Like *A Tale of a Tub*, the *Examiner* addresses two seemingly opposite religious threats, Whig assaults on the Church and the Popish peril, but the first is real and immediate, the second a phantom. Near the end of his tenure as editor he explicitly dismisses Catholicism as "a *weak, remote Enemy*" to combat which "we took a *nearer* and a *stronger* into the *House*." He allows that "*Popery* and *Slavery* are without doubt the greatest and most dreadful of any [threat]; but I may venture to affirm, that the Fear of these, have not, at least since the *Revolution*, been so close and pressing upon us, as that from *another Faction*; excepting only one short Period, when the Leaders of that very Faction, invited the abdicating King to return" (*Works*, 3.166–67, *Examiner* 43). After that brief concession, however, he pushes quickly on to more congenial matters. As in royalist responses to the anti-Popery agitation of the Exclusion Crisis, Catholicism is an acknowledged evil but not the significant one; and Swift reinforces that argument by associating, like Snape, the opposition with Papism. Junto members who invite James II back resemble Snape's Low Church Hoadly who harbors a Jesuit in his house, or the tonsured regicides of Restoration legend – but Swift's version is secularized. The actions and actors are not religious but political, and the two are not the same.[49]

Although employing inherited religious arguments, Swift incorporates them into a political framework changed by twenty years of toleration and war. The *Examiner* condemns "Malcontents" who "bawl out *Popery*,

Persecution, Arbitrary Power, and *the Pretender*" (*Works*, 3.34, *Examiner* 18) as disloyal to Queen Anne, and attacks the party cohesion of "these very Sons of *Moderation* [who] were pleased to *excommunicate* every Man who disagreed with them in the smallest *Article* of their *Political Creed*" (*Works*, 3.39, *Examiner* 19); it instances the Act of Union, of which it was illegal to disapprove, in a transparent analogy, and the inherent Caesarism or Cromwellism of a general for life. In a list of enormities imagined to be passed by Parliament should the Whigs regain control the final item is: "Resolved, *That for a King or Queen of this Realm, to Read or Examine a Paper brought them to be signed by a* Junta *Minister, is Arbitrary and Illegal; and a Violation of the Liberties of the People*" (*Works*, 3.72, *Examiner* 25). This outrage is of course recognizable as modern constitutional monarchy, in which the crown is free to read but not to alter – but the Parliament that elects ministers is only partially democratic, giving point to the allegation of a "Junta." Swift's repeated charge that the Whigs are a "faction" intent on monopolizing power who are more "linked to a certain Sett of *Persons*, than any certain Sett of *Principles*" (*Works*, 3.165, *Examiner* 43) reflects his recognition of a new system of politics arising. The Whigs he attacks are the first modern party, dominating the crown rather than dominated by it, and controlled by political entrepreneurs of a sort who would become familiar throughout the eighteenth century.

In his indictment, which reaches its most ample expansion in *The Conduct of the Allies*, the two components of the Whig party are a cabal of swindlers and a mob of their gulls:

But the common Question is, If we must now Surrender Spain, what have we been fighting for all this while? The Answer is ready; We have been Fighting for the Ruin of the Publick Interest, and the Advancement of a Private. We have been fighting to raise the Wealth and Grandeur of a particular Family; to enrich Usurers and Stock-jobbers; and to cultivate the pernicious Designs of a Faction, by destroying the Landed-Interest. The Nation begins now to think these *Blessings* are not worth Fighting for any longer, and therefore desires a Peace. (*Works*, 6.58–59)

If in *Examiner* 13 we see the beginning statement of Swift's case for peace, in *The Conduct of the Allies* we see its culmination, and in this case religion has no part. Since Swift endured unusually close ministerial supervision of this influential pamphlet, it is impossible to know whether the entire exclusion of religion was his own idea, but, regardless, it is a shrewd one. Because the *Examiner* had a general charge of condemning the previous administration and extolling the present one, there was little it did not have occasion to touch on; the Sacheverell trial and the election were recent. *The Conduct of the Allies* has a single issue to address, and directs all its energies to exposing faithless allies and the suspicious intimacies of a government whose continuance the Dutch and the Bank of England had actively supported. There was no need to insult Dissenters. Enthusiasm for the "Protestant interest," as it had once been called, slips from being the tool of greedy politicians to invisibility, to being implicitly dismissed as irrelevant. In his writings for the Tory ministry under Queen Anne, Swift makes a definitive final statement of legitimist ideology as an alternative to religious and national chauvinism and the imperial ambition that feeds on those chauvinisms. To the rage of the Whigs, the War of the Spanish Succession was ended without total victory.

As Dissenters are a greater threat than Papists in Swift's account in the *Examiner,* so too there are even some allusions to the Civil War, though naturally not nearly so many as when that conflict was fresh in living memory. Like Dryden and other royalist polemicists of thirty years before, Swift presents himself as the champion of loyalty and orthodoxy, but by his repeated mentions of the great Tory majority in the House of Commons he appeals to popular as well as royal sovereignty against a narrow oligarchy. Once George I was king and the alarm of the 1715 Jacobite attempt had allowed the Whigs to consolidate their power, both the popular and royal halves of the legitimating stance of representing crown and people against a Junto were denied him. In exile and under government displeasure, Swift evolved from being the prophet of the eighteenth-century opposition rhetoric of corruption to introduce a discourse of resistance to colonialism to the European metropolis. It is precisely his being a "reactionary," however, his anchoring in an alternative rhetoric of power to that of Enlightenment reason and progress, that enables him to articulate opposition to the emerging imperial regime.

This opposition takes form when, in his Irish tracts, Swift reformulates the relation between England and Ireland from a sectarian divide between virtuous Protestants and evil Catholics that reinforces and sanctifies the national division between English and Irish to an economic model of the illegitimate exploitation of a colony by the metropolitan power. The first of the "Drapier's Letters" opens by declaring that "What I intend now to say to you, is, next to your Duty to God, and the Care of Salvation, of the greatest Concern to your selves, and your Children; your *Bread* and *Cloathing,* and every common Necessary of Life entirely depend on it."[50] "Duty to God" is not at issue; "*Bread* and *Cloathing*" are. The enemy Swift proclaims is not a religion but "*a mean ordinary Man, a Hard-Ware Dealer*" who "was able to attend constantly [at court] for his own Interest; he is an ENGLISHMAN and had GREAT FRIENDS, and it seems knew *very well where to give Money*" (*Works*, 10.4, 5). Mr. Wood, that is, is an ally of a corrupt cabal and thus occupies the same position in the "Drapier's Letters" as the moneyed interest in Swift's ministerial writings – with the crucial addition of a national difference. The plunderers are now battening on Ireland, not on the English "landed interest." By changing the terms of debate in Ireland from religion to money, Swift undercuts the Whig government's chief propaganda weapon, altering the center of discussion from divisive issues that drive Irish Protestants, including most of the upper classes, to ally with England against their compatriots to a national interest that unites all Irish against the English regime. His crucial ideological achievement is to substitute a narrative of national suffering for that of Protestant suffering. In his Irish pamphlets as in his English, he inverts the position of Whiggism, presenting its self-styled champions of liberty as oppressors, but in the Irish context this maneuver metamorphoses from a partisan device into an almost accidental call to national awakening.[51]

III

Addison's *Freeholder* in 1715–16, like Swift's *Examiner* in 1710–11, is a government periodical that develops a rationale to justify a new ministry and discredit the previous one. Covertly in his moralizing journalism as overtly in this political publication, Addison modulates seventeenth-century anti-papistical, anti-monarchical demagoguery into eighteenth-century consumerism – including its diminution of women into objects of fetishization – and assists in secularizing the rationale of gentry power. As Swift's Irish polemics later establish points of resistance against English colonialism, so the writings of his years at the center of English political life are devoted to demythologizing the Whig ideological structures of nationalism, imperialism, and the construction of religion as their servant. Addison's work is effectively a Whig reply. The *Tatler* and *Spectator* profess an absence of partisan motive during the period of Tory government, but indirectly pursue the agenda later explicitly laid out in *The Freeholder*. Whereas Swift's project breaks in two, however, when applied to practical politics, the rights of the crown and of the Irish fragmenting into separate resistances though they share a common opponent, Addison creates an integrated ideology of domestic and imperial dominion.

Like the conversion and accession of James II earlier, the 1715 invasion of the Pretender energized Whig rhetoric and lent plausibility to their reiteration of the identity of Popery and tyranny. The facade of genial good sense, which Swift repeatedly employs in order to expose the insane self-aggrandizement lurking underneath it in works from the early *Tale of a Tub* to *A Modest Proposal* and *Polite and Genteel Conversation*, is Addison's habitual mode in earnest. In *The Freeholder*, however, we find Addison dispensing with indirectness and making a case in which Catholicism plays a major yet, as his editor notes, "unusually petty" role.[52] Anti-Papism thus provides a rent in the veil of Addison's cosmopolitanism. One of his many passages of contemptuous gallantry toward women turns suddenly grotesque with the contrast that, "At least, every one must allow that Fans are much more innocent Engines for propagating the Protestant Religion, than Racks, Wheels, Gibbets, and the like Machines, which are made use of for the advancement of the Roman-Catholick."[53] The conjunction of the ornamental woman and instruments of torture brings direct premodern and indirect modern coercions into conflict: in function, a fan is a gibbet; Protestantism uses the one as Catholicism the other. In his assembling of "innocent Engines" of cultural production, Catholics are the one element he deliberately excludes from his project of reconciliation; as earlier writers cast Catholicism as the antithesis of reason, he makes them the scapegoat who must be excluded from the public sphere as a precondition of its otherwise inclusiveness.[54] After the establishment of the "Protestant succession" of the Hanoverians, the captured crown became a guarantor of oligarchic power, but Papism remained as a phantom of the defeated absolutist state and pre-capitalist social order.

Such a phantom required resurrection only to excite popular passions. In *Tatler* 155, Addison tells a story about an upholsterer bankrupted by his devoting all his attention to politics, particularly war news from abroad, instead of to his business. He "seemed a Man of more than ordinary Application to Business. He was a very early riser, and was often abroad Two or Three Hours before any of his Neighbors. He had a particular Carefulness in his Motions, that plainly discovered he was always intent upon Matters of Importance." Upon inquiry, however, he proved only "the greatest Newsmonger of our Quarter ... He had a Wife and several Children; but was much more inquisitive to know what passed in Poland than in his own Family, and was in greater Pain and Anxiety of Mind for King *Augustus*'s Welfare than that of his nearest Relations."[55] Ruined by his neglect of his business, he reappears later as a strolling beggar and "politician" more concerned with the king of Sweden with than his own elder daughter; untaught by experience, he remains true to his hobby-horse, and the narrator concludes his account with the moral that "This Paper I design for the particular Benefit of those worthy Citizens who live more in a Coffee-house than in their Shops, and whose Thoughts are so taken up with the Affairs of the Allies, that they forget their Customers" (2.373). In this essay of April 6, 1710, less than three weeks after the March 20 conviction of Sacheverell in the House of Lords, Addison ridicules the involvement in politics of persons with other employments nearer to home to occupy them, that is, persons not of the leisured class. In an unmentioned context of High Church enthusiasm at the trial of Sacheverell, and in the twilight of a Whig administration about to be decisively defeated at the polls, Addison deprecates popular political excitement. While walking in the ex-upholsterer's company the narrator encounters "Three or Four very odd Fellows sitting together upon the Bench . . . The Discourse at length fell upon a Point which seldom escapes a Knot of true-born Englishmen, Whether in Case of a Religious War, the Protestants would not be too strong for the Papists? This we unanimously determined on the Protestant Side" (371–72). Addison makes the scene absurd to ridicule the notion that the unpropertied, "Three or Four very odd Fellows," could be fit to judge of "a Religious War." His deprecation of politics has a political object.

In Swift's *A Complete Collection of Genteel and Ingenious Conversation*, Simon Wagstaff proposes that a series of public schools be instituted throughout the country to educate the youth of quality in politeness, and that his work should be the text. The last-cited and weightiest advantage of this collection, "a work so honorable to [its author], and so beneficial to the kingdom," is that

after I have exhausted the whole *in sickly pay-day* (if I may so call it) of politeness and refinement, and faithfully digested it in the following dialogues, there cannot be found one expression relating to politics; that the MINISTRY is never mentioned, nor the word KING, above twice or thrice, and then only to the honor of Majesty; so very cautious were our wiser ancestors in forming rules of conversation, as never to give offence to crowned heads, nor interfere with party disputes in the state. And indeed, although there seem to be a close resemblance between the two words politeness and politics, yet no ideas are more inconsistent in their natures. However, to avoid all appearance of disaffection, I have taken care to enforce loyalty by an invincible argument, drawn from the very fountain of this noble science, in the following short terms that ought to be writ in gold, "MUST is for the King" which uncontrollable maxim I took particular care of introducing in the first page of my book; thereby to instil only the best Protestant loyal notions into the minds of my readers. Neither is it merely my own private opinion that politeness is the firmest foundation upon which loyalty can be supported. For, thus happily sings the never-to-be-too-much-admired Lord H—, in this truly sublime poem, called *Loyalty Defined:*

> Who's not polite, for the Pretender is;
> A Jacobite, I know him by his phiz.
>
> (579–80)

Swift's ardent educational reformer excludes politics, as Addison implicitly suggests that his readers not suffer the sad fate of his bankrupt "politic upholsterer." Once the need for popular passion to remove the royal threat to the gentry is over, at least until the next scare of a Jacobite plot or invasion, storekeepers should mind their books, and leave the business of governing to their betters. Wagstaff's textbook in politeness that empties conversation of politics for a political purpose, the provision of "the firmest foundation upon which loyalty can be supported," constitutes the Addisonian project. The speakers in *Genteel and Ingenious Conversation* have all, as it were, read the *Spectator*. The purpose of this "politeness" is a covert continuation of the indoctrination undertaken by Protestant schools for the Highlands of Scotland: as Swift recognizes, the Whig program of education and cultural uplift represents not disinterested benificence but disguised propaganda. Explicit anti-Papism is a weapon of ideological aggression, designed to neutralize disloyal Highlanders as before to delegitimize Stuarts; once its violent work is done, the more subtle operation of inducing cultural amnesia commences. "[T]he best Protestant loyal notions" reduce religion to partisan politics en route to reducing politics itself to propriety, to forestall the possibility of an imaginative space for oppositional discourse. Politeness is the evacuation of meaning – and popular participation – from politics.

With Addison, as with Swift, the coding of religion is primarily economic: his worry that "Arbitrary Power is so interwoven with Popery" results from concern about "the Change in Property in General, and the utter Extinction of it in our National Funds, the Inundation of Nobles without Estates, Prelates without Bishopricks, Officers Civil and Military without Places," should the Pretender succeed.[56] Still, the partisanship of Addison's agenda in *The Freeholder* can serve as a salutary point of rupture in the superior air he habitually cultivates. The class prejudice is unmistakable when *Freeholder* 3 presents a mock-journal of the march of a cowardly and contemptible rebel, who daydreams of seizing "a noble Country-Seat, which belongs to a *Whig*" (49), and who records that, "Notwithstanding the Magistracy was generally against us, we could discover many Friends among our Spectators; particularly in two or three Balconies, which were filled with several tawdry Females, who are known in that Country by the ancient Name of *Harlots*" (48). An entry in Swift's *Marginalia* provides a revealing glimpse of how the political valence of "loyalty" shifts. Under Anne, Swift is noisily loyal and Addison studies to avoid the explicitly partisan. Under George I Addison writes, "And tho' I should be unwilling to pronounce the Man who is indolent, or indifferent in the Cause of his Prince, to be absolutely perjured; I may venture to affirm, that he falls very short of that Allegiance to which he is obliged by Oath," and in the margin (literally marginalized) Swift comments, "Suppose a King grows a Beast, or a Tyrant, after I have taken an Oath: a 'prentice takes an Oath; but if his Master useth him barbarously, the lad may be excused if he wishes for a better."[57] Unlike Addison with his continued maneuverings to regain power when in opposition, confident in the oncoming Protestant Succession, Swift despairs, reduced from Ministerial confidant and propagandist to Irish exile scribbling a note in a margin that he dare not publish, accurately perceiving that his cause is irrecoverable. It is from the Examiner's despair that the Dean is born.

IV

Eighteenth-century religion is not all a matter of economics, however. Anthony Horneck's anonymous 1678 *A Letter from a Protestant Gentleman to a Lady Revolted to the Church of Rome* forms an exception to the rule that theological tracts are directed toward a male audience. The tract adopts the tone of a superior addressing one within his authority: her apostasy is a "revolt," and he entreats, "Once more therefore I charge you before Almighty GOD, and our lord Jesus Christ, to repent of your Errours, and to return to the bosome of that Church, in which you received your life, and being, and the Principles of Religion and Christianity."[58] A pastor may "charge" his congregation to repent, or to obey the government, but a nonclerical "gentleman," such as the author purports to be, could not "charge" another gentleman in matters of religion; he does a woman, however. He also expresses solicitude for her fallen state, and "should be sorry that this discourse should stand a Witness against you in the Last day, which GOD knows was only intended as a motive to draw you back to that Fold from which you have Wandered and gone astray. I am / Madam, Your Faithful Friend to serve you" (145). The courtliness and authority prescribed for relations between the sexes inflect his discussion; he reproaches her embrace of transubstantiation by conflating the traditional charge of female irrationality with the equally traditional one of Catholic irrationality: "how ill a Logician you are to conclude that this [John 6:53, the crucial text supporting transubstantiation] is spoke of the Sacrament" (65). Nonetheless, he does endeavor to contrast for her "the Doctrines of the Church of ROME ... with the Gospel of our Lord Jesus Christ" (50). Although debarred from participation, women cannot be entirely excluded from being addressed in religious debate, because they have souls, as well as the potential to influence others, particularly if they are persons of means, "ladies." In the generation after Aphra Behn's pioneering work as playwright and propagandist, Mary Astell and Delariviere Manley are active as (like Behn, Tory) pamphleteers on traditionally male subjects in such works as the preface to *Moderation Truly Stated: or, a Review of a Late Pamphlet, Entitul'd, Moderation a Virtue* and *A Modest Enquiry into the Reasons of the Joy Expressed by a Certain Sett of People, upon the Spreading of a Report of Her Majesty's Death*, respectively.[59] Nonetheless, Astell signs her essay "Tom. Single," and Manley maintains the same genderless, which is to say, implicitly male, anonymity in her *Modest Enquiry* as she did in the *Examiner* after she took over its editorship from Swift. Politics and religion remain male fields, so that in Austen when Henry Tilney walks with his sister and Catherine Morland "from politics, it was an easy step to silence"; when Henry Crawford and Edmund Bertram discuss the reading of church services there is no occasion for Fanny Price to intervene beyond a swiftly regretted shake of the head.[60]

In *Mansfield Park*, however, Fanny does claim an independence based on her moral disapproval of Crawford's principles, an independence firm enough for her to defy, however tearfully, the wrath of Sir Thomas Bertram. Conrad Russell has remarked of the pre-Civil War period that, "At one and the same time, the husband was told he must make his wife come to church, and the wife was told she ought to obey God rather than man. If husband and wife disagreed in religion, it was a prescription for chaos."[61] Even after the granting of toleration to Nonconformists, the contradictory impulses of domestic authoritarianism and the Protestant free conscience of the public sphere remained to be reconciled. It is this task that Defoe undertakes in *Religious Courtship*, or, to allow the work its full title, *Religious Courtship: Being Historical Discourses on the Necessity of Marrying Religious Husbands and Wives Only. As also Of Husbands and Wives being of the Same Opinions in religion with one another. With an Appendix of the Necessity Of taking none but Religious Servants, and a Proposal for the better managing of Servants*. This 1722 set of three "Historical Discourses," half-tract, half-novel, written in the midst of Defoe's novel-writing period, proposes a tripartite plan for domestic concord and control that the full title outlines. This didactic narrative presents a widower and his three daughters, all nameless, and "carefully avoid[s saying] ... whether the old gentleman was a churchman or a dissenter."[62] Typically for a Dissenting polemicist, Defoe wishes to emphasize how much Protestants have in common, in order to propitiate Anglican opinion. His preface recognizes that some may "object, that too much is put here upon the woman's part, and that a lady cannot be supposed, in the midst of her lover's addresses, to take upon her to demand such an account of himself as is here suggested" (ix), but argues in justification that in troubled marriages "they are generally the greatest sufferers" (xi). It is because women are the regulators of family morality that they "have the better part of the staff put into their hands" (xi) in this work: the father, "taken up with getting money ... left them [his daughters] wholly to the conduct of their mother," who on her deathbed exacted two promises, that they require a successful suitor to "at least profess to be a religious man" and to have "the same principles and opinion in religion as themselves" (2). Within a few lines the first suitor appears, and Defoe's family fairy tale of three sisters is set in motion. The story breaks into two parts, the wooing of the youngest sister and the marriage of the middle one, with the final section about servants a storyless appendix, domestic in subject and a dialogue in form, but without a narrative subject: after courtship and marriage, all that remains to a woman's lot is household management. Thematically, the first section enforces the necessity of piety, the second that of uniformity, the third that of strict household discipline. Religion becomes a system for regulating domestic economy. Defoe demands on the familial level precisely the uniform religious authoritarianism he had previously resisted on the national level.

In the first section, the youngest daughter keeps "a gentleman of a very good estate" (3) waiting for 170 pages and two years (176) before he can win her hand by converting from irreligion, and he is all the better and respects her the more for her having such high standards. She admits that she loves him, but conscience forbids the union (32): the illicitness of the attractive lover that reappears in Richardson's *Pamela* and *Clarissa* is here a function of belief, not of immoral demands for extramarital relations. The suitor learns "What is religion? And what is it to be a Christian?" (55) from a cottager: as the cottager tells him, "read the Scripture; if God's word reaches your heart, you will not need to be taught to pray" (72). Despite Defoe's coy refusal to name a denomination, that the instructor is a poor layman rather than a clergyman suggests an unstated Dissenting slant.

What is at stake is what Defoe calls "family religion": "family religion is a sociable thing, and God should be worshipped there with one heart, and with one voice: there can be no separation there, without a dreadful breach both of charity and duty" (134). As Ellen Pollak observes, freedom in the male public sphere does not imply an equal freedom in the female domestic one; Defoe's "family religion" is a corrolary of what Locke calls the husband's "Conjugal Power."[63] It is precisely because the wife must submit herself wholeheartedly that her choice must be careful; if policing is to be internal belief must be aligned with duty. The father's widowed sister calls her sisters "ruined by marrying profligate, irreligious husbands" (86). Ruin is not sexual, but religious, and happens as well to a brother with "a wild, giddy, playhouse-bred wife; full of wit, and void of grace" (87). Not only is affection estranged between a couple of mixed faiths, but "some [children] kneel down with the father, some with the mother; till, as they grow up, they really learn not to kneel down at all: family education, united instruction, caution, example, they are all dreadfully mangled and divided, till in the end they come to nothing, and the children grown out of government, past instruction, and are all lost" (136). Indoctrination must possess a united impact. A family is a system of control, the conceptual foundation of government; if faiths differ, not only children but "the servants are left ungoverned" (202).

Like the national polity, such a familial union is implicitly Protestant. The suitor begins his reformation by listening "at a chocolate-house near the court" to a conversation

about the differences . . . then depending between the pope and the French clergy; and of the Sorbonne or faculty of theology, as they are called there, being at that time employed in drawing up a new system of divinity, or body of doctrine, as they called it; and as a consequence, it was hinted how likely it was that such a struct inquiry made by men of learning and virtue into the fundamentals of religion, should lead them at last into protestant principles, and break that whole kingdom off from the errors and ignorance of popery, opening the eyes of the people to Christian knowledge. (50–51)

If the conversation were about matters controverted between Dissenters and Anglicans, or rival Dissenting sects, Defoe would have to give up his pretense of encompassing all Protestants equally. Instead, as in such Restoration pamphlets as Marvell's *An Account of the Growth of Popery, and Arbitrary Government*, he offers an enemy against which all can unite, only this enemy is not the terrifying Papist menace that plotted the execution of Charles I and inserted its hidden agents everywhere, and of which he had written that "the Endeavors of *Popish* and *Jacobite* Agents and Emissaries in diverse arts of *Britain* are to [sic] apparently successful";[64] instead, in 1722, a decade after the Treaty of Utrecht had ended the War of the Spanish Succession, Catholics are merely harmlessly deluded foreigners whom one may hope will someday learn English wisdom. Defoe appears considerably more confident than when he worried *And What if the Pretender should come?* In that 1713 pamphlet, one desperate consequence "if once the Pretender were settled quietly among us, [would be that] an Absolute Subjection, as well of Religious Principles, as Civil Liberties, to the Disposal of the Sovereign, would take Place ... the Slavery of Religion being taken off, and an Universal Freedom of Vice being introduced, what greater Liberty can we enjoy."[65] Popery, vice, and a playhouse "full of wit, and void of grace" – or the opera to which two graceless blades retire instead of listening to edifying religious bigotry (51) – are the contraries of domestic virtue. As "LIBERTIES" and "PROPERTY" require "No *Popery*, no *Slavery*," in Defoe's earlier schematic for public life, so his consolidated domestic regime posits Popery as the unassimilably alien, as the second part develops.[66]

If the first section provides an example of the rewards of heeding the dead mother's monitions, the second demonstrates the penalty for ignoring her teachings. A business connection of the father's appears on the first page of this section, takes "a fancy" to the middle sister on the second, and on the third is described as "not a complete-bred merchant only, but much a gentleman; and to all this was to be added, that he was very sober, grave, and oftentimes, as occasion offered, his discourse upon religious affairs discovered him to be very serious and religious. As to his estate, it was not very well only, but extraordinary" (175). He is a paragon of matrimonial eligibility, that is, in all points but what will fill the hundred pages following. Subsequent to its brief introduction, the second part of *Religious Courtship* divides into three Dialogues, the first a 30-page debate between the two remaining unmarried daughters on the role of religious differences in marriage, the second a series of several short exchanges preceding and following the wedding, and the third an extended post-mortem among all three sisters after the husband's death at the end of eight years. Marriage, the ostensible object of the process, occurs in an ellipsis.

In the first Dialogue, the middle sister feels that "it would be the rudest thing" (195) to ask her suitor his exact denomination, and to press closely is unnecessary since "if he is not of my opinion, I will be of his opinion," which she deems a "very obliging custom" (193). The eldest sister deplores her following "the fashion of our city ladies ... reserving their choice of principles, till they see what principles their husbands are of" (193), warns against blindly uniting with "a strange person coming out of Italy, from the very bowels of superstition, and the very kingdom of popery" (194), insinuates "why he may be a papist for aught you know yet of him" (179), and asks, "suppose he should be a papist?" (193). An Anglican may be lovingly married to a Quaker, though with mutual sorrow (200–4), or a wife of the one faith might conform to the other if unscrupulous, but a Papist exceeds the limits of the permissible, indeed defines those limits by his violation of them.[67] The second Dialogue accomplishes the "ruin" of the middle daughter with a "dull and empty discourse" in which "the girl left it all to her father; and the father, perfectly indifferent as to matters of religion, left it out of his inquiry" (211–12). A daughter has not merely a right but a duty to choose for herself (223); submission to a father's "positive authority" where he is entitled to only a "negative authority" (93) is as wrong for Defoe's sisters as it would later be for Fielding's Sophia Western or Austen's Fanny Price. The marriage ensues in a sentence, and then a brief narrative of a tour through the new husband's house, which is filled with "a noble collection of very fine paintings" – including "a picture of the Crucifixion, extremely valuable and fine, [which] he contrived to have hanged up by the bed-side" (212). The youngest sister asks why it hangs there, and, told that such is the custom in Italy "on a religious account," protests that "methinks they are better anywhere else ... We have the promise of the Spirit of God to assist us, says the sister, very warmly, and need no idolatrous pictures" (213). Discovering a second painting of the crucifixion hidden behind a curtain puts the eldest sister "in no little disorder" because it confirms the dreadful truth: "O sister! I tell you she is undone; the man's a papist!" (215). The youngest sister, now referred to as the *"Mar. Sist.,"* concurs when informed, exclaiming "Poor child! she is ruined indeed" (217), as does the father when he reveals his independent discovery of the truth:

your sister is undone ... She is undone indeed, child; and more than that, I have undone her: the man's a papist.

(*The father burst out into tears as soon as he had spoken the words, and the daughters stood as they were speechless for some time ...*) (221)

The ultimate horror has happened; Quakerism and the Church of England may each have their good and bad points, but Popery is an un-mitigatable evil. Yet any explanation of why it should be taboo has vanished; the defilement remains, but emptied of its former reasons for signifying as it does. Though the husband is kind and generous (227), the father's reaction to his death is that "God has delivered her" (229), and she herself owns that "I am a convert now to my mother's instructions" (231). Upon hearing an instance of his tenderness, the inexorable eldest sister laconically remarks, "Well, sister, 'tis well he's dead" (250), a comment she explains by saying that "her affection to her husband is her worst snare" (251). The "*Wid.* [ow]" middle sister agrees:

O let no woman that values her soul venture into the arms of a husband of a different religion! the kinder he is, the more likely to undo her; everything that endears him to her doubles her danger; the more she loves him, the more she inclines to yield to him; the more he loves her, the stronger are the bonds by which he draws her; and her only mercy would be to have him barbarous and unkind to her. (252)

Like a rake, a Papist is a seducer; his love can only imperil a woman's soul. The toleration that Defoe urged among Protestants in such works as *The True-Born Englishman*, which mocked a nativist hostility toward Dutch William, and *The Shortest Way with the Dissenters*, which reduced High Church concern for the integrity and inclusiveness of the national church to bloodymindedness, in *Religious Courtship* becomes a plea for an interdenominational Protestant exclusiveness. By 1722 Dissenters have enjoyed toleration for over thirty years, the Pretender has been vanquished, the Tories have been routed and excluded from office. The rallying point which all Protestants share in common is still opposition to Catholicism, but they no longer urgently need to justify their opposition. Sexual purity conflates with a despecified ideological purity in the repeated references to a daughter being "ruined" and "undone" by alliance to a Papist.

Unlike Horneck, Defoe sees no occasion to let women participate in doctrinal debate, even in a subordinate capacity. To argue a case would suggest that a counterargument is possible. If the religions were reversed, of course, if Defoe's woman like Horneck's were the Catholic, he would have allowed her to hear gospel truth, to have a chance to save her soul and obey her husband at the same time; but what is unnatural about Catholicism in *Religious Courtship* is precisely how it fouls lines of authority that are supposed to run parallel: a Papist husband is, like a Papist king, an illegitimate authority. A Papist wife of a Protestant would merely have a double duty, as wife and English subject, to convert; a Protestant wife of a Papist faces irreconcilably conflicting loyalties, to the one right religion and the one right sexuality of obedience in patriarchal marriage. What Carol Houlihan Flynn calls "The ideal situation in Defoe's domestic economy, voluntary surrender [by the wife] to God's and the godly husband's will," is impossible if the husband is a Papist and therefore by definition ungodly.[68] Defoe is perfectly willing to see a Popish king ejected, but not a Popish husband: again, the very unity of religious and civil authority which he disallows in the polity he demands in the family. The Protestant family is delimited by its rejection of Popery.

The third part of the work implies a further reason for the empty signifier of Catholicism. Even before this section begins, at the end of the second part the conversation among the sisters turns to the effect upon servants of a family lacking in "family religion." Explaining why, "while I have a family, and can keep any servants, I will entertain none but such as worship God the same way as I worship him," the Papist's widow tells how some servants were Protestant, some Catholic, and "some pagans, for we had three East Indian blacks and one negro among our people" (264–65). An Italian and an English servant each endeavored to convert the Black, Negum, to their respective faiths, but, as the "master" says, "these fellows quarrel continually about this poor man and so in the end he will be brought rather to abhor the Christian religion in general, than to turn Christian at all, while one pulls him one way and one another" (268). Despite his own Catholicism, the owner (Negum's slavery is acknowledged [267]) sends Negum on a pretext to a farm where he will hear only one side and so convert to Protestantism, "for rather than he should not be taught to worship God at all, let him be taught the way of the country where we are" (269). The essence of "family religion" is not doctrine but its role in the internalization of obedience. A work that early on exalts the humble piety of the cottager, and for its only biblical citation chooses "*Not many rich, not many noble are called*; and it is *the poor of this world, that are rich in faith*, James ii.5" (64), concludes by endorsing a religious paternalism:

> [Mary.] I don't meddle with them, let them let me alone, can't they?
> *Bet*[ty]. But it may be, my mistress thinks she ought to govern her servants in religious things, as well as in her house affairs.
> *Ma*. Why let her think what she will, and do what she will, I will have my own way, I shall mind nothing they say to me.
> *Bet*. That's none of my business, Mary; you must do as you will.
> *Ma*. No; and it is none of her business neither, I think.
>   *Bet*. I can't say that, Mary; I think if you were a mistress, and kept a great many servants, as our mistress does, you would talk otherwise too, or else you would soon have a house full of whores and rogues.
>   (283)

Although a Dissenter, Defoe endorses taking the shortest way with servants; in their case, his rejection of religious pluralism is as strict as Laud's. Betty dutifully informs their employer of Mary's disrespect, "upon which her mistress turned her [Mary] out of her house, giving her a month's wages instead of a month's warning, as one not fit to be allowed to stay in the family" (287). Because the "family" includes dependents, only those possessing financial independence are in practice entitled to the freedom supposedly available to all. Popery is intolerable because, like the Pretenders, it suggests the possibility of an alternative to England's rule of Protestant property. Aligning political, religious, and domestic rectitude, Defoe erases differences among Protestants but retains an impenetrable divide between Protestants and Catholics; his advice in seeking husbands is advice also in choosing kings. As in other conduct books, "the retiring and yet ever vigilant domestic woman" forms part of a cohesive regime.[69] Defoe's reason for distinguishing between public and private despotisms, that "there may be divers opinions in a nation, without breach of charity, but I believe it is impossible it should be so in a family, without breach of affection" (134), exemplifies with unusual clarity Nancy Armstrong's dictum that "the power of the middle classes had everything to do with that of middle-class love."[70] Freedom of religion, like freedom to influence the government, is only for the possessing classes.

Comprehensive control of domestic labor is necessary also to maximize the effectiveness of Christianity as a tool for ideological domination also of non-Europeans, as represented by Negum – or Friday. Like Negum, Friday is a pagan whose incorporation into a servile relation to European power is internalized by his adoption of Christianity, but because Friday receives a single message from a single master there is no danger that, "one pull[ing] him one way and one another," conflicting channels will, as on a radio, destroy each other's clarity. (Crusoe, incidentally, is as tolerant of the Catholicism of the Spaniards whom he rescues as the husband in *Religious Courtship* is of the necessity of instructing a pagan in Protestantism in a Protestant country: what is urgent in *Robinson Crusoe* is that Friday "be taught to worship God," which is to say that the New World be remade in the image of the old, the non-European in the image of the European. As the Frenchman and Spaniard in Middleton's Lord Mayor's Day pageant, *The Triumphs of Honor and Industry*, are fundamentally aligned with England's merchants against "Indians" in the very act of being portrayed as commercial rivals, so *Robinson Crusoe* signals that doctrinal differences, though important in Brazil or Europe, still do not cut as deep as a divide between Christendom and paganism that is already becoming racially inflected.) By "carefully avoid[ing saying] . . . whether the old gentleman was a churchman or a dissenter," *Religious Courtship* echoes the strategy of Defoe's 1715 *The Family Instructor*, with its "care [that] is taken to avoid Distinctions of opinion, as to Church of England or Dissenter," which

J. Paul Hunter has observed can be applied also to *Robinson Crusoe*.[71]
"Friday's Christianity" is indeed, as Timothy C. Blackburn argues, "a
model of the essence of reformed Christianity and its necessary civil
theology" – as Defoe chose to represent them.[72] Defoe's infantilization of
the laboring classes at home and abroad constitutes a paternalism
intended not to cherish, as Richard Braverman suggests, but smother.[73]
The vast and complex corpus of Defoe's work, crossing freely between
alleged fact and tacit fiction, may, as Helen Burke argues, not be entirely
reducible to Michael McKeon's "progressive ideology," but its "ability to
invoke providence with conviction" nonetheless is fundamental to the
project of "commercial imperialism."[74] The oligarchy that ruled
eighteenth-century Britain spoke a language of liberty learned in the
previous century's struggles, and, as Linda Colley observes, a coalescing
upper class used religion, most certainly including the Catholic bogey, to
secure popular support.[75] Paula Backscheider remarks that Defoe boasted
of his being "born a Freeman" of London, of the municipal elite eligible
to vote for all offices, including the Lord Mayor, sheriffs, and Members of
Parliament; the "Revolution Principles" of popular sovereignty which he
defends in *Legions Memorial* he readily disowns when the people in question
are Scots resisting the Union of 1707.[76]

v

If Defoe presses religious anxieties into the service of a coercive narrative
of domesticity, however, so in a more fraught fashion does Henry Fielding,
whose Anglican and more explicitly political version also assimilates
sexual, national, and class divisions. That Fielding was politically active as
a writer is not something that could escape critical notice. By and large,
however, such criticism has failed adequately to integrate the journalist
and the novelist. Because "the Richardsonian model" has been perceived
as the wellspring of domestic fiction, and because the mostly male critics
analyzing Fielding as a political journalist represent a separate critical
circle from the mostly female critics exploring the sexuality of the early
English novel, Fielding's interrelation of national and sexual politics has
gone largely overlooked.[77] Brian McCrea reduces the violence of *True
Patriot* 3 to "a call for enlightened self-interest," while Thomas R. Cleary
acknowledges that the essay is "crude, 'scare' propaganda," but argues
that "A vision of London ravaged by highlanders was not utterly mad on
November 19, 1745," and "Fielding was seldom moved to such stridency."[78]
Whereas McCrea dissolves Fielding's highly charged particulars into a

generalized defense of "'stated rules of Property,'" Cleary recognizes them, but declares them an insignificant aberration.[79] Similarly, Cleary's hypothesis of "a politicizing revision of the central books" of *Tom Jones*, while in itself plausible, even probable, operates again to deprecate the extent to which the novel is already political and thus receptive to such revision.[80] The topical references to the Jacobite rebellion fit into *Tom Jones* with minimal disruptiveness because they merely make more explicit a political framework already implicit. A discourse of religiously defined nationalism connects Fielding's "cultural politics" and sexuality.[81]

Fielding relocates Addison's economic anti-Papist rationale in an emotive basis by identifying property with the family and the totemic figure of the upper-class virgin; *Tom Jones* suggests only to suppress an alternative narrative of Papist menace that appears vividly in *True Patriot* 3 as the negation of domesticity. The identification of Popery with Celtic primitivism, familiar from seventeenth-century tracts justifying English imperialism in Ireland, recurs in Fielding's treatment of the Jacobite rebellion of 1745 in *The True Patriot*. The first number is divided into two parts, an introduction of the periodical that opens with the stylish flourish that "Fashion is the great Governor of this World," to which a second section adds "Observations on the Present Rebellion."[82] The latter observes that

> The Rebellion is at present so seriously the Concern of every sensible Man, who wishes well to the Religion and Liberties of his Country, and the Zeal which all the different Sects of Protestants have discovered on this Occasion, is so hearty and unanimous, that it would be a lost Labour to endeavour at inflaming the Minds of my Countrymen on this Occasion ... But let us consider of what Persons this rebellious Rabble consists; and we shall find them to be the savage Inhabitants of Wilds and Mountains, who are almost a distinct Body from the rest of their Country. Some Thousands of them are Outlaws, Robbers, and Cut-throats, who live in a constant State of War, or rather Robbery, with the civilized Part of *Scotland*. The Estates of this Part have been always pillaged by the Thefts of these Ruffians, by whom they are now openly plundered. (113)

As outspokenly confident as any 1660s royal panegyrist, Fielding asserts that his wealthy and imperial England can dismissively characterize dissent on the periphery as "rebellious Rabble." He constructs England as an aristocratic estate to whose august authority "Outlaws, Robbers, and Cut-throats" sneaking about on the outskirts can pose no serious threat. "[T]he civilized Part of Scotland" are "Fellow-Protestants and Fellow-Sufferers with ourselves" (115): Popery, with which Jacobitism is equated, is an intrusion from outside of Whig civilization, not a creed but a stigma of savagery. Protestantism requires adhesion to no belief but in the status quo; the second issue asserts that even "Roman Catholics" themselves may be "less bigotted" or enjoy "Possession of Abby Lands, and of Estates in the Funds," and "There is no Man of Sense, Property, Honour, and Humanity, who can possibly hope to see his Religion introduced by a Banditti of Robbers and Cut-throats, who would certainly make his Country a Scene of Blood and Desolation" (124–25). Catholics must be watched and disarmed, but, so long as they have Sense, which is Property, which is Honour, which is Humanity, extreme measures are unnecessary, since "the Odds are greatly on our Side" (126).

Already a month before beginning publication of *The True Patriot*, however, Fielding takes a dramatically more serious view of "The Rebellion lately begun in *Scotland*, under the Banner of *a Popish Pretender*" in *A Serious Address to the People of Great Britain* (3). The "truly *English* Cause" of resisting "a Rabble of Thieves and Outlaws" who "would by their Swords cut their Way into the Wealth of richer Climates" does not require that he "descend to consider particular Interests: I will not remind all those who are possessed of Abbey-Lands or forfeited Estates, or who are interested in the Funds, how much they are concerned to oppose a Torrent which threatens to overwhelm their Fortunes. The Whole is at Stake" (31, 30). Fielding dredges up every cliché of the Whig cause, from "The suspicious Birth of the Pretender" (3–4) to "Popery and arbitrary Power" (12), in an effort to restore enthusiasm to support for a Hanoverian dynasty that after thirty years in power is difficult to portray heroically. Spanish "Conduct in the *Low Countries*, in the Reign of *Philip* II" is summoned yet once more to underline the horror of "a popish Pretender, educated in all the Tenets of Bigotry," who is moreover "the mere Instrument of *France*" (29). Recycling arguments grown stale before his birth, Fielding is unable to charge them with the old urgency, so that when he returns to "endeavour at inflaming the Minds of my Countrymen" in *True Patriot* 3, he abandons a shopworn argumentation for a dystopic imagination of the future in case of defeat, a "Dream or Vision" (128).

This lurid fantasy of Papistic Stuart terror begins:

Methought, I was sitting in my Study, meditating for the Good and Entertainment of the Public, with my two little Children (as is my usual Course to suffer them) playing near me; when I heard a very hard Knock at my Door, and immediatgely [sic] afterwards several ill-looked Rascals burst in upon me, one of whom seized me with great Violence, saying I was his Prisoner, and must go with him. I asked him for what Offense. Have you the Impudence to ask that, said he, when the Words *True Patriot* lie now before you? I then bid him show me his Warrant. He answered, *there it is,* pointing to several Men, who were in Highland Dresses, with broad Swords by their Sides. My Children then ran towards me, and bursting into Tears, exprest their Concern for their poor Papa. Upon which one of the Ruffians seized my little Boy, and pulling him from me, dashed him against the Ground; and all immediately hurried me away out of my Room and House, before I could be sensible of the Effects of this Barbarity.

My concern for my poor Children, from whom I had beeen torn in the above Manner, prevented me from taking much notice of any Objects in the Streets, through which I was dragg'd, with many Insults. Houses burnt down, dead Bodies of Men, Women and Children, strewed every where as we passed, and great Numbers of Highlanders, and Popish Priests in their several Habits, made, however, too forcible an Impression on me to be unobserved. (128)

The gruesome violence of the Irish massacres imaged by George Fox's *Arraignment of Popery* interrupts an abortive narrative of domesticity. Should Popery and the Pretender triumph, England would become a war zone, would become Ireland, would change from the wealthy colonizer of inferior districts and peoples to itself the colonized, the spoil of "great Numbers of Highlanders, and Popish Priests." Fielding's "Vision" extends not only back to the vulnerable England oppressed by Papism of John Foxe's *Acts and Monuments,* but implicitly forward to the imperial England that is necessary to prevent such horrors. Only an England strong enough to oppress "the savage Inhabitants of Wilds and Mountains" will be itself free of oppression. The author "meditating for the Good and Entertainment of the Public" is the intellectual worker gestating the paradisal Whig future which could be annihilated by "all the Fury which Rage, Zeal, Lust, and wanton Fierceness could inspire into the bloody Hearts of Popish Priests, Bigots, and Barbarians" (133). Popery becomes the inseparable concomitant of not only tyranny, as in the endlessly reiterated seventeenth-century formula, but foreignness and barbarism. The "Chief Justice" of a patently unjust tribunal speaks in "broken English," and the court "proceeded to pass the Sentence usual in Cases of High-Treason, having first made many Eulogiums on the Pope, the *Roman* Catholic Religion, and the King who was to support both, and be supported by them" (130). As the narrator is led away to execution,

The first Sight which occurred to me as I past through the Streets, (for common Objects totally escape the Observation of a Man in my present Temper of Mind) was a young Lady of Quality, and the greatest Beauty of this Age, in the Hands of two Highlanders, who were struggling with each other for their Booty. The lovely Prize, tho' her Hair was dishevelled and torn, her Eyes swollen shut with Tears, her Face all pale, and some Marks of Blood on that and her Breast, which was all naked and exposed, retained still sufficient Charms to discover herself to me, who have always beheld her with Wonder and Admiration. Indeed it may be questioned whether perfect Beauty loses or acquires Charms by Distress. This Sight was Matter of Entertainment to my Conductors, who, however, hurried me presently from it, as I wish they had also from her Screams, which reached my Ears to a great Distance.

After such a Spectacle as this, the dead Bodies which lay every where in the Streets (for there had been, I was told, a Massacre the Night before) scarce made any Impression; nay, the very Fires in which Protestants were roasting, were, in my Sense, Objects of much less Horror . . . The Executioner then attempted to put the Rope round my Neck, when my little Girl enter'd my Bed-chamber, and put an end to my Dream. (132–34)

As in D. W. Griffith's *Birth of a Nation*, the ultimate horror is the rape of civilization, incarnated in a "perfect Beauty" of the master caste, by members of a subject population. As it happens, "perfect Beauty in both Sexes" is a recurring concern in *Tom Jones*, and the opinion of *The True Patriot* that "it may be questioned whether perfect Beauty loses or acquires Charms by Distress" finds an echo in the novel.[83] The narrator explains Lord Fellamar's heightened attraction to Sophia when a tumult drives her from the playhouse with the observation that "Beauty never looks more amiable than in Distress" (785). It is this same Lord Fellamar, of course, who, at Lady Bellaston's instigation, later attempts to rape Sophia; her attractiveness in a lesser distress leads to a greater. Sophia, "the finest Creature in the World" (970) in Allworthy's estimate, who asks her cousin, "'Why, why, would you marry an *Irishman?*'" (601), has much in common with "the greatest Beauty of this Age." If Richardson's *Clarissa* is an extended rape, *Tom Jones* plays a fan dance with its forever-endangered hero and heroine who are yet never in a situation where the wittily omniscient narrator is not perfectly in control and able to rescue them. In *True Patriot* 3, the dreaming narrator is out of control, a prisoner in the hands of pitiless monsters, and equally Fielding himself is out of control, fantasizing a Papist nightmare that negates the perfect order of Whig England. However deliberate the violence of the propaganda, that violence nonetheless ruptures the security of the novelistic narrative of domesticity as much as the Jacobite invasion itself ruptures English "national security." What *Tom Jones* conceals, *True Patriot* 3 reveals. It is the screams of Sophia Western, in a sense, that "reached my Ears to a great Distance."

Like Addison's, Fielding's preferred mode is to assume that resistance to his gentlemanly superiority is inconceivable, but when such resistance does arise, in the Jacobite invasion of 1745, his response is brutal, a determination to destroy the enemy without regard to poise and elegance.

The military threat of the Highlanders compels the stylish spokesmen for imperium to abandon their pretenses of being above the fray. Where Addison argues financial dangers, however, the superiority of English to French tax systems (*Freeholders* 18 and 20) and the perils of the Funds, Fielding emblematizes taxes in the fetishized figure of the upper-class endangered virgin, and the Funds in a family history. The protagonist of *True Patriot* 3 encounters in prison a man there for "stealing a Loaf ... I rose in the Morning with £40000," but "At Noon I found a Royal Decree [repudiating the national debt, the Funds] had reduced me to downright Beggary"; the economic aspect of "stealing a Loaf," however, a crime not unique to ruined patricians, is sentimentalized into his domestic distress: "I had a Wife whom I tenderly loved and three blooming Daughters" (131), and he stole to feed them. Fielding's compassion for a petty thief who once possessed "great Affluence and Splendor" (131) contrasts strikingly with his attitude toward lesser felons in *An Enquiry into the Causes of the Late Increase of Robbers*, in which he notes with bland regret, apropos executions of criminals driven by need, that "This plea of necessity is never admitted in our law; but the reason of that is, says Lord Hale, because it is to difficult to discover the truth."[84] Fielding's approach to poverty in his *Enquiry* has some resemblance to Archbishop Tenison's *Sermon of Alms*, with its reproach of "*foolish pity*"; unless poverty is recent and sudden, like that of the sometime master of £40,000 in *True Patriot* 3, or the highwayman in *Tom Jones*, who also tries robbery to relieve his abruptly ruined family, it is assumed to be the result of laziness and "luxury."

Also in prison – "a large Booth in *Smithfield*" (128) because Newgate is overcrowded – are "many of the most considerable Persons in this Kingdom," two of whom "were in a very particular Manner reviled by the Highland Guards (for all the Soldiers were in that Dress)": Bishop Hoadly, still a Low Church icon thirty years after the Bangorian controversy, and the Archbishop of York, who made a widely reprinted speech to a York county assembly mustering troops against the Pretender, a speech that "emphasized that the jacobite rebellion was part of a larger plan by France and Spain to establish popery in England" (129, 129n).[85] Hoadly and York have no further role to play; they just put in appearances as emblems of the Hanoverian updating of the loyal "King's spiritual militia" of the previous century, intellectuals domesticated to the present regime, in contrast to the "Man who by his Countenance and Actions exprest the highest Degree of Despair ... stamped with his Feet, beat his Face, tore his Hair, and uttered the most horrid Execrations" at the place of execution, "a Nonjuror, who had lent considerable Assistance to the Pretender's Cause, out of

Principle; and was now lamenting the Consequences which the Success of it had brought on such honest Gentlemen as myself. My Informer added, with a Smile, The Wise Man expected his Majesty would keep his Word with Heretics" (133). The Nonjuror, openly such a quisling as Orwell suspected Swift was more covertly, sees too late the fatal effects of not rallying to the patriotic cause, of persisting in an archaic "Principle" that fails to take into account the diabolic treachery and cruelty of Papists toward "Heretics." In 1745 as in 1715, the irrefutable justification for the Georges remains the Protestant Succession.

Relapsing into seventeenth-century verbal violence in response to a seventeenth-century danger, Fielding's phantasmagoria of wartime imagery in *True Patriot* 3 contrasts to the studied urbanity of his narratorial voice in *Tom Jones*, his novel set on the edge of the '45. Tom marches to the war, only to encounter Ensign Northerton's bottle on the way, and Sophia is mistaken for Jenny Cameron, but he needn't go to the front and she possesses infinitely superior virtue to what Honour calls "'a nasty *Scotch* Wh–re'" (604). More curiously still, in the novel's famously "perfect plot," the entire issue of the invasion simply appears when Tom chances upon some soldiers at "(a Circumstance which we have not thought necessary to communicate before) ... the very Time when the late Rebellion was at the highest" (368), then vanishes, never to be revived, as the action approaches London, the core of modernizing, mercantile Whig England. Its importance diminishes to a comic interlude without need of introduction or consequence for the subsequent action. The irruption of the Jacobite peril is deliberately minimized in *Tom Jones* to forestall the possibility of the double and equivalent alternative histories, that Sophia could suffer the fate of her nameless analogue and that any alternative regime could exist to Allworthy's benevolent despotism. The Pretender has no right to rule – "'I believe him to be as much a Protestant as I believe he hath any Right,' says Jones" (439) – but the owner of £40,000, or of a country estate, has an indefeasible right to his possessions. That those who rose beggars in the morning should remain beggars at noon is only natural, yet what is Tom, like the Pretender, but a beggar until he proves his hereditary right? The Pretender has no right because Tom is the true prince of Whig England, where every Protestant lineage and estate is sacred.

Tom Jones does contain a glimpse of an alternative narrative in the history of the Man of the Hill, a story of Restoration debauchery and ruin that contrasts to Tom's harmless frolics and happy ending. The Man of the Hill's account concludes with his participation in the Duke of Monmouth's

1685 rebellion and subsequent exile. He joins Monmouth because "I had been for some Time very seriously affected with the Danger to which the Protestant Religion was so visibly exposed, under a Popish Prince; and thought the Apprehension of it alone sufficient to justify that Insurrection: For no real Security can ever be found against the persecuting Spirit of Popery, when armed with Power, except the depriving it of Power, as woeful Experience presently shewed" (477).[86] Naturally, Tom's reply refers to how, even after the "expelling King *James*, for the preserving of our Religion and Liberties," there remains "a Party among us mad enough to desire the placing his Family again on the Throne" (477). The Man of the Hill is disgusted with the "monstrous Extravagances" of "Human Nature" (478) because, under Charles II, he experienced what Tom calls "'Love derived from the Stews'" and "'Friendship first produced and nourished at the Gaming-Table!'" (485). *Tom Jones* is a comedy, in contrast, because its hero is the child of a happier age than the "'Stews'" and "'Gaming-Tables'" of the Stuarts. McKeon is able to assimilate Fielding to a "conservative ideology" held in common with Swift only by stopping his examination short of *Tom Jones*, where the "extreme skepticism" arguably present in his theatrical works and early satiric novels dissolves, after the fall of Walpole and the Jacobite scare of 1745, into an unproblematized endorsement of "our Religion and Liberties."[87] Only a Partridge (lower-class and therefore foolish and gullible) could believe "'a popish Priest . . . that Prince *Charles* was as good a Protestant as any in *England*; and that nothing but Regard to Right made him [the priest] and the rest of the popish Party to be *Jacobites*'" (439). As Martin Battestin observes, Partridge subscribes to "one of the most preposterous" of "the 'Mysteries' of the Jacobite creed," that, in the words of *The Jacobite's Journal* for January 2, 1748, "*a Popish Prince may be the Defender of a Protestant Church.*"[88] Elkanah Settle's carefully elaborated argument in *The Character of a Popish Successour* in 1681 for the exclusion from the throne of the Duke of York, the future James II, has become a justification of the Georges, and a matter of course. What once needed exposition devolves into "common sense." Tom avers that "Monsters and Prodigies are the proper Arguments to support monstrous and absurd Doctrines. The Cause of King *George* is the Cause of Liberty and true Religion. In other Words, it is the Cause of Common Sense" (440). Liberty and true religion, the great objects of the struggles of the seventeenth century, devolve into mere common sense, "The Cause of King *George*," in a deliberate denial of historical complexity.

The Man of the Hill's story introduces a reminder of a worse past, like the nunnery episode of Marvell's "Upon Appleton House," only Fielding's past isn't pre-Reformation but the profligacy of the Restoration and the Popish threat of James II. In *Tom Jones* as in *True Patriot* 3, a threat from outside – the Stuart, Catholic, Highlander outside – interrupts the English domestic narrative of the ideological reproduction of gentry dominance, as represented by Tom's inheritance of both the Allworthy and Western estates; where *True Patriot* 3 represses the domestic narrative in order to highlight its menacers, however, *Tom Jones* marginalizes the intrusion. The Man of the Hill's story, like Marvell's tale of the nuns, is a digression from the main action; but, whereas Marvell requires a quarter of his poem to deal with the messy history leading to the Commonwealth, Fielding marginalizes history into a tiny sliver of a long novel, and reduces contemporary events into little more than a running joke, an occasion for Tom to show his mettle and Sophia's (virtuous) true Whig princess to be humorously mistaken for the (unchaste) false Jacobite version. Regarding Tom's blank endorsement of "the Cause of common Sense," Peter J. Carlton notes that "Bertolt Brecht remarks somewhere that assertions of naturalness or common sense signal an abandonment of the effort to understand."[89] Fifty years after the Glorious Revolution, and with the '45 defeated in Jacobitism's last hurrah, Fielding no longer needs to make an effort to understand; understanding would itself be dangerous. (That not all Jacobites were broadsword-wielding Catholic Highlanders out to ravish and plunder their betters hardly needs saying: Fielding is deliberately aligning dreadfulnesses together to make sure everyone follows who the bad guys are.) John Allen Stevenson attempts to "imagine a Fielding who may always have chafed at the demands of partisanship," but in *Tom Jones* nonpartisanship itself is a disguised partisan stance designed to forestall the possibility of opposition.[90]

True Patriot 3 and *Tom Jones* are complementary half-narratives portraying respectively the triumphs of Popish darkness and of an Enlightenment that the novel only names as Protestant in moments of contradistinction to Catholicism: one is all but unknown, the other a classic, a great novel, endlessly reprinted and examined. The gap between a short essay and a long novel is wider than that between Milton's *Of True Religion* and *Areopagitica*, but the same cultural dynamic is at work that buoys up the work that tells the flattering history we want to hear and sinks the hatreds and prejudices under the masks of liberty or a gentility disguised by what William C. Dowling calls "benevolist ethical theory."[91] The difference in later generations' response is not a mere misreading, however; it has basis within the works themselves. *Tom Jones* is not, after all, a novel whose greatness must be confined between quotation marks. Even more than Milton's two appeals for Protestants-only toleration, Fielding's two stories of Whig England and the lurking devils on its frontiers are quite unlike. *True Patriot* 3 is not a hundredth the length of *Tom Jones*; its violence, and the fear that underlies that violence, are vestigial, swiftly hidden remnants of the anxiety, the insularity, of the England that in becoming God's vessel contracted Chaucer's cosmopolitanism into the Grand Tour of Pope's "Europe he saw, and Europe saw him too."[92] In *Tom Jones*, Fielding is participating in an ongoing construction of a triumphalist narrative of national redemption in which literature is the ensign run up the rigging of the Royal Navy; *True Patriot* 3 is a flashback, a moment of remembered or invoked terror as Charles Stuart nears London in mid-November, 1745, a relapse into fear that inspires all the greater determination to erect a magnificent edifice for its containment. The atrophy of the narrative of endangerment accompanies the hypertrophy of the narrative of reason and progress. *True Patriot* 3 tells the alternative account repressed in *Tom Jones*, a narrative in which history erupting in horror is the sole alternative to timeless and domesticated Whig power. *Tom Jones* strikes a pose of infinite control, invoking threats only to undercut them, its wise and wisecracking narrator above viewing a "rebellious Rabble" as a serious danger, to minimize the acute alarm of the Jacobite rebellion. The peril horrifically close in *True Patriot* 3 becomes as idle as the words of a "popish Priest," a tragedy repeated as a farce, so that fear itself may be forgotten.

VI

Let us conclude this chapter by observing how the process of amnesia continues in two other works that address, in radically different ways, the relation of anti-Papism and internal regimes of repression. William Shenstone's "The Ruin'd Abbey; or, The Effects of Superstition," reviews Anglo-Papal relations, condemning "artful Rome" and its subjection of a "servile king," how "Pontific fury! English wealth exhaust[ed]" and "pillage[ed] uncontrol'd. / For now with more extensive havoc rag'd / Relentless [Pope] Gregory, with a thousand arts, / And each rapacious, born to drain the world."[93] When "the wanton scene Of monkish chastity" was at last purged from England,

> Nor yet supine, nor void of rage, retir'd
> The pest gigantic; whose revengeful stroke
> Ting'd the red annals of Maria's reign.

When from the tenderest breast each wayward priest
Could banish mercy and implant a fiend!
When Cruelty the funeral pyre uprear'd,
And bound Religion there, and fir'd the base!

(555)

Again, Catholicism is cast as alien and monstrous. Even Mary Tudor's name becomes the Romance-language, un-English Maria. Ritualized outrage at Catholic intolerance contrasts with how James I's "disinclination for ferocious persecution ... produced from the House of Commons protests that the laws were not fully enforced," leading to "'the emboldening of the Papists, and decay of true religion.'"[94] Anti-Catholicism demonizes the target of its hatred to shore up an insecure national identity, and against demons all weapons are fair. Yet Shenstone depicts a long-vanished scene, a memory recalled by a ruin; what Ann Janowitz calls "that peculiar pleasure of ruin which comes from the contemplation of the absolute pastness of the past within the aesthetically controlled shape of temporal transience" requires a superior and safe present.[95] In Shenstone's landscape, as in Marvell's "Upon Appleton House," the aristocratic manor and estate are built upon the ruin of "The pest gigantic" – an independent Church, or incorporated intelligentsia, such as Swift championed.[96]

As Johnson noted, Shenstone was an avid and celebrated landscaper, practicing not as a professional but upon his own small estate, which he ran badly into debt in the process.[97] His poem concludes,

While through the land the musing pilgrim sees
A tract of brighter green, and in the midst
Appears a mouldering wall, with ivy crown'd;
Or Gothic turret, pride of ancient days!
Now but of use to grace a rural scene;
To bound our vistas, and to glad the sons
Of George's reign, reserv'd for fairer times!

(555–56)

The monuments of monkish tyranny have been neutralized through aestheticization; the orderly, English power of the landlord-observer has supplanted Superstition. James Turner observes that "The art of landscape insists on continual harmony; it claims to display a model of the blessed land."[98] Shenstone sees that harmony as requiring as precondition the ruination of the abbey; Catholicism is the transgressive other that must be erased. His work is thus a striking example of Alan Liu's remark that "the picturesque crosses over to begin resembling and expressing historical violence."[99] "The Ruin'd Abbey" less assimilates historical violence to the picturesque, however, than the reverse: the picturesque is the result and validation of historical violence. After an opening celebration of sylvan beauty, the bulk of the poem details the crimes of Catholicism; the iniquity of the past has yielded to "fairer times," and how one condition became the other is omitted. How the bad old days became the Georgian halcyon, the function of historical violence, is what the Whig sublime seeks to obscure. Shenstone is the sort of respectable minor poet the old *Oxford Book of Eighteenth-Century Verse* included, while excluding less seemly writers: no one imagined him a major author, but he was permitted the secondarily canonical position of a recognized minor talent. What made him respectable was precisely his disguising of historical causality, his masking of the origins of Whig triumphalism. The mask he uses is anti-Catholicism. Like Tom Jones and the Hanoverian succession itself, he combines royalism and Protestant orthodoxy, loyalty and the true faith.

Catholicism plays a brief but still essential part in Charlotte Lennox's slightly later *The Sister*. Laurie Langbauer says of Lennox's *The Female Quixote* that

the structural parallel between romance and women remains. Each is the name for qualities the status quo finds transgressive and threatening, and attempts to dispel by projecting into a separate genre or gender. By doing so, the novel or patriarchy shores up its stability, emphasizes its boundaries – romance and women are in the no-novel's no-man's land outside; their very exile is what gives the others shape.[100]

After more than a decade of new historicism, the rhythm of the argument is a familiar one: a hegemonic system defines and empowers itself by what and who it excludes and disempowers. Gender and genre are not, however, the only possible principles and methods of exclusion and disempowerment. In the flurry of interest in *The Female Quixote* in recent years, others of Lennox's works have tended to be overlooked. *The Sister*, one such work, endeavors to reconcile intrigue comedy with the scrupulous moralism of sentimental comedy. To make the intrigue moral, however, requires that its beginning be blameless. The origin of the confusion that is resolved by the double wedding at the end lies in an extraordinary act that Miss Courteney has undertaken: she has fled from her guardian aunt, a scandalous deed that inevitably elicits Clairville's snickering comment that "Her aunt had made some *prudent* choice of a husband for her, perhaps – ."[101] He assumes that woman as a sexual being must have a sexual basis for her actions. The problem that Lennox faces is how to permit her heroine to engage in behavior that by the rules of domestic fiction is at least endangering her virtue, if not actually designed in furtherance of a guilty passion, without any blame attaching. She solves the problem by an appeal to an older tradition. As Nancy Armstrong observes, "in the eighteenth and nineteenth centuries[, m]ost fiction, which represented identity in terms of region, sect, or faction, could not very well affirm the universality of any particular form of desire. In contrast, domestic fiction unfolded the operations of human desire as if they were independent of political history."[102] As her solution, Lennox momentarily de-universalizes her characters, defines them politically and the sister as a religious, not solely domestic, creature: Protestantism is in danger. Courteney explains that his sister did not abscond for an immoral purpose:

No – the old lady is a bigoted Roman Catholick – and, having a large fortune to bestow, attempted to make a proselyte of the poor girl, promising her, in that case, to settle her estate upon her. This failing, she laid a scheme for entrapping her into a convent; which my sister being informed of, fled to me. (4)

As in Defoe's *Religious Courtship*, the one thing that could be as sacred to a woman as her honor is her soul, and that is imperilled by Papistical machinations. This moment of melodrama in the otherwise featherweight (that is, relatively ideologically coherent on its own terms) comedy of mistaken identity plays no further part in the work; it is the donnee that makes the dishonorable honorable. Nonetheless, its allusion to an alternative ideological system generates a Foucaultian discontinuity in the whole, supplying a rupture through which the historical specificity of the action becomes apparent. Anti-Catholicism is the mechanism through which the play violates domestic order in order to validate it, and by that violation falls into history.

Both Shenstone's and Lennox's works betray the distance and lack of urgency to the Catholic threat by their manner of employing the leitmotif. For Shenstone, Catholicism is "a mouldering wall, with ivy crown'd ... Now but of use to grace a rural scene," a ghost of a danger, an ancient bogey of which he recounts thirdhand tales of horror to justify the paradisal present. It may be noted also that, though he repeats the venerable charge of monkish lechery, what he dwells on is Papal extraction of money out of England, "the beggar'd shore ... what Rome might pillage uncontroll'd" (554): for a mercantilist, intent on the accumulation of national wealth, there could be no higher treason. Theological or spiritual issues go unmentioned. Lennox's reduction of the question of faith to a plot device carries the same dynamic still further: apparently converting to Catholicism is something Not Done, but why that should be so goes without saying. The hostility has become residual; religious identity has been conflated with cultural identity for so long as to have lost its religious specificity. By the middle of the eighteenth century, after the passing of the high-Augustan generation but before the French Revolution and Romanticism, Shenstone and Lennox have become insulated from historical process within an ideologically constructed eternal present of mercantilist progress and sentimental virtue. Their comfortable isolation has happened not by accident or destiny, but through a willed forgetting of complexity, a simplification of the ideational, and sometimes social, chaos of the seventeenth century to validate the Whig ascendancy of the eighteenth. In its later stages, as instanced in Shenstone and Lennox, the strategy is one of not only exclusion but preclusion: why the excluded was excluded in the first place has become forgotten, replacing argument with inertia, making active questioning impossible within the system. Extending the process underway in Fielding and Defoe, in these late works invisible coercion is replacing visible; persuasion has come to seem redundant.

Conclusion

History is what you remember, destiny what you desire. In the seventeenth and eighteenth centuries, England had to conquer its Catholic heritage to reinvent itself as a Protestant nation; this passage was literalized in the figure of the ruins or conversions into aristocratic seats of the dissolved monasteries. Moreover, the new identity differed from the old in its conception of England's place in the world; no longer in communion with the Continent, it was no longer a part of a common Christendom, or the multinational, multilingual abortive Plantagenet empire: the petty England that shared even its own islands with several other states and cultures became the Great Britain that projected fleets and finances across the world. "It was Protestantism which gave modern England its sense of manifest destiny," as J. C. D. Clark has noted.[3] The "heroic Protestantism," in Fredric Jameson's phrase, of seventeenth-century Dissent had an historical logic to explain the reformed religion as the precondition of the revolutionary present, but this insurrectionary logic had to be modified to serve the search for stability by the post-Stuart establishment in Church and state.[4] The synthesis of Renaissance form and Reformation content exemplified in Andrew Marvell's "Upon Appleton House" proved little more capable of surviving the revolutions of the seventeenth century than the High Church ideal of a cohesively authoritarian Church and state. In fiction as well, to employ Anthony J. Cascardi's terms to differ with his argument, the novel as it evolved in the eighteenth century represents its culture at once as "discursively heterogeneous and internally divided against itself" yet in a way as "essentializing" as Renaissance poetics.[5]

Annabel Patterson has said of Robert Burns's 1788 "The Fête Champêtre" that it "allegorizes . . . the magic circle of idyllic manners and aesthetic pleasure that were supposed to exclude political experience while implicitly supporting a conservative ideology."[6] Her characterization of the ideology as "conservative" suppresses the degree to which it represents a descendent of what only a century earlier was the "progressive" opposition to the Stuarts. This opposition did not characterize itself as progressive, however, in politics or religion: the English revolutionaries of the seventeenth century professed to be restoring in religion a primitive Christianity and in the state its original constitution, both of which had become corrupted by innovations introduced by corrupt prelates and kings. The progressive/conservative dichotomy, what Robert Markley calls the "us versus them" of "reflexive logics of binarism and progress," proves inadequate to contain the complex historical experience of early imperial England, instead reproducing the oppositional structure of the confessional divide itself.[7] Yet Patterson remains correct that the object of the predominant current in eighteenth-century poetry about the land is to reconcile rather than to agitate; it seeks Bolingbroke's "philosophic detachment," which Fabricant rechristens "selective blindness."[8] The end result of the process of exclusion of the political arrives in the personalized landscape of Romanticism in which, as Marjorie Levinson says, "history . . . ha[s] no room to surface."[9] Allworthy's Paradise Hall in *Tom Jones*, a type of the eighteenth-century country house as ideal society, is like other paradises the exclusive franchise of a jealous god: Eden requires a wall and guardian to keep out the unworthy. Absolute bliss inside the paradisal circle requires as complement absolute deprivation outside. Nor need a king or prince visit, as with Jonson's Penshurst, to ratify the arrangement; ownership is kingship enough.

It is not by coincidence that only by moving from "literary" to "non-literary" texts does the theo-ideological history of a decisive period in the formation of modernity in English society and literature become apparent; literature itself as an ideological system is heir to the methodical forgetting analyzed in this study. The canonizing process is one of sanitizing, the erasure of inconvenient aspects of history to consolidate that history from individual and contradictory textual moments into a metanarrative that justifies the system instituting the process. Anti-Catholicism was the lever by which "progress" and "reason," Fielding's "Cause of King *George*," dislodged Swift's world of sacred monarchy and clerical power – a world already lost when he wrote and that exists in his work perhaps at times as little more than an implied lever with which to dislodge in its turn the corrupt and self-congratulatory society which he confronts. In order to present the modern regime as timelessly true, its ideologues have labored to conceal its origins in the preceding, hieratic system of sectarian divisions, instead positing a dichotomy of rational progress and irrational reaction. As reason came to supplement and even overshadow doctrine in Anglican definitions of the Protestant–Catholic divide after the Restoration, so in the eighteenth century "the Protestant cause" itself becomes generalized into "the Cause of common Sense." Hostility to Catholicism acted as a vital and violent mechanism enabling the Enlightenment to erase the ideological legitimacy of the premodern social order. The political heritage of rationalism lies at the center of the cultural myths of democracy; to acknowledge the origins of this rationalism in the sectarian struggles of the seventeenth century would undercut the legitimacy of the modern state.

Ideology is imperfect, exciting opposition to continue its own existence but by that very excitation compromising its claim to truth value; we know canonical and noncanonical authors alike the better for recognizing what enemies their works contain (in both senses). Observing that Whig pamphleteers of the 1740s associate Jacobitism with "'petticoat government'" and not only "heterosexual promiscuity" but "homoeroticism," Jill Campbell suggests that their "very explicitness ... challenges certain aspects of Armstrong's and others' formulation of the novel's special ideological function: it suggests that the concealment of these connections is not always a crucial feature of their ideological power."[10] While revealing in comparison to works that completely ignore history, *Tom Jones* nonetheless takes its "overt interest in national political conflict"[11] in an attempt to minimize the significance of a conflict that was inescapably present in the minds of all its readers when it appeared in February, 1749, less than three years after the final defeat and brutal suppression of the Jacobite rebels. What *Tom Jones* makes visible to a posterity less conscious of what were current affairs to Fielding is precisely its mechanism of concealment, a mechanism risen from the anonymity of journalism to be preserved in a canonical and literary work. Pamphlets are not novels, but the novel of a journalist becomes touched by his other profession. In order to rebut by ridicule an historical antagonist, *Tom Jones* crosses into history, into journalism, instead of having the leisure to stay suspended entirely in a timeless and inviolable domesticity. *Tom Jones* visibly enacts an effacement rendered wholly invisible in Armstrong's ideal domestic type – but genres consist not of ideals but of discrete works.

Fielding's "Nonjuror, who had lent considerable Assistance to the Pretender's Cause, out of Principle," in *True Patriot* 3 is, like Orwell's Swift, a quisling, a clerical traitor, because he mistakenly supposes that any mere "Principle" could take precedence over the absolute demands of

Protestant England. All of the works examined in this study have to engage political, religious, and cultural issues with a directness that may seem unusual to those who have believed the long-lived Whig assertion that eighteenth-century England faced no serious divisions; and the reason these issues continue to engage these writers is that in High Church and Jacobite claims the regime confronts active and potentially viable alternative discourses of legitimation, alternatives that may seem alien or "reactionary" in their rationale to moderns reared on Lockean social contractualism, but that nonetheless possess a radical impact by the very fact that they *are* alternatives. In Swift's England, after all, if there was a fraud "deliberately contrived, knowingly carried on," to use Marvell's terms – to oppress the poor and the Irish and to discipline wives into the Women's Auxiliary Corps of the Protestant garrison state, whose piety and reason melded into one, like the nation and the state – it was not conducted by a Popery dispossessed two centuries earlier, but by the Tom Allworthies and their propagandists warning of the Popish peril.

The monolithic model of the eighteenth century long remained intact because its principal challengers acted on principles foreign to the inheritors of the Enlightenment. Neither "radical" nor "reactionary" is a term that entirely accurately depicts Swift because Brantley's commonplace assertion that Swift "was first and foremost a man of his age"[12] is more true than he realizes. Both expressions presume the progress/reaction dichotomy, the Left/Right divide that first arose in the French National Assembly – which convened more than half a century after the death of Swift, who indeed "Well remember[ed] Charles the Second."[13] In *An Enquiry Concerning Human Understanding*, Hume begins his discussion "Of Miracles" by citing Archbishop Tillotson against the real presence, and proceeds to a proof one evidence for which is that miracles primarily "abound among ignorant and barbarous nations," but are denied by "the enlightened ages."[14] Hume's dichotomy between "barbarous nations" and "enlightened ages" parallels the developing division between Europe and other peoples whom it is learning to consider inferior. In the battle between Ancients and Moderns, the Ancient Sir William Temple asserts that "There is nothing more agreed than, That all the Learning of the *Greeks* was deduced Originally from *Egypt* or *Phoenicia*," praises "*Indian Brachmans*" for "a strain beyond all *Grecian* wit," and concludes that "whoever observes the Account already given of the Ancient *Indian* and *Chinese* Learning and Opinions will easily find among them the Seeds of all these *Grecian* Productions and Institutions."[15] To respect the intellectual achievements of non-Western cultures is to be an Ancient; to dismiss them as "barbarous" is to be Modern and "enlightened": what is advanced, what retrograde? It is in such a context that Swift's alienation amid corruption and ruthlessness covered by hypocrisy, which seemed mere madness to those eminent Victorians Macaulay and Thackeray, finds a more appreciative response today among a later generation of institutional intellectuals who find themselves excluded and estranged from power.

Skepticism about proclaimed ideals, of course, is prudent with respect to any system of belief and governance. The victors in any struggle always prove their cause is just; the beneficiaries of any social arrangement always devise rationalizations for why that arrangement is superior to any possible alternative. If to err is human, so is complacency in ruling classes. All systems of domination incorporate unequal power relations, subsequent injustices, and more or less plausible justifications for those injustices. As Johnson observes, "To charge those favorable representations, which men give of their own minds, with the guilt of hypocritical falsehood, would show more severity than knowledge. The writer commonly believes himself."[16] The realistic novel comes of age by erasing its origins in a process of "favorable representations." In his 1725 letter to Pope outlining the "great foundation of misanthropy" for *Gulliver's Travels*, Swift makes the distinction that "man" is not "*animal rationale*," a rational animal, but only "*rationis capax*," one capable of reason: a rational animal is one whose reason, whose common sense, is irrefutable by doubt – like the divine right of the propertied, of the English, of the patriarchal family.[17] Discussing the case of Salman Rushdie, Srinivas Aravamudan condemns media coverage focused on "the well-worn dichotomy of religious fanaticism battling secular free speech: (Western) democracy crusading against (Oriental) tyranny."[18] In England anyway, far from the Ottomans, tyranny was identified with Popery long before the Orient impinged seriously on popular consciousness. After 1660, Milton is forced from pamphleteering and public affairs into the indirection of *Paradise Lost*; after 1715, Swift, too, has to retreat from journalism and London politics to the satire of *Gulliver's Travels*: despite the disappearance of formal censorship, the governments of "absolutist" Charles II and "constitutional" George I of the Protestant Succession act to similar effect. Also similar is that neither government's ban is perfectly effective; Milton smuggles his proscribed concerns into *Of True Religion*, as Swift turns from writing on behalf of the independence of the clergy to supporting the in-dependence (though not in any Irish Nationalist sense) of the Irish. In my introduction, I asserted that literature is what can be said, but might it not also be argued that individual works of literature are precisely what *cannot* be said, the fugitive detritus of suppression and evasion? Rushdie in hiding or Swift in Ireland, "the confined satirist is interloper *par excellence*."[19] Silences environ the articulated word. No truths are self-evident, except to a mind predisposed to accept them.

Notes

INTRODUCTION

1 Percy Bysshe Shelley, *The Triumph of Life*, lines 288–92, in *Shelley's Poetry and Prose*, ed. Donald H. Reiman and Sharon B. Powers (New York: Norton, 1977), 463.

2 Samuel Johnson, *Lives of the English Poets*, ed. George Birbeck Hill, 3 vols. (1905; New York: Octagon Press, 1967), 1.410, 421, 422.

3 *Ibid*, 1.408.

4 Interestingly, Hunter himself has noted the suppression of the long eighteenth century in mid-twentieth-century literary criticism: "in many of the most powerful thinkers about literature – Northrop Frye, Frank Kermode, M. H. Abrams, and Stanley Fish, for example – there is room between 1667 and 1787 only for Renaissance leftovers and anticipations of the High Romantics" (J. Paul Hunter, *Before Novels: The Cultural Contexts of Eighteenth-Century English Fiction* [New York: W. W. Norton, 1990], xiii). The same "literary 'line'" (xiii), however, shapes his own anthology, but then theoretical speculations can outrun the marketing imperatives that rule textbook publishing.

5 Jerome J. McGann, *The Romantic Ideology: A Critical Investigation* (Chicago: University of Chicago Press, 1983), 159.

6 Despite the Reform Bills of 1832 and later, and the subordination of the House of Lords in 1911, the fundamental characteristic of the post-1688 regime, the claim to unlimited sovereignty by Parliament, has only recently begun to be seriously challenged, internally by the extra-Parliamentary left and externally by the supranational mechanisms of the European Community.

7 Among the many relevant studies may be listed a special issue of the *Journal of British Studies* (31:4, October 1992) and numerous essays by John Morrill and J. G. A. Pocock such as Morrill's "The Fashioning of Britain," in *Conquest and Union: Fashioning a British State, 1485–1725*, ed. Steven G. Ellis and Sarah Barber (London: Longman, 1995), pp. 8–39, and Pocock's "British History: A Plea for a New Subject," *Journal of Modern History* 47 (1975): 601–28 – besides the Pocock essay in the aforementioned *JBS* issue. Morrill's conception of an expanding centralized control within the respective kingdoms parallel to an increasing ascendancy of England throughout "the Atlantic archipelago" (in Pocock's phrase) in the early modern period is perhaps especially productive. For an exploration of noncanonical Jacobite literature that includes ballads in Gaelic, Welsh, Scots, and Irish, see Murray G. H. Pittock, *Poetry and Jacobite Politics in Eighteenth-Century Britain and Ireland* (Cambridge: Cambridge University Press, 1995).

8 Jonathan Dollimore, *Radical Tragedy: Religion, Ideology and Power in the Drama of Shakespeare and his Contemporaries* (Brighton, Sussex: Harvester Press, 1984), 4.

9 For an account of how the conception of literature was connected to its role as passport to social prestige, see John Guillory, *Cultural Capital: The Problem of Literary Canon Formation* (Chicago: University of Chicago Press, 1993).

10 Charles D. Tarlton, review of Richard Ashcraft, *Revolutionary Politics and Locke's Two Treatises of Government* (Princeton: Princeton University Press, 1986), in *Political Theory* 16 (1988): 335.

11 Alexis de Tocqueville, *Democracy in America*, trans. Henry Reeve, ed. Phillips Bradley, 2 vols. (New York: Knopf, 1960), 1.264.

12 Paul Kleber Monod, *Jacobitism and the English People, 1688–1788* (Cambridge: Cambridge University Press, 1989), 347.

13 Alexander Pope, "Essay on Man" 1.6, quoted and discussed in Samuel Johnson's "Life of Pope" (*Lives of the English Poets*, 3.162).

14 See Michel Serres, *The Parasite*, trans. Lawrence R. Schehr (Baltimore: Johns Hopkins University Press, 1982).

15 Peter Lake, "Anti-Popery: The Structure of a Prejudice," in *Conflict in Early Stuart England: Studies in Religion and Politics 1603–1642*, ed. Richard Cust and Ann Hughes (London: Longman, 1989), 91.

16 Georg Lukacs, *The Historical Novel*, trans. Hannah and Stanley Mitchell (1962; Lincoln: University of Nebraska Press, 1983), 121.

17 Hayden White, *Metahistory: The Historical Imagination in Nineteenth-Century Europe* (Baltimore: Johns Hopkins University Press, 1973), 55.

18 Lukacs, *The Historical Novel*, 26.

19 Roland Barthes, "The Last Happy Writer," in *A Barthes Reader*, ed. Susan Sontag (New York: Hill and Wang, 1982), 156.

20 Edward W. Said, *Orientalism* (New York: Pantheon, 1978), 7, 10.

21 *Ibid.*, 59.

22 *Ibid.*, 60–61.

23 *Ibid.*, 62.

24 Quoted in *ibid.*, 73.

25 Edward Terrar, "Was There a Separation of Church and State in Mid-17th-Century England and Colonial Maryland?," *Journal of Church and State* 35 (1993): 65.

26 At a higher social level, personal tolerance is reflected in the correspondence of one of the most visible of the converts to Catholicism under James II, Dryden. Nearly all of his letters that survive date from the 1690s, but none suggests any personal hostility or slights on the basis of his religion, although like Milton after the Restoration he disliked and felt excluded by the course of public events. See *The Letters of John Dryden, With Letters Addressed to Him*, ed. Charles E. Ward (Durham: Duke University Press, 1942).

27 Frank Felsenstein regards the positions of Jews and Catholics as superficially similar but more significantly different because of the lack of visible stigmata and greater numbers and social integration of Catholics (*Anti-Semitic Stereotypes: A Paradigm of Otherness in English Popular Culture, 1660–1830* [Baltimore: Johns Hopkins University Press, 1995], 247–48). Certainly lay Catholics were not exposed to such daily and gross stereotyping as Jews were, but what

of the widely detested, outlawed, rare, and distinctively clothed and educated clergy?

28 See Terry Eagleton, *Literary Theory: An Introduction* (Minneapolis: University of Minnesota Press, 1983), particularly his conclusion.

29 Jochen Schulte-Sasse and Linda Schulte-Sasse, "War, Otherness, and Illusionary Identifications with the State," *Cultural Critique* 19 (Fall 1991): 85, 95.

30 Terry Eagleton, *Ideology: An Introduction* (London: Verso, 1990), 64.

31 Thomas Tenison, *Dr. Tenison's Sermon of Alms*, 2–3, 45. Published as a separately paginated appendix to [John Williams,] *An Apology for the Pulpits: Being in Answer to a Late Book, Intituled, Good Advice to the Pulpits. Together with an Appendix, containing a Defense of Dr. Tenison's Sermon about Alms; in a Letter to the Author of this Apology* (London, 1688).

32 Max Weber, *The Protestant Ethic and the Spirit of Capitalism* (New York: Charles Scribner's Sons, 1958), 177–79.

33 See Ian Gilmour, *Riots, Risings and Revolution: Governance and Violence in Eighteenth-Century England* (London: Hutchinson, 1992), 427

34 [John Gother,] *Good Advice to the Pulpits* (London, 1687).

35 Terence N. Bowers, "The Production and Communication of Knowledge in William Baldwin's *Beware the Cat*," *Criticism* 33 (1991): 22.

36 Richard Brown, *Church and State in Modern Britain 1700–1850* (London: Routledge, 1991), 98. Paul Langford has an excellent summary discussion of how church property tended to reduce to ordinary property in the eighteenth century in his *Public Life and the Propertied Englishman, 1689–1798* (Oxford: Clarendon Press, 1991), 14–28.

37 J. C. D. Clark, *Revolution and Rebellion: State and Society in England in the Seventeenth and Eighteenth Centuries* (Cambridge: Cambridge University Press, 1986), 7.

38 John Bender, "A New History of the Enlightenment," *Eighteenth Century Life* ns 16 (1992): 1–2.

39 J. G. A. Pocock, "The Significance of 1688: Some Reflections on Whig History," *The Revolutions of 1688: The Andrew Browning Lectures 1988*, ed. Robert Beddard (Oxford: Clarendon Press, 1991), 292.

40 Brook Thomas, *The New Historicism and Other Old-Fashioned Topics* (Princeton: Princeton University Press, 1991), xii.

41 W. H. Auden, "Spain," *Selected Poems*, ed. Edward Mendelson (New York: Vintage, 1979), 55.

I CONSTRUCTING THE NATION, CONSTRUCTING THE OTHER:
MARTYROLOGY AND MERCANTILISM

1 Novalis, quoted in Liah Greenfeld, *Nationalism: Five Roads to Modernity* (Cambridge, MA: Harvard University Press, 1992), 357.

2 William Wordsworth, *The Prelude*, 1805 version, VIII.746–9, in *The Prelude 1799, 1805, 1850*, ed. Jonathan Wordsworth, M. H. Abrams, and Stephen Gill (New York: Norton, 1979), 306.

3 David Cressy notes how the English calendar, unlike those of the rest of

Europe, featured "special days honoring the Protestant monarch and the ordeals and deliverances of the national church" in a manner anticipating that of modern national calendars ("The Protestant Calendar and the Vocabulary of Celebration in Early Modern England," *Journal of British Studies* 29 [1990]: 31). The Reformation served England as a mark of national passage in the same fashion as revolutions have since served other countries.

4 See her *Nationalism*, particularly the introduction and first chapter.

5 Thomas Babington Macaulay, "Van Ranke's History of the Popes," *The Works of Lord Macaulay Complete*, ed. Hannah More (Macaulay) Trevelyan, 8 vols. (London, 1866), 6.476.

6 Daniel Gold, "Organized Hinduisms: From Vedic Truth to Hindu Nation," in *Fundamentalisms Observed*, ed. Martin E. Marty and R. Scott, vol. 1 (Chicago: University of Chicago Press, 1991), 576.

7 Paula Backscheider observes that Defoe's "descriptions of what their nation [Scotland] could become [after the 1707 Union] are the descriptions of what London became after the Great Fire" (Paula Backscheider, *Daniel Defoe His Life* [Baltimore: Johns Hopkins University Press, 1989], 251).

8 Christopher Hill, *Antichrist in Seventeenth-Century England* (London: Oxford University Press, 1971), 174.

9 The following discussion veers closer to Richard Helgerson's account of an emerging "discourse of nationhood" in Foxe than to John R. Knott's focus on "resistance to the church's authority," which largely overlooks the possibility of multiple competing authorities (Richard Helgerson, *Forms of Nationhood: The Elizabethan Writing of England* [Chicago: University of Chicago Press, 1992]; John R. Knott, *Discourses of Martyrdom in English Literature, 1563–1694* [Cambridge: Cambridge University Press, 1993], 3). To oppose one hierarchy need not necessarily imply opposing all. Admitting that "I ignore the literature of Catholic persecution and martyrdom under Elizabeth" (10), Knott neglects the opportunity to examine the covert continuity of repression between the Marian Catholic and Elizabethan Protestant regimes.

10 John Foxe, *Acts and Monuments of Matters most Special and Memorable, Happening in the Church: with an Universal History Of the same*, 9th edn. (London: Printed for the Company of Stationers, 1684), prefatory address, "To all the Professed Friends and Followers of the Popes Proceedings," n.p. Although the precise contents and even title of this work vary among editions, the two sequences of illustrations which form the center of this discussion are present from the earliest editions, "the poysoning of King Iohn" appearing in the first, 1563, edition, "The proud primacie of Popes" in the second, 1570. The 1570 edition also contains the "Pope Alexander treading on the necke of *Fredericke the Emperour*" and "Henricus the Emperour" woodcuts mentioned.

11 William Shakespeare, *The Winter's Tale*, v.ii.22, in *The Riverside Shakespeare* (Boston: Houghton Mifflin, 1974), 1600.

12 The ninth book occurs at the end of the second volume, but pagination begins again at page 1 at its start.

13 Innocent III, Bull dated at Anagni, August 24, 1215, translation on display in

the Magna Carta case in the Manuscript Salon of the British Library Gallery, London.

14 Mark Goldie, "Priestcraft and the Birth of Whiggism," in *Political Discourse in Early Modern Britain*, ed. Nicholas Phillipson and Quentin Skinner (Cambridge: Cambridge University Press, 1993), 214–15.

15 See John N. King, *English Reformation Literature: The Tudor Origins of the Protestant Tradition* (Princeton: Princeton University Press, 1982), 454.

16 Raymond Williams, *The Country and the City* (New York: Oxford University Press, 1973), 297, 298.

17 Anthony Pagden, *Lords of All the World: Ideologies of Empire in Spain, Britain and France c. 1500–c.1800* (New Haven: Yale University Press, 1995), 10.

18 Sheila Williams, "The Lord Mayor's Show in Tudor and Stuart Times," *The Guildhall Miscellany* 1 (1959): 4.

19 Max Weber, *The Protestant Ethic and the Spirit of Capitalism*, trans. Talcott Parsons (New York: Charles Scribner's Sons, 1958), 53.

20 Margot Heinemann, *Puritanism and Theatre: Thomas Middleton and Opposition Drama under the Early Stuarts* (Cambridge: Cambridge University Press, 1980), 4.

21 Theodore B. Leinwand, "London Triumphing: The Jacobean Lord Mayor's Show," *Clio* 11 (1982), 137–53, supplies a useful historical bibliography and summary of the early history of the Lord Mayor's Day fetes. Sergei Lobanov-Rostovsky claims that "Economic power requires political justification" and argues a patronage-driven contrast between Middleton's first, playlike pageant and his later ones (Sergei Lobanov-Rostovsky, "*The Triumphes of Golde*: Economic Authority in the Jacobean Lord Mayor's Show," *ELH* 60 [1993]: 892). While his observation of the destabilizing potential of the theatrical form of Middleton's 1613 pageant resembles mine, however, my study embeds its analysis in a more comprehensive historicity that suggests that to say patronage merely "rendered [Middleton] docile" (891) implies a more antagonistic, coercive relationship between author and the guilds for which he wrote than I find justifiable. There is no more reason to suppose Middleton subduedly "docile," rather than actively and intentionally supportive, in his work for the city than Jonson in his pageants for the court.

22 Thomas Middleton, *The Triumphs of Truth*, in *The Works of Thomas Middleton*, ed. A. H. Bullen, vol. 7 (Boston: Houghton, Mifflin, 1886), 233. All further references to Middleton's Lord Mayor's Day pageants will be made in the text.

23 David Bergeron, "Middleton's *No Wit, No Help* and Civic Pageantry," in *Pageantry in the Shakespearean Theater*, ed. David Bergeron (Athens: University of Georgia Press, 1985), 165–80.

24 It is suggestive that P. J. Cain and A. G. Hopkins begin their study of British imperialism with the year of the Glorious Revolution (P. J. Cain and A. G. Hopkins, *British Imperialism: Innovation and Expansion 1688–1914* [Harlow: Longman, 1993]).

25 Stephen Greenblatt, *Shakespearean Negotiations* (Berkeley: University of California Press, 1988), 22, 136.

26 Franco Moretti, *Signs Taken for Wonders* (London: Verso, 1988), 42; and Jonathan Dollimore, *Radical Tragedy* (Chicago: University of Chicago Press, 1984), 27.

27 Albert H. Tricomi, *Anticourt Drama in England 1603–1642* (Charlottesville: University Press of Virginia, 1989), 152.

28 P. W. Thomas, "Two Cultures? Court and Country under Charles I," in *The Origins of the English Civil War*, ed. Conrad Russell (New York: Barnes and Noble, 1973), 184, and quoted in Christopher Hill's *Milton and the English Revolution* (London: Faber and Faber, 1977), 21.

29 London possessed a pool of concentrated wealth, skills, and manpower found nowhere else in the three kingdoms. Heinemann calls London "the melting-pot for the whole kingdom" (*Puritanism and Theatre*, 3). In his critique of Heinemann, "Thomas Middleton and the Court, 1624: *A Game of Chess* in Context," *Huntington Library Quarterly* 47 (1984): 273–88, Thomas Cogswell attacks Heinemann's use of the idea of a unitary "Parliamentary Puritan opposition." Such revisionist historical analyses as Conrad Russell's *Parliaments and English Politics 1621–1629* (Oxford: Clarendon Press, 1979) have questioned the idea of a simple dichotomy between court and country, government and opposition, as at once "institutionally impossible" and "ideologically impossible" (9), because a Member of Parliament needed both court and country support to get elected (6), and because a heterogeneous court was able to supply a patron for virtually any M.P. (10). Nonetheless, although social and political divisions are rarely neat, and oversimplification of complex social, institutional, and ideological issues ought to be shunned, it is well to keep in mind that the first Parliaments to meet after those of the 1620s were the Long Parliament and its quickly dismissed predecessor. The occurrence of an earthquake suggests the pre-existence of a fault line.

30 John Knowles argues that "Civic ceremony seeks to embody reconciliation and inculcate order, not simply in its explicit rhetoric, but in its very form, especially the processional element, which actually manifested the whole social body and constitution of the City for its citizens" (John Knowles, "The Spectacle of the Realm: Civic Consciousness, Rhetoric, and Ritual in Early Modern London," in *Theatre and Government under the Early Stuarts*, ed. J. R. Mulrayne and Margaret Shewring [Cambridge: Cambridge University Press, 1993], 182). While correct so far as it goes, his analysis fails to consider to what effect the citizenry could – and would – be united against the national government. "Order" is not necessarily unitary. A procession is an organized mob, but so is an army.

31 The Jonson quotation is from Heinemann, *Puritanism and Theatre*, 171.

32 Cogswell, "Thomas Middleton and the Court," cited above.

33 See Annabel Patterson, *Censorship and Interpretation: The Conditions of Writing and Reading in Early Modern England* (Madison: University of Wisconsin Press, 1984) for a detailed account of Stuart censorship.

34 Michael D. Bristol argues, after Bakhtin, that "Plebeian culture ... takes particular note of the arbitrary, ramshackle nature of authority and political

power" (*Carnival and Theater: Plebeian Culture and the Structure of Authority in Renaissance England* [New York: Methuen, 1985], 138).

35 Oliver Goldsmith, "The Traveller," lines 387–88, in *Collected Works of Oliver Goldsmith*, ed. Arthur Friedman, vol. 4 (Oxford: Clarendon Press, 1966), 266.

36 Heinemann, *Puritanism and Theatre*, 259.

37 Greenblatt, *Shakespearean Negotiations*, 29–30.

38 Richard Hakluyt, *The Principal Navigations, Voyages, Traffiques, and Discoveries of the English Nation*, 12 vols. (Glasgow: James Maclehose and Sons, 1903), 10.56, cited in Greenblatt, *Shakespearean Negotiations*, 29.

39 A footnote in the *Diary* of Samuel Pepys, when soon after the Restoration he complains of "earthen pitchers and wooden dishes" at a Lord Mayor's Day feast, observes that "A great deal of city plate had been melted down during the Civil War" (Samuel Pepys, *The Diary of Samuel Pepys*, ed. Robert Latham and William Mattle, vol. 4 [Berkeley: University of California Press, 1970–76], 355). Some of the show of power had been expended in securing more of its substance.

40 Elkanah Settle, *Glory's Resurrection: Being the Triumphs of London Revived* (London, 1698), n.p. Further references to this work will be made in the text.

41 See Nicholas Jose, *Ideas of the Restoration in English Literature* (Cambridge, MA: Harvard University Press, 1984) for a detailed discussion of such panegyrics.

42 Elkanah Settle, *The Triumphs of London* (London, 1701), 6.

43 Terry Eagleton, "Nationalism: Irony and Commitment," in Seamus Deane, Terry Eagleton, Fredric Jameson, Edward W. Said, *Nationalism, Colonialism, and Literature* (Minneapolis: University of Minnesota Press, 1990), 25.

44 Weber, *The Protestant Ethic*, 22, 158–59.

45 Revelation 18:13.

46 John Childs argues that the conspiracy of officers that "wrecked the army [of James II] as an operational machine" in 1688 was motivated primarily by self-interest rather than sectarianism, but concludes, "If England had been involved in a normal foreign war instead of a civil war fomented by intervention from overseas, there is no good reason to suppose that the army would have demonstrated any disloyalty to James II" (John Childs, *The Army, James II, and the Glorious Revolution* [Manchester: Manchester University Press, 1980], 195, 205). What turned an invasion into a civil war, however, was precisely the internal opposition aroused by James's embodiment of "Popery and Tyranny."

47 Ian Gilmour, *Riots Risings, and Revolution: Governance and Violence in Eighteenth-Century England* (London: Hutchinson, 1992), 369, 370.

48 *Ibid.*, 360.

49 Horace Walpole, *Correspondence with the Countess of Upper Ossory*, ed. W. S. Lewis (New Haven: Yale University Press, 1965); quoted in *A Journey to the Western Islands of Scotland*, vol. 9 of *The Yale Edition of the Works of Samuel Johnson*, ed. Mary Lascalles (New Haven: Yale University Press, 1971), 106n.

50 Eagleton, "Nationalism," 33.

51 *Ibid.*, 32, 30.

52 *Ibid.*, 30.

53 Linda Colley, *Britons: Forging the Nation 1707–1837* (New Haven: Yale University Press, 1992), 7, 1.

2 OF TRUE RELIGION AND FALSE POLITICS: MILTON, MARVELL, AND POPERY

1 Nicholas Rowe, "Prologue to *The Non-Juror*," in *Minor English Poets 1660–1780*, ed. David P. French, vol. 3 (New York: Benjamin Blom, 1967), 429, selected from *The English Poets*, ed. Alexander Chalmers (London, 1810).

2 Nahum Tate, "In Memory of Joseph Washington, Esq.; Late of the Middle Temple, an Elegy" (1694), lines 79–80, in *Andrew Marvell: The Critical Heritage*, ed. Elizabeth Story Donno (London: Routledge and Kegan Paul, 1978), 103.

3 In his preface and notes to *Of True Religion* in *Complete Prose Works of John Milton*, vol. 8 (New Haven: Yale University Press, 1982), Keith W. F. Stavely reports only one definite friendly and one probable hostile contemporary allusion to *Of True Religion*, both confined to a phrase, 413–14n, 428n. Further references to *Of True Religion* will be made in the text.

4 In its covert method, the pamphlet resembles the *Observations upon the Articles of Peace*, which, as Thomas N. Corns notes, also "play[s] the Catholic card" as a blind to cover Milton's more controversial intra-Protestant agenda (Thomas N. Corns, "Milton's *Observations upon the Articles of Peace*: Ireland under English Eyes," in *Politics, Poetics, and Hermeneutics in Milton's Prose*, ed. David Loewenstein and James Grantham Turner [Cambridge: Cambridge University Press, 1990], 125).

5 See Stavely, *Complete Prose Works of John Milton*, 408–13, and David Masson, *The Life of John Milton*, vol. 6 (1859; New York: Peter Smith, 1946), 690–99.

6 David Loewenstein and James Grantham Turner, "Introduction," in Loewenstein and Turner, *Politics, Poetics* 2. None of the essays in this volume, it may be noted, addresses *Of True Religion*.

7 Nathaniel Henry, "Milton's Last Pamphlet: Theocracy and Intolerance," in *A Tribute to George Coffin Taylor: Studies and Essays, Chiefly Elizabethan*, ed. Arnold Williams (Chapel Hill: University of North Carolina Press, 1952), 209.

8 Reuben Marquez Sanchez, Jr., "'The Worst of Superstitions': Milton's *Of True Religion* and the Issue of Religious Tolerance," *Prose Studies* 9 (1986): 21.

9 Fredric Jameson, "Religion and Ideology: A Political Reading of *Paradise Lost*," in *Literature, Politics and Theory*, ed. Francis Barker (London: Methuen, 1986), 40. Also relevant is Karl Marx's observation that "Cromwell and the English people had borrowed speech, passions and illusions from the Old Testament for their bourgeois revolution" (Lewis S. Feuer, ed., *Marx and Engels: Basic Writings on Politics and Philosophy* [London, 1969], 361–2, quoted by Terry Eagleton in "The God That Failed," in *Re-membering Milton: Essays on the Texts and Traditions*, ed. Mary Nyquist and Margaret W. Ferguson [New York: Methuen, 1987], 344).

10 Christopher Hill, *The Experience of Defeat* (New York: Viking, 1984), 326–27.

11 N. H. Keeble, *The Literary Culture of Nonconformity* (Leicester: Leicester University Press, 1987), 22.

12 That is, Hill seeks among the Dissenters of the Restoration such works of openly subversive intent as those he had recently examined in "Radical Prose in 17th Century England: From Marprelate to the Levellers," *Essays in Criticism* 32 (1982): 95–118.

13 See Nicholas Jose's *Ideas of the Restoration in English Literature* (Cambridge, MA: Harvard University Press, 1984) for an analysis of 1660s royalist propaganda. Keeble, *Literary Culture of Nonconformity*, 93–126, discusses the post-Restoration censorship.

14 Mary Ann Radzinowicz, *Towards* Samson Agonistes: *The Growth of Milton's Mind* (Princeton: Princeton University Press, 1978), 165.

15 Andrew Marvell, *The Complete Works in Verse and Prose of Andrew Marvell M.P.*, ed. Alexander B. Grosart ([London]: The Fuller Worthies' Library, 1875); The Rehearsal Transpros'd and The Rehearsal Transpros'd The Second Part, ed. D. I. B. Smith (Oxford: Clarendon Press, 1971).

16 Harold Tolliver, "The Critical Reprocessing of Andrew Marvell," *ELH* 47 (1980): 180.

17 W. D. Christie, unsigned review, *Saturday Review* 35 (26 April 1873): 553–54, in *Andrew Marvell: The Critical Heritage*, 238.

18 A. C. Benson, essay from *Macmillan's Magazine* 65 (January, 1892): 203, in *Andrew Marvell: The Critical Heritage*, 262.

19 For all the value of his examination of "the politics of pleasure," Steven N. Zwicker adheres to the traditional bifurcation of the lyrical and satirical, or Renaissance and Restoration, Marvell in considering the *Last Instructions to a Painter* in isolation from the presumedly earlier works on which Marvell's reputation as a poet has primarily rested (Steven N. Zwicker, *Lines of Authority: Politics and English Literary Culture, 1649–1689* [Ithaca: Cornell University Press, 1993], 8).

20 For example, when Gerald M. MacLean incorporates Marvell into an exploration of "a new history of the production, reproduction, and reception of 'English' poetry in the seventeenth century," he discusses the "First Anniversary" at some length, and touches upon the "Horation Ode" and "On the Victory Obtained by Blake," but omits both the prose and less obviously political poetry, such as "Upon Appleton House" (Gerald M. MacLean, *Time's Witness: Historical Representation in English Poetry, 1603–1660* [Madison: University of Wisconsin Press, 1990], 266). As a consequence, although he acknowledges the need to view "'protestant' poetics as central," he is left with a simplistic dichotomy between "opposition poets" and "the new virility of empire which the Restoration helped enunciate" (266, 260, 266), failing to recognize the extent to which both proponents and opponents of the Restoration were attempting to assimilate themselves to a "new virility of empire." "Opposition" writers such as Marvell attacked the Stuarts precisely for being inadequate in Protestantism and thus unmanly and unfit to build God's empire. John Morrill notes an antecedent belief among opponents of Charles I that he was "a negligent king who was oblivious to the threat of popery at home, abroad, and within the church of which he was supreme governor" (John Morrill, *The*

Nature of the English Revolution [London: Longman, 1993], 53). Internal vigilance and external strength were seen as related by both sides.

21 Michael McKeon, "Pastoralism, Pluralism, Imperialism, Scientism: Andrew Marvell and the Problem of Mediation," *Yearbook of English Studies* 13 (1983): 46, 65.

22 Jean-Luc Nancy, "Our History," trans. Cynthia Chase, Richard Klein, and A. Mitchell Brown, *Diacritics* 20.3 (1990): 109.

23 Keeble, *Literary Culture of Nonconformity*, 108–9.

24 I. S., *The Papacy of Paul the Fourth. Or, the Restitution of Abby Lands and Impropriations, An indispensable condition of Reconciliation to the Infallible See, &c.* (London, 1673).

25 Andrew Marvell, *An Account of the Growth of Popery, and Arbitrary Government in England*, in *The Complete Works in Verse and Prose of Andrew Marvell M.P.*, 4.248.

26 Michael G. Finlayson, *Historians, Puritanism, and the English Revolution: The Religious Factor in English Politics before and after the Interrregnum* (Toronto: University of Toronto Press, 1983), 76.

27 Conal Condren, "Andrew Marvell as Polemicist: His Account of the Growth of Popery, and Arbitrary Government," in *The Political Identity of Andrew Marvell*, ed. Conal Condren and A. D. Cousins (Aldershot, Hampshire: Scolar Press, 1990), 177.

28 Annabel M. Patterson, *Marvell and the Civic Crown* (Princeton: Princeton University Press, 1978), 237; William Lamont, "The Religion of Andrew Marvell: Locating the 'Bloody Horse,'" in Condren and Cousins, *The Political Identity of Andrew Marvell*, 150.

29 J. C. D. Clark, *Revolution and Rebellion: State and Society in England in the Seventeenth and Eighteenth Centuries* (Cambridge: Cambridge University Press, 1986), 23; Peter Lake, "Anti-Popery: The Structure of a Prejudice," in *Conflict in Early Stuart England: Studies in Religion and Politics 1603–1642*, ed. Richard Cust and Ann Hughes (London: Longman, 1989), 97.

30 See Elias Canetti on the theatrical audience as crowd (*Crowds and Power*, trans. Carol Stewart [New York: Viking, 1962], 34–38).

31 Don E. Wayne, *Penshurst: The Semiotics of Place and the Poetics of History* (Madison: University of Wisconsin Press, 1984), 16.

32 John N. King, *English Reformation Literature: The Tudor Origins of the Protestant Tradition* (Princeton: Princeton University Press, 1982), 454.

33 Laurence Goldstein observes how "Eighteenth-century authors habitually gave monumental ruins the role of antagonist in the drama of human salvation" (Laurence Goldstein, *Ruins and Empire: The Evolution of a Theme in Augustan and Romantic Literature* [Pittsburgh: University of Pittsburgh Press, 1977], 3). This antagonistic role has its origin in the function of England's most notorious ruins, Shakespeare's "Bare ruined choirs, where once the sweet birds sang," the despoiled monasteries, as the simultaneous enemy and reproach against which the new, Protestant, and imperial England defined itself; it judged and feared that it was judged. John Denham's *Coopers Hill* most famously represents the anti-Puritan elegiac interpretation: "Who sees these dismal heaps, but would demand / What barbarous Invader sackt the land?"

(John Denham, *Coopers Hill* [1655 edition], lines 149–50, in *Expans'd Hieroglyphicks: A Critical Edition of Sir John Denham's Coopers Hill*, ed. Brendan O'Hehir [Berkeley: University of California Press, 1969], 148). Whereas Denham laments "such th'effects of our devotions" (line 156), Marvell's Fairfax represents precisely the idealized secular alternative, "so temperate, so chast, so just" (*Coopers Hill*, line 120), unlike Denham's Henry VIII, to justify the dispossession of the monasteries.

34 Francis Bacon, *Essays and New Atlantis* (Roslyn, NY: Walter J. Black, 1942), 192. Future references to this work will be made in the text.

35 Edmund Burke, *A Philosophical Enquiry into the Origin of our Ideas of the Sublime and Beautiful*, ed. James T. Boulton (Oxford: Basil Blackwell, 1987), 63, 58, 65.

36 Ben Jonson, "To Penshurst," in *The Complete Poems*, ed. George Parfitt (New Haven: Yale University Press, 1975).

37 Patsy Griffin, "'Twas no *Religious House* till now': Marvell's 'Upon Appleton House,'" *Studies in English Literature 1500–1900* 28 (1988): 75, 61. This article is reprinted as chapter 3 of her monograph, *The Modest Ambition of Andrew Marvell: A Study of Marvell and His Relation to Lovelace, Fairfax, Cromwell, and Milton* (Newark: University of Delaware Press, 1995).

38 Daniel P. Jaeckle, "Marvell's Dialogics of History: 'Upon Appleton House,' xi-xxxv," *John Donne Journal* 6 (1987): 261–73.

39 Griffin, "'Twas no *Religious House*," 61, and Jaeckle, "Marvell's Dialogics," 261.

40 A. D. Cousins, "Marvell's 'Upon Appleton House, to my Lord Fairfax' and the Regaining of Paradise," in *The Political Identity of Andrew Marvell*, 66, 67.

41 Douglas D. C. Chambers, "'To the Abbyss': Gothic as a Metaphor for the Argument about Art and Nature in 'Upon Appleton House,'" in *On the Celebrated and Neglected Poems of Andrew Marvell*, ed. Claude J. Summers and Ted-Larry Pebworth (Columbia: University of Missouri Press, 1992), 139–53.

42 John Rogers, "The Great Work of Time: Marvell's Pastoral Historiography," in Summers and Pebworth, *On the Celebrated and Neglected Poems of Andrew Marvell*, 216.

43 Andrew Marvell, "Upon Appleton House," in *Andrew Marvell*, ed. Frank Kermode and Keith Walker (Oxford: Oxford University Press, 1990), 53–77. See Peter Wagner's "Anticatholic Erotica in Eighteenth-Century England," in *Erotica and the Enlightenment*, ed. Peter Wagner (Frankfurt am Main: Peter Lang, 1991), 166–209, for a discussion of monks and nuns in pornography. Vows of chastity and assemblages of unmarried women provided material for pornographic speculation well before the Reformation, as in the first tale of the third day in Boccaccio's *Decameron*. Similarly, John Gay plays on the supposedly lewd celibacy of Catholic clergy in two of his three mildly suggestive tetrameter Tales, "Work for a Cooper" and "The Equivocation," and the third, "The Mad-Dog," has an unchaste woman repeatedly making confession of her sin, indicating that she is Catholic. Gay's setting of his "naughty" poems in Catholic societies is far from venomous, but in its very lack of polemical edge suggests how readily available the association of Catholicism with sexual deviancy was. See John Gay, *Poetry and Prose*, ed. Vinton A. Dearing (Oxford:

Clarendon Press, 1974). William Empson's thesis that Marvell was homosexual is irrelevant to the question of the strategic alignment of sexuality and religion in "Upon Appleton House" (William Empson, "The Marriage of Marvell," in *Using Biography* [London: Chatto and Windus, 1984], 43–95). To assume that a person who is himself homosexual would never use homophobic motifs when to do so would be politically expedient is to assume that sexual identity always trumps political ideology, a highly questionable – and ahistorical – assumption. Certainly male homosexuality was associated with the celibate Catholic clergy; as John Oldham wrote, "Oft have I seen these hallow'd Altars stain'd / With Rapes, those Pews with Buggeries profan'd" (John Oldham, *Satires upon the Jesuits*, 4.293–94, in *The Poems of John Oldham*, ed. Harold F. Brooks [Oxford: Clarendon Press, 1987], 53). For a look at the continuing role of the convent as a site of religious and sexual contestation in nineteenth-century America, see Susan M. Griffin, "Awful Disclosures: Women's Evidence in the Escaped Nun's Tale," *PMLA* 111 (1996): 93–107.

44 See John Sekora, *Luxury: The Concept in Western Thought, Eden to Smollett* (Baltimore: Johns Hopkins University Press, 1977), and more recently Christopher J. Berry, *The Idea of Luxury: A Conceptual and Historical Investigation* (Cambridge: Cambridge University Press, 1994).

45 See Eve Kosovsky Sedgwick, *Between Men: English Literature and Male Homosocial Desire* (New York: Columbia University Press, 1985).

46 Samuel Johnson, *Lives of the English Poets*, ed. George Birbeck Hill, 3 vols. (1905; New York: Octagon Books, 1967), 1.20.

47 Thomas N. Corns, *The Development of Milton's Prose Style* (Oxford: Clarendon Press, 1982), 103.

48 It may be noted that Milton omits to include in his list of those whose errors are only trivial lapses the Quakers, who did not join in the agitation against the Declaration of Indulgence.

49 Christopher Hill, in *Milton and the English Revolution* (New York: Viking, 1978), 404–10, discusses the subterfuges necessary to get a book of politically suspect tendency past the licenser, and Keeble's third chapter of *The Literary Culture of Nonconformity* addresses the overall issue of censorship.

50 Stavely, *Complete Prose Works of John Milton*, 412. Milton had unusual allies to avoid upsetting at this juncture: Stavely notes that the "no Popery" hysteria was "in part engineered by the archbishop of Canterbury and the bishop of London" (410).

51 William Riley Parker, *Milton: A Biography*, vol. 1 (Oxford: Clarendon Press, 1968), 629, cited in Sanchez, " 'The Worst of Superstitions,' " 37.

52 Finlayson, *Historians, Puritanism, and the English Revolution*, 118.

53 *Reliquiae Baxterianae*, 132; cited in Hill, *The Experience of Defeat*, 217.

54 Although *Comus* may be plausibly read as having at least in part a political significance, as Leah Sinanoglou Marcus has argued (in "The Earl of Bridgewater's Legal Life: Notes toward a Political Reading of *Comus*," *Milton Quarterly* 21 [1987], 13–23), a masque performed by children in an aristocratic household in Wales presents a writer with a far different audience, generic task,

and relation to the nation at large than an avowedly polemical pamphlet on current affairs printed for all, or at least all London, to read. *Lycidas* and Milton's refusal to enter the Church are evidence enough that in his youth he was politically aware; but to be politically aware while writing poetry in the house of one's father and to be politically active are not the same. To believe that they are is to fall into the academic fantasizing that confuses monographs and barricades. That Milton himself distinguished *Of True Religion* as an overtly political tract from more ambiguous works is suggested by, again, title pages: whereas his name appears on the cover of *Paradise Lost* and *Paradise Regained* under Charles II, as on his 1645 *Poems* under the Long Parliament, *Of True Religion* identifies its author only by initials. Unless exceptionally transparent, allegorical poems by their nature possess what American political culture calls "deniability."

55 William Riley Parker, "Milton on King James the Second," *Modern Language Quarterly* 3 (1942): 41–44.

56 Roger Pooley, "Language and Loyalty: Plain Style at the Restoration," *Literature and History* 6 (1980): 16.

57 Milton, "In Quintum Novembris," line 1, in *Complete Poems and Major Prose*, ed. Merritt Y. Hughes (Indianapolis: Bobbs-Merrill Educational Publishing, 1957), 15.

58 Milton, *Paradise Lost*, 12.507–14, 524–33, in *Complete Poems and Major Prose*, 455–56.

59 Milton, "In Quintum Novembris," "Lycidas," both in *Complete Poems and Major Prose*, 19, 124.

60 Milton, *Paradise Lost*, 12.539–42, in *Complete Poems and Major Prose*, 455–56.

61 John Illo, "Areopagiticas Mythic and Real," *Prose Studies* 11 (1988): 20.

62 Milton, *Areopagitica*, vol. 4 of *The Works of John Milton* (New York: Columbia University Press, 1931), 303, 302.

63 Illo, "Areopagiticas," 16.

64 Milton, *Paradise Lost*, 7.26, in *Complete Poems and Major Prose*, 346.

65 William Wordsworth, *The Prelude*, 1850 version, 11.109, in *The Prelude 1799, 1805, 1850*, ed. Jonathan Wordsworth, M. H. Abrams, and Stephen Gill (New York: W. W. Norton, 1979), 397.

66 Samuel Johnson, *Samuel Johnson*, ed. Donald Greene (Oxford: Oxford University Press, 1984), 420.

67 Andrew Marvell, "Flecknoe, an English Priest at Rome," in *Andrew Marvell*, 77–81, lines 2, 9–10, 59–62.

68 *Ibid.*, lines 144, 107.

69 Alexander Pope, *The Dunciad*, 4.656, in *Poetical Works*, ed. Herbert Davis (London: Oxford University Press, 1966), 584.

70 Johnson, *Lives of the English Poets*, 3.204.

71 Paul Langford notes that, in the Parliamentary debate on the first Catholic Relief Act in the 1770s, "a law which 'debars a man from the honest acquisition of property . . . needed only to be mentioned in order to excite the indignation of the House'" (John Dunning, speaking in Parliament, cited in Paul Langford

Public Life and the Propertied Englishman, 1689–1798 [Oxford: Clarendon Press, 1991], 8).

3 "THE KING'S SPIRITUAL MILITIA":
THE CHURCH OF ENGLAND AND THE PLOT OF THE PLOT

1 G. S. Minister of God's word in Ireland, *A Brief Declaration of the Barbarous And inhumane dealings of the Northern Irish Rebels.* Published by direction from the State of Ireland (London, 1641), n.p.
2 Jonathan Scott, *Algernon Sidney and the Restoration Crisis, 1677–1683* (Cambridge: Cambridge University Press, 1991), 9.
3 Two recent studies of the rhetoric of the Restoration, it may be noted, both conclude in 1671; see Nicholas Jose, *Ideas of the Restoration in English Literature 1660–71* (Cambridge, MA.: Harvard University Press, 1984), and Nancy Klein Maguire, *Regicide and Restoration: English Tragicomedy, 1660–71* (Cambridge: Cambridge University Press, 1992). Analyses of the Restoration which treat it as an inauguration of an undifferentiated modernity fail to account for the decisive alterations that mark the religious and political negotiations of the later seventeenth century. The monarchy restored in 1660 was an unstable hybrid structure, an only-partial containment of socially centrifugal forces. Tim Harris observes how the ambiguity, the multidimensionality, of anti-Catholicism facilitated both the initial Whig success and their ultimate failure in the Exclusion Crisis (Tim Harris, *London Crowds in the Reign of Charles II: Propaganda and Politics from the Restoration until the Exclusion Crisis* [Cambridge: Cambridge University Press, 1987], chapters 5 and 6). See also Harris, *Politics under the Later Stuarts: Party Conflict in a Divided Society 1660–1715* (London: Longman, 1993); Gary Stuart de Krey, *A Fractured Society: The Politics of London in the First Age of Party* (Oxford: Clarendon Press, 1985); and Steven Pincus, "Popery, Trade, and Universal Monarchy: The Ideological Context of the Outbreak of the Second Anglo-Dutch War," *The English Historical Review* 107 (1992): 1–29.
4 Scott, *Algernon Sidney and the Restoration Crisis*, 8.
5 J. A. I. Champion argues for widening the definition of Popery "to encompass the central idea of the sacerdotal authority of the Church of England," but, while such a definition would have been largely agreed upon by Dissenters, it was anathema to Anglicans themselves (*The Pillars of Priestcraft Shaken: The Church of England and Its Enemies, 1660–1730* [Cambridge: Cambridge University Press, 1992], 16).
6 Thomas Fuller, *The Church-History of England; From the Birth of Jesus Christ, Untill the Year 1648* (London, 1655), "To the Reader," n.p. With only the excuse that it was "Printed for Iohn Williams at the signe of the Crown in St. Paul's Church-yard," this volume's cover page boldly has for illustration a large crown, $2\frac{1}{2}''$ tall and $3\frac{1}{4}''$ wide, suggestive of a royalist political statement at once readable and deniable.
7 *The best fence against Popery: or, a Vindication of the Power of the King in Ecclesiastical Affairs* (London [1670]).

8 [W. Chestlin,] *Persecutio Undecima* (1681), 4, quoted by Christopher Hill, "Irreligion in the 'Puritan' Revolution," in *Radical Religion in the English Revolution*, ed. J. F. McGregor and B. Reay (Oxford: Oxford University Press, 1984), 197.

9 Jürgen Habermas, *The Structural Transformation of the Public Sphere*, trans. Thomas Burger (Cambridge, MA.: MIT, 1989), 7; H. G. Gadamer, *Truth and Method*, trans. and ed. Garrett Barden and John Cumming (New York: Seabury Press, 1975), 125n53 (on 513–14), quoted in Habermas, 7.

10 *Ibid.*, 36–37, 32.

11 Samuel Johnson, *Lives of the English Poets*, ed. George Birbeck Hill, 3 vols. (1905; New York: Octagon, 1967), 2. 129–31; *The Poetical Works of Joseph Addison; Gay's Fables; and Somerville's Chase*, ed. George Gilfillan (Edinburgh, 1859), 51.

12 John Dryden, *Absalom and Achitophel*, in *The Works of John Dryden*, ed. H. T. Swedenberg, Jr. (Berkeley: University of California Press, 1972), 6, 33 and 36, lines 14, 937, and 1030.

13 See Scott, *Algernon Sidney and the Restoration Crisis*, and Mark Knights, *Politics and Opinion in Crisis, 1678–81* (Cambridge: Cambridge University Press, 1994).

14 Michael McKeon notes that "the patriarchalist argument is absent from *Absalom and Achitophel*," and that the poem relies instead for its rationale of legitimacy on an assertion that "the 'Sovereign Sway' of the people (780), once given up, cannot be resumed at will" (Michael McKeon, "Historicizing *Absalom and Achitophel*," in *The New Eighteenth Century: Theory, Politics, English Literature*, ed. Felicity Nussbaum and Laura Brown [New York: Methuen, 1987], 31).

15 Walter Benjamin, *The Origin of Tragic German Drama*, trans. John Osborne (1963; London: NLB, 1977), 65.

16 Samuel Weber, "Taking Exception to Decision: Walter Benjamin and Carl Schmitt," *Diacritics* 22.3–4 (1992): 16.

17 J. G. A. Pocock, "The Fourth English Civil War: Dissolution, Desertion, and Alternative Histories in the Glorious Revolution," in *The Revolution of 1688–1689: Changing Perspectives*, ed. Lois G. Schwoerer (Cambridge: Cambridge University Press, 1992), 59, 62.

18 *A Letter from Mr. S a Romish Priest* (London, 1679), 2.

19 D. G., *A Letter from St. Omars, in Farther Confirmation of the Truth of the Popish Plot* (London, 1679), 1, 3.

20 *Ibid.*, 22.

21 William Lloyd, *The Late Apology In behalf of the Papists, Reprinted and Answered In behalf of the Royalists*, 4th edn. corrected (London, 1675), 46.

22 *The Cabal of several Notorious Priests and Jesuits Discovered* (no city, 1679), 5. This lurid and heavily anecdotal work also dwells on clerical incontinence, including pederastic "horrid Sodomies" and heterosexual child molestation.

23 E. C., *A Full and Final Proof of the Plot* (London, 1680), n.p., 7.

24 T. S. Eliot, "Hamlet and His Problems," in *Selected Essays 1917–1932* (New York: Harcourt, Brace, 1932), 124–25.

25 Titus Otes [sic], *A True Narrative of the Horrid Plot and Conspiracy of the Popish Party* (London, 1679), 63.

26 Nicholas Tyacke, "Anglican Attitudes: Some Recent Writings on English Religious History, from the Restoration to the Civil War," *Journal of British Studies* 35 (1996): 166. As to whether the events of the 1640s were an English civil war or war of the three kingdoms, J. G. A. Pocock observes that they were both ("History and Sovereignty: The Historiographical Response to Europeanization in Two British Cultures," *Journal of British Studies* 31 [1992]: 372).

27 *A Remonstrance of the State of the Kingdom. Die Mercurii 15. Decemb. 1641* (London, 1641), 3. See also *The Petition of the Lords and Commons of England, now Assembled in Parliament: Presented to the Kings most Excellent Majestie with the Remonstrance* (London, 1641).

28 *His Majesties Answer To the Petition which accompanied the Declaration of the House of Commons* (London, 1641), 4–5.

29 *The Bishops Manifest: or, A Comparative Relation of conformitie of the English Prelates to those treacherous and deceitfull ones in the Reign of King Hen. the eighth* (London, 1641), 1.

30 [John Williams,] *The Manner of Impeachment of the XII Bishops Accused of High Treason* (London, 1642), n. p.

31 *A Bloody Massacre Plotted by the Papists* (London, 1641), title page, 1.

32 *The Happiest Newes from Ireland that ever came to England. Since their first Rebellion* (London, 1641), n. p.

33 *A Petition of the Mayor, Aldermen, and Common-Councell of the Citie of London* (London, 1641 [1642 new style]), 2–3.

34 *A True Relation of the unparaleld Breach of Parliament, by his Maiesty* (London, 1641 [1642 new style]), 5.

35 *The Order Of the House of Commons, Declaring the high Breach of Priviledge of Parliament* (London, 1642), n.p.

36 *The Papists Designe against the Parliament and Citie of London discovered* (London, 1642), n.p. As B. Reay notes, "Fear and hatred of popery, a widespread conviction that there was 'some great design in hand by the papists to subvert and overthrow the kingdom,' [John Pym, May 3, 1641, quoted in Anthony Fletcher, *The Outbreak of the English Civil War* (London: E. Arnold, 1981), 26] mobilized the nation in 1642. 'For many contemporary writers,' Robin Clifton has observed, 'the essence of the conflict' between Parliament and King 'was in fact a collision between true religion and popery'" (Robin Clifton, "Fear of Popery," in *The Origins of the English Civil War*, ed. Conrad Russell [New York: Barnes and Noble, 1973], 162, cited in B. Reay, "Radicalism and Religion in the English Revolution: an Introduction," in McGregor and Reay, *Radical Religion in the English Revolution*, 1–2).

37 Ian Gilmour, *Riot, Risings and Revolution: Governance and Violence in Eighteenth-Century England* (London: Hutchinson, 1992), 370. Two important differences between Charles I and George III lay in the degree of unity displayed by the propertied classes and the military forces the government could muster: the mob of 1641 acted under the aegis of Parliament and the city, and could easily overawe the king's few hundred retainers; that of 1780 faced an upper class

that, whatever its internal differences, united against a threat from below, and a government that deployed troops sufficient to slaughter 800 to 1,000 rioters.

38 Clifton, "Fear of Popery," in *The Origins of the English Civil War*, ed. Russell, 144.

39 Mark Goldie, "Danby, the Bishops, and the Whigs," in *The Politics of Religion in Restoration England*, ed. Tim Harris, Paul Seaward, and Mark Goldie (Oxford: Basil Blackwell, 1990), 99.

40 Richard L. Greaves, *Deliver Us from Evil: The Radical Underground in Britain, 1660–1663* (New York: Oxford University Press, 1986), 227–29.

41 John Miller, *Popery and Politics in England 1660–1688* (Cambridge: Cambridge University Press, 1973), 84, 85. Contrast, for instance, William Prynne's *Romes Master-peece. Or, the grand conspiracy* (London, 1643) with his *The Substance of a Speech* ([London], 1649).

42 Peter Du Moulin, *The Great Loyalty of the Papists to K. Charles the I. (Of Blessed Memory.) Discovered, by Peter Du Moulin, D.D., In his Vindication of the Protestant Religion* (London, 1673), 1.

43 O[a]tes, *A True Narrative*, opening address "To His Sacred Majesty," n.p.

44 *The Grand Concernments of England Ensured* (London, 1659), 8, 10, 29–30.

45 Isaac Penington, *A Question Propounded to the Rulers, Teachers, and People of the Nation of England* (London?, 1659), 6–8.

46 *Ibid.*, 5, 1.

47 See Hill, "Irreligion in the 'Puritan' Revolution," in McGregor and Reay, *Radical Religion in the English Revolution*, 207–8.

48 Penington, *The Root of Popery Struck at* (London, 1660), 17, 16.

49 *Philanax Protestant or Papists Discovered to the King As guilty of those Traiterous Positions and Practises which they first Insinuated into the worst Protestants and now Charge upon all* (London, 1663), 6, 3.

50 Thomas Hobbes, *Leviathan*, ed. Richard Tuck (Cambridge: Cambridge University Press, 1991), 482.

51 *Englands Faiths Defender Vindicated* (London, 1660), title page.

52 See Bernard Capp, "The Fifth Monarchists and Popular Millenarianism," in McGregor and Reay, *Radical Religion in the English Revolution*, 167.

53 Steven Zwicker contrasts Dryden's "stak[ing] out the middle ground, posing as impartial physician and scrupulous historian," in *Absalom and Achitophel* to the open partisanship of his *Medall*, written after the royalists had secured victory (*Politics and Language in Dryden's Poetry: The Arts of Disguise* [Princeton: Princeton University Press, 1984], 25, 28).

54 *The Two Associations. One Subscribed by CLVI Members of the House of Commons In the Year 1643. The Other Seized in the Closet of the Earl of Shaftsbury* (London, 1681), 1.

55 Capp, "The Fifth Monarchists," in McGregor and Reay, *Radical Religion in the English Revolution*, 169.

56 Andrew Browning, ed., *English Historical Documents 1660–1714* (London: Eyre and Spottiswoode, 1953), 113.

57 J. F. McGregor, "Seekers and Ranters," in McGregor and Reay, *Radical Religion in the English Revolution*, 138.

58 William B. Hunter, in "The Provenance of the *Christian Doctrine*," *Studies in*

English Literature 1500–1900 32 (1992): 129–42, argues that *Of Christian Doctrine* is by not Milton but an unknown hand. Even if one accepts his view, however, it can hardly be doubted that Milton had a strong proclivity for thinking for himself in matters of religion.

59 Henry Stubbe, *An Account of the Rise and Progress of Mohammedanism*, ed. Hafiz Mahmud Khan Shairani (London: Luzac and Company, 1911), 11ff.

60 Stubbe, *An Account*, 29. Stubbe's vision of early Christians as fractious cultists of decidedly unorthodox tendencies finds an echo in recent scholarship. See Elaine Pagels, *The Gnostic Gospels* (New York: Random House, 1979).

61 Henry Stubbe, *Campanella Revived, Or an Enquiry into the History of the Royal Society, Whether the Virtuosi there do not pursue the Projects of Campanella for the reducing England unto Popery* (London, 1670), 1.

62 Sprat himself, after attacking "The Bishops of *Rome*" as responsible for the destruction of the Roman empire by their "wrest[ing] from it so many privileges," presents as the opposites of experimentalism "the *Schole-men*," who prove "how farre more importantly a good Method of thinking, and a right course of apprehending things, does contribute towards the attaining of perfection in true knowledge, than the strongest, and most vigorous Wit in the World can do without them" (Thomas Sprat, *The History of the Royal Society*, ed. Jackson I. Cope and Harold Whitmore Jones [1667; St. Louis University Studies, 1958], 13, 15). Like clerical pamphleteers, both the advocate and the critic of the Royal Society present their own position as the one opposed to Rome.

63 James R. Jacob, *Henry Stubbe: Radical Protestantism and the Early Enlightenment* (Cambridge: Cambridge University Press, 1983), 1, 2.

64 James R. Jacob and Margaret C. Jacob, "The Anglican Origins of Modern Science: The Metaphysical Foundations of the Whig Constitution," *Isis* 71 (1980): 260.

65 James R. Jacob, *Henry Stubbe*, 5.

66 *Ibid.*, 69.

67 Henry Stubbe, *An Account of the Rise and Progress of Mohammedanism*, 181–82, 47, quoted in James R. Jacob, *Henry Stubbe*, 65, 69.

68 James R. Jacob, *Henry Stubbe*, 164.

69 *Ibid.*, 162.

70 John Milton, *Areopagitica*, in *Complete Prose Works of Milton*, vol. 2 (New Haven: Yale University Press, 1959), 565.

71 Champion, *The Pillars of Priestcraft Shaken*, 124.

72 Sir John Temple, *The Irish Rebellion* (London, 1646), 9–10.

73 George Fox, *The Arraignment of Popery* (London, 1667), table of contents, n.p.

74 Andrew Hamilton, *A True Relation of the Actions of the Inniskilling-Men From Their First Taking up of Arms* (London: Richard Chiswell, 1690), vii.

75 Gilmour, *Riot, Risings and Revolution*, 427.

76 Ian Higgins demonstrates, however, that Swift's trope of cannibalism in *A Modest Proposal* has parallels in English domestic, specifically, Jacobite, political rhetoric (*Swift's Politics: A Study in Disaffection* [Cambridge: Cambridge

University Press, 1994], 190–92). See my last chapter for an account of the continuity between Swift's rhetoric on English and Irish politics.

77 Simon Schama, *Citizens: A Chronicle of the French Revolution* (London: Viking, 1989), 792.

78 See Greaves, *Deliver Us from Evil*, on radical republicans' hostility toward Catholics in the early 1660s.

79 Greaves, *Deliver Us from Evil*, 229. See also his *Enemies under His Feet: Radicals and Nonconformists in Britain, 1664–1677* (Stanford: Stanford University Press, 1990), 4.

80 Jonathan Scott, "England's Troubles: Exhuming the Popish Plot," in *The Politics of Religion in Restoration England*, ed. Tim Harris, Paul Seaward, and Mark Goldie (Oxford: Basil Blackwell, 1990), 111.

81 Alan Liu, "The Power of Formalism: The New Historicism," *ELH* 56 (1989): 752.

82 [Charles Hutchinson,] *Of the Authority of Councils and the Rule of Faith* (London, 1687), 107.

83 *Ibid.*, 109, 110.

84 John White, *The First Century of Scandalous, Malignant Priests* (London, 1643), 36. Julian Davies notes that "Those 'scandalous' clergy who were eventually deprived were singled out, often randomly, in response to pressure for purges from the center rather than selected on the weight of local evidence or because of the singularity of their complicity in the Caroline changes" (*The Caroline Captivity of the Church: Charles I and the Remoulding of Anglicanism 1625–1641* [Oxford: Clarendon Press, 1992], 310). See also I. Green, "The Persecution of 'Scandalous' Ministers and 'Malignant' Parish Clergy during the English Civil War," *English Historical Review* 94 (1979): 507–31.

85 *A new Test of the Church of England's Loyalty* (London, 1687), 8.

86 *The New Test of the Church of England's Loyalty, Examined by the Old Test of Truth and Honesty* (London, 1687).

87 Daniel Defoe, "A new Test of the Church of England's Loyalty, or Whiggish Loyalty and Church Loyalty compar'd," in *A true Collection of the Writings of the Author of the True Born English-man* (London, 1703), 417–18. Defoe, of course, was more than willing to object vehemently to laws if he disapproved of them.

88 John Dryden, letters to Mrs. Steward of April 11, 1700, and March 12, 1699/1700, *The Letters of John Dryden, with Letters Addressed to Him*, ed. Charles E. Ward (Durham, NC: Duke University Press, 1942), 135, 134.

89 John Gother, *A Papist Mis-represented and Represented: or, A Twofold Character of Popery* (no city, [1685]; the date given is 1665), 109.

90 Mary Cowper, *Diary of Mary Countess Cowper, Lady of the Bedchamber to the Princess of Wales* (London, 1864), October 20, 1716, quoted in James Leheny's Introduction to Joseph Addison, *The Freeholder*, ed. James Leheny (Oxford: Clarendon Press, 1979), 3.

91 Ellis Archer Wasson observes that "In 1715 over half of all MPs had fathers who were MPs," a trend which only intensified: "The dominance of the Commons by the hereditary political elite was at its height in the eighteenth

century. In 1774, 82 per cent of all members of the House of Commons came from parliamentary families" ("The House of Commons, 1660–1945: Parliamentary Families and the Political Elite," *The English Historical Review* 106 [1991]: 638, 643). After the Reform Bill of 1832, the proportion dropped, but it remained large into this century.

92 Michel Serres, *Rome: The Book of Foundations*, trans. Felicia McCarren (Stanford: Stanford University Press, 1991), 93.

93 William Sancroft, *A Sermon preached to the House of Peers, Novem. 13.1678* (London, 1678). The *Term Catalogues, 1668–1709* (Edward Arber, ed. [London: privately printed, 1903]) provide an excellent index of the reflux of literally "licensed" opinion; between the June 22, 1678, and the December 6, 1678, Quarterly List the number of pages devoted to "Divinity" swells from just over one to four, with a vast influx of anti-Papist titles representing the difference; as throughout the late seventeenth and early eighteenth centuries, their strongly cyclical occurrences form an index of the level of political tension.

94 Walter Benjamin, "The Work of Art in the Age of Mechanical Reproduction," *Illuminations*, ed. Hannah Arendt, trans. Harry Zohn (New York: Harcourt, Brace, and World, 1968), 243.

4 "REASON AND RELIGION": THE SCIENCE OF ANGLICANISM

1 Michel Serres, *Rome: The Book of Foundations*, trans. Felicia McCarren (Stanford: Stanford University Press, 1991), 19–20.

2 Christopher Hill, *The Intellectual Origins of the English Revolution* (Oxford: Clarendon Press, 1965), 254, cited in Philip Corrigan and Derek Sayer, *The Great Arch: English State Formation as Cultural Revolution* (Oxford: Basil Blackwell, 1985), 94

3 J. R. Jones, *The Revolution of 1688 in England* (New York: W. W. Norton, 1972), 76. Jones regards the potential impact of opportunistic conversions by the ambitious devastating, given the incentives available to absolute monarchs, but also concludes that the Revocation of the Edict of Nantes by Louis XIV doomed the project of conversion in England (91).

4 Richard Sherlock, "The Theology of Leviathan: Hobbes on Religion," *Interpretation: A Journal of Political Philosophy* 10 (1982): 58.

5 Edward Stillingfleet, *A Rational Account of the Grounds of Protestant Religion* (London, 1665), 109, 111.

6 Keith Thomas noted that from its beginning the Reformation attacked the magical element of pre-Reformation Catholicism, "their masses and other socerous witchcraft" in the words of Bishop Bale (Keith Thomas, *Religion and the Decline of Magic* [New York: Charles Scribner's Sons, 1971], 54).

7 Richard W. F. Kroll, *The Material Word: Literate Culture in the Restoration and Early Eighteenth Century* (Baltimore: Johns Hopkins University Press, 1991), 16.

8 Terry Eagleton, *Ideology: An Introduction* (London: Verso, 1990), 64. For instance, Margaret C. Jacob discusses the "pantheistic and materialistic" *Traite des trois imposteurs* without noting how its "God of the theologians and the impostors," whose "'priests have wanted to enrich themselves by the sale of an infinity of

chimeras which they sell dearly to the ignorant'" expresses a condemnation of false priests strongly reminiscent of the Protestant case against Catholicism (Margaret C. Jacob, *The Radical Enlightenment: Pantheists, Freemasons, and Republicans* [London: George Allen and Unwin, 1981], 217, 221). On the other hand, J. G. A. Pocock has argued that "in post-Puritan and Whig England, philosophes are not much needed" ("Post-Puritan England and the Problem of Enlightenment," in *Culture and Politics: From Puritanism to the Enlightenment*, ed. Perez Zagorin [Berkeley: University of California Press, 1980], 93).

9 [John Williams], *A Discourse Concerning the Celebration of Divine Service in an Unknown Tongue* (London, 1685), 56.

10 Edward Stillingfleet, *Originae Sacrae, or a Rational Account of the Grounds of Christian Faith* (London, 1662); *A Rational Account of the Grounds of Protestant Religion* (London, 1665); *The Unreasonableness of Separation* (London, 1681); *The Doctrine of the Trinity and Transubstantiation Compared, as to Scripture, Reason, and Tradition* (London, 1687). Both works of the 1660s are systematic elaborations exceeding 600 pages; both 1680s ones are much shorter and more pointedly controversial tracts.

11 See Michel Serres, *The Parasite*, trans. Lawrence R. Schehr (Baltimore: Johns Hopkins University Press, 1982).

12 G. S. Rousseau and Roy Porter, eds., *Exoticism in the Enlightenment* (Manchester: Manchester University Press, 1990), 1.

13 Mark Goldie, "Ideology," in *Political Innovation and Conceptual Change*, ed. Terence Ball, James Farr, and Russell L. Hanson (Cambridge: Cambridge University Press, 1989), 285. See also Goldie, "The Theory of Religious Intolerance in Restoration England," in *From Persecution to Toleration: The Glorious Revolution and Religion in England*, ed. Ole Peter Grell, Jonathan Israel, and Nicholas Tyacke (Oxford: Clarendon Press, 1991), 331–68; "Priestcraft and the Birth of Whiggism," in *Political Discourse in Early Modern Britain*, ed. Nicholas Phillipson and Quentin Skinner (Cambridge: Cambridge University Press, 1993), 209–31.

14 William Chillingworth, *The Religion of Protestants a Safe Way to Salvation. Or an Answer to a Book Entitled Mercy and Truth, Or, Charity Maintain'd by Catholiques, Which pretends to prove the Contrary* (Oxford, 1638), the 8th and 9th pages of the unpaginated "Preface to the Author of Charity Maintained, with an Answer to his Pamphlet."

15 *Ibid.*, 9th page of "Preface to the Author."

16 Jean-François Lyotard, *The Postmodern Condition: A Report on Knowledge*, trans. Geoff Bennington and Brian Massumi (Minneapolis: University of Minnesota Press, 1984), 30.

17 Michel de Certeau, *The Writing of History*, trans. Tom Conley (New York: Columbia University Press, 1988), 2.

18 De Certeau notes that the antithesis of past and present is not a universal but a specifically Western pattern. "Far from being self-evident, this construction is a uniquely Western trait. In India, for example, 'new forms never drive the older ones away.' Rather, there exists a 'stratified stockpiling,' Louis Dumont has noted" (Certeau, *The Writing of History*, 4, quoting Louis Dumont, "Le

Problem de l'histoire," in *La Civilization indienne et nous* (Paris: Colin, Coll. Cahier des Annales, 1964), 31–54.

19 De Certeau, *The Writing of History*, 3, 33.

20 [Samuel Johnson], *The Absolute Impossibility of Transubstantiation Demonstrated* (London, 1688), iii.

21 De Certeau, *The Writing of History*, 4.

22 Margaret C. Jacob, *The Newtonians and the English Revolution, 1689–1720* (Ithaca: Cornell University Press, 1976), 272. Because Jacob's study covers the period following the Glorious Revolution, it finds its subjects in a very different situation from that under James.

23 *Ibid.*, 16, 73.

24 Margaret C. Jacob, *The Cultural Meaning of the Scientific Revolution* (Philadelphia: Temple University Press, 1988), 112, 106.

25 *Ibid.*, 106–7. In her account, precapitalist methods of organization and pre-experimentalist systems of rhetorical logic diminish together to "the capriciousness of Continental absolutism," the "doctrinal orthodoxy ... of Aristotelian natural philosophy," and "the doctrinal rigidity of the French Catholic church, or of fundamentalist Calvinism" (112, 111). Burdened by repeated descriptions as "rigid," "orthodox," or "clinging" to an unnaturally prolonged existence, such systems are implicitly weighed in the humanist balance and found wanting.

26 Robert Markley, "Objectivity as Ideology: Boyle, Newton, and the Languages of Science," *Genre* 16 (1983): 369.

27 Robert Markley, *Fallen Languages: Crises of Representation in Newtonian England, 1660–1740* (Ithaca: Cornell University Press, 1993), 98.

28 *Ibid.*, 95. While James R. Jacob mentions the role of "Catholic enemies" and the threat "by Catholics from outside," in neither article does he expand on the subject, preoccupied as he is with Protestant English internal dynamics (James R. Jacob, "Restoration, Reformation, and the Origins of the Royal Society," *History of Science* 13 [1975]: 171; James R. Jacob and Margaret C. Jacob, "The Anglican Origins of Modern Science: The Metaphysical Foundations of the Whig Constitution," *Isis* 71 [1980]: 260). The latter article notes both that "Newton led the anti-Catholic opposition to James II in Cambridge" (264) and that Henry Stubbe accused the Royal Society of being "tantamount to popery" in upholding "natural religion" (260), but de-emphasizes the connection that both the Anglican and "Radical" Enlightenments define themselves as progressive representatives of the modern in contrast to archaic Popery.

29 Martin Greig observes how latitudinarian theology must be at once "rational" and anti-intellectual to reconcile the competing demands for scriptural sufficiency and clarity (Martin Greig, "The Reasonableness of Christianity? Gilbert Burnet and the Trinitarian Controversy of the 1690s," *Journal of Ecclesiastical History* 44 [1993]: 637).

30 Following William Sancroft's deprivation for refusal to swear the Oath of Allegiance to William and Mary, John Tillotson was consecrated as Archbishop of Canterbury in 1691, Thomas Tenison in 1695, and William Wake in 1716.

31 [Robert Boyle?], *Reasons Why a Protestant Should Not Turn Papist* (London, 1687), 23. Edward B. Davis argues that David Abercromby, an ex-Jesuit who enjoyed Boyle's substantial patronage in the 1680s, not Boyle himself as hitherto supposed, wrote this tract. Davis has located a contemporary attribution to Abercromby by someone who "may have known Abercromby personally" (624) – or may not, given that the only evidence of such acquaintance is that both are Scots – but he strains unduly for certainty because of a bias (of the romanticizing sort which Margaret Jacob criticized) which he ingenuously admits: "that Boyle had such a magnanimous spirit is the main reason why I have never believed that he wrote *Protestant and Papist*" ("The Anonymous Works of Robert Boyle and the *Reasons Why a Protestant Should not Turn Papist* [1687]," *Journal of the History of Ideas* 55 [1994]: 622). That *Reasons* resembles other anti-Catholic writings by Abercromby in some respects does not support Davis's case, however, since the tract is remarkable only for its unremarkability, as this chapter later indicates. Additionally, the exact provenance of this tract is less important than that the attitude toward Catholicism of this pamphlet is far from alien to the worldview implicit in Boyle's ouevre.

32 Steven Shapin and Simon Schaffer provide a detailed account of the beginnings of Restoration experimentalism in Robert Boyle's contention with Thomas Hobbes's plenist ontology in *Leviathan and the Air-Pump: Hobbes, Boyle, and the Experimental Life* (Princeton: Princeton University Press, 1985). See also Barbara J. Shapiro, *Probability and Certainty*, and Shapin, *A Social History of Truth: Civility and Science in Seventeenth-Century England* (Chicago: University of Chicago Press, 1994).

33 The appropriateness of "Baconianism" as a shorthand term for anti-Aristotelianism in science is a vexed question which I need not attempt to answer here.

34 Francis Bacon, "Preface to The Great Instauration," in *Novum Organum With Other Parts of The Great Instauration*, trans. and ed. Peter Urbach and John Gibson (Chicago: Open Court, 1994), 19, 8.

35 *A Catalogue of all the Discourses Printed against Popery* (1689), cited in W. A. Speck, *Reluctant Revolutionaries: Englishmen and the Revolution of 1688* (Oxford: Oxford University Press, 1988), 182.

36 Examining how the ideal of comprehension within the Church yielded to that of toleration of those outside it between the Restoration and the Revolution, John Spurr notes that doctrinal agreement between the Church and moderate Dissenters was more piously believed in than actual (John Spurr, "The Church of England, Comprehension and the Toleration Act of 1689," *The English Historical Review* 104 [1989]: 931n). Analyzing how toleration of Dissent came about, Richard Ashcraft concludes, "Toleration, in short, was in its realization less the fulfillment of a tendency toward cultural rationalism than the product of deep-rooted fears and prejudices directed against Catholicism which, momentarily, produced a political alliance between Anglicans and dissenters in their common struggle against James II's attempt to reclaim the throne following the Glorious Revolution" (Richard Ashcraft, "Latitudinarianism

and Toleration: Historical Myth versus Political History," in *Philosophy, Science, and Religion in England 1640–1700*, ed. Richard Kroll, Richard Ashcraft, and Perez Zagorin [Cambridge: Cambridge University Press, 1992], 152). See also W. M. Spellman, *The Latitudinarians and the Church of England, 1660–1700* (Athens, GA: University of Georgia Press, 1993).

37 Thomas Babington Macaulay, *The History of England*, in *The Works of Lord Macaulay Complete*, ed. Hannah More (Macaulay) Trevelyan (London, 1866), 1.606.

38 For a discussion of the connection between the rhetoric of common sense and the experimentalist stance, see Kevin Dunn, *Pretexts of Authority: The Rhetoric of Authorship in the Renaissance Preface* (Stanford: Stanford University Press, 1994).

39 [George Savile, first Marquess of Halifax], *A Letter to a Dissenter, Upon occasion of His Majesties Late Gracious Declaration of Indulgence* (London, 1687), 15–17.

40 [William Penn,] *Good Advice to the Church of England, Roman Catholick, and Protestant Dissenter* (London, 1687), 54, 55, 56. See also his *A Third Letter From a Gentleman in the Country, To his Friends in London, Upon the Subject of the Penal Laws and Tests* (London, 1687).

41 [Penn,] *Good Advice*, 48.

42 [Richard Baxter,] *Fair-Warning: or, XXV Reasons Against Toleration and Indulgence of Popery* (London, 1663). Mark Goldie observes that Baxter "had the cussedness to preach coercive uniformity while suffering as its victim" (Mark Goldie, "The Theory of Religious Intolerance in Restoration England," in *From Persecution to Toleration: The Glorious Revolution and Religion in England*, ed. Ole Peter Grell, Jonathan Israel, and Nicholas Tyacke, 338).

43 John Milton, "On the New Forcers of Conscience under the Long Parliament," *Complete Poems and Major Prose*, ed. Merritt Y. Hughes (Indianapolis: Bobbs-Merrill Educational Publishing, 1957), 145.

44 [Matthew Tindal,] *New High-Church Turn'd Old Presbyterian* (London, 1709), 4, 6.

45 [Penn], *Good Advice*, 52.

46 *An Essay upon the Nature of a Church and the Extent of Ecclesiastical Authority* (York, 1718), 9, 23.

47 [Joshua Bassett,] *Reason and Authority: or the Motives of a Late Protestants Reconciliation to the Catholic Church* (London, 1687), 8.

48 *Ibid.*, 9.

49 [William Sherlock,] *An Answer to a Discourse Intituled, Papists Protesting against Protestant-Popery; Being a Vindication of Papists not Misrepresented by Protestants* (London, 1686), 116.

50 As John Spurr notes, "The vital, but limited, role of reason in religion meant that the emphasis given to reason could be varied to suit the needs of controversy: it could be elevated against enthusiasts, fideists and reasoning atheists, and played down against Socinians" (*The Restoration Church of England* [New Haven: Yale University Press, 1991], 255).

51 [John Gother,] *An Agreement between the Church of England and Church of Rome* (London, 1687), 60–61, 3.

52 [John Williams,] *An Apology for the Pulpits* (London, 1688), 3.

53 [John Gother], *An Amicable Accommodation of the Difference Between the Representer and the Answerer* (London, 1686), 13–33; *A Reply to the Answer of the Amicable Accommodation. Being A Fourth Vindication of the Papist Misrepresented and Represented* (London, 1686), 29–32.

54 [Gother], *A Reply to the Answer*, 12.

55 [William Wake], *A Defense of the Exposition of the Doctrine of the Church of England, Against the Exceptions of Monsieur de Meaux, Late Bishop of Condom, and his Vindicator* (London, 1688), 85. "*The Papist Represented*" (85), John Gother's anonymous *A Papist Misrepresented and Represented* (no city, [1685]; the date printed is 1665) is specified as the offender, though his is not the work to which Wake is replying.

56 Jeremy Collier, *A Short View of the Immorality and Profaneness of the English Stage* (London, 1698).

57 Margarita Stocker's analysis of the deprecation of "'fanaticism,' 'enthusiasm' and 'imagination'" as "interchangeable terms" in the late seventeenth century is vitiated by her dichotomizing of "'fanatics'" and "the conservative alliance against enthusiasm" (Margarita Stocker, "From Faith to Faith in Reason? Religious Thought in the Seventeenth Century," in *Into Another Mould: Change and Continuity in English Culture 1625–1700*, ed. T. G. S. Cain and Ken Robinson [London: Routledge, 1992], 84). Papists, too, were dangerous fanatics; Anglicanism is not merely "conservative" on a left-right spectrum, but fends off contradictory challenges. The significance of the controversies of the reign of James II is the degree to which they must qualify such binarism, revealing the complexity of the ideological battlefield.

58 [William Sherlock], *An Answer to the Amicable Accommodation of the Difference between the Representer and the Answerer* (London, 1686), 17–24, 22.

59 [Thomas Tenison], *A Discourse Concerning a Guide in Matters of Faith* (London, 1683), 43.

60 [William Sherlock], *A Papist Not Misrepresented by Protestants* (London, 1686), 65.

61 [Sherlock], *An Answer to the Amiable Accommodation*, 16.

62 Jonathan Swift, *The Examiner and Other Pieces Written in 1710–11*, vol. 3 of *The Prose Works of Jonathan Swift*, ed. Herbert Davis (Oxford: Shakespeare Head Press, 1940), 143.

63 [William Wake], "Preface," *A Second Defense of the Exposition of the Doctrine of the Church of England: Against the New Exceptions of Monsieur de Meaux, Late Bishop of Condom, and his Vindicator* (London, 1687), i.

64 In another example, Daniel Whitby condemns Catholic doctrines as "very grateful to Men of covetous and greedy Minds" and supplying "full Opportunity to lord it over all Mens Consciences and keep them in an absolute Subjection to their Wills" ([Daniel Whitby], *A Treatise of Traditions* [London, 1688], xliii, xliv). However strong his theoretical arguments, however, they become problematic because of the simple fact that in England the path of ease for a cleric was in the Church of England, certainly not with persecuted Rome.

65 [Wake], *A Second Defense*, 66. Wake's double standard is hardly unique to him. William Clagett displays the same combination of assuming Catholic bad faith and expressing indignation that such a thing could be suspected of Anglicans:

a work that begins, "you *conjure the* Defender *by all that is Sacred,* &c. *by the Eternal God, and his Son Christ Jesus,* &c. Reverend Sir! Men that are not in earnest may use the most amazing Expressions to make the World believe they are. But *be not deceived, God is not mocked;* as you will find" (n.p.; 10th page of Preface) ends: "Or do you believe us to be Hypocrites . . . *We are Ministers of Christ, and Stewards of the Mysteries of God, no less than* they . . . neither our Doctrine nor our Conversation in the World, carry the marks of Hypocrisy. Had we any other Interest to serve, but that of Truth, we also [i.e. like Papist priests] should contend for Mysteries, by which the People get Ease and Liberty, and the Priest *Power*" ([William Clagett], *A Discourse Concerning the Pretended Sacrament of Extreme Unction* [London, 1687], n.p., 135).

66 Milton, "Lycidas," lines 109, 119, in *Complete Poems and Major Prose*, 123.

67 Henry Burton, *The Grand Impostor Unmasked* (London, [1644]), 20.

68 William Sherlock, *A Vindication of some Protestant Principles of Church-Unity and Church-Communion, From the Charge of Agreement with the Church of Rome* (London, 1688), 7.

69 *Ibid.*, 17.

70 *Ibid.*, 24.

71 George Bernard Shaw, *Saint Joan*, in *Collected Plays with Their Prefaces*, vol. 6 (London: The Bodley Head, 1973), 205.

72 Sherlock, *A Vindication of some Protestant Principles*, 63, quoting [Isaac Chauncy], *The Catholick Hierarchie, or the Divine Right of a Sacred Dominion* (London, 1681), 76.

73 Jonathan Swift, *A Tale of a Tub*, in *Jonathan Swift*, ed. Angus Ross and David Woolley (Oxford: Oxford University Press, 1984), 159.

74 [Charles Leslie], *A Discourse; shewing, Who they are that are now Qualified to Administer Baptism and the Lord's Supper. Where in the Cause of Episcopacy Is briefly Treated* (London, 1698), 20.

75 Jaques Benigne Bossuet, *A Pastoral Letter From the Lord Bishop of Meaux, to The New Catholics Of His Diocess* (London, 1686), 36.

76 Gilbert Burnet, *A Pastoral Letter writ by The Right Reverend Father in God Gilbert, Lord Bishop of Sarum, to the Clergy of his Diocess* (London, 1689), 3.

77 Sherlock, *A Vindication of some Protestant Principles*, 127.

78 Robert Boyle, *The Excellence of Theology, Compar'd with Natural Philosophy, (as both are Objects of Men's Study.) Discourse'd of In a Letter to a Friend* (London, 1671/2), 139.

79 Robert Boyle, *Of the High Veneration Man's Intellect Owes to God*, in *The Works of the Honourable Robert Boyle*, ed. Thomas Birch (London, 1772), 5.131, 130.

80 Robert Boyle, *Some Considerations about the Reconcileableness of Reason and Religion*, in *Works*, 4.163. Locke argues similarly that "If you do not understand the Operations of your own finite Mind, that thinking Thing within you, do not deem it strange, that you cannot comprehend the Operations of that eternal infinite Mind, who made and governs all Things, and whom the Heaven of Heavens cannot contain" (John Locke, *An Essay Concerning Human Understanding*, ed. Peter H. Nidditch [Oxford: Clarendon Press, 1975], 630).

81 Boyle, *Some Considerations about the Reconcileableness of Reason and Religion*, in *Works*, 4.163.

82 Shapin and Schaffer, *Leviathan and the Air-Pump*, 7, 8.
83 Boyle, *Some Considerations about the Reconcileableness of Reason and Religion*, in *Works*, 4.157.
84 F. Toussain Bridoul, *The School of the Eucharist Established* [trans. William Clagett?], (London, 1687), "Preface to the Translation," vii. This Preface is half as long as the body of the work: it is essential that the reader be reminded that these miracles are presented to discredit, not to win credit. [Samuel Johnson,] *Purgatory Prov'd by Miracles: Collected out of Roman-Catholick Authors* (London, 1688), "Preface," n.p.
85 [John Hartcliffe,] *A Discourse against Purgatory* (London, 1685), 12.
86 Andrew Marvell, *An Account of the Growth of Popery, and Arbitrary Government in England*, in *The Complete Works in Verse and Prose of Andrew Marvell M.P.*, ed. Alexander B. Grosart ([London]: The Fuller Worthies' Library, 1875), 251.
87 [Hartcliffe], *A Discourse against Purgatory*, 35.
88 [William Payne,] *A Discourse of the Sacrifice of the Mass* (London, 1688), 7. Jean-François Lyotard notes that Louis Marin considers transubstantiation as "the essence of terroristic power," and that Michelet compares Robespierre's assertion that "'Those who speak like ultra-Leftists are reactionary agents'" to the Eucharist; "'*No reality is real compared to Robespierre's word*'" (Louis Marin, *La Critique du discours: sur la "Logique de Part-Royal" et les "Pensées" de Pascal* [Paris: Minuit, 1975], and Jules Michelet, "Le Tyran," preface to 1869 edition of *La Terreur*, cited in Jean-François Lyotard, "Futility in Revolution," trans. Kenneth Berri, in *Toward the Postmodern*, ed. Robert Harvey and Mark S. Roberts [Atlantic Highlands, NJ: Humanities Press, 1993], 88).
89 [Robert Boyle?], *Reasons Why a Protestant Should not Turn Papist*, 23.
90 [John Williams], *The Protestant's Answer to the Catholick Letter to the Seeker* (London, 1688), 36.
91 [Henry Wharton], *A Brief Declaration of the Lord's Supper, Written By Dr. Nicholas Ridley, Bishop of London, During his Imprisonment* (London, 1688), "Preface," n.p.
92 Jean de La Placette, *Of the Incurable Skepticism of the Church of Rome* (London, 1688), "Preface," n.p.
93 [Jean de La Placette], *Six Conferences concerning the Eucharist* (London, 1687), 4.
94 [Henry More], *A Brief Discourse of the Real Presence of the Body and Blood of Christ*, 2nd edn (London, 1686), 86.
95 [William Payne], *A Discourse Concerning the Adoration of the Host* (London, 1685), 65.
96 Gerard Reedy, *The Bible and Reason: Anglicans and Scripture in Late Seventeenth-Century England* (Philadelphia: University of Pennsylvania Press, 1985), 142.
97 *A Dialogue Between a New Catholic Convert and a Protestant, Shewing the Doctrine of Transubstantiation To be as Reasonable to be Believed as the Great Mystery of the Trinity* (London, 1686), 6.
98 [Richard Kidder], *A Second Dialogue Between a New Catholick Convert and a Protestant. Shewing why he cannot believe the Doctrine of Transubstantiation, Though he do firmly believe the Doctrine of the Trinity* (London, 1687), 4–6.

99 [William Sherlock], *An Answer to a late Dialogue Between a New Catholic Convert and a Protestant, To prove the Mystery of the Trinity to be as absurd a Doctrine as Transubstantiation* (London, 1687), 13.

100 [Edward Stillingfleet], *The Doctrine of the Trinity and Transubstantiation Compared, as to Scripture, Reason, and Tradition, in a New Dialogue between a Protestant and a Papist. The Second Part* (London, 1687), 43. Nicholas Hudson observes that Hume asserted that his skepticism merely extended the logic of the critique of transubstantiation in John Tillotson's 1684 *Discourse of Transubstantiation* (*Samuel Johnson and Eighteenth-Century Thought* [Oxford: Clarendon Press, 1988], 8).

101 [John Patrick,] *Transubstantiation no Doctrine of the Primitive Fathers* (London, 1687), 72.

102 [Samuel Johnson], *The Absolute Impossibility of Transubstantiation Demonstrated* (London, 1688), i.

103 Boyle, *The Christian Virtuoso*, in *Works*, 5.515; *Reflections upon a Theological Distinction. According to which it is said, That some Articles of Faith are above Reason, but not against Reason*, in *Works*, 5.542.

104 Boyle, *Reflections*, in *Works*, 5.542–43.

105 *Ibid.*, 5.542.

106 John Trenchard and Thomas Gordon, *Cato's Letters: Essays on Liberty, Civil and Religious, and Other Important Subjects* (New York: Da Capo Press, 1971), 3.9, 118, 91.

5 POLEMIC AND SILENCE: JEREMY COLLIER, ELKANAH SETTLE, AND THE IDEOLOGICAL APPROPRIATION OF MORALITY

1 Walter Benjamin, "Theses on the Philosophy of History," *Illuminations*, ed. Hannah Arendt, trans. Harry Zohn (New York: Harcourt, Brace and World, 1968), 263.

2 Brian Corman, "What *is* the Canon of English Drama, 1660–1737?," *Eighteenth-Century Studies* 26 (1992–93): 318, 319. As Austen's Henry Crawford says, Shakespeare "'is a part of an Englishman's constitution,'" and a constitution is what constitutes both a person and a polity (Jane Austen, *Mansfield Park*, in *The Novels of Jane Austen*, ed. R. W. Chapman, vol. 3 [1923; Oxford: Oxford University Press, 1988], 338).

3 *The English Prelates Practizing the Methods and Rules of the Jesuits, for Enervating and Altering the Protestant Reform'd Religion in England, and Reducing the People to Popery* (no city, 1661), 9.

4 In 1719, John Matthews, one of the printers of a Jacobite pamphlet, *Vox Populi, Vox Dei*, was executed for high treason. The satire angered the authorities by arguing that most of the people favored the Stuarts, so that if the Whigs supported popular sovereignty they should be Jacobites. The slogan of the Glorious Revolution was "liberty and property" because in effect the "liberty" championed was limited to the propertied. As Paul Kleber Monod observes, the Whigs "simply substituted one-party rule for divinely

sanctioned monarchy" (Paul Kleber Monod, *Jacobitism and the English People, 1688–1788* [Cambridge: Cambridge University Press, 1989], 349; see 40–41 for a discussion of the pamphlet).

5 Annabel Patterson, *Censorship and Interpretation: The Conditions of Reading and Writing in Early Modern England* (Madison: University of Wisconsin Press, 1984); Richard Burt, *Licensed by Authority: Ben Jonson and the Discourses of Censorship* (Ithaca: Cornell University Press, 1993); within the corpus of Michel Foucault see particularly *The History of Sexuality, volume I: An Introduction* (New York: Vintage, 1980). Foucault's distinction between the spectacularly overt premodern model of authority and the modern textual, internalizing one in *Discipline and Punish: The Birth of the Prison* (New York: Vintage, 1979) is also relevant to this discussion.

6 A teleological history constructing a narrative of progress has received extensive criticism from "revisionist" historians. J. C. D. Clark's *Revolution and Rebellion: State and Society in England in the Seventeenth Centuries* (Cambridge: Cambridge University Press, 1986) argues for continuity between seventeenth- and eighteenth-century governance.

7 Toward the end of the long, peaceful, and thoroughly undemocratic Walpole administration, however, the Licensing Act of 1737 reintroduced a more formal mechanism of control, complete with prior examination of scripts, but restricted it to the theater. That this Act precedes by so short a period the famed "rise of the novel" after 1740 is, of course, to say the least suggestive.

8 Terry Eagleton, *The Function of Criticism: From the "Spectator" to Post-structuralism* (London: Verso, 1984), 9, 124.

9 *Ibid.*, 123.

10 *Ibid.*, 13, quoting Peter Uwe Hohendahl, *The Institution of Criticism* (Ithaca: Cornell University Press, 1982), 12.

11 Umberto Eco's characterization of "the lesson of Foucault," in Stefano Rosso, "A Correspondence with Umberto Eco," trans. Carolyn Springer, *Boundary 2* 12.1 (1983): 4.

12 Burt, *Licensed by Authority*, xiii.

13 Charlotte Brontë, *Jane Eyre*, 2 vols. (Oxford: Shakespeare Head Press, 1931), 1.106.

14 Eagleton, *The Function of Criticism*, 12–13.

15 Nancy Armstrong and Leonard Tennenhouse argue that the very proliferation of discourse after the lapse of censorship reflects the circumstance that "It was not enough for members of the emergent class, decidedly in the minority, to testify to their own unique humanity. To become dominant, they had to universalize their self-definition; they had to define other people as more or less lacking their humanity" (Nancy Armstrong and Leonard Tennenhouse, "A Novel Nation; or, How to Rethink Modern England as an Emergent Culture," *MLQ* 54 [1993]: 342).

16 Alexis de Tocqueville, *Democracy in America*, trans. Henry Reeve, ed. Phillips Bradley, 2 vols. (New York: Knopf, 1960), 1.264. De Tocqueville's characterization of bourgeois democracy corresponds remarkably closely, as it happens, to

Marx's assertion in the same period, in his 1844 *Contribution to the Critique of Hegel's Philosophy of Right*, that Luther "liberated man from exterior religiosity by making man's inner conscience religious. He emancipated the body from chains by enchaining the heart" (Karl Marx, *Karl Marx: Selected Writings*, ed. David McLellan [Oxford: Oxford University Press, 1977], 69).

17 Liah Greenfeld discusses at length England's precedence in evolving a "modern" nationalism; see her *Nationalism: Five Roads to Modernity* (Cambridge, MA: Harvard University Press, 1992). Geoffrey Gart Harpham argues how in its "nascent modernity" the Spanish Inquisition was at once "Manifestly the 'other' of the Enlightenment" and "Enlightenment without denial, its 'counter' elements displayed in full view" (Geoffrey Gart Harpham, "So ... What Is Enlightenment? An Inquisition into Modernity," *Critical Inquiry* 20 [1994]: 542, 549, 550).

18 Nancy Klein Maguire, *Regicide and Restoration: English Tragicomedy, 1660–1671* (Cambridge: Cambridge University Press, 1992), 219.

19 Michael D. Bristol, *Carnival and Theater: Plebeian Culture and the Structure of Authority in Renaissance England* (New York: Methuen, 1985), 213.

20 Robert D. Hume, "Opera in London, 1695–1706," *British Theater and the Other Arts, 1660–1800*, ed. Shirley Strum Kenny (Washington: Folger, 1984), 73, 74.

21 Lisa Moore, "'She was to fond of her mistaken bargain': The Scandalous Relations of Gender and Sexuality in Feminist Theory," *Diacritics* 21.2–3 (1991): 91.

22 "Review of Reviews," *The Christian Observer* 7 (1808): 390. The attacked review, in the previous month's issue, questions whether plays, even an expurgated Shakespeare, ought to be allowed in a Christian family's library at all; in this context, the man who gave us the adjective "bowdlerized" appears as the champion of art and aesthetic liberty.

23 Similarly, the General Assembly of the Church of Scotland, as Paula Backscheider observes, "defined the goals of the Edinburgh SPCK [Society for the Propagation of Christian Knowledge] to be to found charity schools and to bring 'the Protestant religion and morality to the Highlands'" in 1707 because "Resistance to the Union came in large part from the Catholic Highlands" (Paula Backscheider, *Daniel Defoe His Life* [Baltimore: Johns Hopkins University Press, 1989], 238).

24 Peter Stallybrass and Allon White, *The Politics and Poetics of Transgression* (London: Methuen, 1986), 106.

25 *Ibid.*, 202.

26 The *Empress of Morocco* controversy, about which see Robert D. Hume, *The Development of English Drama in the Late Seventeenth Century* (Oxford: Oxford University Press, 1976), 288–89, and Frank C. Brown, *Elkanah Settle: His Life and Works* (Chicago: University of Chicago Press, 1910), 51–59. Brown quotes Dennis's "Preface to *Remarks upon Mr. Pope's Translation of Homer*": Settle "was then a formidable Rival to Mr. Dryden: And ... not only the Town but the University of Cambridge, was very much divided in their Opinions about the

Preference that ought to be given them; and in both Places, the Younger Fry, inclined to Elkanah."

27 Bonamy Dobree, *William Congreve* (London: Longman, Green, 1963), 9.

28 See the first chapter of G. V. Bennett's *The Tory Crisis in Church and State 1688–1730: The Career of Francis Atterbury Bishop of Rochester* (Oxford: Clarendon Press, 1975), 3–22, for an account of "The Anglican Crisis" of the 1690s.

29 J. Douglas Canfield, "Royalism's Last Dramatic Stand: English Political Tragedy, 1679–89," *Studies in Philology* 82 (1985): 236; Janet Clare, "'All run now into Politicks': Theater Censorship During the Exclusion Crisis," in *Writing and Censorship in Britain*, ed. Paul Hyland and Neil Sammells (London: Routledge, 1992), 48.

30 Frank Brown, *Elkanah Settle*, 108.

31 Susan Staves, *Players' Scepters* (Lincoln: University of Nebraska Press, 1979), 79; Canfield, "Royalism's Last Dramatic Stand," 247–48.

32 Richard Brown, "Nathaniel Lee's Political Dramas," *Restoration* 10 (1986): 46.

33 Elkanah Settle, "Epistle Dedicatory," *The Female Prelate: Being the History of the Life and Death of Pope Joan. A Tragedy*, ([no city], 1680, n. p.).

34 Frank Brown, *Elkanah Settle*, 73. Brown observes that, similarly, Settle's *Female Prelate* "was perhaps referred to more often in dedication, prologue, and epilogue, than any other dramatic work produced between 1680 and 1700" (21).

35 Elkanah Settle, *The Character of a Popish Successour, and What England may expect from such a One* (1681), 2–3.

36 Elkanah Settle, *A Narrative. Written by E. Settle* (London, 1683). In this publication Settle's name is stated prominently, in large letters in the upper center, on the title page. His name had value as a turncoat's, and on this title page enjoys an exaltation related to its subsequent need for a low profile.

37 [Elkanah Settle], "Remarks on Algernon Sidney's Paper, Delivered to the Sherriffs at his Execution" (London, 1683), n. p.

38 Michael McKeon, "Marxist Criticism and Marriage à la Mode," *The Eighteenth Century: Theory and Interpretation* 24 (1983): 153.

39 Alexander Pope, "Argument of Book the Second," *Dunciad*, in *Poetical Works*, ed. Herbert Davis (London: Oxford University Press, 1966), 496.

40 Aubrey Williams, "No Cloistered Virtue: Or, Playwright versus Priest in 1698," *PMLA* 90 (1975): 234–46.

41 Jeremy Collier, "Preface," *A Short View of the Immorality, and Profaneness of the English Stage* (London: 1698), n. p.

42 William Congreve, *Amendments of Mr. Collier's False and Imperfect Citations*, in *The Complete Works of William Congreve*, ed. Montague Summers (Soho: Nonesuch Press, 1923), 173.

43 *Ibid.*, 171.

44 *Ibid.*, 173–4.

45 Samuel Johnson, "Life of Congreve," *Lives of the English Poets*, ed. George Birbeck Hill, 3 vols. (1905; New York: Octagon Press, 1967), 2. 222.

46 For a discussion of Congreve's dramaturgy as a reimposition of authoritarian values on comedy, "a sophisticated attempt to redefine the ideology of comic

conventions, to justify the ways of hierarchical society to men – and women," (250), see Robert Markley, *Two-Edg'd Weapons: Style and Ideology in the Comedies of Etherege, Wycherley and Congreve* (Oxford: Clarendon Press, 1988), 195–250.

47 James Drake, *The Ancient and Modern Stages surveyed. Or, Mr. COLLIERs View of the Immorality and Profaneness of the English Stage Set in a TRUE LIGHT* (London, 1699), 131, 180, 218.

48 Curt A. Zimansky conclusively established Settle's previously-disputed authorship of these tracts by reporting variant copies of the two works bound together with a dedication signed "E. SETTLE" and "E. S." (*The Critical Works of Thomas Rymer* [New Haven: Yale University Press, 1956], 287).

49 [Elkanah Settle,] "Preface," *A Farther Defense of Dramatic Poetry: Being the Second Part of the Review of Mr. Collier's View of the Immorality and Profaneness of the Stage,* "Done by the same Hand" (London: Eliz. Whitlock, 1698), n. p.

50 [Elkanah Settle,]"Preface," *A Defense of Dramatick Poetry: Being a Review of Mr. Collier's View of the Immorality and Profaneness of the Stage* (London, 1698), n. p.

51 Settle, *A Defense,* 14. He is admitting that Sparta, unlike Athens and Rome, did prohibit plays.

52 Johnson, "Life of Congreve," *Lives of the English Poets,* 2.192.

53 The only points in either *A Defense* or *A Farther Defense* to which Collier responds in *A Defense of the Short View* (London, 1699) is the silence of scripture and St. Paul's quoting of Menander. Collier does not allow one moral sentence delivered by one playwright to justify the entire institution of the stage (132–33).

54 Sir John Vanbrugh, *A Short Vindication of the Relapse and the Provok'd Wife, from Immorality and Profaneness* (London: 1698).

55 For a chronology of publications, see Sister Rose Anthony, *The Jeremy Collier Stage Controversy* (Milwaukee: Marquette University Press, 1937), 60, 92. Vanbrugh's pamphlet also discusses *The Provok'd Wife.*

56 Elkanah Settle, "To the Reader," *City-Ramble: or, a Play-House Wedding* (London: 1711), n. p. The only study available of this play is Jackson I. Cope, "Settle's *City Ramble:* A Yet Farther Defense of the Stage," in *Rhetorics of Order/Ordering Rhetorics in English Neoclassical Literature,* ed. J. Douglas Canfield and J. Paul Hunter (Newark, DE: Delaware University Press, 1989), 68–81. His argument locates *City-Ramble* in the context of Settle's relations with the City of London, particularly some threatened new restrictions on Bartholomew Fair.

57 J. Douglas Canfield, "The Ideology of Restoration Tragicomedy," *ELH* 51 (1984), 447–64.

58 William Shakespeare, *The Tragedy of Hamlet, Prince of Denmark,* II.ii.586–87, in *The Riverside Shakespeare* (Boston: Houghton Mifflin, 1974), 1159.

59 Eve Kosovsky Sedgwick mentions the progression from Catholic aristocratic matriarchy to Protestant bourgeois patriarchy in *Henry Esmond,* a passage portrayed as from darkness to light, without further examining the religious–political significance of the priest who acts as desexed father surrogate in the Catholic matriarchy of the novel's beginning (*Between Men: English Literature and Male Homosocial Desire* [New York: Columbia University

Press, 1985], 146–47). The relationship of sex roles and political patriarchalism has been much discussed in recent years, but the function of the Catholic other as paralleling the sexual other has gone comparatively unexamined. Gregory W. Bredbeck, for instance, groups together "papists, bodily mutilation, and cross-dressed marauders" as threats/alternatives to "the voice of patriarchy" in the seventeenth century, but like Kosovsky does not develop the idea of Papism as deviancy (*Sodomy and Interpretation: Marlowe to Milton* [Ithaca: Cornell University Press, 1991], 231).

60 Elkanah Settle, *The Empress of Morocco* (London, 1673). See Maximillian E. Novak's introduction to *The Empress of Morocco and Its Critics* (Los Angeles: Clark Library, 1968), i–xix, for the background of the controversy this play aroused.

61 Elkanah Settle, *The Female Prelate: Being the History of the Life and Death of Pope Joan. A Tragedy* (London: 1679), 24. This work will hereafter be referred to in the text.

62 Sir George Etherege, *The Man of Mode*, ii.ii, ed. John Conaghan (Edinburgh: Oliver and Boyd, 1973), 48.

63 *Ibid.*, 43–44.

64 W. H. Auden, "Spain," in *Selected Poems: New Edition*, ed. Edward Mendelson (New York: Vintage, 1979), 54.

65 Maurice Levy, *Le roman 'gotique' anglais* (Toulouse, 1968), 600ff., cited in Victor Sage, *Horror Fiction in the Protestant Tradition* (New York: St. Martin's Press, 1988), xiii.

66 See Sage, *Horror Fiction*, particularly chapter 2, "The Unwritten Tradition: Horror and the Rhetoric of Anti-Catholicism," 26–69.

67 Charles Maturin, *Melmoth the Wanderer*, ed. William F. Axton (Lincoln: University of Nebraska Press, 1961), 174.

68 "Of the Kingdome of Darkness," the fourth and last of the major divisions of Thomas Hobbes's *Leviathan*, consists of an extended attack on "the Spirit of Rome" exorcized by Henry VIII and Elizabeth I.

6 *"POLITENESS* AND *POLITICS"*: THE LITERATURE OF EXCLUSION AND THE "TRUE PROTESTANT HEART"

1 Blackstone, *Commentaries*, quoted in Basil Thomson, *The Story of Scotland Yard* (London: Grayson and Grayson, 1935), 3; cited by Philip Corrigan and Derek Sayer, *The Great Arch: English State Formation as Cultural Revolution* (Oxford: Basil Blackwell, 1985), 95.

2 J. G. A. Pocock parallels the "commonwealthsmen" of the seventeenth century with the "Tory satirists" of the eighteenth as discontented intellectuals, despite their opposite positions on a retrospectively imposed left–right spectrum (J. G. A. Pocock, "Post-Puritan England and the Problem of Enlightenment," in *Culture and Politics: From Puritanism to the Enlightenment*, ed. Perez Zagorin [Berkeley: University of California Press, 1980], 108).

3 Rose A. Zimbardo, "At Zero Point: Discourse, Politics, and Satire in Restoration England," *ELH* 59 (1992): 796, 790.

4 Jean-François Lyotard, *The Postmodern Explained: Correspondence 1982–1985*, trans. Don Barry et al., ed. Julian Pefanis and Morgan Thomas (Minneapolis: University of Minnesota Press, 1992), 95; Daniel Defoe, *A Tour Through the Whole Island of Great Britain*, ed. G. D. H. Cole and D. C. Browning, vol. 1 (London: Dent, 1974), 140, cited in Alistair M. Duckworth, "'Whig' Landscapes in Defoe's Tour," *Philological Quarterly* 61 (1982): 458.

5 Richard Steele, *The Englishman: A Political Journal by Richard Steele*, issue 1.46, January 19, 1714, ed. Rae Blanchard (Oxford: Clarendon Press, 1955), 185. For an exploration of the relationship between the ideologies of progress and capitalism see Hiram Caton, *The Politics of Progress: The Origins of the Commercial Republic, 1600–1835* (Gainesville: University of Florida Press, 1988). That Irish Presbyterians were frequently Scottish in origin and Church of Ireland adherents aboriginally English helped complicate the Irish situation.

6 Daniel Defoe, *The Present State of Jacobitism Consider'd* (London, 1701), 21; cited in Manuel Schonhorn, *Defoe's Politics: Parliament, Power, Kingship, and Robinson Crusoe* (Cambridge: Cambridge University Press, 1991), 15.

7 Gary Hentzi, "Sublime Moments and Social Authority in *Robinson Crusoe* and *A Journal of the Plague Year*," *Eighteenth-Century Studies* 26 (1993): 434.

8 Ines G. Zupanov, "Aristocratic Analogies and Demotic Descriptions in the Seventeenth-Century Madurai Mission," *Representations* 41 (1993): 142.

9 Irvin Ehrenpreis's attempt to divide doctrine from form, and thus to claim that *A Tale of a Tub* "celebrate[s] the Church of England," while valid insofar as it goes, implicitly rejects examination of the project as a totality ("The Doctrine of *A Tale of a Tub*," in *Proceedings of the First Munster Symposium on Jonathan Swift*, ed. Hermann J. Real and Heinz J. Vienken [Munich: Wilhelm Fink Verlag, 1985], 71). If the *Tale* had been as conventional in impact as Ehrenpreis finds it in a detextualized "doctrine," after all, it would not have outraged Anglican opinion. It was precisely Swift's estrangement of the familiar, his translation of the orthodox into the outrageous, that kept him from the bishopric he expected. The contraditions of his rhetorical position paralleled those of the Church he served, and they were contradictions which those less bold than Swift preferred not to acknowledge.

10 George Orwell, "Politics vs. Literature," *The Collected Essays, Journalism, and Letters of George Orwell*, ed. Sonia Orwell and Ian Angus, vol. 4 (New York: Harcourt, Brace, and World, 1968), 207.

11 What Mark Goldie calls "the long clericalist tradition of the Church's corporate rights" is equivalent to neither automatic support of nor opposition to the crown, nor to any particular dynasty ("The Nonjurors, Episcopacy, and the Origin of the Convocation Controversy," in *Ideology and Conspiracy: Aspects of Jacobitism, 1689–1759*, ed. Eveline Cruickshanks [Edinburgh: John Donald, 1982], 30). Bishop John Tanner, for instance, displaying a corporatist clerical loyalty resembling Swift's, presents a largely sympathetic account of the suppressed English monasteries, as parts of a Church not decisively differentiated from his own, in the introduction to *Notitia Monastica* (London, 1744).

12 William Makepeace Thackeray, "Swift," in *The English Humourists of the Eighteenth Century* (London: Macmillan, 1924), 23.

13 Edward Said briefly notes the confluence in Swift of active engagement in these two widely different political formations, and also remarks that to characterize such Whigs as Marlborough or Godolphin as democrats would be a gross distortion, so that Orwell's identification of Swift with a transhistorical reactionaryism is simplistic (*The World, the Text, and the Critic* [Cambridge, MA: Harvard University Press, 1983], 83, 77).

14 Laura Brown, *Ends of Empire: Women and Ideology in Early Eighteenth-Century English Literature* (Ithaca: Cornell University Press, 1993), 200.

15 Ricardo Quintana, *The Mind and Art of Jonathan Swift* (1936; Gloucester, MA: Peter Smith, 1965), vii.

16 John Traugott, "*A Tale of a Tub*," in *The Character of Swift's Satire: A Revised Focus*, ed. Claude Rawson (Newark: University of Delaware Press, 1983), 124.

17 F. P. Lock, "Swift and English Politics," in Rawson, *The Character of Swift's Satire*, 127.

18 Joyce Lee Malcolm, "Charles II and the Reconstruction of Royal Power," in *The Historical Journal* 35 (1992): 328.

19 Joseph McMinn, *Jonathan Swift: A Literary Life* (Basingstoke, Hampshire: Macmillan, 1991), 47.

20 Paul S. Fritz, *The English Ministers and Jacobitism between the Rebellions of 1715 and 1745* (Toronto: University of Toronto Press, 1975), 28.

21 John Dryden, *The Vindication of the Duke of Guise*, in *Dryden: The Dramatic Works*, ed. Montague Summers, 6 vols. (1932; New York: Gordian Press, 1968), 5.311, 322.

22 *Ibid.*, 320, 336.

23 *Ibid.*, 322.

24 See [Daniel Defoe?], *His Majesty's Obligations to the Whigs Plainly Proved* (London, 1715). After challenging in general the reliability of attributions to Defoe in *The Canonisation of Daniel Defoe* (New Haven: Yale University Press, 1988), P. N. Furbank and W. R. Owens proceeded in *Defoe De-Attributions: A Critique of J. R. Moore's* Checklist (London: Hambledon Press, 1994) to specify which attributions they viewed as unreliable. Of all the works attributed to Defoe which this chapter examines, they regarded only *His Majesty's Obligations* as not his (79).

25 As David Hume notes, the Parliamentary resolution declaring the throne vacant accused James II of "'having, by the advice of Jesuits and other wicked persons, violated the fundamental laws, and withdrawn himself out of the kingdom'"; and Hume himself argues that the Stuart claim was superior to the Hanoverian except for the obnoxiousness of their religion, at least until the Hanoverians enjoyed incumbency (*History of England* and "Of the Protestant Succession," in *Political Essays*, ed. Knud Haakonsson [Cambridge: Cambridge University Press, 1994], 237, 218–19).

26 Roger Schmidt, "Roger North's Examen: A Crisis in Historiography," *Eighteenth-Century Studies* 26 (1992): 57. The significance of "Jacobitism as a viable option in its day" has gained force as a parallel to socialism as an

alternative in the twentieth century in the wane of former certainties of progress (J. C. D. Clark, "On Moving the Middle Ground: The Significance of Jacobitism in Historical Studies," in *The Jacobite Challenge*, ed. Eveline Cruickshanks and Jeremy Black [Edinburgh: John Donald, 1988], 177).

27 Quoted in Bruce Lenman, *The Jacobite Risings in Britain 1689–1746* (London: Eyre Methuen, 1980), 27.

28 Bishop Hooper, cited in Ian Gilmour, *Riot, Risings and Revolution: Governance and Violence in Eighteenth-Century England* (London: Hutchinson, 1992), 55.

29 Gilbert Burnet, *Two Sermons, Preached in the Cathedral Church of Salisbury* (London, 1710), 7, 8, 9.

30 F. P. Lock, *Swift's Tory Politics* (London: Duckworth, 1983), 133, vii, 68.

31 Ellen Pollak, *The Poetics of Sexual Myth: Gender and Ideology in the Verse of Swift and Pope* (Chicago: University of Chicago Press, 1985), 187.

32 Carole Fabricant, "The Battle of the Ancients and (Post)Moderns: Rethinking Swift through Contemporary Perspectives," *The Eighteenth Century: Theory and Interpretation*, 32 (1991): 257. Perry Anderson, *Arguments within English Marxism* (London: Verso, 1980), 97. See also Fabricant's *Swift's Landscape* (Baltimore: Johns Hopkins University Press, 1982) and "Swift in His Own Time and Ours," in *The Profession of Eighteenth-Century Literature*, ed. Leo Damrosch (Madison: University of Wisconsin Press, 1992), 113–34. For another Marxist view of Swift as simply a reactionary in his politics, see Warren Montag, *The Unthinkable Swift: The Spontaneous Philosophy of a Church of England Man* (London: Verso, 1995).

33 See *William Law's Defense of Church Principles: Three Letters to the Bishop of Bangor, 1717–1719*, ed. J. O. Nash and Charles Gore (Edinburgh: John Grant, 1909), 13–35.

34 Carole Fabricant, *Swift's Landscape* (Baltimore: Johns Hopkins University Press, 1982), 95, 271; quotation from Mark Girouard, *Life in the English Country House: A Social and Architectural History* (New Haven: Yale University Press, 1978), 2.

35 Will Brantley, "Reading Swift as a Modernist: A Polemical Investigation," *Essays in Literature* 19 (1992): 21.

36 Similarly, what Kenneth Craven calls Swift's "unabated challenge to the seductive scientific millenarian myth" is at once reactionary in its questioning of modern rationalism from the vantage of a premodern "priest system," and radical because what he interrogates is, after all, very much the modern establishment (*Jonathan Swift and the Millennium of Madness: The Information Age in Swift's* Tale of a Tub [Leiden: E. J. Brill, 1992], xi, 2).

37 Benjamin Hoadly, *Preservative against the Principles and Practices of the Non-jurors*, in *Works*, 2.588, quoted in Nash and Gore, *William Law's Defense of Church Principles*, 26–27.

38 William Sherlock, *A Preservative against Popery: Being some Plain Directions to Unlearned Protestants, How to Dispute with Romish Priests. The First Part* (London, 1688) and *The Second Part of the Preservative against Popery* (London, 1688); Edward Aspinall, *A Preservative against Popery. Being an easy Method of Conviction from Scripture and Reason* [ed. Edmund Gibson, Bishop of London] (London, 1715).

39 Andrew Snape, *A Second Letter to the Lord Bishop of Bangor, in Vindication of The Former* (London, 1717), 66. The title page states that Snape is "Chaplain in Ordinary to His Majesty," but Snape proved correct that, despite "a due regard to your episcopal character ... the 'engines of the world' [quoting Hoadly] would be made use of against me": along with three other Chaplains in Ordinary, he lost the position in punishment for his part in the dispute (Nash and Gore, *William Law's Defense of Church Principles*, 28, 33).

40 Ian Gilmour, *Riot, Risings and Revolution: Governance and Violence in Eighteenth-Century England* (London: Hutchinson, 1992), 394.

41 Ronald Paulson notes that Nicholas Amhurst, later of *The Craftsman*, charged the 1717 Convocation with "Protestant Popery" for resisting government control. His language places High Church clergy in the same usurping position as the earlier-discussed illustration in Foxe's *Acts and Monuments* placed "The Proud Primacy of Popes": "Th'ambitious, upstart, sacrificing Priest / Reigns absolute, and lords it o'er his CHRIST; / On a new Foot projects the sov'reign Scheme, / His *Prince* a Subject, and himself *Supreme*" (Nicholas Amhurst, *Protestant Popery: or, the Convocation* (1718; 3rd edn, 1724), cited by Ronald Paulson, "Putting Out the Fire in Her Imperial Majesty's Apartment: Opposition Politics, Anticlericalism, and Aesthetics," *ELH* 63 (1996): 84. Paul Kleber Monod observes how a nonjuring cleric's new liturgy was called Papist (Paul Kleber Monod, *Jacobitism and the English People, 1688–1788* [Cambridge: Cambridge University Press, 1989], 141).

42 Noting that Swift mentioned the Queen in every issue of the *Examiner*, Frank H. Ellis observes that "He wrapped himself in the panoply of the throne and made himself invulnerable" (Introduction to *Swift vs. Manwaring:* The Examiner *and* The Medley, ed. Frank H. Ellis [Oxford: Clarendon Press, 1985], xlv) – so long as the crown was in friendly hands.

43 Jonathan Swift, *The Prose Works of Jonathan Swift*, ed. Herbert Davis, 14 vols. (Oxford: Shakespeare Head Press, 1939–68), 3.4–5. Further references to this edition will be made in the text as *Works*.

44 Francis Bacon, *Essays and New Atlantis* (Roslyn, NY: Walter J. Black, 1942), 59n.

45 *Ibid.*, 64.

46 Richard Ashcraft, *Revolutionary Politics and Locke's Two Treatises of Government* (Princeton: Princeton University Press, 1986), 264, quoting *A Character of Popery and Arbitrary Government* (London, 1681), 6–7; Penn, *England's Great Interest in the Choice of This New Parliament* (London, 1680), 3–4; Bethel, *The Interest of Princes and States* (London, 1680), 15.

47 Jonathan Swift, *A Tale of a Tub*, in *Jonathan Swift*, ed. Angus Ross and David Woolley (Oxford: Oxford University Press, 1984), 145.

48 Swift, "An Argument against Abolishing Christianity," in *Jonathan Swift*, 225.

49 Whig writers also address economic concerns, but in a manner that reinforces the dichotomy of Protestant and Catholic; for them, Catholicism is not only evil but expensive. Defoe warns that "*If the Pretender comes, the Credit of* OUR FUNDS IS GONE; *all the Money lent upon the Publick Security is lost at once* ... If ye will not keep him out to save your Money, I believe nothing will move you to it"

(*Review* 1.68 [March 10, 1713], in *Defoe's Review*, volume [9], ed. Arthur Wellesley Secord [New York: Columbia University Press, 1938], 22.135). Steele quotes Burnet's warning that, as in France, should Catholicism triumph "'impious'" conversion would not suffice to preserve ex-Protestants' fortunes, because, "'The enriching of Shrines and Relicts, the adorning Churches and Images, an affected Devotion to Saints, with the Pomp of Endowments, will be then the Tests by which Men's Affections will be Judged. The bare doing what is commanded will not serve turn: The Wealth with which God blesses any, must be applied to the Endowing of Altars, the Founding of perpetual Masses, and the Redemtion of Souls out of Purgatory. A Multitude of Holidays must take Men off from their Labour'" (Richard Steele, *The Reader*, no. 1, in *Richard Steele's Periodical Journalism, 1714–1716*, ed. Rae Blanchard [Oxford: Oxford University Press, 1959], 145). The last expression suggests that the intended audience is less laborers, who might not object to holidays, but their employers. To participate in the public sphere one must have the price of admission.

50 Swift, "A Letter to the Shop-Keepers, Tradesmen, Farmers, and Common-People of Ireland, Concerning the Brass Half-Pence Coined by Mr. Woods," in *The Prose Works of Jonathan Swift*, ed. Davis, 10.3.

51 Sir Walter Scott called the furore over Wood's halfpence "the first grand struggle for the independence of Ireland" (Sir Walter Scott, ed., *The Works of Jonathan Swift, D.D., Dean of St. Patrick's Dublin*, 12 vols., 2nd edn [1824], 1.301; in *Swift: The Critical Heritage*, ed. Kathleen Williams [New York: Barnes and Noble, 1970], 288).

52 Introduction to Joseph Addison, *The Freeholder*, ed. James Leheny (Oxford: Clarendon Press, 1979), 16.

53 Addison, *The Freeholder*, 105. Leheny observes that even C. S. Lewis, not the most vehement of feminists, criticized Addison's "playful condescension towards women" (C. S. Lewis, *Selected Literary Essays* [Cambridge: Cambridge University Press, 1969], 167, quoted in Leheny's introduction to Addison, *The Freeholder*, 26).

54 Similarly, Richard Ashcraft notes the "glaring intellectual inconsistency" that Locke not only thought Dissenters likely to be less dangerous subjects than Catholics but, whereas Dissenters were to be subject only to "persuasion" as presumed immune to threats, Catholics were supposed possible to coerce, in contrast to his general system – probably because Catholicism was assumed not to be a "rational" belief (Richard Ashcraft, *Revolutionary Politics and Locke's Two Treatises of Government* [Princeton: Princeton University Press, 1986], 100).

55 *The Tatler*, ed. Donald F. Bond, vol. 2 (Oxford: Clarendon Press, 1987), 369.

56 Addison, *The Freeholder*, 95.

57 *Ibid.*, no. 6, Jan. 9, 1715–16, with Swift's marginal commentary, in Swift, *Marginalia*, in *Prose Works*, 5.252.

58 [Anthony Horneck], *A Letter from a Protestant Gentleman to a Lady Revolted to the Church of Rome* (London, 1678), 144. John Spurr notes Horneck's activity in

both moral reformation and the defense of Protestantism in the 1670s and 1680s ("The Church, the Societies, and the Moral Revolution of 1688," in *The Church of England, c. 1689–c. 1833: From Toleration to Tractarianism*, ed. John Walsh, Colin Haydon, and Stephen Taylor [Cambridge: Cambridge University Press, 1993], 132). As in Defoe's *Religious Courtship*, Popery and impiety are alike threats.

59 [Mary Astell], preface to *Moderation Truly Stated: or, a Review of a Late Pamphlet, Entitul'd, Moderation a Virtue* (London, 1704); [Delariviere Manley], *A Modest Enquiry into the Reasons of the Joy Expressed by a Certain Sett of People, upon the Spreading of a Report of Her Majesty's Death* (London, 1714).

60 Jane Austen, *Northanger Abbey*, in *The Novels of Jane Austen*, ed. R. W. Chapman, 6 vols. (Oxford: Oxford University Press, 1933), 5.111; *Mansfield Park*, in *The Novels of Jane Austen*, 3.340–41.

61 Conrad Russell, *Unrevolutionary England, 1603–1642* (London: Hambledon Press, 1990), xxii.

62 Daniel Defoe, *Religious Courtship*, in *The Novels and Miscellaneous Works of Daniel Defoe*, vol. 14 (1840; New York: AMS Press, 1973), 1. This work will hereafter be referred to in the text.

63 Pollak, *The Poetics of Sexual Myth*, 26; John Locke, *Two Treatises of Government*, ed. Peter Laslett, 2nd edn., bk. 1, chap. 5, sec. 48, line 12 (Cambridge: Cambridge University Press, 1963), 210.

64 [Daniel Defoe], *An Answer to a Question That No body thinks of, viz. But what if the Queen should die?* (London, 1713), 26.

65 [Daniel Defoe], *And What if the Pretender should come?* (London, 1713), 23.

66 [Defoe], *An Answer to a Question*, 32, 34, 27.

67 Defoe's dislike of wives' complying with their husbands' religion parallels his opposition to occasional conformity – the practice of some Dissenters of attending Anglican services just enough to qualify for public employment – as betokening a lax conscience. See [Daniel Defoe], *An Enquiry into Occasional Conformity* (London, 1702). Dissenters, Defoe argues, have no interest in permitting occasional conformity because no Dissenter of sincere beliefs would stoop to dissimulation of his religion for worldly profit.

68 Carol Houlihan Flynn, "Defoe's Idea of Conduct: Ideological Fictions and Fictional Reality," in *The Ideology of Conduct: Essays on Literature and the History of Sexuality*, ed. Nancy Armstrong and Leonard Tennenhouse (New York: Methuen, 1987), 74.

69 Nancy Armstrong, *Desire and Domestic Fiction: A Political History of the Novel* (New York: Oxford University Press, 1987), 71.

70 *Ibid.*, 4.

71 J. Paul Hunter, *The Reluctant Pilgrim: Defoe's Emblematic Method and Quest for Form in Robinson Crusoe* (Baltimore: Johns Hopkins University Press, 1966), 176n, quoted in Timothy C. Blackburn, "Friday's Religion: Its Nature and Importance in *Robinson Crusoe*," *Eighteenth-Century Studies* 18 (1985): 360.

72 Blackburn, "Friday's Religion," 361.

73 Richard Braverman, "Locke, Defoe, and the Politics of Childhood," *English Language Notes* 24 (1986): 47.

74 Helen Burke, "Roxana, Corruption, and the Progressive Myth," *Genre* 23 (1990): 103–20; Michael McKeon, *The Origins of the English Novel, 1600–1740* (Baltimore: Johns Hopkins University Press, 1987), 337; Duckworth, "'Whig' Landscapes in Defoe's Tour," 460. One might say of Defoe's protagonists, all omnivores of experience, what Stephen Greenblatt says of *Henry V*, that "the play's central figure seems to feed on the doubts he provokes" (*Shakespearean Negotiations: The Circulation of Social Energy in Renaissance England* [Berkeley: University of California Press, 1988], 63.)

75 Linda Colley, *Britons: Forging the Nation 1707–1837* (New Haven: Yale University Press, 1992), 50.

76 Paula Backscheider, *Daniel Defoe His Life* (Baltimore: Johns Hopkins University Press, 1989), 23, 249.

77 Armstrong, *Desire and Domestic Fiction*, 50.

78 Brian McCrea, *Henry Fielding and the Politics of Mid-Eighteenth-Century England* (Athens, GA: University of Georgia Press, 1981), 140; Thomas R. Cleary, *Henry Fielding: Political Writer* (Waterloo, Ont.: Wilfred Laurier University Press, 1984), 214.

79 McCrea, *Henry Fielding and the Politics of Mid-Eighteenth-Century England*, 127.

80 Cleary, *Henry Fielding: Political Writer*, 267.

81 Brean S. Hammond uses the phrase "cultural politics" to attempt to define Fielding as neither "nonpartisan and apolitical" nor simply Whig or Tory, but his concluding vision of Pope and Fielding "united under Allworthy's extensive roof" reproduces the very illusion of Allworthy's all-embracing beneficence that Fielding endeavors to engender ("Politics and Cultural Politics: The Case of Henry Fielding," *Eighteenth-Century Life* 16 [1992]: 77, 91).

82 Henry Fielding, *The True Patriot and Related Writings*, ed. W. B. Coley (Middleton, CT: Wesleyan University Press, 1987), 103, 113. Further references to this work will be made in the text.

83 Henry Fielding, *The History of Tom Jones, A Foundling*, ed. Martin C. Battestin and Fredson Bowers (Middleton, CT: Wesleyan University Press, 1975), 870. Future references to this work will be made in the text.

84 Henry Fielding, *An Enquiry into the Causes of the late Increase of Robbers*, in *The Complete Works of Henry Fielding*, ed. William Ernest Henley, vol. 13 (New York: Croscup and Sterling, 1902), 126.

85 Coley suggests that the presence of Hoadly "is nostalgic and probably personal," but it is unnecessary to speculate that Fielding "may have known Hoadly and his two sons Benjamin and John from his own early days in Salisbury" to account for the presence in *True Patriot* 3's prison of so eminent, if semi-retired, a controversialist (Coley, *The True Patriot and Related Writings*, 129n).

86 Battestin and Bowers's Wesleyan edition of *Tom Jones*, like most modern editions, follows the first and fourth original editions for the Man of the Hill's story; in the third edition, the rhetoric against Catholicism and the Stuarts is still stronger.

87 McKeon, *The Origins of the English Novel, 1600–1740*, 392, 393.

88 Martin C. Battestin, footnote in *The History of Tom Jones, A Foundling*, 439n. As he notes, Addison's *Freeholder* 14 makes the same point about the Old Pretender.

89 Peter J. Carlton, "*Tom Jones* and the '45 Once Again," in *Studies in the Novel* 20 (1988): 361.

90 John Allen Stevenson, "*Tom Jones* and the Stuarts," *ELH* 61 (1994): 588.

91 William C. Dowling, *The Epistolary Moment: The Poetics of the Eighteenth-Century Verse Epistle* (Princeton: Princeton University Press, 1991), 107.

92 Pope, "The Dunciad," 4.294, *Poetical Works*, ed. Herbert Davis (London: Oxford University Press, 1966), 566.

93 William Shenstone, "The Ruin'd Abbey; or, The Effects of Superstition," in *Minor English Poets 1660–1780*, ed. Alexander Chalmers and David P. French, vol. 4 (New York: Benjamin Blom, 1967), 554–55.

94 John J. La Rocca, S. J., "James I and his Catholic Subjects, 1606–1612: Some Financial Implications," in *Recusant History* 18 (1987): 251.

95 Ann Janowitz, *England's Ruins: Poetic Purpose and the National Landscape* (Cambridge, MA: Basil Blackwell, 1990), 1.

96 The description of the neighborhood of "Mr. *Allworthy*'s House" also includes "one of the Towers of an old ruined Abbey, grown over with Ivy, and Part of the Front which remained still entire" (Fielding, *Tom Jones*, 42, 43).

97 Johnson, "Shenstone," in *Lives of the English Poets*, 3.351–52.

98 James Turner, *The Politics of Landscape: Rural Scenery and Society in English Poetry 1630–1660* (Oxford: Basil Blackwell, 1979), 115.

99 Alan Liu, *Wordsworth: The Sense of History* (Stanford: Stanford University Press, 1989), 58.

100 Laurie Langbauer, "Romance Revised: Charlotte Lennox's The Female Quixote," *Novel* 18 (1984): 49. See also her *Women and Romance: The Consolations of Gender in the English Novel* (Ithaca: Cornell University Press, 1990).

101 Charlotte Lennox, *The Sister: A Comedy* (London, 1769), 3.

102 Armstrong, *Desire and Domestic Fiction*, 9.

CONCLUSION

1 André Malraux, "The Cultural Heritage" (1936), cited in F. O. Matthiessen, *American Renaissance: Art and Expression in the Age of Emerson and Whitman* (London: Oxford University Press, 1941), xv(n).

2 *The Humble Address of the Publicans of New England, to which King you please* (London, 1691), 20.

3 J. C. D. Clark, "Sovereignty: The British Experience," *Times Literary Supplement* (November 29, 1991): 15.

4 Fredric Jameson, "Religion and Ideology: A Political Reading of *Paradise Lost*," in *Literature, Politics, and Theory*, ed. Francis Barker (London: Methuen, 1986), 40.

5 Anthony J. Cascardi, "A Response by Anthony J. Cascardi" (to Timothy J. Reiss, "The Limits of Discursive Idealism," *MLQ* 54 [1993], 409–13), *MLQ* 54

(1993): 416. See also Anthony J. Cascardi, *The Subject of Modernity* (Cambridge: Cambridge University Press, 1993).

6 Annabel Patterson, "Pastoral and Ideology: The Neoclassical *Fête Champêtre*," *Huntington Library Quarterly* 48 (1985): 321.

7 Robert Markley, "The Rise of Nothing: Revisionist Historiography and the Narrative Structure of Eighteenth-Century Studies," *Genre* 23 (1990): 80.

8 Carole Fabricant, *Swift's Landscape* (Baltimore: Johns Hopkins University Press, 1982), 192.

9 Marjorie Levinson, *Wordsworth's Great Period Poems: Four Essays* (Cambridge: Cambridge University Press, 1986), 2.

10 Jill Campbell, "Tom Jones, Jacobitism, and Gender: History and Fiction at the Ghosting Hour," *Genre* 23 (1990): 162, 175, 162. See also her *Natural Masques: Gender and Identity in Fielding's Plays and Novels* (Stanford: Stanford University Press, 1995).

11 Campbell, "Tom Jones, Jacobitism, and Gender," 163.

12 Will Brantley, "Reading Swift as a Modernist: A Polemical Investigation," *Essays in Literature* 19 (1992): 32.

13 Swift, "Verses on the Death of Dr. Swift, D.S.P.D.," line 108, *Jonathan Swift*, ed. Angus Ross and David Woolley (Oxford: Oxford University Press, 1984), 517.

14 David Hume, *An Enquiry Concerning Human Understanding / A Letter from a Gentleman to His Friend in Edinburgh*, ed. Eric Steinberg (Indianapolis: Hackett, 1977), 79, 80.

15 Sir William Temple, "An Essay upon the Ancient and Modern Learning" (1690), in *Critical Essays of the Seventeenth Century*, vol. 3, 1685–1700, ed. J. E. Spingarn (Bloomington: Indiana University Press, 1957), 33, 39, 44.

16 Samuel Johnson, "Pope," in *Lives of the English Poets*, ed. George Birkbeck Hill, vol. 3 (1905; New York: Octagon Books, 1967), 207–8.

17 Swift, letter of September 29, 1725, in *Jonathan Swift*, 470.

18 Srinivas Aravamudan, "'Being God's postman is no fun, yaar': Salman Rushdie's *The Satanic Verses*," *Diacritics* 19.2 (1989): 3.

19 *Ibid.*, 19.

Index